South University Library
Richmond Campus
2151 Old Brick Road
Glen Allen, Va 23060

Y0-AJL-449

MAR 2 7 2018

International Perspectives on Social Policy, Administration, and Practice

Series Editors
Sheying Chen
Pace University, New York, USA

Jason L. Powell
University of Lancashire, Preston, Lancashire, United Kingdom

The Springer series International Perspectives on Social Policy, Administration and Practice puts the spotlight on international and comparative studies of social policy, administration, and practice with an up-to-date assessment of their character and development. In particular, the series seeks to examine the underlying assumptions of the practice of helping professions, nonprofit organization and management, and public policy and how processes of both nation-state and globalization are affecting them. The series also includes specific country case studies, with valuable comparative analysis across Asian, African, Latin American, and Western welfare states.The series International Perspectives on Social Policy, Administration and Practice commissions approximately six books per year, focusing on international perspectives on social policy, administration, and practice, especially an East-West connection. It assembles an impressive set of researchers from diverse countries illuminating a rich, deep, and broad understanding of the implications of comparative accounts on international social policy, administration, and practice.

More information about this series at http://www.springer.com/series/7

Leonid Grinin • Andrey Korotayev
Arno Tausch

Economic Cycles, Crises, and the Global Periphery

With a foreword by William R. Thompson

Springer

Leonid Grinin
National Research University Higher
  School of Economics
Moscow, Russia

Institute of Oriental Studies of the Russian
  Academy of Sciences
Moscow, Russia

Andrey Korotayev
National Research University Higher
  School of Economics
Moscow, Russia

Institute of Oriental Studies of the Russian
  Academy of Sciences
Moscow, Russia

Arno Tausch
Corvinus University
Budapest, Hungary

International Perspectives on Social Policy, Administration, and Practice
ISBN 978-3-319-41260-3   ISBN 978-3-319-41262-7   (eBook)
DOI 10.1007/978-3-319-41262-7

Library of Congress Control Number: 2016944156

© Springer International Publishing Switzerland 2016
This work is subject to copyright. All rights are reserved by the Publisher, whether the whole or part of the material is concerned, specifically the rights of translation, reprinting, reuse of illustrations, recitation, broadcasting, reproduction on microfilms or in any other physical way, and transmission or information storage and retrieval, electronic adaptation, computer software, or by similar or dissimilar methodology now known or hereafter developed.
The use of general descriptive names, registered names, trademarks, service marks, etc. in this publication does not imply, even in the absence of a specific statement, that such names are exempt from the relevant protective laws and regulations and therefore free for general use.
The publisher, the authors and the editors are safe to assume that the advice and information in this book are believed to be true and accurate at the date of publication. Neither the publisher nor the authors or the editors give a warranty, express or implied, with respect to the material contained herein or for any errors or omissions that may have been made.

Printed on acid-free paper

This Springer imprint is published by Springer Nature
The registered company is Springer International Publishing AG Switzerland

Foreword: Of Cycles, Changes, and Transformations

There are many orthodoxies about how economic processes work. That such knowledge has become orthodox does not make them either accurate or useful. When it comes to longer-term economics, orthodoxy tends to give way to mystery. Why have some states become so much more affluent than others? Why do some places remain impoverished while others flourish? Why do economic growth rates fluctuate so much? Why do economies move back and forth between years of prosperity and years of recession and depression? Once in recession or depression, what does it take to get back to prosperity? Of course, it is not the case that there are no answers to these questions. There are multiple answers but much less consensus about what works and does not work.

One of the non-orthodoxies that addresses these types of questions contends that long-term economic growth has come to be characterized by crudely cyclical processes of 40–60 years duration that are driven by the emergence of new ways of doing things. Periodically, Schumpeter's "creative destruction" occurs as older practices give way to newer practices. Sunset industries fall away. Sunrise industries blossom. New waves of investment sustain the newer practices and starve more routine and less profitable ways of making money. New waves of infrastructure undergird fundamental changes in how commodities, information and people are transported from place to place. Radical changes in life styles gradually emerge. Where people once walked, they now drive automobiles. In the next iteration, the automobiles will drive themselves. Where people once endured hot and cold weather, they now are capable of insulating themselves from the vagaries of inclement climate. People that once communicated by relatively slow messengers and mail now exchange messages instantaneously using telephones and the internet. Cities and water systems that were once filthy with human and animal waste products need no longer be polluted. After centuries of relatively constant living conditions, modern economies have created some ability to re-invent themselves periodically.

We are all aware of these changes in some respects and some even seek to account for them explicitly but that does not mean that we agree on how exactly they come about. The source(s) of long-term changes has been attributed to new technology, new types of energy, clusters of investment, profits, war, demographic changes, and generational changes, among other things. We disagree about how long these crudely cyclical processes have been in play and whether they are likely to persist into the future. Most authors argue for the emergence of long economic cycles (or waves) with the advent of industrialization. Some, however, suggest that one can find earlier precedents even if industrialization certainly made the periodicity and impacts of change more evident. In turn, such an auxiliary argument raises other questions. How uneven are the waves of change? Do some have great impact while others bring about only fairly weak changes. Why? Is the pace of change uniform over time? Is it speeding up or slowing down? If the waves preceded industrialization, is the cyclical behavior likely to persist or take the same format as leading economies move into a post-industrialization phase?

We know economics does not occur in a political vacuum. Yet we diverge when it comes time to acknowledge the political structures that provide a framework for these changes. Is it coincidence that some of the states that have become so rich are also the places where new technology and new sources of energy are introduced? Is it also coincidence that these same states assume disproportionate roles in world politics? Yet their rise to prominence and pre-eminence is finite. They decline and are supplanted by rivals. Why does that happen? One might think that once a group has ascended to the top of the stratification system, it could figure out how to stay on top. But that does not seem to be the case. Britain predominated in the nineteenth century. The United States eclipsed Britain and was most pre-eminent in the twentieth century. Some observers think that China will do something similar in the twenty-first century. Is this a function of larger populations? Or, is there a strong link between the economic cycles and political cycles? Moreover, is there a strong link between patterns of economic growth, the rise and decline of pre-eminent political-military actors, and the vagaries of world politics?

There probably is literally no corner of human behavior that is immune to re-consideration once one adopts a view that economics (and other activities) are characterized by long-term cycles that are not precisely regular in periodicity. The authors of this book, Grinin, Korotayev, and Tausch, prefer to focus on the economic manifestations and choose to break down the longer cycles (the Kondratieffs, sometimes called K-waves) into shorter variations (Kitchins, Juglars, Kuznets cycles) that have been examined before (although they stress the Juglar here) and highlight one that has received little explicit attention, which they label Akamatsu cycles after a Japanese economist who wrote about the process in question decades earlier. Akamatsu cycles refer to movements toward divergence and convergence between center and periphery. The basic process in play is that the center initially produces finished goods while the periphery supplies raw materials. Some of the technology developed in the center diffuses to the periphery as peripheral agents attempt to produce more technologically advanced products. This process has been going on for (see in particular Grinin and Korotayev 2015) a couple of centuries but the authors think a "Great Convergence" is imminent in which the periphery will replace (or, at least, join) the center as the focus of industrialization. China and India, once deemed the richest economies in the world not that many years ago (in long-term terms) will re-assert themselves as leading centers of economic wealth. The West, once clearly dominant, will recede accordingly in global economic and political significance. Presumably, if the convergence is widespread, we would eventually no longer be able to distinguish between a center and a periphery.

The authors believe that the next concentration of new technology will be centered initially on medical technology to address an ageing population and its many problems. But this next technology cluster will be moving away from old school industrialization production to an emphasis on a more cybernetic, production on demand phase that could eliminate the tendency for new technology to cluster in space and time. These technological changes in combination with the "Great Convergence" merging center and periphery are likely to radically alter the world as we know it. Kondratieff waves could disappear abruptly or with a whimper. The Global North's relatively brief ascendancy (since the British Industrial Revolution) will also come to an end. The authors are even willing to date these changes to midtwenty-first century—a point in time not all that far away.

Are they right? Who knows? We will have to wait until mid-century to find out. Still, they develop theoretical arguments and empirical evidence that should be taken seriously. What is more important in the present is that we consider the implications of their interpretation for how we understand the past, the present, and the immediate future. Big questions are being asked. Equally big answers are being proposed. We need more of these questions (and, of course, answers) and it helps all the more if authors choose to stray from current orthodoxies that decline to address such questions.

Yet even if the predictions made in this book are deemed plausible (which, of course, they are), there are other dragons lurking in our future that could alter the future suggested by Grinin, Korotayev, and Tausch. Global warming will affect the Global South or periphery more than it will harm the Global North. Much the same can be said about water shortages that are sure to come, with or without global warming. What will these multiple whammies do to center-periphery convergence? There is also a Sino-American rivalry underway that could have greater impact on the Global North. A Chinese hegemonic ascendance could be seen as a step towards the general ascent of the periphery. Yet it need not work that way. The Chinese are by no means guaranteed to supplant the U.S. position. But that does not mean, either, that the United States will maintain its own leading position. Perhaps the propensity towards hierarchical stratification in the world system will also diminish in the coming decades. Certainly, if the tendency for technology to cluster goes away, so, too, must the tendency for one state to emerge as pre-eminent based on its technological lead.

Whether the future is knowable to any limited extent depends on how well we are able to discern the dynamics of the past/present and calculate the probable impacts of various possible developments that have not yet happened. We are not there yet. Maybe we never will be. None of that precludes trying to read what may be coming based on what we think we know now. If readers disagree with the authors' predictions, let them develop their own theoretical bases and data to address the same or similar questions differently. We will all be better off should that occur.

In many respects this book is an outstanding event. It is based on solid theoretical foundations; on the other hand, it contains a lot of reach factual material. It successfully combines a variety of research methods. This monograph covers a rather long period since the end of the fifteenth century up to the late twenty-first century. But perhaps its main virtue is the ability of authors to link the past and the modern processes in a solid conceptual whole, so that it becomes possible on this basis to make interesting and quite plausible forecasts. The readers will undoubtedly benefit greatly from this book, each chapter of which opens a new dimension for the understanding of economic and social reality of our complex world.

Indiana University, Bloomington, IN, USA　　　　　　　　　William R. Thompson

Preface

Although the global economy has more or less recovered from the most severe manifestations of the global financial and economic crisis, it is obvious that the economy of many Western and non-Western countries continues to be influenced by depression. Indeed, we are dealing with such symptoms of economic depression as a very slow pace of economic growth; ongoing high unemployment; low inflation (or even deflation); lack of investment growth; increasing public debt; strong volatility of stock markets; decreasing prices of raw materials; slow rates of global trade growth; and many other negative phenomena. Even China has started to be heavily influenced by these factors after for a long time it appeared immune to global economic perturbations. Further, it appears that such a phase of weak growth and economic stagnancy will continue for a relatively long time.

These phenomena can be more or less explained by a number of theories, but one of the most important for us is the theory of medium-term cycles, bearing the name of the French economist Clement Juglar. In 2008–2009, we have seen a classic cyclic Juglar crisis that gained huge and destructive dimensions due to the rapid growth of unregulated global capital. According to the theory of medium-term cycles, the acute phase of the crisis gives way to socio-economic depression. However, the medium-term cycle usually lasts 7 to 11 years. Does this mean that soon a new cyclical upturn will begin? In fact, one can hardly expect a strong recovery. Actually, we have sufficient grounds to expect sluggish and short economic recoveries and prolonged depressions for the next 10–15 years. A depressive period of this kind is well explained by the theory of long cycles, according to which a sufficiently long period of strong economic growth with a small number of crisis-depression years (for about 20–25 years) is followed by a period of lower growth, in which the number of years of depression increases dramatically. The World System experienced a period of relatively rapid growth in the 1990s and 2000s. Now we are confronting a downswing phase.

Economic development is for many reasons cyclical whereas many cycles[1] end with economic crises and depressions and then it becomes necessary to work hard to prepare for a new economic rise. This book is dedicated to the analysis of

---

[1] First of all, the Juglar cycles.

different cycles and crises including signs of a systemic crisis, which is in some respects increasingly affecting Western economies.

The background for this study is the current stagnation on the European continent and in several other regions of the world economy since the 2007–2009 crisis. What does our scientific knowledge tell us about the regularity of such crises? What conclusions does this knowledge suggest as regards the relationship between center and periphery on a global scale and also for the probable future continuing decline of peripheral regions in Europe?

Within Europe, the spirit of the day uniformly maintains that there is no alternative for the European periphery but to continue to be members of the Eurozone and to be subjected to the *phlebotomy* (bloodletting) by austerity packages under the auspices of the European Commission and "the institutions", while in reality new organizing principles for rationalizing the complexities of stagnation and recession are needed.

Our analysis is influenced by a most unusual source: the path-breaking advances in cancer research described by Hanahan and Weinberg (2000, 2011). It is from cancer research, then, that we have taken the above ideas—however, instead of "hallmarks of cancer", we use the insights gained from cancer research to diagnose the "hallmarks of economic crisis." In the future, these insights may include, like in medicine, sustaining future crisis signaling, coming to terms with and controlling the spread of economic growth suppressors, resisting the death of economic and social networks and agendas, especially in the most peripheral regions of the European periphery. Underlying the economic hallmarks of stagnation and decline are potentially long-run political, social and economic instabilities, which might generate the loss of economic and social diversity, and the "inflammation" of social, economic and political processes by corruption and organized crime, which more likely than not foster multiple hallmark functions of crisis. Already today Europe faces very strong political and social problems connected with a number of challenges (among them the migrant crisis is the sharpest one). Even this one is able to shake the very foundations of European integration. This is demonstrated by the recent "Brexit" referendum in the United Kingdom and the rise of nationalist parties in France and some other EU countries suggest that the future of united Europe may be even more gloomy if it has such a future altogether.

In addition to economic "cancer cells", we might discover that "economic" tumours exhibit another dimension of complexity: they might contain a repertoire of ostensibly normal "cells" that contribute to the acquisition of hallmark traits by creating the "tumour microenvironment". Recognition of the widespread applicability of these concepts will, like in medicine, increasingly affect the development of new means to treat the "economic cancer" of peripheral stagnation.

The present monograph was written by two Russian scholars and an Austrian scholar precisely to fill this gap. The idea of this book emerged at a time of world political tensions in many places around the world, after the start of the longest and most profound recession in the developed western democracies in the period after the Second World War.

Preface

When two of the three authors, Andrey V. Korotayev and Arno Tausch, met in person for the first time during an IIASA[2] seminar in 2006 in the idyllic castle of Laxenburg situated in the beautiful park with the same name near Vienna, both would not have imagined that only years after a chilly political "Kondratieff winter" would start; a few years after the onset of the 2008 depression it seems that world political and world economic cycles go in parallel.

Even without any official "*IIASA umbrella*" the two authors initiated a far-reaching and long-standing fruitful cooperation, soon also joined by Leonid E. Grinin. In times like these, which threaten to throw back "East-West" or "West-East" relations (as you prefer) to the times of the Cold War, it is worthwhile to remember the still valid words from IIASA's official website:

> "*In October 1972 representatives of the Soviet Union, United States, and 10 other countries from the Eastern and Western blocs met in London to sign the charter establishing the International Institute for Applied Systems Analysis (IIASA). It was the culmination of 6 years' effort by US President Lyndon Johnson and USSR Premier Alexey Kosygin, and marked the beginning of a remarkable project to use scientific cooperation to build bridges across the Cold War divide and to confront growing global problems on an international scale.*
>
> *In the 1970s most research organizations focused on national issues. Few encouraged researchers from different countries or disciplines to work together for the greater good. To achieve its ambitious research vision, IIASA would have to break down the barriers between nations and disciplines. This it did, building international interdisciplinary teams that used advanced systems analysis to study innumerable global challenges, both long-standing and emerging. For example, a study on water pollution carried out by a team of IIASA chemists, biologists, and economists in the 1980s is still the basis of modern water policy design in Japan, the USA, and the former USSR.*
>
> *The refurbished Schloss Laxenburg near Vienna was made available by the Austrian government shortly after the foundation of IIASA in 1972. The Schloss has been the Institute's home for nearly four decades.*
>
> *When the Cold War ended, IIASA's sponsoring countries could have said 'mission accomplished' and disbanded the Institute. However, as well as helping foster mutual understanding among scientists from East and West, IIASA had shown the scientific benefits of different nationalities and disciplines working together toward common goals*".[3]

Global governance responsibility and the leadership styles of Lyndon Johnson and Alexey Kosygin are still needed on many fronts. The geographical setting of the place of residence of the authors is also not a coincidence and it points to the Schumpeterian subject of our investigation. About half-way between Moscow and Vienna—symbolic locus for our times of the most serious world political tension since the end of Communism in Europe—there is the Ukrainian town of Chernivtsi (by road, 1376 km from Moscow and 925 km from Vienna), where that great admirer of Nikolay Kondratieff, the Austrian economist Joseph Alois Schumpeter, was professor of economics from the winter semester 1909/1910 to the end of the summer semester 1911, when Schumpeter took up his position as professor of

---

[2] International Institute for Applied System Analysis (http://www.iiasa.ac.at/).
[3] http://www.iiasa.ac.at/web/home/about/whatisiiasa/history/history_of_iiasa.html.

economics in Graz. At that time, Chernivtsi was a border town of the Austro-Hungarian Empire and Russia.[4]

Since the time of Schumpeter economics has advanced considerably. But still its predictions remain largely close to fortune-telling. And the world is still developing in a largely chaotic way, from crisis to crisis, from cycle to cycle; so, despite the enormous difficulties in the way, one would like to look for more scientifically grounded methods of long-term forecasting to try to see a little further. This book is a humble attempt of the authors to contribute to this movement.

***

This monograph consists of six chapters dealing with long economic cycles (or Kondratieff waves) as well as other types of economic cycles and crises, their interconnectedness and their connection with changes in the World System core and periphery. It covers a rather long period since the mid-eighteenth century (and for some aspects even since the end of the fifteenth century) up to the late twenty-first century.

Moscow, Russia	Leonid Grinin
Moscow, Russia	Andrey Korotayev
Budapest, and Vienna, Austria	Arno Tausch

---

[4] For the "consolidated" English language versions of Schumpeter's main works which are of relevance here, see, among others: Schumpeter 1934, 1939, 1954, 2010.

Acknowledgements

We would like to express our deepest gratitude to Antony Harper (USA), Peter Herrmann (China–Germany), Victor de Munck (USA–Lithuania), Elena Emanova (Russia), and Kseniya Uchova (Russia) for their invaluable help with the editing of this book. This monograph is an output of a research project implemented as part of the Basic Research Program at the National Research University Higher School of Economics (HSE) in 2016 with support by the Russian Science Foundation (Project No. 14-11-00634).

Contents

1	**Introduction. Cyclical and World-Systemic Aspects of Economic Reality with Respect to Contemporary Crisis**...............	1
	Origins of Modern Economic Cyclicity..	1
	The System of Economic Cycles	5
	Kondratieff Waves	5
	Juglar Cycle	5
	About This Book and Its Structure	11
2	**Kondratieff Waves in the World System Perspective**	23
	Long Waves in the World Economic Dynamics	24
	How Real are Kondratieff Waves? Discussions and Empirical Evidence..	29
	Kondratieff Waves in the Post-World War II GDP Data.........................	30
	Kondratieff Waves in the Pre-1945/50 World GDP Data	33
	Kondratieff Waves in the Pre-1870 World GDP Dynamics	39
	Kondratieff Waves in the World Technological Innovation Dynamics.....	42
	World System Effects and K-Wave Dynamics	44
	Change of K-Wave Phases Against the Background of the World System Core–Periphery Interaction	46
	Core and Periphery	46
	First Wave: The Late 1780s/Early 1790s–1844/1851	47
	Phase A: The Late 1780s/Early 1790s–1810/1817	47
	Phase B (Downswing): 1810/1817–1844/1851	47
	Second Wave: 1844/1851–1890/1896	48
	Phase A: 1844/1851–1870/1875	48
	Phase B: 1870/1875–1890/1896	48
	Third Wave: 1890/1896–1945	48
	Phase A: 1890/1896–1914/1928	48
	Phase B: 1914/1928–1939/1950	49
	Fourth Wave: 1939/1950–1984/1991...	49
	Phase A: 1939/1950–1968/1974	49

	Phase B: 1968/1974–1984/1991	49
	Fifth Wave: 1984/1991–the 2020s(?)	49
	Phase A: 1984/1991–2006/2008	49
	Phase B: 2006/2008–the 2020s(?)	50
	Possible Causes of the Expansion	50
	During Upswings the Resource Movement Balance Tended to be in Favor of the Core	51
3	**Interaction Between Kondratieff Waves and Juglar Cycles**	**55**
	Introductory Notes	55
	The Phases of Medium-Term Juglar Cycles (J-Cycles)	62
	On the Importance of Further Research on the Theory of J-Cycles	65
	Correlation Between K-Waves and J-Cycles	68
	Preliminary Discussion	68
	Juglar Cycles as Structural Elements of the K-Waves	76
	How Many J-Cycles Are There per a K-Wave Phase? An Analysis of Empirical Data	76
	Verbal Model of K-Waves	84
	General Outline	84
	Notes on Dynamics	85
	The Main Principles for the Development of the K-Wave Model	87
	Phase Alteration in the K-Wave Model	87
	Relationships between K-Waves and J-Cycles	88
	K-Waves and J-Cycle Clusters	88
	On the Correlation Between J-Cycles and K-Wave Phases	90
	General Causes and Mechanisms of Economic Cycles	91
	Mechanism of Influence of J-Cycles on the Temporal Rhythm of K-Wave Alteration	92
	Emergence and Resolution of Societal Structural Crisis within A- and B-Clusters of J-Cycles	92
	Additional Notes	96
	An Example of More Active Social Activities During K-Wave B-Phases in Comparison with K-Wave A-Phases	96
	Social Innovations as a Factor of K-Wave Interphase Transitions at the Level of Individual Societies, the Level of Intersocietal Interactions, and the World System Level	97
	What Limits the Length of the K-Wave A-Phases?	99
	Exhaustion of Growth Factors	100
	Excessive Business Optimism About the Prospects for Growth and the Revaluation of Assets	102
	The Long Depression Pause Emerging Within Border J-Cycles and the Change of Development Strategy	102
	The World System Dimension	104
	Modernization and World-System Socioeconomic Crises	104
	World-System Crises and Obstacles for the Emergence of the World-System Innovations. World-System Innovations and Their Delays	104

	How Does the K-Wave Synchronicity in the World System Emerge?	106
	General Characteristics of K-Wave Evolution, Factors, Mechanisms, and Indicators	107
	How and Why Do the Main K-Wave Dynamics Indicators Change?	107
4	**From Kondratieff Cycles to Akamatsu Waves? A New Center-Periphery Perspective on Long Cycles**	**111**
	Preliminary Remarks	111
	Background	113
	From Kondratieff Waves to Akamatsu "Flying Geese" Model	114
	Arrighi's Center-Periphery Model	121
	The Analysis of Economic Disasters and the Analysis of Economic Convergence	128
	New Evidence on Economic Cycles in 31 Countries of the World System, the Discovery of the Akamatsu Cycle and the Relationship of the Akamatsu Perspective with Long-Run Tendencies of Inequality	129
	The Global Maps of Convergence During World Depressions	137
	Conclusions	139
5	**Kondratieff Waves and Technological Revolutions**	**143**
	Production Principles, Production Revolutions and K-Waves	143
	Structural Model of Production Revolutions	144
	The Structure of the Production Principle	147
	The Cybernetic Revolution, Scientific-Cybernetic Production Principle, the Fourth, Fifth and Sixth K-Waves	150
	The Cybernetic Revolution	150
	Peculiarities of the Fourth K-Wave in Connection with the Beginning of the Cybernetic Revolution	153
	The Fifth K-Wave and the Delay of the New Wave of Innovations	154
	Characteristics of the Cybernetic Revolution	156
	What Are Self-Regulating Systems and Why Are They So Important?	156
	Medicine as a Sphere of the Initial Technological Breakthrough and the Emergence of MANBRIC-technology Complex	158
6	**Afterword: New Kondratieff Wave and Forthcoming Global Social Transformation**	**161**
	Problems of Population Ageing and Their Possible Solutions	163
	Global Population Ageing and the Sixth Technological Paradigm	167
	The Crisis and the Characteristics of the Financial System	169
	Pensioners and Pension Funds	171
	Reflections on a Possible Global Pension System	173
	Changing Global Order and the World System Reconfiguration	176
	Once Again about the Sixth K-wave and Cybernetic Revolution	178
	There Is Another Scenario	179
	The End of the Cybernetic Revolution and Possible Disappearance of K-Waves	179

**Appendix A: Biographies of Nikolay Kondratieff
and Kaname Akamatsu** 181

**Appendix B: The Results of Spectral Analysis and Application
of Other Statistical Approaches to the Study of Cycles
with Different Lengths**... 191

References.. 233

Index.. 261

Chapter 1
Introduction. Cyclical and World-Systemic Aspects of Economic Reality with Respect to Contemporary Crisis

Origins of Modern Economic Cyclicity

Our book is based on a number of theories. At the center stands the world-systems aspect of research.[1] It is not surprising due to the fact that many trends are more visible at the world-system level rather than at the level of a single country. The authors repeatedly show this with reference to different examples. But overall, this book is about a system of interrelated economic cycles (and crises as they are integral parts of those cycles). Our understanding of the nature of these cycles gives us the ability to anticipate crises and pitfalls that most certainly await us in the future. Perhaps the knowledge provided in this book will supply means to avoid falling into the deepest troughs of future economic crises

No matter how attractive the idea of linear progress (that was actively developed since the second half of the eighteenth century Nisbet, 1980) is—nevertheless, it has become apparent that the world evolves in a nonlinear fashion. Among the nonlinear phenomena, cyclical movements in various forms constitute one of the most common patterns.

It is obvious that the movement toward qualitatively new forms cannot continue endlessly—linearly and smoothly. It always has limitations, accompanied by the emergence of imbalances, increasing resistance to environmental constraints, competition for resources, etc. These endless attempts to overcome the resistance of the environment created conditions for a more or less noticeable advancement in particular societies. Historically, relatively short periods of rapid growth (which could be expressed as

---

[1] World-system approach emerged in the 1960s and 1970s emerging from the work of Fernand Braudel, Andre Gunder Frank, Immanuel Wallerstein, Samir Amin and Giovanni Arrighi (see, e.g., Arrighi and Silver, 1999; Amin, Arrighi, Frank, & Wallerstein, 2006; Braudel, 1973; Chase-Dunn & Hall, 1994, 1997; Frank, 1990, 1993; Frank & Gills, 1993; Wallerstein, 1974, 1987). In some way it acted as a direct development of the civilization approach (for more detail see Гринин и Коротаев, 2009a).

logistic, exponential, or power-law curves) tended to be followed by stagnation, different types of crises and setbacks, which led to the creation of complex patterns of historical dynamics, within which trend and cyclical components were usually interwoven in intricate ways (see, e.g., Grinin, Korotayev, & Malkov, 2010; Korotayev, 2007б; Korotayev & Grinin, 2012, 2014; Korotayev, Malkov, & Khaltourina, 2006a; Markov & Korotayev, 2007; Гринин и Коротаев, 2010). Hence, in history we see a constant interaction of cyclical dynamics and dynamics of trends, including some long-term trends.

If we observe in some society a long-time regular repetition of cycles of the same type, ending with grave crises and significant setbacks, this means that this society confronts some strong systemic and environmental constraints that it is unable to overcome.

Cyclical dynamics was noticed a long time ago. Already ancient historians (see, e.g., the second Chapter of Book VI of Polybius' *Histories*) described the cyclical component of historical dynamics, whereas new interesting analyses of such dynamics also appeared in Medieval and Early Modern periods (see, e.g., Ibn Khaldūn, 1958 [1377], or Machiavelli, 1996 [1531]). This is not surprising as cyclical dynamics were dominant in the agrarian social systems. With modernization, trend dynamics became much more pronounced and, naturally, students of modern societies pay more attention to these trends.[2]

The cyclical nature of economic development was, for a long time, not traced because it was indiscernibly weak and irregular.[3] This is no accident. We believe that the cyclical effect in economy only appears in a really clear way with the advent of regular extended reproduction (first, in the financial and trade sector, and then in the manufacturing). It would be useful to give a brief summary of how modern cyclical dynamics originated in the economy.

It is no coincidence that the first clear manifestations of the long-wave processes of economic dynamics coincided with the industrial revolution, namely the 1780s (see, e.g., Grinin, 2007a; Grinin & Korotayev, 2015a). We can assume that the transition to machine industry created the phenomenon of Kondratieff waves (or K-waves) in the economy (or allowed at least the ability to see them clearly).[4]

---

[2] Trends may be described by various equations—linear, exponential, power-law, etc. On the other hand, the cliodynamic research has demonstrated that the cyclical historical dynamics can be also modeled mathematically in a rather effective way (see, e.g., Chu & Lee, 1994; Korotayev, 2007a, 2007б; Korotayev & Komarova, 2004; Korotayev & Khaltourina, 2006; Korotayev, Malkov, & Grinin, 2014; Korotayev, Malkov, & Khaltourina, 2006a; Korotayev, Zinkina, Kobzeva et al., 2011; Nefedov, 2004; Turchin, 2003, 2005a, 2005b; Turchin & Korotayev, 2006; Turchin & Nefedov, 2009; Usher, 1989), whereas the trend and cycle components of historical dynamics turn out to be of equal importance.

[3] However, in complex agrarian systems one could detect rather regular sociodemographic cycles (see, e.g., Коротаев, 2006, 2007a, 2007б; Korotayev & Khaltourina, 2006; Korotayev & Komarova, 2004; Korotayev, Malkov, & Khaltourina, 2006a; Коротаев, Комарова и Халтурина, 2007; Korotayev, Zinkina, Kobzeva et al., 2011; Korotayev, Malkov, & Grinin, 2014; Nefedov, 2004; Turchin, 2003, 2005a, 2005b; Гринин, 2007а; Гринин и Коротаев, 2012; Turchin & Korotayev, 2006; Turchin & Nefedov, 2009).

[4] See Гринин, 2013а; Гринин и Коротаев, 2014а. In any case, most researchers agree with this dating, though there are ones who find long waves in prices (and not only in prices) starting from

The reason for this statement is seen in the fact that during this period the productive forces began to acquire a new fundamental characteristic—a "desire" for steady and continuous expansion (on this property see, e.g., Abramovitz, 1961; Gellner, 1983; Grinin, 2007a; Kuznets, 1966; Гринин, 2006a, 2010a, 2012a, 2013a; Гринин и Коротаев, 2010, 2012). The emergence of this property led to the emergence of various forms of cyclical dynamics connected with various limitations (that hinder such an expansion) and attempts to overcome them. This forward movement, of course, could not be uniform, and must obey different rhythms; their common property was the alteration of acceleration and deceleration phases caused by the exhaustion of available resources for growth, market saturation, reduced profit margins and so on.

Those rhythms were already present in the development of trade in the eighteenth century. The birth of the first K-wave at the final phase of the Industrial Revolution meant the emergence of a new form of cyclical dynamics that was specific for the industrial production principle (see *Chap. 5*). Completion of the Industrial Revolution in Britain and consolidation of the extended production pattern were marked by the emergence of a new and more explicit form of cycling—the medium-term cycles (ending with cyclical crises). The first cycle of such kind can be dated to 1818–1825. It is rather symptomatic that this cycle occurred after the completion of the upswing phase of the first K-wave. There is every reason to believe that K-waves may be fully realized only through the medium-term cycles, as aggregated depressions of medium-term cycles determine the overall downward trend at the B-phases of K-waves, whereas aggregated booms of medium-term cycles determine the upswing dynamics of K-wave A-phases (see Grinin & Korotayev 2014c; Коротаев и Гринин, 2012; Гринин, 2010a; Гринин и Коротаев, 2012, as well as *Chap. 3* of the present monograph for more details; see also Grinin, Korotayev, & Malkov, 2010).

Thus, both the Kondratieff long waves and medium-term Juglar cycles are associated with the same fundamental change—the transition to a new pattern of development of production, i.e., extended reproduction based not only on the involvement of new resources (this happened as well within complex pre-modern agrarian systems), but on the economic growth through regular investments, innovations and improvements. In other words, the relationship between the long and medium-term cycles, on the one hand, and the tendency of the modern productive forces toward their continued expansion on the other has a common denominator, which includes innovation as an important component. Hence, it is evident that both types of the economic cycle are associated with a longer (and deeper) cyclic change of the productive forces—production revolutions that are leading to the movement from one principle of production to another (for more details see *Chap. 5*; see also Grinin & Grinin, 2014; Гринин, 2012a, 2013a; Гринин и Гринин, 2015a).

1825 was the year when a typical cyclical crisis of the Juglar type engulfed for the first time the entire British economy and to some extent economies of many other countries. It was preceded by the rise, which in 1824 and early 1825 grew into

---

the twelfth (or even tenth) century (see, e.g., Goldstein, 1988; Моуги, 1992; Modelski & Thompson, 1996; Modelski, 2006, 2008a, 2012; Пантин, 1996; Пантин и Лапкин, 2006).

a real boom of investment and speculation (see Гринин и Коротаев, 2010 for more details). The crises that took place until 1825 in the industry were not universal; they were connected with specific problems in trade caused by different factors (inflation, wars and others).

Researchers of medium-term cycles and crises of the nineteenth century often paid much attention to the crises of the eighteenth century—finding them very instructive, and saw them—most importantly—as similar to those that occurred during the nineteenth century. Indeed, the similarities (excessive lending, unexpected bankruptcies, credit crunch, panic and bust) are very clearly visible. And it is no coincidence—a number of necessary elements for modern economic cycles had already emerged by that time.

As mentioned above, the imperative of the continuous expansion of economic turnover emerged. Therefore cyclicality (inherent in the industrial production principle) was substantial. The role of credit also increased. And since the mid-term cycles and crises are associated with fluctuations in credit, a certain prototype of medium-term cycles (with a characteristic period of about 10 years) can be seen in the eighteenth century, especially in its second half (see Braudel, 1973; Hansen, 1951).

In 1763, the crisis began in Hamburg against the background of the depreciation of currency during the Seven Years' War, but then as a result of the huge bankruptcy of the Neufville brothers in Amsterdam this crisis acquired a pan-European character (Braudel, 1973; Wirth, 1883). Then there was the crisis of 1772–1773, which took place against the background of severe crop failures in 1771–1772 and, like the previous crisis, included a large bankruptcy (the Cliffords bankruptcy of December 1772—which became the detonator of collapse). Finally, the crisis of 1780–1783 also acquired a large scale as a result of another major bankruptcy in 1780 (see Braudel, 1973).[5]

Crises could grow to include all of Europe largely because trade and economic relations in the Western (or rather, Atlantic) part of the World System had significantly increased and become more intense. Against this background it is hardly surprising that any market fluctuations in one place also influenced other places (see, e.g., Wirth, 1883). It is no coincidence, that the crises in the nineteenth century were called commercial/industrial, as they particularly and quickly hit commerce (which tends to depend heavily on the credit). Still, we note that there was a significant difference between the eighteenth and nineteenth centuries. In the eighteenth century, crises were mainly trade-related and based on a "disorder of the credit;" that is a violation of trust in the credit sector which were a result of failures in the functioning of the financial system. Until 1825, industrial crises (of overproduction) were observed in the cotton-textile industry (Мендельсон, 1959–1964, vol. 1), but they are more likely to be considered local, and the normal cycle period had not yet emerged. Thus, there was a certain preparatory period, during which the mechanism of K-waves and J-cycles formed.

---

[5] Then, however, crises became more frequent occurring every three to four years. For example, mention may be made of the crises of 1787–1788, 1793, 1797, 1803. But, as has been mentioned above, they were of transitional type.

The System of Economic Cycles

As has already been mentioned, this book will show the relationship between a number of cycles (Kondratieff, Kuznets, Akamatsu, Juglar and others). However, analysis of the different cycles is given with different levels of completeness. Therefore, in the first chapter, we would like to introduce to the reader some system of those cycles, to give some explanations that will be useful for the perception of the remaining chapters and to say a bit about the economists who made the most important contributions to the study of those cycles.

We start with some definitions. A more detailed analysis of the notions of Kondratieff waves and Juglar cycles is offered in the forthcoming chapters of the present monograph, so here we restrict ourselves to rather brief definitions.

Kondratieff Waves

Kondratieff waves (Kondratieff cycles, long waves, long economic cycles) are repeated fluctuations of important economic variables with a characteristic period of about 40–60 years, within which at one (upswing) phase growth rates of indicators tend to accelerate, and at the other (downswing) phase they tend to slow down.

Juglar Cycle

Juglar cycle (or "business cycle") is a medium-term economic cycle with a characteristic period between 7 and 11 years. Juglar cycles may be regarded as macroeconomic fluctuations when economic growth and boom is replaced by economic downturn, which is regularly followed by a new period of economic growth (thus starting a new economic cycle). This cycle can be subdivided into four phases: (1) phase of recovery, when, after the fall of production and stagnation, economic growth begins; (2) expansion phase, when economic growth is accelerating up to an economic boom; (3) phase of recession, during which the euphoria of prosperity is replaced by panic accompanying collapse, and after that comes the economic downturn; (4) phase of depression or stagnation, during which a balance is achieved: the decline has stopped, but any pronounced growth is absent yet.

One more type of economic cycle (its period is identified by various students in the range between 15 and 25 years) is named after Nobel laureate Simon Kuznets who first discovered and described them (Abramovitz, 1961; Kuznets, 1930). These are known as **Kuznets swings** (see, e.g., Abramovitz, 1961: 226; Diebolt & Doliger, 2006; Solomou, 2008b). Kuznets himself first connected these cycles with demographic processes, in particular with immigrant inflows/outflows and the changes in construction intensity that resulted from these demographic in and out flows. That is why he denoted them as "demographic" or "building" cycles/swings. However, there are a number of more general models of Kuznets swings. For example, Forrester connected Kuznets swings with major investments in fixed capital, whereas he accounted for the Kondratieff waves through the economic and physical connections between the capital producing and capital consuming sectors (Forrester, 1977: 114; Румянцева, 2003: 34–35). Note also the interpretation of Kuznets swings as infrastructural investment cycles (e.g., Shiode, Batty, Longley, & Maguire, 2004: 355). So **Kuznets swings** *(with period in the range between 15 and 25 years) are connected with infrastructural investment or other changes in economy.* However, there is no agreement regarding the nature of such changes, they can be connected with oscillation in technologies, long-term investments in infrastructure, construction or other spheres (On Kuznets swings see also *Appendix B*).

A number of influential economists deny the presence of any economic cycles altogether.[6] Below in the following chapters, we will discuss such views. Anyway, we believe this is not a constructive approach, as it hinders our ability to make predictions based on the theory of cycles, as well as to provide full and adequate explanations of the past crises.

On the other hand, economists make important and valuable attempts to find the relationship between different types of cycles (see *Chaps. 2–4* and *Appendix B* below for more detail). However, there are some grounds to maintain that Nikolay Kondratieff really started this direction of research (for more biographic detail on Kondratieff see *Appendix A;* for the most recent biography of Nikolay Kondratieff see Kopala & Budden, 2015: Part 1).

In 1922, in his book *The World Economy during and after the War* Nikolay Kondratieff first formulated the basic tenets of the theory of long cycles (Кондратьев, 1922). Until that time the economic literature hardly knew any cycles other than ones with a characteristic period between 7 and 11 year (which were called industrial, commercial cycles, and so on), and Kondratieff quite logically called them "short cycles" (Кондратьев, 2002 [1922]: 323 etc.). However, already in 1925 in the "Big cycles of conjuncture" (Кондратьев, 1925, 1993в [1925]: 25, 26), he began to call them "medium cycles".[7] Why? The fact is that in those years a British businessman and statistician Joseph Kitchin (1923) discovered some cycles (with a characteristic period between 3 and 4 years) manifested in fluctuations in inventories that could be denoted as truly "short cycles". Later, they became known as **Kitchin cycles.**

Thus, the Kitchin cycles are cycles with a period between 40 and 59 months that are believed to be manifested in the fluctuations of enterprises' inventories.[8]

---

[6] For example, the title of the respective section in a classical *Principles of Economics* textbook by N. Gregory Mankiw—"Economic Fluctuations are Irregular and Unpredictable" (Mankiw, 2008: 740) is rather telling in this respect; see also, e.g., Zarnowitz, 1985: 544–568.

[7] Incidentally, this is Kondratieff who appears to be the first economist to call those cycles "medium-term".

[8] "The logic of this cycle can be described in a rather neat way through neoclassical laws of market equilibrium and is accounted for by time lags in information movements affecting the decision making of commercial firms. As is well known, in particular, firms react to the improvement of commercial situations by increasing output through the full employment of the extent fixed capital assets. As a result, within a certain period of time (ranging between a few months to 2 years) the

Due to the fact that the medium-term cycles often have internal ups and downs, Harvard School headed by Wesley Mitchell, started to consider cycles statistically. They did not consider the logical causes or intensity of cycles but rather measured them by the presence of recessions, from a recession to another recession, regardless of the point that different recessions may be significantly different as regards their strength and nature. As a result, they also detected some cycles with a period between 3 and 4 years (that to a certain extent coincided with Kitchin cycles).

Somewhat later, as has been mentioned above, Simon Kuznets discovered construction cycles lasting 17–30 years (Abramovitz, 1961; Kuznets, 1930, 1958; see above with respect of the nature of Kuznets cycles).

In 1937 the Japanese economist Kaname Akamatsu discovered specific links between the rise and decline of the global peripheries to the larger Kondratieff cycle (for more biographic detail on Akamatsu see *Appendix A*). Now this type of swing is known as **Akamatsu waves**. *They are cycles (with a period ranging from 20 to 60 years) connected with convergence and divergence of core and periphery of the World System and explaining cyclical upward and downward swings (at global and national levels) in the movements of the periphery countries to catch up with the richer ones.*

Thus, in the 1920s and 1930s one could observe within Economics the formation of an idea of a whole system of economic cycles.

It seemed logical to try to consider the different cycles as having a single nature. Such an attempt was made by Joseph Schumpeter in his monograph *Business cycles* (Schumpeter, 1939).[9] However, due to the fact that he tried to consider the structure of the long wave to be identical with the structure of the medium-term cycle, his attempt to create a general theory of cycles failed. Note, on the other hand, that it is due to Schumpeter that the medium term cycles are known now as "Juglar cycles" after the French economist Klement Juglar (see also *Chap. 3*), whereas the long-term cycles are denoted now as "Kondratieff waves".

The Great Depression intensified interest by economists in cyclical dynamics. As was noted by Gottfried Haberler (1964), never before in the history of economics had the problem of the economic cycle been studied so hard. Haberler himself, before the Second World War, and on the instructions of the League of Nations, compiled an exhaustive analysis of all the theories of business cycles, but he was skeptical about the idea of long cycles.

However, the emergence of the Keynesian theoretical framework turned economists' attention to other aspects. On the one hand, Keynesian ideas have contributed to the understanding of the internal predisposition of the capitalist economy to recession and booms (i.e., cycles), but on the other — the attractiveness of the

---

market gets 'flooded' with commodities whose quantity becomes gradually excessive. The demand declines, prices drop, the produced commodities get accumulated in inventories, which informs entrepreneurs of the necessity to reduce output. However, this process takes some time" (Румянцева, 2003: 23–24). Currently, due to the development of logistics and information technologies, Kitchin cycles lost their importance. About Kitchin cycles see also *Appendix B*.

[9] But of course Schumpeter did not know about Akamatsu waves.

opportunity to influence the course of cycles through public policies led to the fact that economic thought focused mainly on instruments of such an influence, and the problems of nature and the root causes of cyclical changes gradually went to the periphery of economic science.

This was facilitated by the fact that in the second half of the twentieth century (especially at the upswing phase of the fourth Kondratieff wave in the 1950s and 1960s) the flow of cycles significantly changed (primarily under the impact of active external influences on the economic situation).[10] Recessions ceased to be as deep as before. Not surprisingly, the researchers began to pay more attention to such issues as monetary regulation rather than to Juglar cycles.

Such disregard for the study of Juglar cycles is, of course, counterproductive. In our opinion, the current crisis in many respects is very similar in type to the classic crisis as an integral part/phase of Juglar cycle (for more detail see Grinin, Korotayev, & Malkov, 2010).[11]

Yet, investigations of long cycles continued, especially in the period of the K-wave downswing of the 1970s and 1980s, when substantial research based on the ideas of Schumpeter was produced (e.g., Barr, 1979; Bieshaar & Kleinknecht, 1984; Cleary & Hobbs, 1983; Dickson, 1983; Glismann, Rodemer, & Wolter, 1983; Eklund, 1980; Freeman, 1987; Gordon, 1978; Kleinknecht, 1981; Mandel, 1975, 1980; Marchetti, 1980, 1986; Mensch, 1979; Senge, 1982; van Duijn 1979, 1981; van der Zwan, 1980; van Ewijk, 1982). But although the topic concerned sometimes very prominent scientists such as Forrester, Rostow, or Wallerstein (Forrester, 1978, 1981; Rostow, 1975, 1978; Wallerstein, 1984), on the whole this area has never been among the top interests of economists. Nevertheless, interest in this process continues, a new surge of interest has been associated with the work of Tessaleno Devezas.

There are rather diverse opinions regarding the long cycles. For example, the London-based *Economist* claims that most currents in standard economic theories do not give lots of credit to Kondratieff cycle research:

> *"Kondratieff cycle: a 50-year-long BUSINESS CYCLE, named after Nikolai Kondratieff, a Russian economist. He claimed to have identified cycles of economic activity lasting half a century or more in his 1925 book, The Long Waves in Economic Life. Because this implied that CAPITALISM was, ultimately, a stable system, in contrast to the Marxist view that it was self-destructively unstable, he ended up in one of Stalin's prisons, where he died. Alas, there is little hard evidence to support Kondratieff's conclusion" (http://www.economist.com/economics-a-to-z/k)*

Now we might lean back and say, if prestigious magazines such as *The Economist* issue such a verdict, our labors are completely in vain.

Katherine Yester in *Foreign Policy,* No. 172, May–June 2009, however, puts it differently by saying:

---

[10] For a more detailed analysis of post-World War II cycles (see Гринин, 2013а; Гринин и Коротаев, 2010).

[11] Fast, sometimes explosive booms (that produced a huge strain on the economy), and then even more precipitous busts were typical for the industrial cycles of the nineteenth century.

"AS NIKOLAI KONDRATIEV SHIVERED before his executioners... in 1938, he could scarcely have imagined that, 71 years later, his name would be resurrected by a new generation of business theorists and management gurus seeking to understand the first Great Recession of the twenty-first century.

A prime mover behind Lenin's 1921 New Economic Policy, which briefly rehabilitated capitalism in order to save a young Soviet Union from imminent collapse, Kondratiev was an intellectual insurgent in a time and place where heresy could get one killed. Kondratiev theorized that economic activity took place in long waves: 50- or 60-year periods of creativity and growth followed by briefer contractions, after which the cycle would begin anew.

So taken was Joseph Schumpeter, the Harvard University economist best known for coining the term 'creative destruction', with the idea of long waves that he named the concept for Kondratiev. Schumpeter's view was that innovation tends to arrive in clumps: 'discrete rushes which are separated from each other by spans of comparative quiet.' These bursts of creativity, he wrote, 'periodically reshape the existing structure of industry by introducing new methods' of production, organization, and supply. As for the negative effects of depressions—unemployment, the loss of wealth, economic dislocation—they were just creative destruction at work.

Today, with the pillars of capitalism falling all around us, it might seem odd to wonder what world-changing shifts this Great Recession will help bring to life—what Next Big thing?" (http://www.foreignpolicy.com/articles/2009/05/01/the_next_big_thing)

This paragraph from one of the most prestigious mainstream U.S. foreign policy journals reveals another aspect in the Kondratieff legacy, which is surfacing again and again almost 80 years after his cruel death in the Gulag: political classes—for good or for bad—seem to take Kondratieff's theories more seriously than established, mainstream economists. Kondratieff cycles or K-cycles remind the political elites of the temporal character of political, economic and social conditions and the power relationships characteristic of them. This seems also to be true for the think tanks and research institutes, working for the political, economic or security establishments around the globe.

In this book, a lot of attention is paid to the aspects of the relationship between the medium and long term cycles. External connection between them is very clearly seen in the fact that temporal datings of Kondratieff waves and their phases are closely connected with the generally accepted datings of Juglar cycles. Overall, however, even this aspect of the relationship between Kondratieff waves and Juglar cycles has been studied insufficiently and rather superfluously (see, e.g., Аврамов, 1992: 66–68; Полетаев and Савельева, 1993: 11–12). In particular, for reasons of lack of time and opportunity, Kondratieff did not study those relationships in any detail, although from time to time he touched upon this point. Schumpeter (1939) paid more attention to this relationship, but, as has been said, his approach proved insufficiently productive.

In contrast to Schumpeter, more recent researchers of Kondratieff waves in the vast majority disregarded the medium-term cycles. Some of them have focused only on one side of the heritage of Schumpeter (the mechanism of creation and implementation of basic innovations), the other part which had been leaning toward the study of the connection of K-waves with even more long-term military-political cycles that are even more controversial than the original Kondratieff cycle.

Thus, studies of medium and long cycling are generally proceeding in different planes—relative independently of each other. However, one of the most promising areas could be a return to the analysis of the connection between long waves and medium-term cycles. We believe that such an analysis will be able to shed light on the causes of the most mysterious moment—relatively stable duration of Kondratieff waves and their phases (respectively 40-60 years and 20-30 years).

In addition to the analysis of the organic relationship between Juglar cycles and Kondratieff waves, it appears absolutely necessary to investigate also the connection of these two types of cycles with some processes taking place at the World System level.

True enough, world-systems scholars, especially in the research traditions of Arrighi, Attinà and Wallerstein, have always talked about "Kondratieff cycles", but, as yet, have not presented sufficient advanced statistical evidence of their own, to convince the writers of encyclopedic articles like the ones quoted above that the evidence in favor of K-cycles is sufficiently solid. Now, to combine a highly contested economic term—Kondratieff cycles—with a term which might be even more contested today—*"center-periphery relationships"*—might be more daring still. But in a more recent standard social science encyclopedia we read under the heading *"Dependency Theory" (International Encyclopedia of the Social Sciences, 2008.* Encyclopedia.com. 21 Oct. 2014) the following:

"In the early 1950s, a group of economists stationed at the United Nations Economic Commission for Latin America (ECLA) in Santiago, Chile, launched a rigorous research program around one pressing question: What accounts for the growing divergence in living standards and gross domestic product (GDP) between the wealthy countries of the industrialized North and the poorer developing countries of the South? In 1850, for example, Argentina was among the richest nations of the world and GDP per capita in Latin America was $245, compared to $239 in North America. A century later, Argentina was mired in debt and poverty, and GDP per capita in Canada and the United States had quickly outpaced that of Latin America as both had firmly joined the ranks of the developed-country bloc.

According to neoclassical economic theory, strong trade and investment linkages between North and South should lead to a positive-sum outcome for all participants. However, by the 1950s it was difficult to ignore the widening global cleavages between North and South, as well as the growing gap between rich and poor within the developing countries. This latter trend, characterized by an uneasy coexistence between a modern urbanized sector of the economy with strong global ties and a largely rural traditional sector where production modes sorely lagged, was increasingly referred to as dualism.

[…] At heart, most dependency theorists saw the problem of underdevelopment as the inherently exploitive and contradictory nature of the capitalist system, which pitted capitalists and workers against each other as both sought to maximize their respective economic well-being. The North, with its capital abundance and accumulation of wealth, was the oppressor, while the South, with its ready supply of cheap labor and vastly rich land and natural resources, was the oppressed. It was the external sector that perpetuated underdevelopment, as well as the various private (multinational corporations) and public entities (the World Bank, the International Monetary Fund, and industrial-bloc governments) that represented it.

[…] While few of the dependency school's theoretical assertions have stood the test of time, this perspective continues to offer a powerful description of the political and economic plight of the majority of countries that remain on the periphery of the world economy. A full understanding of the causal mechanisms and policy solutions for remedying underdevelopment may still be a long way off; however, the dependency school's specifica-

tion of concrete problems like dualism, inequality, diminishing returns to trade, and the North-South divide have enriched debates about development and helped them to move forward." (http://www.encyclopedia.com/topic/Dependency_Theory.aspx)

Revisiting these old questions of social science theory—long cycles and the center-periphery relationship and the interaction between them—is the theme of this book. The authors are united in their admiration for the great legacy of Kondratieff's work and personality, they are united in their long-term interest in globalization studies and investigations of the center-periphery relationships, and they all share the methodological premises of applying rigorous quantitative and statistical research to questions, which are often highly contested on the global political terrain.

Of course we try to take into account all investigations of long and other cycles in English, German, and Russian as well as some other languages (readers will see this in the next chapters). In many ways, the present volume is indebted to the legacy of the great volume, Devezas, 2006, which is a unique encounter of Russian and Western Kondratieff cycle research and Kondratieff research, and which is now present at a truly staggering number of global libraries (960 libraries; see http://classify.oclc.org/classify2/ClassifyDemo?search-author-txt=%22Devezas%2C+Tessaleno+C.%22). On the other hand, in many ways, the present volume builds on earlier publications by the authors on the subject, but specifically develops the center-periphery aspect of the debate about Kondratieff cycles.[12] So it makes available the main thrust of the thinking of the three authors on Kondratieff cycles with a major European publisher. True enough, the current volume also builds on recent advances in mainstream economics, which now evaluate long-term economic development data series and which recently discovered the economic disaster cycle (see, especially, Barro, 2012, 2013; Barro & Ursúa, 2008; Barro, Nakamura, & Ursúa, 2011; Gourio, 2012; Maddison, 1995, 2001, 2003, 2007, 2010).

About This Book and Its Structure

This monograph consists of six chapters (including this introduction) and two appendices.

In the second chapter *"Kondratieff Waves in the World System Perspective"*, it is shown that the analysis of long economic cycles allows us to understand long-term

---

[12] See Grinin, 2008, 2009a, 2009b, 2010, 2011; Grinin & Korotayev, 2010a, 2010b, 2014a, 2014b; Grinin, Devezas, & Korotayev, 2012; Grinin, Markov, & Korotayev, 2009; Гринин, 2005, 2006а, 2007а, 2008а, 2008б, 2008в, 2008г, 2009д, 2010а, 2012б, 2013а; Korotayev, 2005, 2006, 2007а, 2007б, Korotayev & Grinin, 2012; Korotayev & Khaltourina, 2006, Коротаев и Халтурина, 2009, Korotayev & Tsirel, 2010; Коротаев и Цирель, 2010а; Коротаев и Халтурина, 2009; Korotayev, Malkov, & Khaltourina, 2006a; Korotayev, Zinkina, & Bogevolnov, 2011; Korotayev, Zinkina, Bogevolnov & Malkov, 2011a, 2011b; Korotayev, Zinkina, & Bogevolnov, 2011; Коротаев, Халтурина и Малков и др., 2010; Tausch, 2006b, 2007, 2010, 2012, 2013; Гринин и Коротаев, 2010, 2009а, 2012; Гринин, Коротаев и Цирель, 2011; Tausch & Heshmati, 2011, 2014; Tausch, Heshmati, & Bajalan, 2010; see also Тауш, 2002, 2003, 2007, 2008, 2009, 2012.

world-system dynamics, to develop forecasts, to explain crises of the past, as well as the current global economic crisis. This chapter offers a sketch of the history of research on K-waves; it analyzes the nature of Kondratieff waves. It offers a historical and theoretical analysis of K-wave dynamics in the World System framework; and in particular, it studies the influence of the long wave dynamics on the changes of the world GDP growth rates during the last two centuries.

K-waves are considered as one of the most important components of the World System dynamics. The driving forces of K-waves can be adequately understood only if we take into account the dynamics, phases, and peculiarities of the World System development. Kondratieff waves are most relevant when considered at the World System scale. As those waves always manifest themselves at supra-societal scales, the World System processes turn out to be very important for the understanding of the K-wave dynamics.

The expansion and intensification of the World System economic links lead to the formation of preconditions for new upswings. Kondratieff himself noticed that *"the new long cycles usually coincide with the expansion of the orbit of the world economic ties"* (Кондратьев, 2002: 374). The start of the new cycles implies not only expansion of those ties, but also the change in their character.

World System processes are bound to influence economic processes including medium period business cycles (e.g., Grinin & Korotayev, 2012b; Гринин и Коротаев, 2009a). Hence, they are bound to influence K-wave dynamics. However, there is a reverse influence of those waves on World System development. Kondratieff himself noticed the growth in the intensity of warfare and revolutionary activity during K-wave upswings (e.g., Kondratieff, 1935: 111; Кондратьев, 2002: 373–374). On the other hand, it is quite clear that those processes themselves influenced K-wave dynamics in a very significant way and world wars provide salient illustrations. It is also quite clear that those K-wave students who pointed to the important role of military expenses (and inflation shocks produced by them) identified a significant (though in no way sole) cause of price growth (and decline) in the course of Kondratieff cycles (see, e.g., Goldstein, 1988).

Breakthrough inventions (producing new technological systems) tend to be made during downswings, whereas their wide implementation is observed during subsequent upswings. The diffusion of those innovations throughout the World System is bound to affect significantly the course of K-waves, as the opening of new zones of economic development is capable of changing the world dynamics as a whole. Thus large-scale investments of British capital in the railway construction in the United States, Australia, India, etc. in the last third of nineteenth and the beginning of twentieth centuries contributed to periodical stagnations within Great Britain (and, finally, to the change of the World System hegemon). Technological changes that start in one zone of the World System after their diffusion to other zones may produce such consequences that could hardly be forecasted. Thus, the development of oceanic and railway transportation led to vigorous exportation of cereal crops from the USA, Russia, and Canada that caused in the 1870s, 1880s, and 1890s the so-called world agrarian crisis (which affected significantly the second K-wave downswing but helped several countries to escape from the Malthusian trap).

Important events that take place within the World System may lead to an earlier (or later) switch from downswing to upswing (or, naturally, from upswing to downswing) within K-wave dynamics. For example, as is well-known, the discovery of gold in California and Australia contributed in a rather significant way to the world economic (and price) growth during the second K-wave upswing, which was already noticed by Kondratieff (e.g., Kondratieff, 1935: 111, 113–115; Кондратьев, 2002: 384–385).

It the chapter we contend that the change of K-wave upswing and downswing phases correlates significantly with the phases of fluctuations in the relationships between the World System Core and Periphery, as well as with World System Core changes– the growth or decline of its strength, emergence of competing centers, their movements, and so on. Currently, the World System Periphery, in contrast with what was observed not so long ago, tends to develop more rapidly than the core (Grinin & Korotayev, 2015a, 2015b). This has become especially salient during the current global economic crisis.

Thus, what is the correlation between structural changes of the World System and periodic fluctuations within the K-wave dynamics? Authors suggest that during the K-wave downswings the Core tended to subjugate, integrate, and pull up the Periphery to a greater extent than what was observed during the K-wave upswings. It is during the K-wave downswings that the Core tended to expand vigorously (in various way) to the Periphery by investing resources into it and by actively modernizing it. Those efforts and resource flows made a rather important contribution in the slow-down of the Core growth rates. In contrast, during K-wave upswings the Core's activities were concentrated within the core part of the World System; in the meantime the balance of resource movement turned out to be in favor of the Core. Such a situation led to the acceleration of the growth rates of the Core countries (As reader will see in *Chap. 4*, this approach in some respect correlates with Akamatsu's theory). However, this regularity changed at the A-phase of the Fifth K-wave as during this period the main economic growth was generated not by the Core, but rather by the Periphery whose strongest countries moved to the Semiperiphery and even became new centers of growth. This tendency is also continuing at the B-phase of the current Fifth K-wave.

In the third chapter *"Interaction between Juglar Cycles and Kondratieff Waves"* the authors describe Juglar cycles, provide a brief history of their study, and then concentrate on aspects of the relationship between the medium-term (7–11 years) Juglar cycle (J-cycle) and long (40–60 years) Kondratieff cycle (K-waves). In their opinion, such an approach can greatly clarify the causes of alternation of upward and downward phases within the Kondratieff waves, and the reasons for the relative stability of the length of these waves. They proceed from the fact that long-term processes must have appropriate causes. For K-waves such causes are rooted in the very nature of the expanded reproduction of the economy, but less long pulses (associated with alternating J-cycles) streamline periodicity. In their opinion, J-cycles are the only real factor that can set the rhythm of Kondratieff waves and their phases.

The point is that adjacent 2–4 medium cycles form a system that affects dynamics of economic trend. The latter can be an upswing (active) or a downswing (depressive). The mechanisms of formation of such medium-term trends and changing tendencies are explained in this chapter. The presence of such clusters of medium cycles (general duration of which is 20–30 years) determines to a large degree the long-wave dynamics and its timing characteristics. It also can provide certain means for forecasting, and the respective chapter contains such forecasts.

This chapter provides a verbal model of Kondratieff waves, based on the close relationship between the medium-term (7–11 years) Juglar cycles and K-waves. As has already been mentioned, the relative duration and regularity of change of K-wave phases is determined by the nature of nearby chains or clusters of J-cycles.

A chain-cluster of J-cycles with less pronounced depressions, and more durable pronounced expansions is denoted as "A-cluster", whereas a chain-cluster of J-cycles with more pronounced depressions and less intense and less prolonged expansions is denoted as "B-cluster".

During the K-wave A-phase the fast economic expansion leads inevitably to the necessity of societal change; as a result, B-phase starts. But the possibilities of societal transformation lag behind the demands of the economy, that is why periods of such a restructuring correspond to periods of more difficult development, that is, to K-wave downswings.

The model proposed in this chapter suggests that one can observe an evident negative feedback between the K-wave trends, which strengthens with each new medium-term cycle (until the trend does not change), since the nature and results of each J-cycle is a signal for a particular type of action of active participants in the process (from individual entrepreneurs to whole states and supranational organizations).

The model also shows that for an adequate understanding of the nature of Kondratieff waves it is necessary to consider their effect firstly at the World System level. The World System scale allows to support long-term positive feedbacks and to delay the manifestation of negative feedbacks. During the A-phase positive feedbacks emerge due to the acceleration of modernization within the World System as a whole, while during the B-phase they emerge due to the complexity of finding anti-crisis measures.

In this chapter authors also analyze the transmission of impulses from the leading countries to the less developed or less actively developing ones throughout the K-wave, and the connection with the J-cycles. During the period of one J-cycle (7–11 years) advantages of new technologies, organizational arrangements, and other achievements (that have appeared in the leading country or countries) become more obvious. The second cycle initiates, with great intensity, the modernization of a large number of countries. The third cycle extends modernization, but at this level there are already difficulties associated with the complexity of sharing as well as a fall in the rate of profit, and—very importantly—the transformation of institutions and relationships both within individual countries and across the World System.

The authors also focus on how and why the main K-wave dynamics indicators change. Kondratieff himself and many researchers after him believed that the main indicators of the upswing/downswing dynamics within the K-waves are associated with the directions of price trends. But in recent decades this role is rather played by relative GDP growth rate dynamics.

The analysis of the dynamics of K-waves for over two hundred years suggests that within this apparent incompatibility one may still trace some organic link, if we assume that the factors that define K-wave phases change (at least, according to their importance) in a natural way. K-waves change their manifestations in connection with the development of industrial production, as well as with the expansion of the World System and the World System links. In addition, the role of the state grows. It is worth noting that van Duijn puts forward a very plausible hypothesis that long waves in economic growth emerged in the second half of the nineteenth century, replacing long waves in price movements (van Duijn, 1983: 91).

If we accept the idea of natural changes in the K-wave factors, it allows us to move to an organic synthesis of all the major theories explaining K-waves through monetary, technological, investment, external and military factors. But of course, such a change of the driving forces of long-term trends could not be either rapid or complete.

It seems that price changes, as the main K-wave indicator, started to be replaced by the fluctuations in economic growth rates sometime in the early twentieth century. This, in particular, is reflected in the competition between Britain and Germany. Finally, this became clear after the First World War and the postwar crisis of 1920, and it is no accident that in the period preceding the Great Depression, prices barely rose, which even was a cause of some forecast errors. Such a radical change in the oscillation factors coincided (but not coincidentally): (a) with an almost complete expansion of the World System, (b) with the change of its leader, (c) with the weakening of the gold standard, and (d) with the fact that the industry, including heavy industry, began to play a decisive role in the pace and direction of economic growth.

During the nineteenth century the role of the state changed significantly: it stopped being neutral, as states became more and more interested in high economic growth rates (some states showed interest in the development of trade and industry quite long ago, in particular, parliamentary commissions in England analyzed reasons for the decline of industry during the 1825 crisis, see for example: Туган-Барановский, 2008 [1913]). Prior to this, states at best cared for maintaining stability of the currency and government securities, and partly for the construction of communications. We should also note the state's role in the development of military technology and military organization. Starting from the Great Depression the economic growth became one of the main concerns of the state. However the price upswings and downswings have not vanished completely; indeed, the current deflation trend demonstrates this quite convincingly.

Chapter 4 *"From Kondratieff cycles to Akamatsu waves? A new center-periphery perspective on long cycles"* highlights "dual" or even "triple" structure of cycles—global ups and downs, national ups and downs, and ups and downs in the relative position of countries in the global economy. We study the relationship between the cycles of convergence of the economies of the World System with the overall economic fluctuations. The chapter presents the thought of the Japanese economist Kaname Akamatsu, and puts it into a larger perspective, it also develops and details some ideas explored in *Chap. 2*.

We present Akamatsu's theory, and the links between his "flying geese" (*Gankō Keitairon*) model and Kondratieff's ideas. Akamatsu's original new contribution to the Kondratieff cycle debate is his analysis of the "differentiation" of the world economy (Akamatsu, 1961, 1962; see also Arrighi, Silver, & Brewer, 2003; Kasahara, 2004; Krasilshchikov, 2014; Ozawa, 2004, 2013; Schroeppel & Nakajima, 2002).

The rising A-phase of the global Kondratieff cycle will be a period of differentiation in the world economic structure, while the B-phase of the cycle coincide with a process of "uniformization" in the world economic structure.

For Akamatsu, the characteristic structure of the Center-Periphery relationship, which he more deeply analyze in his publication (Akamatsu, 1962), is characterized by the fact that the underdeveloped nation will export primary products and will import industrial goods for consumption. Later on, an underdeveloped nation will attempt to produce goods which were hitherto imported, first in the field of consumer goods, and later on in the area of capital goods. As the fourth stage of the process, the underdeveloped nation will attempt to export capital goods. There will be a tendency of "advanced" differentiation in the world economy, because the capital goods industries in advanced nations will still advance further, giving rise to "extreme differences of comparative costs". The wild-geese flying pattern will include three sub-patterns: the first is the sequence of imports—domestic production—exports; the second will be the sequence from consumer goods to capital goods and from crude and simple articles to complex and refined articles; the third will be the re-alignment from the advanced nations to backward nations according to their stages of growth.

Akamatsu foresaw the huge discrepancies in the structure of the world economy caused by imports to the periphery, which lead to discrepancies in the balance of payments, and the pressure to increase exports of primary products to improve the balance. Discrepancies will also lead to a shift of production away from domestic industries in the underdeveloped country towards the export sector. This leads to problems of excessive supply capacities in the underdeveloped country.

Chapter 4 compares these theoretical advances with the analyses put forward by Arrighi, Silver, & Brewer (2003) and Vernon (1966). Arrighi and associates correctly foresaw that the zones of prosperity in the world economy not only cluster in time, but also in space. The innovation process will be highly unequal. High incomes create a favorable environment for product innovations; high costs create a favorable environment for innovations in techniques; and cheap and abundant credit creates a favorable environment for financing these and all other kinds of innovations. Up to the onset of the Great Convergence (see Grinin & Korotayev, 2015a), there tended to be a "virtuous circle" of high incomes and innovations in the wealthy countries as opposed to the tendency in the poorer countries to reap few, if any, of the benefits of the innovations. However, in the recent decades, after the start of the Great Convergence, the situation has changed dramatically (*ibidem*).

In *Chap. 4*, as well as in *Appendix B*, we not only analyze cycles, but also long-run trends, with a turning point for many countries taking place in the present decade. Much more ill-fated is the trajectory of the European center and the European semi-periphery. Their upward ascent definitely came to a halt, implying a very long-run shift in the socio-geographical structure of the world economy.

The free availability of the Maddison data set (Bolt & van Zanden, 2013) with its long time series about real income in purchasing power per capita since the nineteenth century in 31 countries,[13] really invites global research to think beyond the boundaries of national economic cycles and to relate the "national swings" to the upward and downward more long-term movements of national societies in the global center-periphery structure.

Chapter 4 compares the effects of the recent two world depressions and the decline of real incomes in many countries in the periods 1929–1933 and 2007–2011, underlining how dramatically different the experience of the European periphery is in comparison to the BRICS countries.

We show the severity of the Great Depression in the 1930s, which so deeply struck at North America, Poland, Austria and several but not all nations of Latin America. Interestingly enough, several countries, starting from Scandinavia, the UK, several Latin American countries, Portugal, Turkey, Russia, China, India, Japan et cetera did relatively well and dived out from the 1930s depression in an often remarkable way.

The tsunami of the depression 2008/2011 swept most severely over the economic landscapes of Greece and Ireland as well as a great number of other countries—such as Italy, Denmark, Spain, United Kingdom, New Zealand, Norway, Finland, Japan, Portugal, United States, Hungary, France, Venezuela, Belgium, Netherlands, El Salvador, Canada, and Mexico. We establish empirical comparisons between the effects of the 1929 and 2008 depressions, and finally highlight the issue of economic convergence and disaster cycles in the work of neo-classical contemporary economics (Barro & Ursúa, 2008; Jaeger & Springler, 2012; Mankiw, Romer, & Weil, 1992; see also Barro, 2012; Berthold & Kullas, 2009; Gennaioli, La Porta, Lopez-de-Silanes, & Shleifer, 2014). We also highlight the relationship of the Barro "economic disaster cycle" and the Kondratieff cycle.

The chapter tries to link the issue of long cycles with the issue of economic convergence and divergence in the World System, because (as it is discussed in *Chap. 4*) there are very strong cyclical ups and downs of relative convergence in the world system, observable not just in the "national" growth rates and "national" economic cycles (Akamatsu waves).

The Fifth chapter "*Kondratieff Waves and Technological Revolutions*" has been prepared the basis of the theory of production principles and production revolutions. In this chapter we reveal the interrelation between K-waves and major technological

---

[13] Argentina; Australia; Austria; Belgium; Brazil; Canada; Chile; Colombia; Denmark; Finland; France; Germany; Greece; India; Indonesia; Italy; Japan; Netherlands; New Zealand; Norway; Peru; Portugal; Russia; Spain; Sri Lanka; Sweden; Switzerland; UK; Uruguay; USA; and Venezuela.

breakthroughs in history (such as the Industrial Revolution) and make forecasts about features of the sixth Kondratieff wave in the light of the theory of Cybernetic Revolution that, from our point of view, started in the 1950s and will be completed in the 2060s or 2070s.

We have established a close correlation between Industrial and Scientific-Cybernetic production principles' cycles and Kondratieff cycles. Taking into account that K-waves arose only at a certain level of economic development of societies (see above), we can consider K-waves as a specific mechanism connected with the emergence and development of the Industrial production principle and the expanded reproduction of industrial economy. Given that each new K-wave does not just repeat the wave motion, but is based on a new technological system, K-waves in a certain aspect can be treated as phases of the development of the Industrial production principle and the first phases of development of the Scientific-Cybernetic production principle.

There is a special section that demonstrates specific features of the Fourth and Fifth K-waves and their phases. It explains on the basis of the theory of production revolutions why the Fourth wave was so powerful and why there is no comparably strong technological breakthrough during the Fifth K-wave. The theory of production revolution also can explain the contemporary phenomenon when periphery of the World System develops faster than its core.

We assume that the sixth K-wave in the 2030s and 2040s will merge with the final phase of the Cybernetic Revolution (which we call a phase of self-regulating systems). This period will be characterized by the breakthrough in medical technologies which will be capable of combining a number of other technologies into a single system of new and innovative technologies. The chapter offers some forecasts concerning the development of these technologies. The drivers of the final phase of the Cybernetic Revolution will be medical technologies, additive manufacturing (3D printers), nano- and biotechnologies, robotics, IT, cognitive sciences, which will together form a sophisticated system of self-regulating production. We can denote this complex with an acronym 'MANBRIC'.[14] Thus, we suppose that medical technologies will be a sphere of the initial technological breakthrough and the emergence of the MANBRIC-technology complex. It is worth remembering that the Industrial Revolution began in the rather narrow area of cotton textile manufacturing and was connected with the solution of quite concrete problems—at first, liquidation of the gap between spinning and weaving, and then, after increasing weavers' productivity, searching for the ways to mechanize spinning (see Allen, 2009; Grinin & Korotayev, 2015a). However, the solution of these narrow tasks caused an explosion of innovations conditioned by the existence of a large number of the major elements of machine production (including abundant mechanisms, primitive steam-engines, quite a high volume of coal production, etc.) which gave

---

[14] The order of the letters in the acronym does not reflect our understanding of the relative importance of areas of the complex. For example, biotechnologies will be more important than nanotechnologies, let alone additive manufacturing. The order is determined simply by the convenience of pronunciation of the respective acronym.

an impulse to the development of the Industrial Revolution. By analogy, we assume that the Cybernetic Revolution will start first in a certain area. Given the general vector of scientific achievements and technological development and taking into account that a future breakthrough area should be highly commercially attractive and have a wide market, we forecast that the final phase of this revolution (the phase of self-regulating systems) will begin somewhere at the intersection of medical technologies and many other technologies connected with them.

Certainly, it is almost impossible to forecast the concrete course of innovations. However, the general vector of breakthrough can be defined as a rapid growth of opportunities for correction or even modification of the human biological nature. In other words, it will be possible to extend our opportunities to alter a human body, perhaps, to some extent, its genome; to widen sharply our opportunities of minimally invasive influence and operations instead of the modern surgical ones; to use extensively means of cultivating separate biological materials, bodies or their parts and elements for regeneration and rehabilitation of an organism, and also artificial analogues of biological material (bodies, receptors), etc.

This will make it possible to radically expand the opportunities to prolong the life and improve its biological quality. It will be technologies intended for common use. Certainly, it will take a rather long period (about two or three decades) from the first steps in that direction (in the 2030–2040s) to their common use.

The Sixth chapter "*Afterword: New Kondratieff wave and forthcoming global social transformation*". This final chapter in many respects continues the subject which has been analyzed in the previous chapter. It analyzes some aspects of the population ageing and its important consequences for particular societies and the whole world with respect to the new (sixth) K-wave and its forthcoming technologies. Population ageing is important for both the World System core and many countries of the global periphery and it has turned into a global issue. In the forthcoming decades population ageing is likely to become one of the most important social processes determining the future characteristics of society and the direction of technological development.

Based on this analysis and the conclusion (in *Chap. 5*) that the future technological breakthrough (which we define as the final phase of the Cybernetic Revolution) is likely to take place in the 2030s, we offer some important forecasts.

As demonstrated in *Chap. 5*, in the 2020s and 2030s we expect the upswing of the forthcoming Sixth Kondratieff wave, which will introduce the sixth technological paradigm (system).

The main conclusion of the chapter is that the process of global ageing will be both one of the main reasons and one of the main driving forces for the formation of a new technological paradigm of the Sixth K-wave as well as the final phase of the Cybernetic revolution. That is why all those revolutionary technological changes will be connected, first of all, with breakthroughs in medical and related technologies, and the first direction of this new innovative breakthrough will be medical technologies.

So, by the 2030s, the number of middle-aged and elderly people will increase; the economy will desperately need additional labor resources while the state will be interested in increasing the working ability of elderly people, as the population of wealthy and educated people will grow in a rather significant way. In other words, the unique conditions for the stimulation of business, science and the state to make a breakthrough in the field of medical technologies will emerge, and just these unique conditions are necessary to start the innovative phase of a revolution.

It is extremely important to note that enormous financial resources will be accumulated for the technological breakthrough, such as: the pension money whose volume will increase at high rates; spending of governments on medical and social needs; growing expenses of the ageing population to support health. All this can provide initial large investments as it has high investment appeal for respective venture projects and long-term high demand for innovative products. That is, there will be a full set of favorable conditions for a powerful technological breakthrough.

To decide the problem of supplying means of subsistence and social services for a growing number of ageing pensioners, the world needs a new system of financial-economic regulation at the global scale. However, such a global regulation cannot emerge from nowhere. It can be realized only in the fight against the crisis-depressive phenomena, and as a result of the reconfiguration of the World System. In the chapter we draw the picture of future changes of the world order.

We also present our ideas about the financial instruments that can help to solve the problem of pension provision for the growing elderly population in the developed countries. We think that a more purposeful use of pension funds' assets together with their allocation (with necessary guarantees) into education and upgrade of the skills of young people in the World System periphery may partially solve the indicated problem in the developed states.

The chapter offers some forecasts concerning the development of these technologies and its social consequences. One of our forecasts concerns the future of long cycles. The sixth K-wave (*c.* 2020 — the 2060/2070s), like the first K-wave, will proceed generally during completion of the production revolution. However, there is an important difference. During the first K-wave the duration of the one phase of the industrial production principle significantly exceeded the duration of the whole K-wave. But now one phase of the K-wave will exceed the duration of one phase of production principle. This alone should essentially modify the course of the sixth K-wave; the seventh wave will be feebly expressed or will not occur at all. Such a forecast is based also on the fact that the end of the Cybernetic Revolution and distribution of its results will promote integration of the World System, considerably increasing the influence of new universal regulation mechanisms. It is quite possible, considering the fact that the coming final phase of the revolution will include the revolution of the regulating systems. Thus, the management of the economy should reach a new level. So, K-waves appeared at a certain stage of social evolution and they are likely to disappear at its certain stage.

In Appendix A *"Biographies of Nikolay Kondratieff and Kaname Akamatsu"* we provide biographic sketches of Kondratieff and Akamatsu, describe some of their ideas and plans, and show how Kondratieff theory influenced Akamatsu's scholar carrier.

Appendix B *"Spectral analysis and other statistical approaches to the study of cycles with different lengths"* is connected with *Chap. 4*. It is based on a variety of standard econometric techniques, and aims to be a fairly comprehensive test of the hypotheses about long Kondratieff cycles. The appendix presents the econometric results of our analyses in a user-friendly fashion. 31 countries of our sample make up approximately 40.8% of global population and 57.8% of global purchasing power. Our data for world industrial production growth are an extension of the materials, first presented by Goldstein (1988), updated by Tausch and Ghymers (2007), relying on UNIDO data on world-wide industrial production growth from the mid-1970s to the turn of the millennium, now updated by open access figures from the United States Central Intelligence Agency.

Our figures on major power wars were first presented by Goldstein (1988), updated by PRIO data (major power wars) until 2002 (Tausch & Ghymers, 2007). The online appendices further highlight our freely available data.

After debating the methodological issues in a non-mathematical fashion, we present the main results.

(1) Our results on the level of the world economy are a resounding "yes" for the hypotheses voiced by Kondratieff, but with several additional qualifications and extensions. (2) Kondratieff was right in analyzing a 54 year cycle of the real economy, but there are other important cycles too; some of them very well known to social science research, others perhaps still more to be explored. (3) On the level of industrial production growth in the world economy, there is—parallel to the Kondratieff cycle—a 140 year "logistic" cycle, first analyzed by Immanuel Wallerstein; and in addition, there is evidence on a new 36 year disaster cycle, correctly predicted by the neoclassical contemporary economist Robert Barro. (4) For sure, there is also evidence—although somewhat weaker than expected—for a 22–23 year Kuznets cycle and the shorter, well-known real estate cycles, Juglar cycles and Kitchin cycles. (5) We also analyze the connection between the 75-year rolling correlation trend of the war cycle and the 75-year rolling correlation trend of the Wallerstein economic cycle.

We also re-analyze contentions about war cycles and their relationships to the Kondratieff cycles. In addition, we discuss exit strategies from economic crises and the implications of our analysis for Russia. In the final part of this appendix a reader will find "A primer on spectral analysis and time series analysis".

In many ways, the modern world is entering a very turbulent era, during which the old economic and political world order will change significantly and features of the new world order are likely to emerge. This turbulence will no doubt be expressed in various crises. That is why to a certain extent the expression "hallmarks of crises", mentioned in the *Preface* refers not just to the present moment, but also to the near future. As we have said, the study of different cycles and their interactions with each other, as well as the application of sophisticated methods of analyzing economic statistics are not an end in itself, but only an opportunity to improve our understanding of the modern trends of economic development and the basic characteristics of the modern economic system. It is also an opportunity to improve our forecasting potential, and, thus, to make future trials a bit less severe.

Chapter 2
Kondratieff Waves in the World System Perspective

This chapter offers an historical and theoretical analysis of K-wave dynamics within the World System framework; in particular, it studies the influence of long wave dynamics on the changes of the world GDP growth rates during the last two centuries. This chapter concludes with a section that presents an hypothesis that the change of K-wave upswing and downswing phases correlates significantly with the phases of fluctuations in the relationships between the World System Core and Periphery, as well as with changes in the World System Core.

As we have already mentioned above, qualitative movement toward new unknown forms and levels cannot proceed infinitely because of inevitable limitations. As a result, such movement is accompanied by the emergence of disproportions as well as growth of competition for resources, etc. On the other hand, continuous human effort to overcome environmental resistance to such a movement has created conditions for the continuous emergence of more and more complex and effective structures at the level of both individual societies and the World System as a whole. However, relatively short periods of fast development gave place to periods of stagnation, crisis, and sometimes even collapse. This was one of the main causes that led to the formation of cyclical components of social macrodynamics that in the pre-industrial epoch could include cycles with many different periods, including secular and even millennial ones (e.g., Korotayev & Khaltourina, 2006; Korotayev, Malkov, & Khaltourina, 2006a, 2006b; Коротаев et al., 2010; Nefedov, 2004; Гринин и Коротаев, 2012; Turchin, 2003, 2005a, 2005b; Turchin & Korotayev, 2006; Turchin & Nefedov, 2009).

As we said in *Chap. 1*, in the industrial period we see the emergence of new cyclical components including Juglar cycles with a characteristic period between 7 and 11 years that manifest themselves in energetic booms and crises that suddenly

---

Electronic supplementary material The online version of this chapter (doi:10.1007/978-3-319-41262-7_2) contains supplementary material, which is available to authorized users.

engulf social systems. At the same time cyclical dynamics in undustrial societies is represented by cycles with a characteristic period of 40 to 60 years known as Kondratieff waves (or just K-waves).

In this chapter we will analyze the emergence of K-waves in the World System economic dynamics in the nineteenth century and the changes that can be traced within K-wave patterns in the twentieth century, but especially after the Second World War. We will also analyze the peculiarities of the study of K-waves within the World System scale and will demonstrate that an adequate understanding of the nature of the modern K-wave dynamics can only be achieved if this phenomenon is studied precisely within this framework.

Long Waves in the World Economic Dynamics

As it has been already said, in the 1920s Nikolai Kondratieff observed that the historical record of some economic indicators then available to him appeared to indicate a cyclic regularity of phases of gradual increases in the values of these respective indicators followed by phases of decline and produced a systematic analysis of these data (Kondratieff, 2004 [1922]: Chap. 5, 1935 [1925], 1926; Кондратьев, 1922: Chap. 5; 1925, 2002). The period of these apparent oscillations seemed to him to be around 50 years. This pattern was found by him with respect to such indicators as prices, interest rates, foreign trade, coal and pig iron production (as well as some other production indicators) for some major Western economies (first of all England, France, and the United States). Whereas the long waves in pig iron and coal production were claimed to be detected since the 1870s at the world level as well[1].

Kondratieff himself (in his seminal article "Long Cycles of Conjuncture" Кондратьев, 1925) mentioned the following scientists who had managed to detect before him to some degree these long waves of economic dynamics: Aftalion (1913), Layton (1922), Lescure (1907, 1912), Moore (1914, 1923), Motylev (Мотылев, 1923), Spiethoff (1925), and Trotsky (Троцкий, 1923); however, Trotsky was not sure that those waves could be regarded as a regular phenomenon (see Кондратьев, 1993а: 27–29). He also mentioned a number of economists who refused to identify long waves as a regular phenomenon, but actively discussed them, such as Cassel (1918), Kautsky (Каутский 1918), Osinsky (Осинский, 1923а, 1923б) (*Ibidem*: 29). In his study "Dynamics of prices of manufactured and

---

[1] Note that as regards the production indices during decline/downswing phases we are dealing with the slowdown of the growth of production rather than with actual declines in production that rarely last longer than 1–2 years, whereas during the upswing phase we are dealing with a general acceleration of production growth rates in comparison with the preceding downswing/slowdown period (see, e.g., Modelski 2001, 2006 who prefers quite logically to designate 'decline/downswing' phases as 'phases of take-off', whereas the upswing phases are denoted by him as 'high growth phases').

agricultural commodities" published in 1928 (Кондратьев, 2002: 450–451) Kondratieff provided an even larger list of economists who noticed the long wave phenomenon.

Among important Kondratieff predecessors one should also mention J. van Gelderen (1913), M. A. Bunyatyan (Бунятян 1915), and S. de Wolff (1924). One can also mention William Henry Beveridge (better known, perhaps, as Lord Beveridge, the author of the so-called Beveridge Report on Social Insurance and Allied Services of 1942 that served after the Second World War as the basis for the British Welfare State, especially the National Health Service), who discovered a number of cycles in the long-term dynamics of wheat prices, whereas one of those cycles turned to have an average periodicity of 54 years (Beveridge, 1921, 1922).

In any case, it is clear that long waves started to be mentioned quite frequently in the 1900s, but starting from the 1920s they began to be mentioned especially actively. One of Kondratieff's teachers, Tugan-Baranovsky also mentioned them, in particular in his study "Paper Money and Metal" (Туган-Барановский, 1998 [1917]). However, none of the abovementioned economists had studied the long waves systematically, and none of them offered a systematic theory of the long cycles. Thus, the real contribution of Kondratieff was not the discovery of the long wave phenomenon as is frequently believed, but the systematic study of this phenomenon and the development of a long wave theory on this basis.

In many respects Kondratieff's discovery can well be compared with Edwin Hubble's discovery of the expanding Universe that was made also in the 1920s. Let us recollect that the redshift phenomenon had been known long before the seminal work of Hubble. But it was Hubble who was able to produce a systematic theory of the expanding Universe on the basis of the systematic analysis of the redshift data. Similarly, the long wave phenomenon in economic dynamics had been known well before Kondratieff, but it was Kondratieff who was able to produce a systematic theory of the long cycles of global dynamics on the basis of a systematic analysis of scattered observations of long waves within the economic dynamics of various countries.

Kondratieff himself identified the following long waves and their phases (see Table 2.1).

The subsequent students of Kondratieff cycles identified additionally the following long-waves in the post-World War 1 period (see Table 2.2).

Table 2.1 Long waves and their phases identified by Kondratieff

Long wave number	Long wave phase	Dates of the beginning	Dates of the end
I	A: upswing	'The end of the 1780s or beginning of the 1790s'	1810–1817
	B: downswing	1810–1817	1844–1851
II	A: upswing	1844–1851	1870–1875
	B: downswing	1870–1875	1890–1896
III	A: upswing	1890–1896	1914–1920
	B: downswing	1914–1920	

Table 2.2 'Post-Kondratieff' long waves and their phases

Long wave number	Long wave phase	Dates of the beginning	Dates of the end
IV	A: upswing	1939–1950	1968–1974
	B: downswing	1968–1974	1984–1991
V	A: upswing	1984–1991	2006–2008
	B: downswing	2006–2008	the 2020s?

(*Sources:* Ayres, 2006; Бобровников, 2004: 47; Dickson, 1983; Goldstein, 1988: 67; Jourdon, 2008: 1040–1043; Linstone, 2006: Fig. 1; Mandel, 1980; Modelski & Thompson, 1996; Пантин и Лапкин, 2006: 283–285, 315; Tausch, 2006b: 101–104; Thompson, 2007: Table 5; Van Duijn, 1983: 155; Wallerstein, 1984. The last date is suggested by the authors of the present book. It was also suggested earlier by Lynch, 2004; Пантин и Лапкин, 2006: 315; see also Акаев, 2010; Акаев и Садовничий, 2010; Akaev, Fomin, Tsirel, & Korotayev, 2010; Акаев et al., 2011; about the forthcoming sixth wave see *Chaps. 5* and *6*).

A considerable number of explanations for the observed Kondratieff wave (or just K-wave Modelski, 2001; Modelski & Thompson, 1996) patterns have been proposed. From the initial stages of K-wave research, the respective K-wave pattern was detected in the most affirmative way with respect to price indices (see below). Most explanations proposed during this period were monetary, or monetary-related. For example, K-waves were connected with the inflation shocks caused by major wars (e.g., Åkerman, 1932; Bernstein, 1940; Silberling, 1943, etc.). In recent decades such explanations went out of fashion, as the K-wave pattern stopped being traced in the price indices after the Second World War (e.g., Бобровников, 2004: 54; Goldstein, 1988: 75).

Kondratieff himself accounted for K-wave dynamics first of all on the basis of capital investment dynamics (see Kondratieff, 1928, 1984; Кондратьев, 2002: 387–397). This line was further developed by Jay W. Forrester and his colleagues (see, e.g., Forrester, 1978, 1981, 1985; Senge, 1982 etc.), as well as by A. van der Zwan (1980), Hans Glismann, Horst Rodemer, and Frank Wolter (1983) etc.

However, in the recent decades the most popular explanation of K-wave dynamics was the one connecting them with the waves of technological innovations.

Kondratieff himself noticed that 'during the recession of the long waves an especially large number of important discoveries and inventions in the technique of production and communication are made, which, however, are usually applied on a large scale only at the beginning of the next long upswing' (Kondratieff, 1935: 111, see also, e.g., Кондратьев, 2002: 370–374).

This direction of reasoning was used by Schumpeter (1939) to develop a rather influential 'cluster-of-innovation' version of K-waves' theory, according to which Kondratieff cycles were predicated primarily on discontinuous rates of innovation (for more recent developments of the Schumpeterian version of K-wave theory see, e.g., Ayres, 2006; Berry, 1991; Dator, 2006; Devezas and Modelski, 2003; Dickson,

1983; Freeman, 1987; Hirooka, 2006; Маевский, 1997; Mensch, 1979; Modelski and Thompson, 1996; Modelski, 2001, 2006; Papenhausen, 2008; Perez, 2011; Яковец, 2001; Tylecote, 1992; Глазьев, 1993) for the most recent presentation of empirical evidence in support of Schumpeter's cluster-of-innovation hypothesis see Kleinknecht & van der Panne, 2006; Коротаев и Гринин 2013). Within this approach every Kondratieff wave is associated with a certain leading sector (or leading sectors), technological system(s) or technological style(s). For example, the third Kondratieff wave is sometimes characterized as 'the age of steel, electricity, and heavy engineering. The fourth wave takes in the age of oil, the automobile and mass production. Finally, the current fifth wave is described as the age of information and telecommunications' (Papenhausen, 2008: 789); whereas the forthcoming sixth wave is sometimes supposed to be connected first of all with nano- and biotechnologies (e.g., Акаев, 2010, 2011; Dator, 2006; Lynch, 2004; Прайд и Коротаев, 2008; for a detailed analysis of the possible technological basis of the sixth K-wave see *Chaps. 5* and *6* below).

There were also a number of attempts to combine capital investment and innovation theories of K-waves (e.g., Акаев, 2010; Rostow, 1975, 1978; van Duijn, 1979, 1981, 1983 etc.). Of special interest is the Devezas–Corredine model based on biological determinants (generations and learning rate) and information theory that explains (for the first time) the characteristic period (50–60 years) of Kondratieff cycles (Devezas & Corredine, 2001, 2002; see also Devezas, Linstone, & Santos, 2005).

Many social scientists consider Kondratieff waves as a very important component of modern world-system dynamics. As has been phrased by one of the most important K-wave students,

> long waves of economic growth possess a very strong claim to major significance in the social processes of the world system... Long waves of technological change, roughly 40–60 years in duration, help shape many important processes... They have become increasingly influential over the past thousand years. K-waves have become especially critical to an understanding of economic growth, wars, and systemic leadership... But they also appear to be important to other processes such as domestic political change, culture, and generational change. This list may not exhaust the significance of Kondratieff waves but it should help establish an argument for the importance of long waves to the world's set of social processes (Thompson, 2007).

Against this background it appears rather significant that evidence of the very presence of the Kondratieff waves in the world dynamics remains quite controversial. The presence of K-waves in price dynamics (at least till the Second World War) has found very wide empirical support (see, e.g., Cleary & Hobbs, 1983; Gordon, 1978: 24; van Ewijk, 1982 etc.). However, as has been mentioned above, the K-wave pattern stopped being traced in the price indices after the Second World War (e.g., Бобровников, 2004: 54; Goldstein, 1988: 75).

On the other hand, as has already been demonstrated (Щеглов, 2009; Гринин, Коротаев, и Цирель, 2011: 75–77), when inflation is taken into account, and the price indices are expressed in grams of gold rather than in dollars, those indices continue to correspond to the K-wave pattern (see Fig. 2.1). Starting from the early

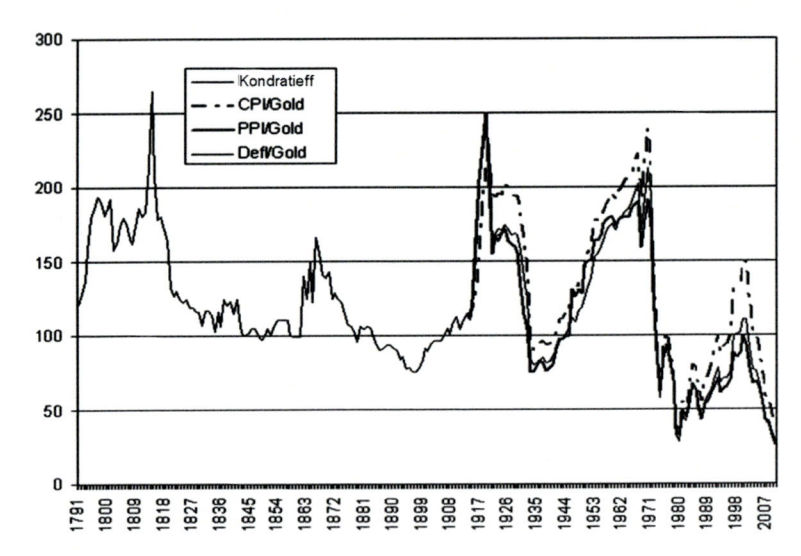

Fig. 2.1 The USA producer price index used by Kondratieff and extended to 2010 in the gold equivalent (100 = 1900–1910 level). *Sources:* (Щеглов, 2009; Гринин, Коротаев и Цирель, 2011: 76)

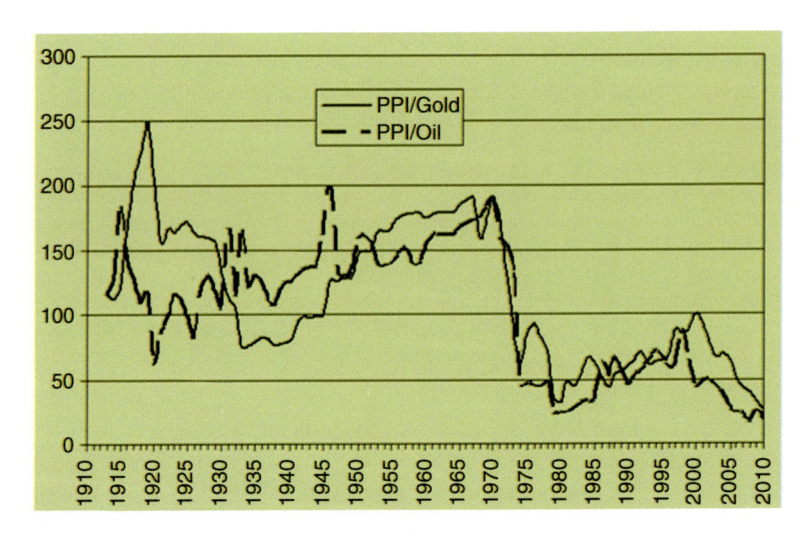

Fig. 2.2 The USA producer price index in gold and oil equivalent (100 = 1900–1910 level). *Sources:* (BP 2010; Щеглов, 2009; Гринин, Коротаев, и Цирель, 2011: 77)

1970s, energy resources (and, first of all, oil) served as a sort of 'reserve currency' comparable with gold, and the Kondratieff waves started to be traced in the price index dynamics when expressed in oil equivalent (see Fig. 2.2).

How Real are Kondratieff Waves? Discussions and Empirical Evidence

Regarding long waves in production dynamics, we will restrict ourselves to analyzing evidence for the presence of K-waves in world production indices. As Kondratieff waves tend to be considered an important component of the World System social and economic dynamics, one would expect to detect them with respect to the major world macroeconomic indicators; first of all with respect to the world GDP dynamics (Chase-Dunn & Grimes, 1995: 405–411). However, till now attempts to detect them in the world GDP (or similar indicators') dynamics record have brought controversial results.

Kondratieff himself claimed to have detected long waves in the dynamics of the world production of coal and pig iron (e.g., Kondratieff, 1935: 109–110). However, his evidence of the presence of long waves in these series (as well as in all the production dynamics series on national levels) was criticized most sharply:

> Foremost among the methodological criticisms have been those directed against Kondratieff's use of trend curves. Kondratieff's method is first to fit a long-term trend to a series and then to use moving averages to bring out long waves in the residuals (the fluctuations around the trend curve).

But 'when he eliminated the trend, Kondratieff failed to formulate clearly what the trend stands for' (Garvy, 1943: 209). The equations Kondratieff uses for these long-term trend curves… include rather elaborate (often cubic) functions.[2] This casts doubt on the theoretical meaning and parsimony of the resulting long waves, which cannot be seen as simple variations in production growth rates (Goldstein, 1988: 82; see also, e.g., Barr, 1979: 704; Eklund, 1980: 398–399, etc.).

However, quite a few scientists presented later new evidence supporting the presence of long waves in the dynamics of the world economic indicators. For example, Mandel (1975: 141; 1980: 3) demonstrated that, in full accordance with Kondratieff's theory, between 1820 and 1967 during the A Phases of K-cycles, the annual compound growth rates in world trade were on average significantly higher than in adjacent Phases B. Similar results were arrived at by David M. Gordon (1978: 24) with respect to world *per capita* production for 1865–1938 based on world production data from Duprież (1947, 2: 567), world industrial dynamics (for 1830–1980) taken from Thomas Kuczynski (1982: 28), and average growth rates of the world economy (Kuczynski, 1978: 86) for 1850–1977; similar results were obtained by Joshua Goldstein (1988: 211–217).

Of special interest are the works by Marchetti and his co-workers at the International Institute for Advanced System Analysis who have shown extensively the evidence of K-waves using physical indicators, as for instance energy consumption, transportation systems dynamics, etc. (Marchetti, 1980, 1986, 1988 etc.). However, empirical tests produced by a few other scholars failed to support the hypothesis of the K-waves' presence in world production dynamics (see, e.g., Chase-Dunn & Grimes, 1995: 407–409; van der Zwan, 1980: 192–197, reporting the results of Peter Grimes' research).

---

[2] For example, for the trend of English lead production the function used by Kondratieff looks as follows: $y = 10^{(0.0278 - 0.0166x - 0.00012x^2)}$.

There were a few attempts to apply spectral analysis in order to detect the presence of K-waves in the world production dynamics. Thomas Kuczynski (1978) applied spectral analysis in order to detect K-waves in world agricultural production, total exports, inventions, innovations, industrial production, and total production for the period between 1850 and 1976. Though Kuczynski suggests that his results 'seem to corroborate' the K-wave hypothesis, he himself does not find this support decisive and admits that 'we cannot exclude the possibility that the 60-year-cycle… is a random cycle' (1978: 81–82); note that Kuczynski did not make any formal test of statistical significance of these K-waves tentatively identified by his spectral analysis. K-waves were also claimed to have been found with spectral analysis by Rainer Metz (1992) both in the GDP production series of eight European countries (for the 1850–1979 period) and in the world production index developed by Hans Bieshaar and Alfred Kleinknecht (1984) for 1780–1979; however, later he denounced those findings (Metz, 1998, 2006).

A few scientists using spectral analysis have failed to detect K-waves in production series on the national levels of quite a few countries (e.g., Diebolt & Doliger, 2006; Metz, 1998, 2006; van Ewijk, 1982 see *Chap. 4* and *Appendix B* below for more detail).

Against this background we (together with Sergey Tsirel) have found it appropriate to check the presence of K-waves in the world GDP dynamics using the most recent datasets on these variable dynamics covering the period between 1870 and 2007 (Maddison, 1995, 2001, 2003, 2010; World Bank, 2016) and applying an upgraded methodology for the estimation of statistical significance of detected waves (see, e.g., Korotayev & Tsirel, 2010, Коротаев и Цирель, 2010а, 2010б; Гринин, Коротаев и Цирель, 2011); it is worth stressing that for the first time our analysis made it possible to estimate the statistical significance of Kondratieff waves in the world GDP dynamics; we have demonstrated the presence of K-waves in the world GDP dynamics at a generally quite acceptable 5% level. We will return later to the issue of Kondratieff wave detection using spectral analysis methods below in *Chap. 4* and *Appendix B*.

Kondratieff Waves in the Post-World War II GDP Data

Note that the Kondratieff-wave component can be seen quite clearly in the post-World War II dynamics of the world GDP growth rates quite directly, and without the application of any special statistical techniques (see Fig. 2.3)[3]:

---

[3] Note that for recent decades K-waves (as well as Juglar cycles) are also quite visible in the world dynamics of such important macroeconomic variables as the world gross fixed capital formation (as % of GDP) and the investment effectiveness (it indicates how many dollars of the world GDP growth is achieved with one dollar investments) — see online Appendix to this chapter, Figs. S1 and S2. The dynamics of both variables are connected to the world GDP dynamics. Actually, the world GDP dynamics is determined to a considerable extent by the dynamics of those two variables.

Kondratieff Waves in the Post-World War II GDP Data 31

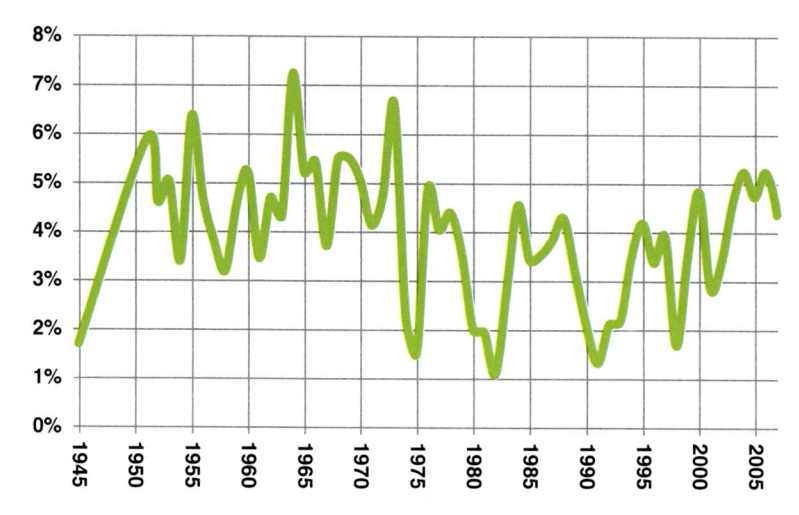

Fig. 2.3 Dynamics of the Annual World GDP Growth Rates (%), 1945–2007; 1945 point corresponds to the average annual growth rate in the 1940s. *Initial series*: Maddison/World Bank empirical estimates

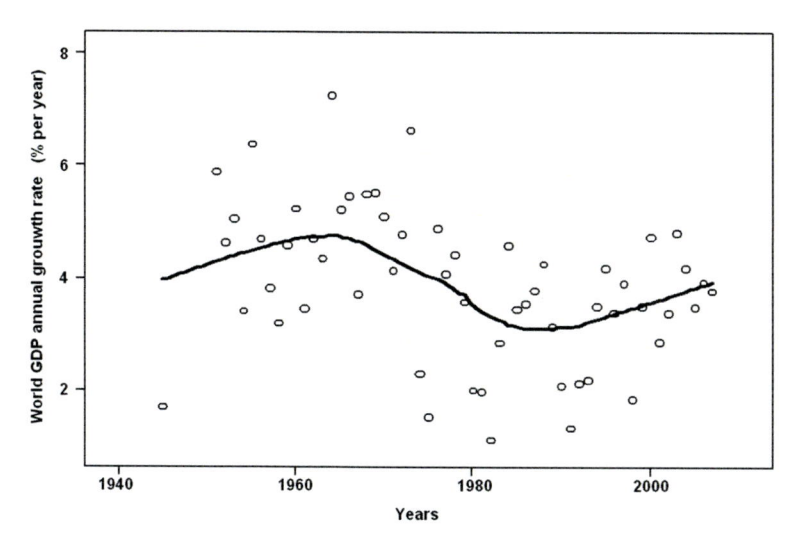

Fig. 2.4 Maddison/World Bank empirical estimates with fitted LOWESS line. Kernel: Triweight. % of points to fit: 50

However, the Kondratieff wave component becomes especially visible if a LOWESS (=*LOcally WEighted Scatterplot Smoothing*) line is fitted (see Fig. 2.4).

As can be seen, Figs 2.3, and 2.4 indicate:

1. That the Kondratieff-wave pattern can be detected up to the present in a surprisingly intact form (though, possibly, with a certain shortening of its period, suggested by a few authors [see, e.g., Бобровников, 2004; Tausch, 2006a; Пантин и Лапкин, 2006; van der Zwan, 1980]).
2. That the present world financial-economic crisis might indeed mark the beginning of a new Kondratieff Phase B (downswing see also Table 2.2 above). Indeed, consider the post-World War II dynamics of the world GDP growth rates taking into account the 2008–2014 period (see Fig. 2.5).

As we see, according to its magnitude the 2008–2009 global financial-economic crisis does not appear to resemble a usual crisis marking the end of a Juglar cycle amidst an upswing (or even downswing) phase of a Kondratieff cycle. Instead it resembles particularly deep crises (similar to the ones of 1973–1974, 1929–1933, mid 1870s or mid 1820s) that are found just at the border of phases A and B of the K-waves (see, e.g., Grinin & Korotayev, 2010a, 2010b).

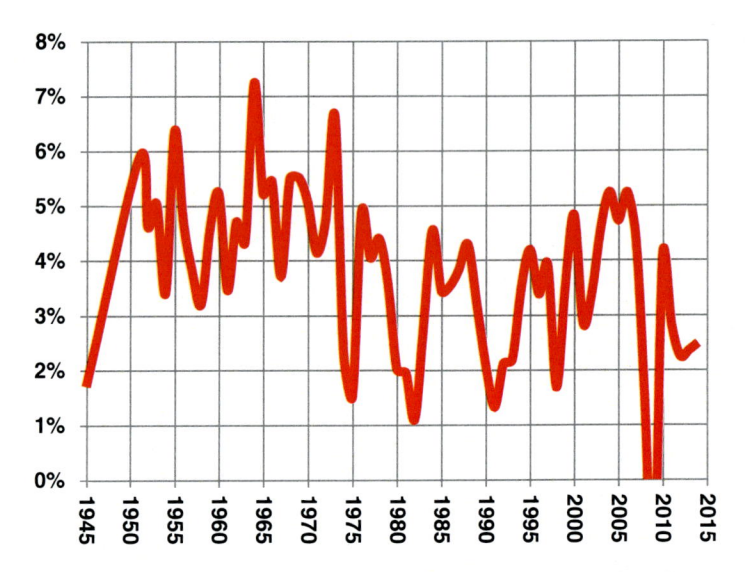

Fig. 2.5 Dynamics of the Annual World GDP Growth Rates (%), 1945–2014. *Sources:* (World Bank, 2016: NY.GDP.MKTP.PP.KD; Maddison, 2010; Conference Board, 2016)

Kondratieff Waves in the Pre-1945/50 World GDP Data

As can be seen in Fig. 2.6, for the 1870–1945/50 period the K-wave pattern is not as easily visible as after 1945/50. The turbulent 2nd, 3rd and 4th decades of the twentieth century are characterized by an enormous magnitude of fluctuations of world GDP growth rates (not observed either in the previous or subsequent periods).

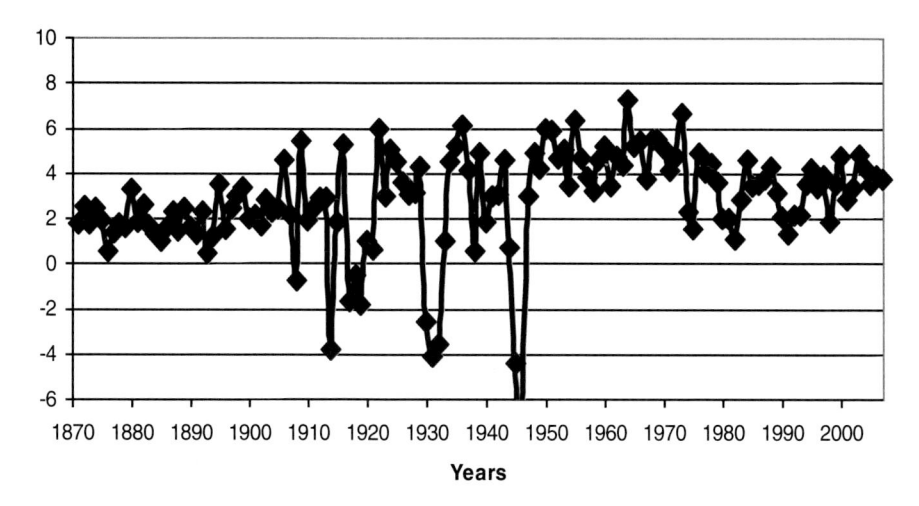

Fig. 2.6 Dynamics of the World GDP Annual Growth Rates (%), 1871–2007. *Source*: (Korotayev and Tsirel, 2010: 6)

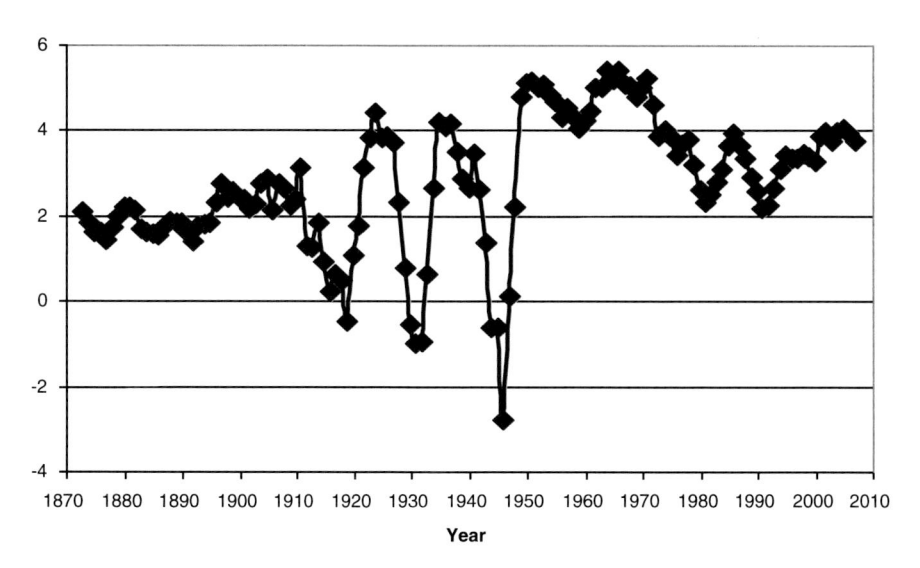

Fig. 2.7 Dynamics of the World GDP annual growth rates (%), moving 5-year averages, 1871–2007. *Sources:* World Bank, 2016; Maddison, 2010. *Note:* 1873 point corresponds to the average annual growth rate in 1871–1875, 1874 to 1872–1876, 1875 to 1873–1877… 2005 to 2003–2007; 2006 and 2007 points correspond to the annual growth rates in years 2006 and 2007 respectively

The lowest (for 1871–2007) figures of the world GDP annual rates of change are observed just in these decades (during the Great Depression, World Wars I and II as well as immediately after the end of those wars). On the other hand, during the mid-20s and mid-30s booms, the world GDP annual growth rates achieved historical maximums (they were only exceeded during the K-wave 4 Phase A, in the 1950s and 1960s, and were generally higher than during both the pre-World War I and recent [1990s and 2000s] upswings). This, of course, complicates the detection of the long-wave pattern during those decades.

Actually, this pattern is somehow more visible in the diagrams for 5-year moving averages, and, especially, for simple 5-year averages (see Figs 2.7 and 2.8):

The application of the LOWESS technique reveals a specific K-wave pattern in the pre-1950 series (see Fig. 2.9):

In fact, the LOWESS technique reveals quite clearly the K-wave pattern prior to World War I (in the period corresponding to Phase B of the second Kondratieff wave and major part of Phase A of the third wave) (see Fig. 2.10).

However, the third K-wave (apparently strongly deformed by World War I) looks much less clear (see Fig. 2.11).

The main problem is presented by Phase B of the third Kondratieff cycle—as the timing of its start remains unclear (1914, or mid-1920s?). Our analysis does not make it possible to choose explicitly between two options—either that the K3 Phase B started in 1914 and was interrupted by the mid-1920s boom; or that the K3 Phase A continued until the mid-1920s, having been interrupted by the WWI bust.

However, the LOWESS technique produces an especially neat K-wave pattern with the second assumption—that is that it materializes when we omit the WWI influence (see Fig. 2.12).

This figure reveals rather distinctly the double peaks of the upswings. With a stronger smoothing (see Fig. 2.13) the form of the peaks becomes smoother, and as well the waves themselves become more distinct.

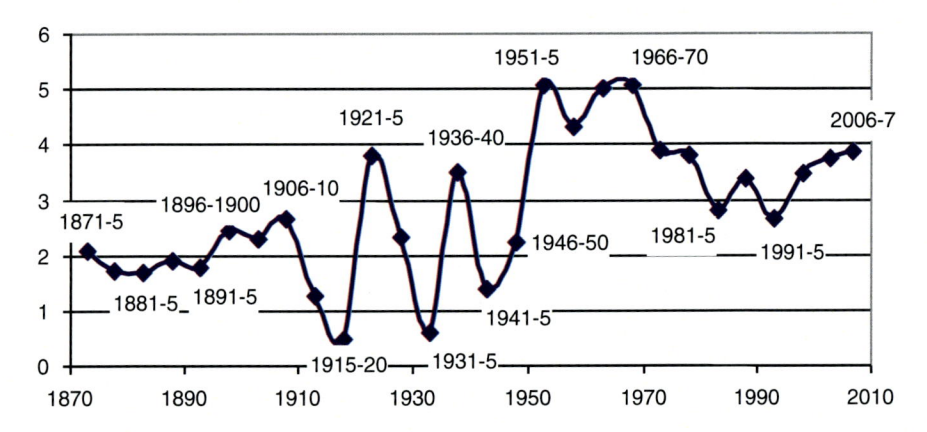

Fig. 2.8 Dynamics of the World GDP annual growth rates (%), 5-year averages, 1871–2007. *Sources:* (World Bank, 2016; Maddison, 2010)

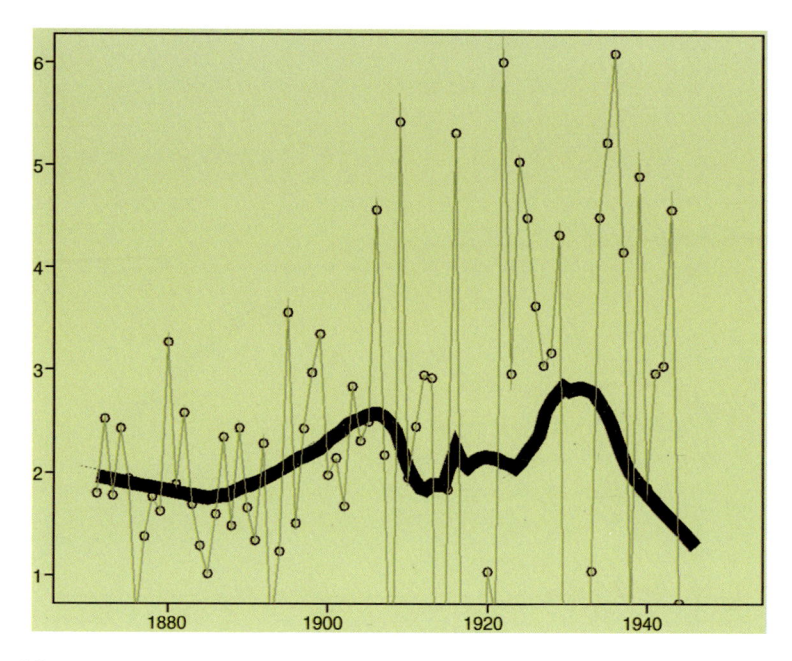

Fig. 2.9 World GDP annual growth rate dynamics, % per year (1870–1946): Maddison empirical estimates with fitted LOWESS line. *Note:* Maddison-based empirical estimates with fitted LOWESS line. Kernel: Triweight. % of points to fit: 40

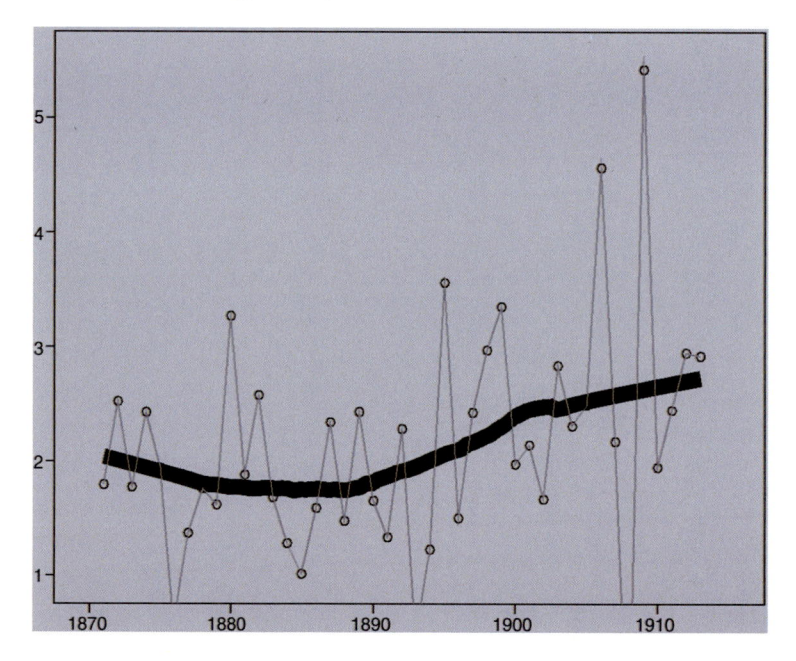

Fig. 2.10 World GDP annual growth rate dynamics, % per year: Maddison-based empirical estimates with fitted LOWESS line. **Phase B (Downswing) of the Second Kondratieff Wave and Phase A (Upswing) of the Third Wave, 1871–1913.** *Note:* Maddison-based empirical estimates with fitted LOWESS line. Kernel: Triweight. % of points to fit: 50

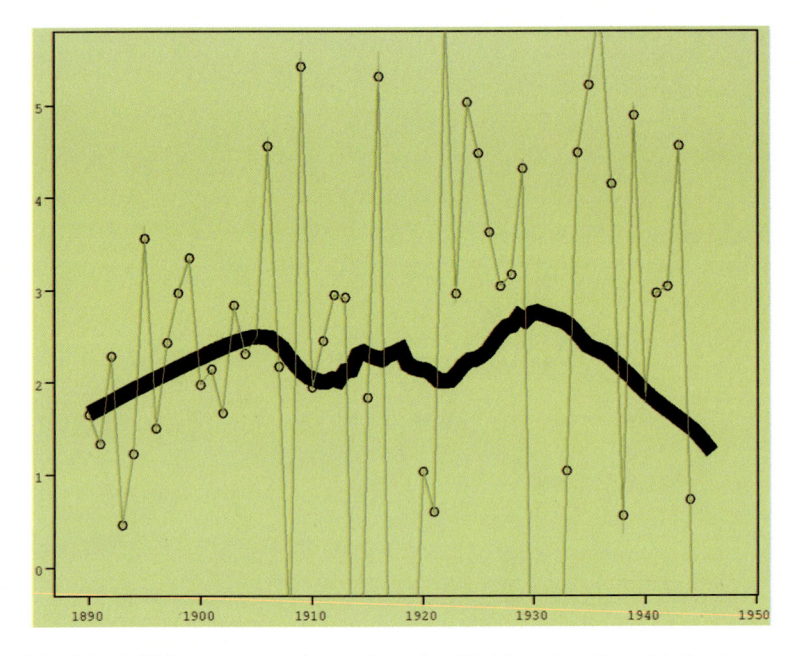

Fig. 2.11 World GDP annual growth rate dynamics: Maddison-based empirical estimates with fitted LOWESS line. **The Third Kondratieff Wave.** *Note:* Maddison-based empirical estimates with fitted LOWESS line. Kernel: Triweight. % of points to fit: 60

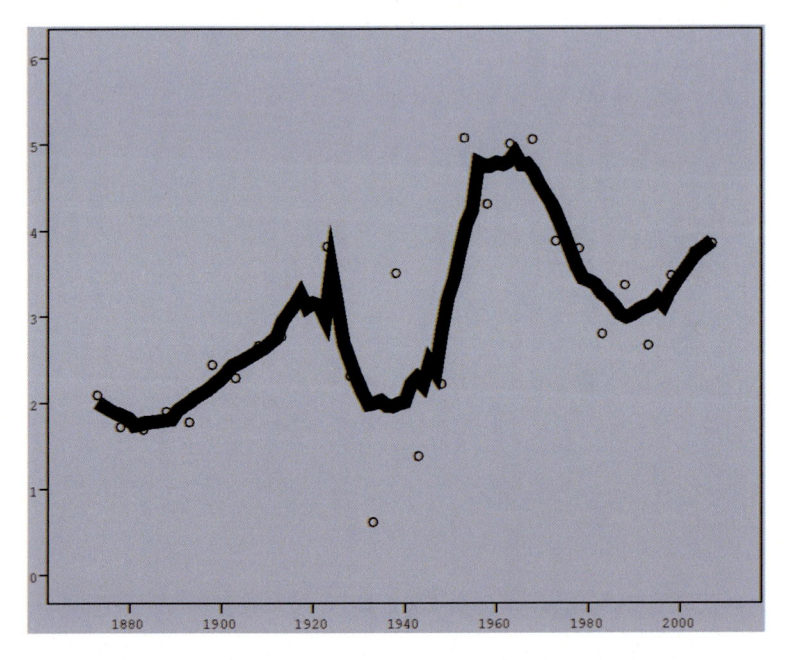

Fig. 2.12 World GDP annual growth rate dynamics, % per year, **5-year averages**: Maddison-based empirical estimates with fitted LOWESS line. **1870–2007, omitting World War I influence.** *Note*: Maddison-based empirical estimates with fitted LOWESS line. Kernel: Triweight. % of points to fit: 20

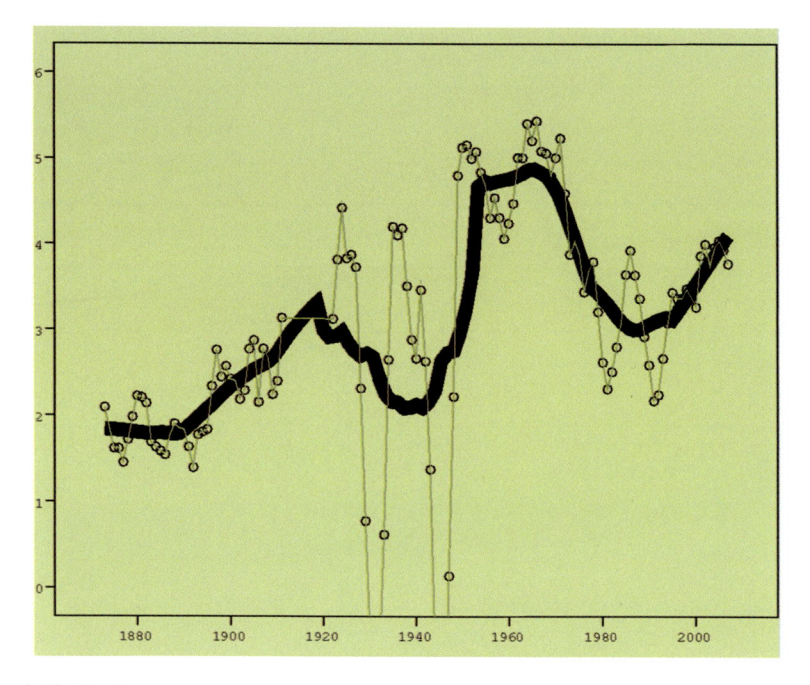

Fig. 2.13 World GDP annual growth rate dynamics, **5-year moving average**: Maddison-based empirical estimates with fitted LOWESS line. **1870–2007, omitting World War I influence**. *Note:* Maddison-based empirical estimates with fitted LOWESS line. Kernel: Triweight. % of points to fit: 20

Hence, it looks a bit more likely that K3 Phase A lasted until the mid-1920s (having been interrupted by WWI). Incidentally, if we take the WWI years of influence (1914–1921) out, we arrive at a quite reasonable K3 Phase A length—26 years, even if we take 1929 as the end of this phase:

1929–1895 = 34

34−8 = 26

Note that with the first assumption (K3 Phase B started in 1914 and was interrupted by the mid-1920s boom) we would have an excessive length of K3 Phase B—32 years (that would, however, become quite normal, if we take out the mid-1920s boom years).

Yet, it seems necessary to stress that we find overall additional support for the Kondratieff pattern in the world GDP dynamics data for the 1870–1950 period. First of all, this is manifested by the fact that both Phases A of this period have relatively higher rates of world GDP growth, whereas both Phases B are characterized by relatively lower rates. Note that this holds true without taking out either the effect of World War I, or the effect of the 1920s boom influence, and this is irrespective

Table 2.3 Average annual World GDP growth rates (%) during phases A and B of Kondratieff waves, 1871–2007

Kondratieff wave number	Phase	Years Version 1	Years Version 2	Average annual World GDP growth rates (%) during respective phase Version 1	Version 2
II	End of Phase A	1871–1875	1871–1875	2.09	2.09
II	B	1876–1894	1876–1894	1.68	1.68
III	A	1895–1913	1895–1929	2.57	2.34
III	B	1914–1946	1930–1946	1.50	0.98
IV	A	1947–1973	1947–1973	4.84	4.84
IV	B	1974–1991	1974–1983	3.05	2.88
V	A	1992–2007	1984–2007	3.49	3.42

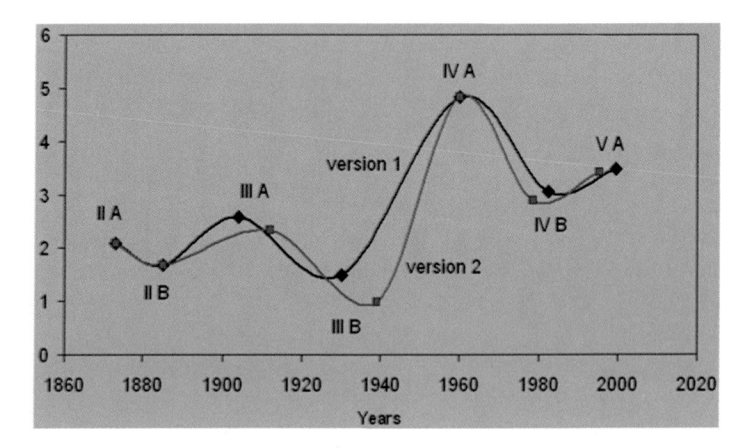

Fig. 2.14 Average annual World GDP growth rates (%) during phases A and B of Kondratieff waves, 1871–2007

of whatever dating for the beginnings and ends of the relevant phases we choose (see Table 2.3 and Fig. 2.14).

With different dates for the beginnings and ends of various phases we have understandably different shapes of long waves, but the overall Kondratieff wave pattern remains intact. Note that the difference between these two versions can be partly regarded as a continuation of the controversy between the following two approaches: (1) 'the K-wave period is approximately constant in the last centuries'; (2) 'the period of K-waves becomes shorter and shorter').[4]

---

[4] See, e.g., Бобровников, 2004; Tausch, 2006a; Пантин и Лапкин, 2006; van der Zwan, 1980.

Kondratieff Waves in the Pre-1870 World GDP Dynamics

There are some grounds to doubt that Kondratieff waves can be traced back in the world GDP dynamics for the pre-1870 period (though for this period they appear to be detected for the GDP dynamics of the West).

Note that for the period between 1700 and 1870 Maddison provides world GDP estimates for one year only—for 1820. What is more, for the period before 1870 Maddison does not provide annual (or even per decade) estimates for many major economies, which makes it virtually impossible the construction of the world GDP annual (or even per decade) growth rates during this period. However, it appears possible to reconstruct a world GDP estimate for 1850, as for this year Maddison does provide his estimates for all the major economies. Thus, it appears possible to estimate the world GDP average annual growth rates for 1820–1850 (that is the period that more or less coincides with K1 Phase B) and for 1850–1870/1875 (that is K2 Phase A), and, consequently, to make a preliminary test as to whether the Kondratieff wave pattern can be observed for the 1820–1870 period **or not**.

The results look as follows (see Table 2.4):

Thus, whatever dating of the end of K2 Phase A we choose, we observe a rather strong deviation from the K-wave pattern. Indeed, according to this pattern one would expect that in the 1850–1870/5 period (corresponding to Phase A of the second Kondratieff wave) the World GDP average annual growth rate should be higher than in the subsequent period (corresponding to Phase B of this K-wave). However,

Table 2.4 Average annual World GDP growth rates (%) during phases A and B of Kondratieff waves, 1820–1894

Kondratieff wave number	Phase	Years Version 1	Years Version 2	Average annual World GDP growth rates (%) during respective phase Version 1	Average annual World GDP growth rates (%) during respective phase Version 2	Average annual World GDP growth rate predicted by Kondratieff wave pattern	Observed
I	B	1820–1850	1820–1850	0.88	0.88		
II	A	1851–1875	1851–1870	1.26	1.05	To be significantly higher than during the subsequent phase	Significantly lower than during the subsequent phase
II	B	1876–1894	1871–1894	1.68	1.76	To be significantly lower than during the subsequent phase	Significantly higher than during the subsequent phase

Table 2.5 Average annual World GDP growth rates (%) of the West during phases A and B of Kondratieff waves, 1820–1894

Kondratieff wave number	Phase	Years	Average annual World GDP growth rates (%) during respective phase	Average annual World GDP growth rate predicted by Kondratieff wave pattern	Observed
I	B	1820–1850	2.04	To be significantly lower than during the subsequent phase	Significantly lower than during the subsequent phase
II	A	1851–1875	2.45	To be significantly higher than during the subsequent phase	Significantly higher than during the subsequent phase
II	B	1876–1894	2.16	To be significantly lower than during the subsequent phase	Significantly lower than during the subsequent phase
III	A	1895–1913	2.94	To be significantly higher than during the previous phase	Significantly higher than during the previous phase

the actual situation turns out to be squarely the opposite—in 1870/75–1894 the World GDP average annual growth rate was significantly higher than in 1850–1870/75.

Note, however, that the K-wave pattern still seems to be observed for this period with respect to the GDP dynamics of the West[5] (see Table 2.5 and Fig. 2.15).

Note: Data are for 12 major West European countries (Austria, Belgium, Denmark, Finland, France, Germany, Italy, the Netherlands, Norway, Sweden, Switzerland, the United Kingdom) and 4 'Western offshoots' (the United States, Canada, Australia, New Zealand).

We believe that the fact that K-wave pattern can be traced backward in the GDP dynamics of the West for the pre-1870 period and that it is not found for the world GDP dynamics is not coincidental, and cannot be accounted for simply on the basis of the unreliability of the world GDP estimates for this period. In fact, it is not surprising that the Western GDP growth rates were generally higher in 1851–1875 than in 1876–1894, and the world growth rates were not. The proximate explanation is very simple. The world GDP growth rates in 1851–1875 were relatively low (in comparison with 1876–1894) mostly due to the enormous economic decline observed in China in 1852–1870 due to a social-demographic collapse in connection with the Taiping Rebellion and accompanying events of additional episodes of internal warfare, famines, epidemics, catastrophic inundations and so on (Непомнин,

---

[5] What is more, this pattern appears to be observed in the socio-economic dynamics of the European-centered world-system for a few centuries prior to 1820 (see, e.g., Beveridge, 1921, 1922; Goldstein, 1988; Jourdon, 2008; Modelski, 2006; Modelski & Thompson, 1996; Пантин и Лапкин, 2006; Thompson, 1988, 2007).

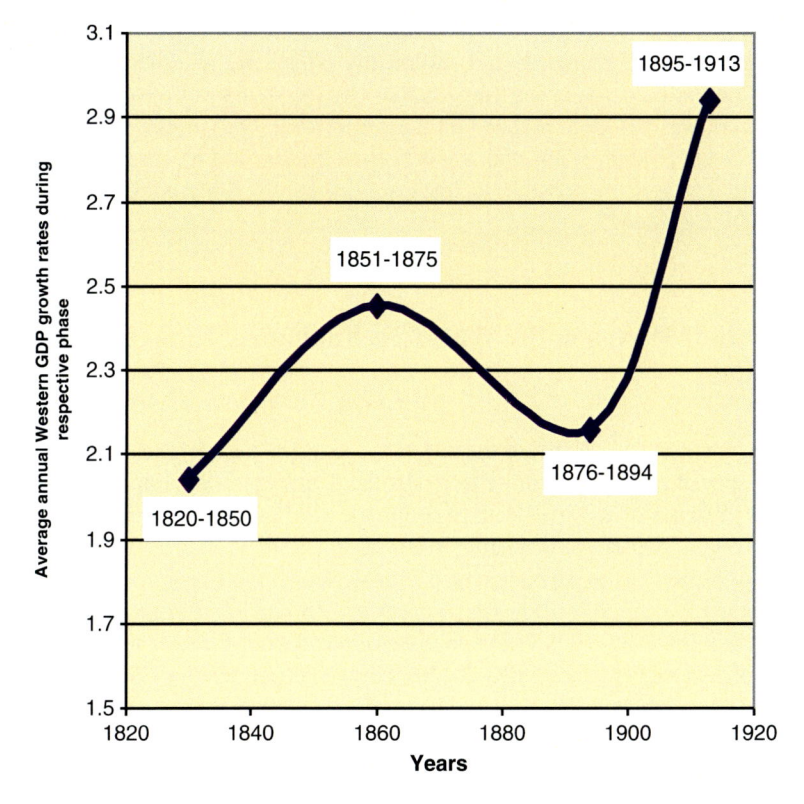

Fig. 2.15 Average annual World GDP growth rates (%) of the West during phases A and B of Kondratieff waves, 1820–1913

2005; Ларин, 1986; Kuhn, 1978; Liu, 1978; Илюшечкин, 1967; Perkins, 1969: 204 etc.) that resulted, for example, in the human death toll as high as 118 million human lives (Huang, 2002: 528). Note that in the mid-nineteenth century China was still a major world economic player, and the Chinese decline of that time affected the world GDP dynamics in a rather significant way. According to Maddison's estimates, in 1850 the Chinese GDP was about 247 billion international dollars (1990, PPP), as compared with about 63 billion in Great Britain, or 43 billion in the USA. By 1870, according to Maddison, it declined to less than $190 billion, which compensated up to a very high degree for the acceleration of economic growth observed in the same years in the West (actually, Maddison appears to underestimate the magnitude of the Chinese economic decline in this period, so the actual influence of the Chinese 1852–1870 sociodemographic collapse might have been even more significant). The effects of K2 Phase A in the Western GDP dynamics started to be felt on the world level only at the very end of this phase, in 1871–1875, after the end of the collapse period in China and the beginning of the recovery of growth in this country.

In more general terms, it seems possible to maintain that in the pre-1870 epoch the Modern World System was not sufficiently integrated, and the World System core was not sufficiently strong yet—that is why the rhythm of the Western core's development was not quite realized on the world level. Only in the subsequent era does the World System reach such a level of integration and its core acquires such strength that it appears possible to trace quite securely Kondratieff waves in the World GDP dynamics.[6]

Kondratieff Waves in the World Technological Innovation Dynamics

Naturally, the connection between the K-waves and technological innovation processes deserves special attention. In order to re-test the Kondratieff–Schumpeter hypothesis about the presence of K-waves with regard to the world invention activities, we have used the World Intellectual Property Organization (WIPO) Statistics Database information on the number of patents granted annually in the world per one million of the world population in 1900–2008 (see Korotayev, Zinkina, & Bogevolnov, 2011 for more details). For 1985–2008 WIPO publishes direct data on the total number of patent grants in the world per year (WIPO 2012a). For the period, 1900–1985, we calculated this figure by summing up the data for all the countries (that are provided by the WIPO in a separate dataset WIPO, 2012b). We used as our sources of data on the world population dynamics the databases of Maddison (2010), UN Population Division (2016), and U.S. Bureau of the Census (2016).

The results of our calculations are presented in Fig. 2.16.

It is easy to see that the figure above reveals an unusually clear K-wave pattern (Note that a similar pattern has been detected in the dynamics of patent applications by Plakitkin (Плакиткин, 2011) who, however, did not appreciate that he was dealing with K-wave dynamics). In general, we see rather steady increases in the number of patent grants per million during K-wave A-phases ('upswings'), and we observe its rather pronounced declines during K-wave B-phases ('downswings'). Thus, the first period of the growth of the variable in question and revealed by

---

[6] The phenomenon that K-waves can be traced in Western economic dynamics earlier than at the world level has already been noticed by Reuveny and Thompson (2008) who provide the following explanation: if one takes the position that the core driver of K-waves is intermittent radical technological growth primarily originating in the system leader's economy, one would not expect world GDP to mirror K-wave shapes as well as the patterned fluctuations that are found in the lead economy and that world GDP might correspond more closely to the lead economy's fluctuations over time as the lead economy evolves into a more predominant central motor for the world economy. Reuveny and Thompson also argue that to the extent that technology drives long-term economic growth, the main problem (certainly not the only problem) in diffusing economic growth throughout the system is that the technology spreads unevenly. Most of it stays in the already affluent North and the rest fell farther behind the technological frontier. Up until recently very little trickled down to the global South (Reuveny & Thompson, 2001, 2004, 2008, 2009). Our findings also seem to match this interpretation.

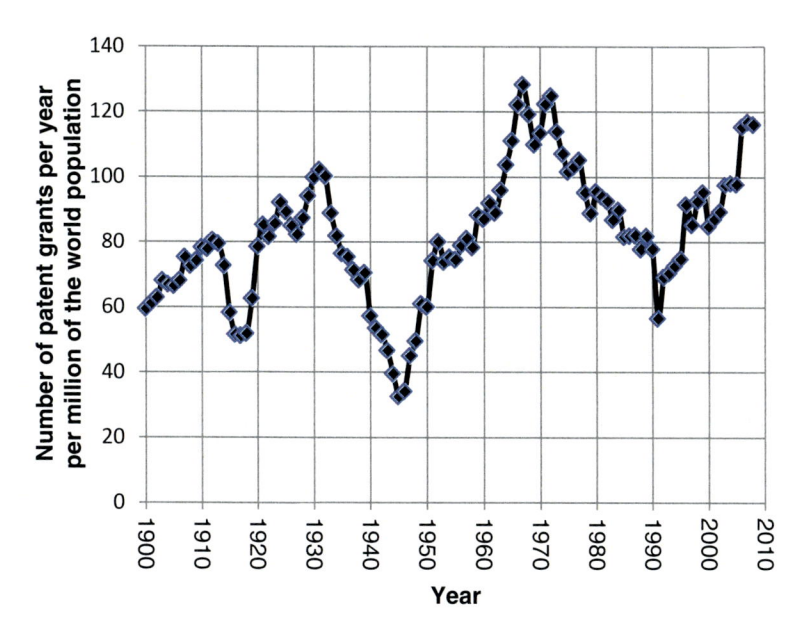

Fig. 2.16 Dynamics of number of patent grants per year per million of the world population, 1900–2008

Fig. 2.16 more or less coincided (with a rather slight, about 2–3 years, lag) with the A-phase of the third K-wave (1896–1929); it was only interrupted by the First World War when the number of patent grants per million experienced a precipitous but rather short decline—whereas after the war the value of the variable in question returned as quickly to the A-phase-specific trend line. The first prolonged period of the decline of the number of patent grants per million corresponds rather neatly (except for the above mentioned 2–3 year lag) to the B-phase of this wave (1929–1945); the second period of steady increase in the value of the variable in question correlates almost perfectly with the A-phase of the fourth K-wave (1945–1968/74), whereas the second period of decline corresponds rather well to its B-phase (1968/74–1984/1991); finally, the latest period of the growth of the number of patent grants per million correlates with the A-phase of the fifth K-wave.

Note, however, that this pattern apparently goes counter to the logic suggested by Kondratieff, Schumpeter and their followers who expected increases in invention activities during B-phases and decreases during A-phases. Yet, this contradiction is only apparent. Indeed, as we have mentioned above, Kondratieff maintained that 'during the recession of the long waves, an especially large number of *important* discoveries and inventions in the technique of production and communication are made, which, however, are usually applied on a large scale only at the beginning of *the next long upswing*' (Kondratieff, 1935: 111, our emphasis).

It has been suggested that it is necessary to distinguish between 'breakthrough' and 'improving' inventions (e.g., Акаев, 2010); breakthrough inventions are those that during a B-phase of a given K-wave create the foundations of a new technological system corresponding to a new K-wave. As suggested by Kondratieff, they find their large-scale application during the A-phase of this new K-wave based on this new technological system, which is accompanied by a flood of improving innovations that are essential for the diffusion of technologies produced by breakthrough inventions made during the B-phase of the preceding K-wave (*Ibid.*; Hirooka, 2006). Thus, it appears important to distinguish between breakthrough inventions, which involve a paradigm shift, and innovations which represent improvements, adaptations, and modifications of the breakthrough inventions.

Note that of the total number of patents a negligible proportion has been granted for breakthrough inventions, whereas the overwhelming majority of all the inventions for which patents are granted are nothing else but 'improving' inventions. The exhaustion of the potential of a given K-wave's technological system leads to a decrease of the number of inventions that actually realize the potential created by the breakthroughs which created the respective technological system. On the other hand, this very exhaustion of the previous technological system's potential for improvement creates powerful stimuli for new paradigm shifting inventions. However, the increase in the number of breakthrough inventions in no way compensates the dramatic decrease of the number of innovations improving the potential of the previous technological system. Hence, on the basis of this logic there are theoretical grounds to expect that during the B-phases of K-waves the total number of inventions (and patent grants) per 1 million of population should decrease, whereas during A-phases we should observe a pronounced increase in this number (as some decrease in the number of breakthrough inventions is by far compensated by a dramatic increase in the number of improving inventions).

As we have seen, this pattern is what has been revealed by our test.

World System Effects and K-Wave Dynamics

As has already been mentioned above, adherents of the world-system approach consider K-waves as one of the most important components of the World System dynamics.

We quite agree with Thompson (2007), who maintains that K-waves may help to clarify many important points in World System processes. However, one could also trace another kind of logic—the analysis of the World System processes can contribute a lot to the clarification of the nature of the Kondratieff waves themselves. We believe that the driving forces of the K-waves can be adequately understood only if we take into account the dynamics, phases, and peculiarities of World System development. That is why we have tried to analyze K-waves on a World System scale. Clearly, such an approach can integrate different points of view on the nature of Kondratieff waves.

Actually, we can consider the following five points:

1. Kondratieff waves are most relevant when considered at the World System scale. As those waves always manifest themselves at supra-societal scales, the World System processes turn out to be very important for the understanding of the K-wave dynamics.

2. The expansion and intensification of the World System economic links lead to the formation of the preconditions for new upswings. Note that Kondratieff himself notice that 'the new long cycles usually coincides with the expansion of the orbit of world economic ties' (Кондратьев, 2002: 374). We would add that the start of these new cycles implies not only the expansion of those ties, but also a change in their character (We will discuss this in more details below).
3. In general, World System processes are bound to influence economic processes (including medium period business cycles [e.g., Гринин и Коротаев, 2010]), hence, they are bound to influence K-wave dynamics. However, we also observe a reverse influence of those waves on World System development (which was actually noticed by Thompson). Kondratieff himself noticed the growth in the intensity of warfare and revolutionary activities during K-wave upswings (Кондратьев, 2002: 373–374). On the other hand, it is quite clear that those processes themselves influenced K-wave dynamics in a very significant way and world wars provide salient illustrations). It is quite clear that those K-wave students who pointed to an important role of military expenses (and inflation shocks produced by them) identified a significant (though in no way sole) cause of price growth (and decline) in the course of Kondratieff cycles.
4. As we have already mentioned above, breakthrough inventions (producing new technological systems) tend to be made during downswings, whereas their wide implementation is observed during subsequent upswings. The diffusion of those innovations throughout the World System is bound to affect significantly the course of K-waves, as the opening of new zones of economic development is capable of changing the world dynamics as a whole. Thus, in *Chap. 1* of our monograph on periodic economic crises (Гринин и Коротаев, 2010), we paid a considerable attention to the point that the vigorous railway construction of the last decades of the nineteenth century produced a major vector in world economic development (see, e.g., Лан, 1975; Мендельсон, 1959, vol. 2; Трахтенберг, 1963; Туган-Барановский, 2008 [1913]). Large-scale investments of British capital in the railway construction in the United States, Australia, India, etc. contributed to stagnation within the World System hegemon (and, finally, to the change of the center of this hegemony). Technological changes that start in one zone of the World System after their diffusion to other zones may produce such consequences that could hardly be forecasted. Thus, the development of oceanic and railway transportation led to vigorous exportation of cereal crops from the USA, Russia, and Canada that caused in the 1870s, 1880s, and 1890s the so-called world agrarian crisis (which affected significantly the second K-wave downswing but helped several countries to escape from the Malthusian trap [see, e.g., Grinin, Korotayev, & Malkov, 2010]).
5. Important events that take place within the World System may lead to an earlier (or later) switch from downswing to upswing (or, naturally, from upswing to downswing) within K-wave dynamics. As is well-known, the discovery of gold in California and Australia contributed in a rather significant way to the world economic (and price) growth during the second K-wave upswing, which was already noticed by Kondratieff (Кондратьев, 2002: 384–385).

Change of K-Wave Phases Against the Background of the World System Core–Periphery Interaction

Core and Periphery

We contend that the change of K-wave upswing and downswing phases correlates significantly with the phases of fluctuations in the relationships between the World System Core and Periphery, as well as with World System Core changes (the growth or decline of its strength, emergence of competing centers, their movements, and so on). Below we will describe our suppositions regarding possible causes of such a correlation. However, it turns out to be necessary to study the following questions: does this correlation emerge as a result of the casual link between the two processes? Is it caused by some other processes? Is not the causation pattern here even more complex? In any case this correlation appears especially important, as in the recent years one can observe a clear change in the interaction between the Core and Periphery of the World System. In particular, the World System Periphery (in contrast with what was observed not so long ago) tends to develop more rapidly than the core (see, e.g., Grinin & Korotayev, 2010b, 2015a; Korotayev, Zinkina et al., 2011a, 2011b, 2012; Коротаев и Халтурина, 2009; Коротаев, Халтурина, Малков et al., 2010; Малков, Божевольнов et al., 2010; Гринин, 2013б, 2013д; Гринин и Коротаев, 2010; Халтурина и Коротаев, 2010). This has become especially salient during the current global economic crisis.

Thus, what is the correlation between structural changes of the World System and periodic fluctuations within the K-wave dynamics?

We suggest that during the K-wave downswings the Core tended to subjugate, integrate, and pull up the Periphery to a greater extent than was observed during the K-wave upswings. It was during the K-wave downswings that the Core tended to expand vigorously (in various ways) into the Periphery by investing resources into it and by actively modernizing it. Those efforts and resource flows made a rather important contribution to the slow-down of the Core growth rates.

In contrast, during K-wave upswings the Core's activities were concentrated within the core part of the World System; in the meantime the balance of resource movement turned out to be in favor of the Core. Such a situation led to the acceleration of the growth rates of the Core countries (note, however, that this situation was not observed during the upswing of the most recent [fifth] K-wave).

The resource flow from the World System Core to the Semiperiphery and Periphery may proceed in various forms (military expenditures, FDI, aid, emigration, and so on). Of course, usually such actions are undertaken by the Core countries in order to obtain certain concrete gains: to get colonies, to obtain profits, to get influence in certain countries, to open markets, to get access to raw materials and so on (though the philanthropic component tended to become more and more pronounced with the passage of time). However, it takes any long-term investments a long time to pay for themselves (and sometimes these investments do not pay—

especially when they are made by politicians rather than businessmen). Often such a resource flow will proceed in the form of loans many of which are never paid back.

The resource flow to the Core could also be achieved in various forms – ranging from a direct plunder of colonies to importing very cheap commodities from them; it was also achieved through monopoly prices, unfair loans, and so on. The second K-wave upswing (the late 1840s to the 1870s) was supported to a very considerable extent by the flow of gold from such peripheral areas as California and Australia. In recent years one could observe certain exportation of capitals from the Periphery and Semiperiphery to the Core, as has been observed for China, Brazil, and Russia as regards the US securities; one may also note cheap Chinese exports, brain drain from India, etc.

Consider how this worked with respect to particular K-waves and their phases.

First Wave: The Late 1780s/Early 1790s–1844/1851

Phase A: The Late 1780s/Early 1790s–1810/1817

By this period the main colonial conquests of the pre-industrial epoch were already finished, the independence wars of the New World colonies had begun, and the main interests of the European powers were focused on internal affairs. In this period the resource flow from the Core to the Periphery was rather insignificant, whereas the one from the Periphery to the Core remained quite substantial. The Periphery and Semiperiphery (the USA, first of all) acted as suppliers of raw materials (cotton) for the development of the most advanced industrial sectors (Бурстин, 1993а, 1993б; Севостьянов, 1983; DiBacco, Mason, & Appy, 1992; Zinn, 1995).

Phase B (Downswing): 1810/1817–1844/1851

Europe (first of all, Britain and France) engaged in a rather active expansion in the Periphery – China, Algeria, Egypt, Turkey, and Latin America. British loans and investments went to Latin America and the USA (Мендельсон, 1959; Туган-Барановский, 2008 [1913]). There was a massive emigration from Europe (and especially Britain) to the West European offshoots; one could observe the active opening of Australia (e.g., Малаховский, 1971) as well as the South and the West of the USA. In this period, resources moved from Britain rather than to Britain. This partly accounts for the relatively bad conditions of the working class in Britain at this time (vividly described by Engels, 2009 [1845]).

Second Wave: 1844/1851–1890/1896

Phase A: 1844/1851–1870/1875

Europe again concentrated on its internal affairs (including the Crimean War, the unification of Germany and Italy and so on). Both the USA and Russia were also tied by internal struggles and reforms. A free trade system was established (e.g., Held, McGrew, Goldblatt, & Perraton, 1999). The flow of Australian and Californian gold reached Europe; one could observe a rather active catch-up of the European Semiperiphery (Гринин и Коротаев, 2010).

Phase B: 1870/1875–1890/1896

Europe actively expanded to the Periphery, actually the world was mostly divided between the Core powers through the final wave of colonial conquests (this involved some semiperipheral countries, first of all Russia conquered most of Central Asia). One could observe an active opening of agricultural lands in the American West (Бурстин, 1993а, 1993б; Севостьянов, 1983; DiBacco, Mason, & Appy, 1992; Zinn, 1995) and a very rapid development of Australia (e.g., Малаховский, 1971), as well as significant investments in the Periphery (especially in the railroad construction). Actually, during this period resources moved rather actively from Britain and some other European countries to the Periphery—for example, as loans for Latin America (e.g., Мендельсон, 1959; Tugan-Baranovsky, 1954; Туган-Барановский, 2008 [1913]).

Third Wave: 1890/1896–1945

Phase A: 1890/1896–1914/1928

During this phase Europe was concentrated on internal competition within itself (resulting finally in outright warfare), the USA was also concentrated on its own internal affairs (with the exception of a war with Spain); the preparations for the war and competition between Germany and Britain stimulated a technological race and economic growth (e.g., Grenville, 1999). One could observe a significant flow of resources from the Periphery, as well as the start of the transition of World System hegemony to the USA that, however, continued to be an importer of capital for a long time (e.g., Лан, 1975). Resources also flowed actively to Russia, Japan and some other semiperipheral countries where investors could find opportunities to introduce new technologies and receive high profits.

Phase B: 1914/1928–1939/1950

This phase saw activation of the Periphery and Semiperiphery, their struggle with the Core in various forms (India, China, Egypt, the USSR, Japan, etc.), the finalization of the transition of World System hegemony from Europe to the USA (see, e.g., Лан, 1976; Modelski & Thompson, 1996; Гринин и Коротаев, 2010). The continuation of the Core countries' control over their colonies required more and more effort and expense.

Fourth Wave: 1939/1950–1984/1991

Phase A: 1939/1950–1968/1974

The Core lost direct political control over the Periphery and was concentrated on its own internal affairs (including the West European integration); as a result of this concentration and the redistribution of capitals and technologies within the World System Core one could observe the Japanese, German, Italian, and Spanish economic miracles, as well as the consolidation of the Western world under US hegemony (e.g., Лан, 1978); one could also observe the emergence of new centers of development, including the Eastern Block and Japan (e.g., Попов, 1978).

Phase B: 1968/1974–1984/1991

The Core was 'attacked' by the Periphery economically — first of all through a radical increase in oil and some other raw material prices. In the meantime the West invested rather actively in the Periphery (especially, through loans to the developing countries).

Fifth Wave: 1984/1991–the 2020s(?)

Phase A: 1984/1991–2006/2008

This phase displays certain peculiarities in comparison with previous upswings, as during this period the main economic growth was generated not by the Core, but rather by the Periphery whose strongest countries moved to the Semiperiphery and even became new centers of growth.[7] Many Core countries (especially in Europe) were concentrated

---

[7] This somehow resembles the situation during the third K-wave upswing, when the growth was generated in still semiperipheral Germany, the USA, and Russia, rather than in still hegemonic Britain.

on their internal affairs. In the meantime, one could observe a rather active exchange of resources between the Core and the Periphery. On the one hand, industrial production moved from the Core to the Periphery; on the other hand, one can observe a vigorous flow of cheap manufactured products from the Periphery to the Core, whereas the Western countries became financial net importers (especially, through the movement of petrodollars). The USA actively exchanged 'paper' dollars for manufactured goods from the periphery, which contributed to the explosive growth of the US public debt (see, e.g., Akaev, Korotayev, & Fomin, 2012). One may also take into account the Periphery—Core labor migration. Thus, at the first glance the balance of exchange looked as if being in favor of the Core. On the other hand, one should take into account the fact that those processes were accompanied by the acceleration of the economic growth in the Periphery and at the same time its slowdown in the Core—so, actually the Periphery was favored by those processes more than the Core. One may suppose that this was supported by a substantial transformation of national sovereignty that in turn opened borders for the flows of foreign capitals and technologies.[8]

Phase B: 2006/2008–the 2020s(?)

By the end of this phase we are likely to observe the weakening of the Core and the activation of new Core centers; one can expect a search for a new balance of power and new coalitions within the World System at this time (see Grinin, 2010, 2011; Grinin & Korotayev, 2010b; Grinin et al. 2016; Гринин, 2009a for more details).

Consider now some characteristics and causes of those processes.

Possible Causes of the Expansion

It is natural to suppose that particularly strong Juglar crises and depressions typical of K-wave downswings in the Core countries could stimulate the Core expansion into the Periphery.[9] Such an expansion can be considered a result (and as a part) of counter-crisis measures undertaken by the Core countries. In addition, one may take into account the competition imitation effect—that the intensification of expansion efforts by one state would tend to provoke such an intensification on the part of competing states.

---

[8] See Гринин, 2005, Grinin, 2008, 2009a, 2009b, 2010, 2012a, 2012b; Grinin & Korotayev, 2010b; Гринин, 2008а, 2008б, 2008в, 2008г; Grinin et al. 2016; Гринин и Коротаев, 2009б, 2010 on the processes of decrease of sovereignty prerogatives.

[9] On the other hand, the weakening of the Core makes it possible for the Periphery to undertake counter-expansion, as was observed in the 1970s and early 1980s as regards fuel prices. Their explosive growth led to the flow of resources from the Core to the Periphery.

In what way does the expansion contribute to the additional slow-down of economic development during the downswing?

1. In the course of such an expansion the energy of the Core will tend to become exhausted.
2. In addition, the Core powers could be exhausted by their struggles over their control over the World System Periphery. In any case the growth of this control involved substantial expenses (and sometimes serious destruction). In the previous periods this could have additionally weakened the Periphery. On the other hand, results of mutually beneficial expansion may be felt only with a substantial lag.
3. On the other hand, the rapid development was often hindered by the insufficient congruence of the economic structures of the Core and Periphery, a huge gap in the levels of economic development that was observed in many cases.
4. One cannot exclude that we are dealing here with a sort of positive feedback: the worsening of the economic situation in the Core stimulated its expansion to the Periphery, whereas the growing expenses to support this expansion may have worsened the situation in the Core.
5. As a result of the active integration of the Periphery into the World System, the transformation of the Hinterland into Periphery, a part of the Periphery into Semiperiphery, and the formation of new centers in the Semiperiphery, the World System expanded, the number of links and contact intensity within it increased explosively, etc.; this, however, led to a certain slowdown of World System economic growth.
6. Downswings are also connected with the weakening of the old Hegemon. This weakens the structural congruence of the World System and supports the trend toward the slowdown of economic growth rates. We are likely to observe such a pattern in the forthcoming years. On the other hand, it appears virtually impossible to replace the USA as the World System Hegemon, because the USA is a multifunctional Hegemon, whereas no other power will be able to play such a role in the forthcoming decades. That is why there are grounds to expect the reconfiguration of the World System as a whole (see Grinin, 2010; Grinin & Korotayev, 2010b; Grinin et al. 2016; Гринин, 2009a, 2012a for more details).

Slowdowns of the world economic growth are often connected with the slowdown of the economic growth of the Hegemon.

During Upswings the Resource Movement Balance Tended to be in Favor of the Core

1. During the upswing, the World System Core tended to concentrate on its internal affairs (including the struggles between the Core countries), and consequently it tended to move less resources to the Periphery.

2. Resource accumulation, restructuring of relationships within the core, as well as the emergence of new (and especially military) technologies stimulated the escalation of hegemonic struggles within the Core.
3. By themselves those struggles and wars contributed to the acceleration of both inflation and economic growth (thus we are dealing here with a certain positive feedback).
4. An important factor regarding the change of resource movement balance in favor of the Core was constituted by the fact that the previous investment started to produce returns; in particular, long-term investments in the infrastructure started to produce results; the trade-financial links started to work, scarcely populated territories were peopled (as was observed, e.g., in Australia in the first half of the nineteenth century), and so on.
5. On the other hand, new peripheral regions were involved in global trade. Those regions in order to maintain their participation in global trade had to export their commodities with reduced prices (which often implied unequal exchange — see Гринин и Коротаев, 2012 for more detail).[10]

It is also essential to take into consideration the fact that in the last two decades the balance of economic power in the world (between the Core and Periphery of the World System) changed dramatically under the influence of various factors, including the deindustrialization of the West (see Grinin & Korotayev, 2015a). So the mechanisms of these long cycles of interaction between the World System core and periphery (as well as those cycles closely associated with them, i.e. Akamatsu cycles, spelled out in *Chap. 4*) can change. As a result, the movement of capital and industries within the World System is described by such models less adequately now than before.

In any case it is worth mentioning that such core-periphery long cycles strongly influence processes of the Great Divergence and the Great Convergence (see Grinin & Korotayev, 2015a). In particular, these processes (together with the scientific and technological progress and changing technological modes) affect the transformation of technological paradigms and influence the diffusion of technologies from the Core of the World System to its Periphery and Semi-periphery. They can be considered as an important reason for the shift to convergence, especially starting from the 1980s when an active phase of the so-called deindustrialization of the West began. It appears appropriate to reproduce here the following passage from our earlier Springer monograph:

---

[10] Note, however, that during the fourth K-wave downswing and the fifth K-wave upswing one could observe the change of the World System trend toward the growing divergence between the Core and Periphery to the trend toward convergence. Before this switch of the global trends the gap between the Core and the Periphery tended to increase; now it tends to decrease (Grinin & Korotayev, 2015a; Korotayev, Zinkina et al., 2011a; Коротаев и Халтурина, 2009; Малков, Божевольнов et al., 2010; Коротаев, Халтурина и Божевольнов, 2010; Гринин, 2013б; Халтурина и Коротаев, 2010). As a result, as has been mentioned above, we could observe the decrease of the gap between the Core and the Periphery already during the fifth K-wave upswing. Note, that if the hypothesis that we have spelled out above is true, then we should expect the acceleration of the Core–Periphery convergence during the current (fifth) K-wave.

"Deindustrializationcan be defined as a decline in the share of industry in the GDP of the countries of the West, as well as in employment in manufacturing. The process of deindustrialization actually started in the mid-1960s, first in the USA; however, in Japan and Europe this process lagged behind. The share of manufacturing employment in the USA declined from 28 % in 1965 to 16 % in 1994. In general, in developed countries the share of manufacturing employment declined from 28 % in 1970 to 18 % in 1994 (Rowthorn & Ramaswany, 1997). At the same time, the share of services employment rapidly grew. However, this phase of deindustrialization was mainly connected not only with a transfer of industrial technologies to developing countries or the preferential establishment of new factories there, even though the process was under way (see Amsden, 2004) but also with the rapid growth of other economic sectors including information production and services. For this reason, many economists mistakenly believed that North–South trade had very little to do with deindustrialization and with the growing share of low-skilled workers in the developing countries (Bhagwati, 1995; Krugman, 1996; Krugman & Lawrence, 1994; Lawrence & Slaughter, 1993). Later the researchers had to admit that in this respect the role of external trade with low-wage economies showed some signs of strengthening in the 1990s and early 2000s (Debande, 2006).[11] On the whole, the rapid growth of the service sector, including complex and qualified services (e.g. informational, medical, financial, etc.) together with the extension of free trade, free capital transfer (see below), strict environmental laws, demographic deterioration in the countries of the First World, and the growth of the human capital development level in the Third World made the transfer of production to peripheral countries more profitable. So, the initiation of the active phase of deindustrialization turned out to be an active phase of industrialization in many developing countries. Let us point out once again that TNCs played the most important, actually a defining, role in this process, as under free-trade conditions it was more profitable and even simply necessary for them (in order to produce competitive products) to substitute high-paid workers of their own countries with the low-paid workers from the developing countries. As a side note, this slowed down the development of robotics which was actively developed in the 1960s, 1970s, and 1980s. Since the productivity in services grew less rapidly than manufacturing productivity (Rowthorn & Ramaswany, 1997); this process contributed greatly to Convergence. First, the industrial share in the developing countries' GDP grew very quickly; second, working efficiency grew faster than in developed countries. Thus, due to the shortage of demographic resources, scientific and technological progress supported the move of production from the First World countries to the Third World countries, at the same time making it profitable. The economy of every country is known to comprise different sectors, starting with agriculture. Yet, their hierarchy changes together with the development of innovative spheres within the economy. The less innovative sectors lose their share in economy, while the new ones expand. But within the global economy, due to the international division of labor, the situation is different, and the economic share of less innovative sectors might even increase. The reason is that the former technologically leading sectors, when leaving the World System Core, move to other parts of the World System, not as leaders with the prefix 'ex-' but as actual leaders there.[12] First, this occurs in underdeveloped countries via the development of their own production in the ex-leading sectors by means of adopted (imported) technologies. Second, this happens due to the actual transfer of old sectors to the less-developed countries (as has already been mentioned, this process has been going on during the last two or three decades within the process of the deindustrialization of the West). Thus, the structure of the international division

---

[11] For the analysis of the waves of scholarship in the studies in deindustrialization, change of vectors of researchers' interests and estimations during the last 40 years see High, 2013.

[12] The problem of the leading sector has been considered in different aspects in Kuznets, 1926, 1930; Modelski, 1987; Modelski & Thompson, 1996; Rostow, 1975; Rasler & Thompson, 1994; van Duijn, 1983; Thompson, 1990; Thompson, 2000, see also: Rennstich, 2002.

of labor, which is generally the World System's most important axis, to a certain extent reflects the historical succession of leading sectors and makes it possible for a new mode of production to emerge in the World System core. But the new wave of technologies requires not only the presence of an innovation cluster but also a 'free space' in the leading countries in order to re-orient the workforce. While capital and labor are being reoriented, the old basic commodities should be produced elsewhere in sufficient quantity so that the economy with an emerging new leading sector could have more opportunities. This means that it should get rid of the less-innovative commodities. Otherwise, in the situation of basic commodities shortage, it would be more difficult to concentrate on innovative ones which, despite their importance, becomes less connected with people's basic needs (compare food, clothes, and even metals, on the one hand, with Internet and specific services, on the other). Such a release becomes possible due to the import of goods whose production becomes unprofitable. Far from everything is logical here; the process of transformation proceeds with difficulty, but the logic of the process contributes to the World System's economic growth and provides opportunities for innovative breakthroughs in different regions of the World System. In fact, this is a way to introduce new economies into the operating arena of a new production principle. Even if a number of societies do not fit the principle yet (as at present many countries of the world do not really achieve the appropriate level for the scientific and information production principle), anyway to a certain extent they are getting involved in it (at least in large cities where there already exist some advanced technology centers). Moreover, they become a part of the international division of labor which is formed under the influence of a new principle of production. Therefore, the adaptation of new waves of innovations should be supported by technology and capital transfer to the less developed parts of the World System in order to compensate for the volume and range of commodities not produced anymore in the core" (Grinin & Korotayev, 2015a: 131–133).

One of the mechanisms of such shifts within technological modes can be interpreted within the flying geese paradigm which was developed in the late 1930s by the Japanese scientist Kaname Akamatsu (in the early 1960s his works appeared in English [Akamatsu, 1961, 1962]), for a detailed discussion of this theory see *Chap. 4* below.

Chapter 3
Interaction between Kondratieff Waves and Juglar Cycles

Introductory Notes

This chapter addresses some important correlations between medium-term economic cycles (7–11 years) known as Juglar cycles and long-term (40–60 years) Kondratieff cycles. The research into the history of this issue shows that this particular aspect has been insufficiently studied. In our opinion, our research can significantly clarify both the reasons for the alternation of upswing and downswing phases in K-waves and the reasons for the relative stability of the length of these waves. Further, our research can also contribute to the development of more precise means of long-term global forecasting.

'It appears that crises, like diseases, are one of the conditions of the existence of those societies where trade and industry are prevalent. One can predict them, alleviate them, delay them up to a certain moment, one can facilitate the recovery of economic activities; but it has turned to be impossible to eliminate them notwithstanding all the possible methods that have been applied'. Unfortunately, those well forgotten words of Clement Juglar (1862: VII), who was one of the first to demonstrate that economic crises follow the a periodical/cyclical pattern, became very relevant again in 2008, that is about 150 years after they had been written about.

We will start this chapter with our analysis of the main features of medium-term cycles of business activity, or business cycles (7–11 years)[1] that are also known as

---

[1] Many economists maintain that business cycles are quite regular with the characteristic period of 7–11 years. However, some suggest that economic cycles are irregular (see, for example, Fischer et al., 1988). As we suppose, comparative regularity of business cycles is observed rather at the World System scale than in every country taken separately. This corroborates the important role of exogenous factors for the rise and progress of business cycles (for more details see below).

Juglar cycles after the prominent nineteenth-century French economist Clement Juglar (1819–1905), who investigated these cycles in detail (Juglar, 1862, 1889).[2]

Juglar investigated fluctuations of prices, discount rates, and gold reserves of banks in France, England, and the USA and showed their correlation with cycles of increasing business activity, investments (and speculations), and employment (Juglar, 1862, 1889). The first edition of his book discussing these cycles was published in 1862. Juglar's most important achievement lay in presenting substantial evidence that crises were periodic, that is in support of 'the law of crises' periodicity'. According to this law, crisis is preceded by epochs of recovery, well-being, and price growth, which are followed by years of price decrease and the slowing of trade that brings the economy into a depressed state (*Idem* 1889: xv). It is specifically with Juglar's contribution to the analysis of periodic crises that the transition of economics as a whole from crisis theory to business-cycle theory is frequently connected (Besomi, 2005: 1).

Thus, crisis does not occur randomly (It is erroneous to ascribe its occurrence to random factors.).[3] Economic crisis is preceded by an intensive increase in business activities and prices, which sometimes allows one to predict a crisis in advance.[4] According to Tugan-Baranovsky (Туган-Барановский, 2008 [1913]: 294), Juglar successfully coped with this task on a number of occasions.

A few notes on Juglar cycles (which will also bedenoted as **J-cycles** below). Let us turn to a brief description by Tugan-Baranovsky of the economic cycle scheme proposed by Juglar:

> "Industrial crisis never comes unexpectedly: it is always preceded by a special heated state of industry and trade whose symptoms are so specific that an industrial crisis may be forecasted in advance… What causes these regular changes of booms and busts? Juglar indicates one main cause: periodic fluctuations of commodity prices. The prosperous epoch that precedes the crisis is always characterized by the growth of prices: 'Annual savings of civilized nations (that enlarge their wealth) also lead and sustain the constant growth of prices: this is a natural state of the market, a prosperous period. The crisis approaches when the upward movement slows down; the crisis starts when it stops… The main cause (one may even say—the only cause) of the crises is the interruption of the growth of prices' (Juglar, 1889: 33). The overall mechanism of crisis development is specified by Juglar in the following way. The increase in commodity prices naturally tends to impede the sales of respective commodities. That is why, with the growth of prices, the foreign trade balance becomes less and less favorable for the respective country. The gold starts to move abroad to pay for the imports whose amounts start to exceed those of exports. At the beginning the amounts of

---

[2] As we have already mentioned above, Medium-term cycles (7–11 years) were first named after Juglar in works by Joseph Schumpeter, who developed the typology of different-length business-cycles (Schumpeter, 1939, 1954; see also Kwasnicki, 2008).

[3] Notwithstanding the belief of some influential modern economists in the contrary (see, e.g., Mankiw, 2008: 740; Zarnowitz, 1985: 544–568).

[4] It is worth mentioning here that, before Juglar, prevailing views were based on Adam Smith's ideas of 'invisible hand' and on Say's law of markets. According to such views, equilibrium state is considered to be the main one for the market, various shifts from it being caused by some external factors. Consequently, crises are also caused by random factors. However, currently these ideas (those of external shocks) are rather popular again. We will consider this issue in more detail further on.

gold moving abroad are negligible and nobody pays attention to this. However, the higher the prices, the greater the amount of gold that moves abroad. Finally, the commodity prices reach such a high level that selling the respective goods abroad becomes highly problematic. As the traders cannot cover the import expenses with the export revenues, they have to renew their promissory notes in banks after the payment deadline, and this accounts for the intensification of the discounting operations of the banks in the period that directly precedes the crisis. Yet, the payments cannot be delayed forever; sooner or later they should be made. The commodity prices fall immediately, this is followed by bankruptcies of banks and traders, and the industrial crisis begins" (Туган-Барановский, 2008 [1913]: 294–295).

It can be seen that the central mechanism of cyclical fluctuations, in Juglar's opinion, is the fluctuation of prices, their increase leading to recovery and upswing, their decrease being followed by crisis and depression. The exceptionally important role of price fluctuations is indisputable; it has been noticed by economists belonging to various schools (see, e.g., Haberler, 1964 [1937]). Among them one can mention such contemporaries of Juglar as Karl Marx and Friedrich Engels. In Tugan-Baranovsky's opinion (Туган-Барановский, 2008 [1913]), with which we are ready to agree, Juglar's theory, however, does not explain adequately enough the main point, namely the increase in commodity prices in the period that precedes the crisis. Subsequent researchers described numerous mechanisms of such an increase ranging from interest rate fluctuation, credit expansion and reinvestment to the behavior of aggregate demand and aggregate supply curve, as well as psychological factors such as ungrounded optimism. Nevertheless, the issue is still subject to vigorous academic discussions. Tugan-Baranovsky himself suggests that crises are caused by lack of capital, as in the upswing period capital is spent faster than it is accumulated. As a result, both credit and impulse to development are exhausted, while structural disproportions lead to crisis phenomena (not necessarily in the form of an acute crisis; he was right in stating that the crisis intensity depends on the intensity of the upswing). Tugan-Baranovsky emphasizes (and we would agree with him on this point to a certain degree) that the school of Marx and Engels suggested the deepest understanding of crisis for their time. According to them, crises are caused by over-production (which is a consequence of the main contradiction of capitalism). Overproduction itself is stipulated, first of all, by the anarchic character of capitalist production; secondly, by the poverty of the masses, their exploitation, and the tendency of salaries to decrease. As a consequence of the constant growth of capital's organic structure (i.e. the decline of the proportion of salaries in total production expenses), according to Marx, the profit rate falls.[5] Capitalists try to overcome the profit rate reduction by introducing new machines, which in turn leads to labor productivity growth. This leads to the expansion of the commodities' supply and, consequently, to their overproduction (because of the 'anarchy' of capitalistic production). Crisis is namely the explosion of capitalistic production contradictions, and, consequently, the restoration of equilibrium. Some Marxist economists provided fundamental descriptions of the history of crises (see, e.g., Варга, 1937; Мендельсон, 1959–1964; Трахтенберг, 1963 [1939]). However, Marx and Engels,

---

[5] Phenomenon marked by economists of various schools but explained differently.

in our view, did not manage to show the true connection between the processes of production and circulation (the latter was ignored as an allegedly less fundamental part). Thus, they were not capable of revealing the causes of crisis explosiveness and the dramatic change of situation at so-called turning points (i.e. from boom to acute crisis and from the bust to recovery and boom).

In the first half of the twentieth century, numerous theories explaining economic cycles were already present. In fact, the under-consumption theory was one of the oldest, as such views appeared long ago (actually, together with the science of political economy itself). Among its earliest followers, Lord James Lauderdale, Thomas Malthus and Jean Sismondi were the most prominent. In the first half of the twentieth century, a significant contribution to scientific re-consideration and diffusion of the under-consumption theory was made by John Atkinson Hobson, William Foster, Waddill Catchings, and Emil Lederer. Essentially concordant with the ideas of this theory were some of the abovementioned approaches of the Marxist orthodox school, which assumed that the working class condition, according to the law of working class absolute impoverishment put forward by Marx, must worsen.[6]

Monetary theories saw causes of cyclicity mainly in the cumulative character of business activity expansion and contraction depending on the amounts of money in the economy.[7] The most vivid example is Hawtrey's theory (see, e.g., Hawtrey, 1926, 1928). For him, trade-industrial crises appeared to be purely monetary phenomena, as, in his opinion, monetary flow change suffices to explain the transitions from upswings to depressions (and vice versa). On the whole, undoubtedly, the monetary component of cyclicity and crises is very important. However, representatives of monetary theories attributed a too dominant role to monetary factors, thus ignoring non-monetary causes.

One of the versions of the over-accumulation theory is based on the ideas of Tugan-Baranovsky. Haberler (1964) divides representatives of the theory into followers of its monetary and non-monetary versions. The first group includes those economists who suggest that monetary factors, acquiring great importance with credit expansion, cause strong disproportions between economy sectors producing consumer items and capital goods (or, more exactly, between sectors of the whole manufacturing chain). The followers of this version of the theory in question have made a particularly valuable contribution to the analysis of disproportions in production structure caused by the credit expansion at the phase of boom and prosperity, as well as to the interpretation of crisis as a result of those disproportions. Representatives of this direction include Friedrich von Hayek, Fritz

---

[6] However, such explanation has become an anachronism long ago. The given theory correlates very badly indeed with a long-term trend to an unprecedentedly fast (against the general historical background) increase in life standards (and real incomes) of 'direct producers' in general, and of the 'working class' in particular. This trend is rather typical for 'capitalist' countries and is observed in reality.

[7] It should be noted that, from the point of view of General Systems Theory, this point is essentially related to the issue of positive feedback loops, which will be considered in more detail further on. The action of these feedbacks can lead to phenomena perceived as 'booms', 'collapses', and 'breakdowns' (see, e.g., Sornette, 2003).

Machlup, Lionel Robbins, Wilhelm Roepke, and Richard von Strigl. Numerous representatives of this direction belong to the so-called Austrian School, which started from the works by Ludwig von Mises (1981 [1912]; фон Мизес, 2005). It sees the most important cause of crises as state interference into economic processes, particularly in artificial credit expansion. Special attention is given to the role of central banks in crisis generation (see, e.g., Huerta de Soto, 2006; Rothbard, 1969; Shostak, 2002; Skousen, 1993).[8]

The other, non-monetary direction of over-accumulation theory is represented by the authors whose theories are based on taking into account non-monetary factors: inventions, discoveries, creation of new markets etc., that is factors securing favorable conditions for new investments. This direction is represented by Gustav Cassel, Peter Hansen, Arthur Spiethoff, and Knut Wicksell. Works by Arthur Pigou and Joseph Schumpeter are essentially close to this direction as well.

Psychological theories are also worth mentioning. Even though every economic phenomenon has its psychological aspect, some theories (not without grounds) when interpreting different cycle phases assign a special importance to 'psychological reaction' that can considerably increase disproportions, make a new phase occur faster or slower, contribute to business activity increase or hinder it, etc. Among the representatives of psychological theory, one may mention such prominent economists as, for example, John Keynes, Frederick Lavington, Arthur Pigou, and Frank Taussig. In some aspects they ascribe to psychological factors (such as optimism, pessimism, euphoria, panic) a capacity to produce a relatively independent impact (for more details see Гринин, 2009г).

Theories of economic crises can be classified in a variety of ways. For example, they can be segregated into exogenous and endogenous ones (see, e.g., Morgan, 1991), which is closely connected with approaches to the explanation of the nature of equilibrium state in economy. We take it as a basis that, though cyclicity has an endogenous structure being connected to occurrence of structural disproportions, still crises cannot occur without exogenous impacts. Essentially, the economy of a given country cannot be regarded in an isolated way, as the economic field is always much broader than the one of an isolated economy. It serves as a part of the World System economic field, so in reality external impacts must necessarily be observed (see for more details Гринин и Коротаев, 2010). The following important aspect must also be taken into consideration: while a crisis in a given country may have a primarily endogenous character, its process and characteristics may possess substantial peculiarities in comparison to crisis in countries where it is caused by exogenous factors. In particular, in modern conditions many countries, for example, China, India, or Russia, had not exhausted

---

[8] As a separate direction, a group of economists may be specified who developed the so-called 'acceleration principle'. According to this principle, the changes in consumer goods production cause, due to technological reasons, much sharper fluctuations in production goods sector, as investments into main capital require much more time and expenses. This causes a general demand increase, which eventually turns out to be greater than required for optimal development, which creates prerequisites for crisis origin (see, e.g., Haberler, 1964).

their resources for development by 2008. In 2008–2009, the crisis in these countries occurred simply under the influence of a sharp change in external conditions. And, as external conditions of every country form a unique combination, crisis would have important peculiarities in each particular case. At the same time, in the USA the crisis was more due to endogenous origins, as the country's economic development resources had been worn out to a greater extent than those in many developing countries. Such a situation is generally (though, of course, not always) typical for the development of crises in the World System core, on the one hand, as opposed to crises in its periphery, on the other. In the center, crises have a more endogenous character, while in the periphery their origins are usually more exogenous, as they tend to be caused by economic fluctuations in the World System center. Thus, every crisis always has both endogenous and exogenous causes, but their combination is specific for each particular society in every particular period, which makes the situation unique for any society and for any crisis.

We will now turn our attention to the work of Kondratieff. He divided all approaches firstly into ones regarding economic phenomena as static, i.e. considering a static equilibrium state in an economy as normal, and all deviations from such an equilibrium as disturbances (Кондратьев, 2002: 11–14). Among the followers of this approach Kondratieff named William Jevons, Leon Walras, Vilfredo Pareto, Gregory Clark, Alfred Marshall, Knut Wicksell, etc. Secondly, in Kondratieff's view, the research of some other economists was oriented mostly at the study of economic dynamics. These economists state that the equilibrium moment is not a basic one; they may even consider it as random, whereas, according to them, the economic dynamics go through a whole range of regular developmental phases. Among those economists Kondratieff mentions Karl Marx, Clement Juglar, Mikhail Tugan-Baranovsky, Arthur Spiethoff, Jean Lescure, Albert Aftalion, and George Mitchell. He indicates, however, that these researchers elaborated on particular problems of economic dynamics, their work standing somewhat apart from the general development of economic theory. Nevertheless, it should be added here that specifically these researchers made an especially important contribution to the development of the economic cycle theory.

As regards the above-mentioned division, it should be noted that, in the view of some economists, the essence of the Keynesian revolution is in Keynes' ideas (1936) destroying the belief in the existence of perfect inner regulatory forces of the market mechanism (Adam Smith's 'invisible hand'), which meant the true end of the laissez-faire doctrine (see, e.g., Blaug, 1985). Discussions between the Keynesians and Neoclassicists are centered mainly on the question whether the economy possesses self-regulating forces.[9] Classical theory pays particular attention to long-term economic growth, dwarfing the meaning of economic cycles. Keynesians insist that crisis-less economic growth is only possible in the presence of adequate monetary

---

[9] In classical economic theory, self-regulating forces are stated to be ones connected with the behavior of economic agents: entrepreneurs, workers, buyers, sellers, etc., stipulated by elasticity of salaries and prices, which are capable of supporting the economy in a state of full employment.

and fiscal policies playing the role of countercyclical stabilizers. In other words, Keynesians maintain that economic growth directly depends on *the state's* economic policy, without which such growth may not occur at all. As Samuelson and Nordhaus note (Samuelson & Nordhaus, 2009: 486–487), in Keynesians' opinion, the economy is prone to lengthy periods of recurring unemployment followed by speculation and growth of inflation. While for a classical economist the economy is similar to a person leading a healthy way of life, for a Keynesian, the economy is a manic-depressive personality periodically inclined either to boundless rage and groundless gaiety, or to hopeless sullenness.

Since the 1950s, but especially in 1970–1990s, discussions concerning cyclicity problems were connected with choosing the parameters that economists proposed would influence economic cycles in order to diminish the negative consequences of uneven economic development. Expansion and development of the Keynesian theory contributed to the advancement of the idea about the economy's immanent proneness to booms and busts (i.e., to cycles). However, on the other hand, the popularity of the idea about the possibility of influencing cycles through state policy led to economic thought focusing mainly on influence instruments. The problems of the cycles' nature and their deep causes gradually shifted to the periphery of the economic science.

Best-known in modern economic thought are the Keynesian (more exactly, neo-Keynesian) and monetary schools. The first post-war decades showed that the state policy of influencing economic parameters (such as aggregate demand, aggregate supply, discount rates, etc.) is not entirely successful. First of all, it is not always effective; secondly, it is not always based on long-term economic interests; thirdly, it has a certain lag, as necessary laws and decisions must be subject to a long procedure of coordination, approval, and enforcement. This led to the growing popularity of the monetarist theory, which suggests that the state should exercise less direct influence on the economy, while its interference must be more subtle and concentrate mainly on regulating money supply, money circulation velocity, state debt volume, and interest rates.[10] An important contribution of this school to macroeconomic theory is in the development of the idea about the necessity of following stable rules of money circulation and not relying on voluntary fiscal and monetary policy.

Thus, the main difference between the views of Keynesians and monetarists lies in their approaches to defining aggregate demand. Keynesians suggest that aggregate demand changes are influenced by numerous factors, while monetarists believe the main factor having impact on output and prices to be the change of money supply. Monetarists believe that the private sector is stable, and state interference often simply takes resources from it; macroeconomic fluctuations appear mainly because of fluctuations of money supply. In general, one can observe different views as

---

[10] It is no coincidence that dominating positions in global economic science (and practice) went from Keynesians to monetarists in the early 1970s at a transition period from upswing to a downswing phase of fourth Kondratieff cycle. On the other hand, such position transition was stipulated by refusal from attachment to the gold standard in dollar, which led to great changes in behaviour of finances devoid of such an anchor.

regards the questions of which instruments should be used to influence economic cyclicity, and what should be the role and economic policy of a state from both short-term and long-term perspectives.

However, some more radical views on direct state interference into the economy are also present within the neoclassical theory. One of its tenets is based on the so-called theory of rational expectations (Robert Emerson Lukas and others), which essentially suggests that, as people use all available information, they can figure out in advance the predictable state policy and use it for their own benefit, as a result of which state policy turns out to be ineffective. Roughly speaking, 'no government can outwit the taxpayers'. Neoclassicists also assume price and salary flexibility (that is why the theory is called neoclassical, as, similar to the classical pre-Keynesian one, it is based on the idea of economic self-regulation). Like monetarists, they suppose that state influence should concentrate mainly on indirect economic regulation via various monetary instruments.

However, it is important to understand that in the last 10–15 years the process of definite and substantial synthesis of old and new economic theories has been going on (for more details see Самуэльсон и Нордхаус, 2009: 505–507).[11] In particular, economists have started paying more attention to expectations, as neoclassical theory suggests.

The Phases of Medium-Term Juglar Cycles (J-Cycles)

Some modern economists single out only two main phases of the business cycle: upswing and downswing (there are some other names for those phases–e.g., 'expansion' and 'contraction'), whereas moments corresponding to the crisis (emerging at the peak of the overheating) and the trough of the downswing/recession are interpreted as inflection points (see, e.g., Samuelson & Nordhaus, 2009; Гринин, Коротаев, 2014а).[12]

However, it is not rare when the cycle is subdivided into four phases[13] (and we prefer to do this within our model). For more details on our model of the Juglar cycle (see Grinin, Korotayev, & Malkov, 2010).[14]

---

[11] Actual synthesis of Keynesian and monetary theories started much earlier.

[12] Yet, generally speaking, the number of phases may depend on how detailed the respective analysis is (as well as a number of other factors). Thus (see below), we subdivide each cycle into four big phases (basing ourselves on Schumpeter's approach to the distribution of cycle phases), and then single out eight subphases (two subphases per every phase), whereas Burns and Mitchell (1946) only identify two big phases (expansion and contraction) subdividing each phase into three subphases, and consider turning points (peak and trough) as separate short phases. Thus, they get eight stages too (as the ninth stage belongs actually to the next cycle).

[13] On the other hand, it appears possible to single out two sub-phases in each phase.

[14] This model takes into account a number of approaches to the analysis of such cycles that are specified in the publications by Abel and Bernanke (2008a); Варга (1937); Haberler (1964 [1937]); Hicks (1946 [1939]); Hilferding (1981 [1910]); Juglar (1862, 1889); Keynes (1936); Lescure (1907); Marx (Маркс, 1961 [1893, 1894]); Mitchell (1927), Мендельсон (1959–1964); Minsky

Fig. 3.1 The model of a Juglar cycle

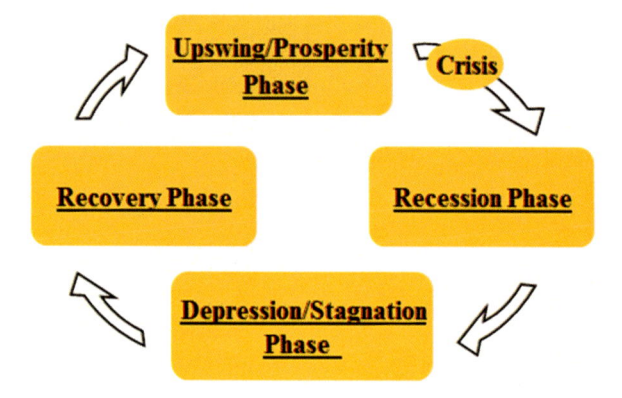

Thus, in our model a J-cycle consists of four phases:

- recovery phase (which we could sub-divide into a start sub-phase and an acceleration sub-phase);
- upswing/prosperity/expansion phase (which we sub-divide into the a growth sub-phase and a boom/overheating sub-phase);
- recession phase (within which we single out a crash/bust/acute crisis sub-phase and a downswing sub-phase);
- depression/stagnation phase (which we could subdivide into a stabilization sub-phase and the a breakthrough sub-phase) (Fig. 3.1).

Recovery phase starts after (and as a result of) the liquidation of disproportions (and the establishment of new proportions) that almost inevitably take place during the preceding phases of recession and stagnation (which often lead to a significant restructuration). That is why a new cycle starts at a new level of equilibrium (Schumpeter, 1939). The recovery and certain growth can start because, as a result of the preceding downswing, excessive commodity inventories have been dissolved and have come into correspondence with extant demand, some unsatisfied demand for commodities has been formed, problematic firms have disappeared, bad debts and fictive capitals have been 'burnt out', and businessmen have become much more cautious (see, e.g., Minsky, 1983, 1985, 1986, 2005), etc.

At the expansion phase the growth accelerates, whereas the recovery becomes general. The phase of active expansion often needs some external factor (e.g., the emergence of some major new market). Demand for resources and commodities grows, and investments increase in a really substantial way. This tends to lead to the growth of prices. The demand for credit also grows, new enterprises emerge, active speculations at stock and commodity exchanges take place. If the growth continues and becomes very fast, the economy moves to the

---

(1983, 1985, 1986, 2005); Samuelson and Nordhaus (2005: 403–552); Schumpeter (1939); Tugan-Baranovky (1954; Туган-Барановский, 2008 [1913]); von Hayek (1931, 1933); von Mises (1981 [1912]); Cassel (Кассель 1925); Fridman (Фридман 2002); Pigou (1929) as well as a number of other economists.

boom (overheating) sub-phase, which leads to an overstrain of the financial markets, as free liquidity is absent. As a result, prices grow very fast, 'bubbles' emerge, and speculations increase.

Recession phase. Finally, some factors interfere (for example, a sudden drop of demand or prices, a bankruptcy of a large firm or bank, a default of some foreign state, additional demand for funds in the context of a worsening political situation, or a new law that changes 'rules of the game'); as a result one observes bust and acute crisis. This is accompanied by a decline of industrial production, waves of bankruptcies, a decline of orders for various products, shut-downs of many enterprises, explosive growth of unemployment, and so on.

Depression phase is a period of stagnation and very slow economic growth, when the economy moves from overheating and bust, the over-accumulated inventories are dissolved, prices decrease (though in modern times prices may behave in somewhat different way during this phase). The depression phase involves the process through which the market economy becomes adapted, it eliminates extremes and distortions of the previous inflationary boom and restores a stable economic state. Within this perspective, depression turns out to be an unpleasant but necessary reaction to the distortions and extremes of the preceding boom (e.g., Rothbard, 1969).

Causes of cyclical crises. Economic crisis (bust, recession, and depression) is the most dramatic part of the medium-term J-cycle. The crisis is always a result of the preceding active growth, because this growth inevitably produces structural strains not only in the economy, but also in the society as a whole (as the current social institutions are 'designed' for a certain scale of phenomena and processes). However, notwithstanding all the similarities, every crisis, naturally, has certain unique individual features.

Characteristic features of classical J-cycles can be presented as follows: at the expansion phase they were characterized by very fast (sometimes even explosive) growth (boom) that involved a tremendous strain within the economic system, which was followed by an even more impressive bust.

The phase of expansion (that included the sub-phase of boom and overheating) was accompanied by the following phenomena:

(a) a very strong growth of prices of raw materials and real estate;
(b) excessive demand for credit and the expansion of investment over any reasonable limits;
(c) an outbreak of speculations with commodities and bonds;
(d) enormous growth of risky operations.

All these are salient features of the Juglar cycle that have been described on many occasions by representatives of various schools of this particular mode of economic thought. On the other hand, they can also be easily found in the recent global economic crisis of 2008–2009.

Our analysis has also demonstrated that during the expansion phase a special role is usually played by some new financial technology or some new type of financial assets.

Sharp transitions from booms to busts were connected with a spontaneous economic development that was regulated by almost nothing except market forces, as state interference in the economic development was not sufficient. Within such a context (and taking into consideration the presence of the gold standard) acute crises became inevitable.[15]

On the Importance of Further Research on the Theory of J-Cycles

After the Great Depression the interest in Juglar cycles grew sharply, and, as it was said in *Chap. 1,* according to Haberler (Хаберлер, 2008: 431), there was no other period in the history of economic thought when the problems of economic cycles were studied so intensively. However, later, in the second half of the twentieth century (especially, during Phase A of the fourth Kondratieff Cycle), the dynamics of business cycles experienced a significant change (first of all as a result of the active interference of the state into the economic life),[16] recessions became less deep than before (whereas the crisis became less dramatic), the recovery came relatively fast, etc. As a result, economists began paying more attention to long waves of business activities (Kondratieff cycles) than to Juglar cycles, though, mostly by tradition, macroeconomics textbooks still tend to include a chapter on those cycles (yet, they are mostly denoted simply as 'business cycles').[17] We believe that such neglect with respect to the study of J-cycles is unproductive. In our opinion, the modern crisis is quite similar in type to a classical Juglar's cycle crisis.

The cyclical dynamics of Juglar-type cycles in their most pronounced form (that is, not smoothed by state intervention) was determined by the following factors: (a) the presence of the gold standard in transactions within a country, as well as at the international level; (b) uncontrolled dynamics of prices and interest rates; (c) relatively weak interference of the state during upswings and even crises and recessions (though gradually such interference increased). These resulted in fast (sometimes

---

[15] Thus, with the excessive growth of credit and swelling of financial assets, the amount of money substitutes (shares, bills, bonds, etc.) greatly increased. As a result, with a decrease in confidence in these securities a sudden demand for gold and cash increased so much that destroyed the entire banking system.

[16] Even some Soviet economists had to acknowledge this, e.g., Varga, a Hungarian by origin, who was influenced originally by the Austrian Economic School (e.g., Варга, 1974: 366–400). In particular, he noticed that the depression phase had contracted in a very significant way. The change in crisis patterns in England since the late nineteenth century was first noticed by Tugan-Baranovsky (Туган-Барановский, 2008 [1913]). Mitchell also showed that, though recession is a necessary part of the cycle, not every cycle should be necessarily connected with an acute crisis (Митчелл, 1930: 391–392). For a more detailed analysis of post-war cycles see Гринин и Коротаев, 2010.

[17] See, e.g., Мэнкью, 1994: Chap. 14; Abel & Bernanke, 2008a: Chap. 8; Сакс и Ларрен, 1996: Chap. 17, even though such chapters are present not in all textbooks of the kind. For example, in the textbook by Дорнбуш и Фишер (1997) such a chapter is absent.

even explosive) upswings (that demanded a great tension on the part of the economic system) and equally rapid downswings. The upswing, boom and overheating were accompanied by rapid and inadequate growth of prices of raw materials and real estate; an increase in intensity of speculations with commodities and stock assets; a dramatic expansion of credit and risky operations; and the growth of investments beyond any reasonable limits. All these are salient features of the J-cycles that were described many times in the writings of representatives of various schools of economic thought (see, e.g., Abel & Bernanke, 2008; Haberler, 1964; Juglar, 1862, 1889; Hicks, 1946 [1939]; Hilferding, 1981 [1910]; Keynes, 1936; Lescure (Лескюр, 1908); Marx [Маркс, 1961/1893, 1894]; Samuelson & Nordhaus, 2005, 2009; Tugan-Baranovsky, 1954).

Such an expansion of assets tended to lift temporarily limitations produced by the metallic standard. This is almost always that during the upswing phase we observe the effect of some new financial technology (naturally, in addition to the old ones), or some new type of assets (e.g., in the nineteenth century this could be railway shares), that could drive the credit and speculations, amplifying the overheating of the economic system.[18] The monetary component of the Juglar cycles was always exceptionally important (though this was the driving force of the dynamics of the real economy that was at the basis of cyclical upswings).

The above indicated factors were the main ones to engender very sharp and vividly expressed cyclic features. However, gradually under the impact of the Keynesian recipes (in the framework of national economic development) it became possible to minimize these dramatic distortions of rises and falls and to put speculation under a certain amount of control (e.g., after the Great Depression in the USA the Glass-Steagall Act was passed, forbidding banks, investment firms and insurance companies to speculate at stock exchanges [see Суэтин, 2009: 41]; Лан, 1976; Samuelson & Nordhaus, 2005, 2009). This led to smoothing of cyclical fluctuations and to less explosive crises.[19]

However, currently, the crisis has rather overgrown national borders, occurring namely as an international crisis, where national norms act in an obviously weakened form, while international regulations have not yet been worked out. That is why a number of old features recur at this new stage, because regulation methods

---

[18] For example, by the Charter of the Bank of England (as renewed in 1833), it was permissible to establish deposit joint stock banks everywhere. As a result, their number started growing rapidly which greatly contributed to the growth of capital accumulation, speculation, and at the same time to the accumulation of conditions for the 1836 crisis (for more detail see Туган-Барановский, 2008 [1913]: 110–111). For more detail on the development of various new financial technologies from cycle to cycle see Гринин и Коротаев, 2010.

[19] In 1999 in the USA the law on financial services modernization was passed, which annulled the Glass-Steagall Act that was in force for more than 60 years (see Суэтин, 2009: 41). As a basis for introducing the law on financial services modernization, it has been claimed that American credit organizations are inferior to foreign rivals, especially European and Japanese 'universal banks' which were not subject to such limitations (Гринспен, 2009: 200).

applicable to separate countries would not work at the World System scale, and still more so that the rules of such regulation have not been worked out yet.

We suggest that the current recurrence of some features of Juglar's cycle is connected namely with the following features of anarchy and arrhythmia of the non-regulated market economy:

1. Subjects of international law (and their economic agents) largely behave the same way as subjects of national law and the market previously did. As they use foreign currency and foreign currency rates in their dealings, this invariably leads to sharp distortions in international trade, devaluations, etc.
2. In the last decades capital movement between countries became free, that is. it is relatively weakly regulated by national law and almost not regulated at all by international law. This causes huge and exceedingly fast capital movements, which lead to a very rapid growth in some places and then to a sharp decline and corresponding crisis phenomena.
3. In the modern economy not only have new financial technologies been developed, but the modern economy itself largely started producing values namely in the financial sphere (financial services). Thus, the financial component of crisis has increased dramatically; this differs from previous decades, when the main economic growth went on in the sphere of manufacturing. (These processes are analyzed in greater detail in the following publications: Grinin, 2012a; Grinin, Korotayev, & Malkov, 2010; Гринин, 2009б, 2009в; Гринин и Коротаев, 2010; Гринин, Малков и Коротаев, 2010а, 2010б).

We would like to conclude the present section with the following important note. Activities of modern financial corporations and funds lead to an uncontrollable growth of financial assets and anarchy in their movements; that is why it is criticized quite convincingly by various authors (e.g., Schäfer, 2009: 279–280), including ourselves (Akaev, Fomin, Tsirel, & Korotayev, 2010; Akaev, Sadovnichy, and Korotayev, 2011, 2012; Grinin & Korotayev, 2010a, 2010b; Grinin, Korotayev, & Malkov, 2010; Гринин, 2008д, 2009б, 2009г, 2012б; Гринин, Малков и Коротаев, 2010б; Гринин, Коротаев и Малков, 2010). That is why we are absolutely convinced in the necessity to look for ways to minimize the respective risks at the global scale, to regulate activities of financial actors, and to restrict them in their most risky operations (*Ibidem*). However, it is highly erroneous to claim that modern financial technologies are immanently destructive, that they only lead the world economy to various calamities, and that they are only useful to parasitic financiers and speculators. Contrary to this, the modern financial sector performs a lot of generally useful important functions at the global scale. Our own analysis has demonstrated quite convincingly that the global financial system, notwithstanding all its negative points, still performs certain important positive functions including the 'insurance' of social guaranties on a global scale (Гринин, 2009а; Grinin, 2010, Grinin et al., 2012; Grinin & Korotayev, 2010a).

Correlation Between K-Waves and J-Cycles

Preliminary Discussion

Introductory Notes

The main goal of this section is to study the interaction between K-waves and J-cycles. We believe that the analysis of this interaction may help to clarify significantly both the causes of the alternation of upswing and downswing phases in K-waves and the relative stability of their characteristic period.

As we have already noticed previously, there are quite numerous explanations as regards the origins of the medium-term Juglar cycles with their characteristic period between 7 and 11 years[20]; however, there is a substantial degree of unanimity as regards the main factors that are responsible for the emergence of the Juglar fluctuations (though this unanimity is absent as regards the contribution of each of those factors). There is much less clarity and unanimity as regards the causes of the emergence and recurrence of the K-waves (long cycles), as this field is still mostly dominated by various hypotheses (see, e.g., Korotayev & Grinin, 2012).[21]

Notwithstanding substantial advances in the study of wave-like periodic fluctuations, there is no unanimity among researchers as regards many important points (see, e.g., Goldstein, 1988 for a reviewer of earlier literature on this subject, or Korotayev & Grinin, 2012); those points include the total number of attested Kondratieff cycles; their periodization (this includes the issue of the presence/absence of the K-waves before the industrial revolution of the eighteenth century[22]); which parameters should be used to trace periodic fluctuations; which spheres are subject to those fluctuations (whether they are observed in the economic subsystem only, or also in political and cultural spheres).[23] There is no unanimity either as

---

[20] See, e.g., Abel & Bernanke, 2008a: 361–502; Варга, 1937; Hicks, 1946 [1939]; Haberler, 1964 [1937]; Juglar, 1862, 1889; Lescure, 1907; Маркс, 1961 [1893, 1894]; von Mises, 1981 [1912]; Мендельсон, 1959–1964; Minsky, 1983, 1985, 1986, 2005; Mitchell, 1913, 1927; Tugan-Baranovsky, 1954 [1913]; Pigou, 1929; von Hayek, 1931, 1933; Keynes, 1936; Schumpeter, 1939; Samuelson & Nordhaus, 2009; Трахтенберг, 1963, etc.

[21] Some of those hypotheses even suggest climatic change as the main factor generating the K-waves (see, e.g., Моуги, 1992).

[22] For the evidence supporting the existence of the preindustrial K-waves see, e.g., Goldstein, 1988; Моуги, 1992; Modelski, 2006, 2008a, 2008b, 2012; Модельски и Томпсон, 1992; Modelski & Thompson, 1996; Modelski, Thompson, & Devezas, 2008; Пантин, 1996; Пантин и Лапкин, 2006, etc. Some scholars, while not rejecting some long-term fluctuations in the pre-industrial period, consider the K-waves in this period as certain historical excesses produced by various exogenous factors (see, e.g., Маевский 1992: 60).

[23] See an incomplete list of such problems in the following publications: Аврамов, 1992: 64–66; Маевский, 1992: 58–60; Румянцева, 2003: 11–12.

regards the issue of the main factors affecting the formation of the waves and the change of their phases[24] (for more details see Grinin, Devezas, & Korotayev, 2012).

Notwithstanding the abovementioned difficulties, we may base our further research on the fact that K-wave dynamics were actually observed at least during the last two centuries; that we do observe some fairly periodic fluctuations of some important economic indicators (technological innovations, prices, GDP, trade turnover, etc. — see, e.g., Berry & Dean, 2012; Devezas, 2012; Helenius, 2012; Husson & Louça, 2012; Korotayev & Tsirel, 2010, Коротаев и Цирель, 2010а, 2010б; Korotayev, Zinkina, & Bogevolnov, 2011; Korotayev & Grinin, 2012a; Modelski, 2012; Ternyik, 2012; Thompson, 2012; Гринин, Коротаев и Цирель, 2011; Гринин и Коротаев, 2012).

We believe that one of the most promising directions of the K-wave research is constituted by the analysis of the connections between the K-wave and J-cycle dynamics. It appears a bit strange that these relations between K-waves and J-cycles have not been studied sufficiently yet, which indicates that the importance of these relationships is still underestimated.[25]

The relationships between K-waves and J-cycles are visible rather saliently in the following point: the most widely accepted dates of the Kondratieff waves and their phases are tightly connected with the most widely accepted dates of Juglar cycles. However, even this aspect of the relationship between Kondratieff and Juglar cycles has been studied rather superfluously and insufficiently (see Аврамов, 1992: 66–68; Полетаев и Савельева, 1993: 11–12); note that Kondratieff himself did not pay much attention to this relationship (Кондратьев, 2002: 379–380) though Schumpeter (1939) paid significantly more attention to it. However, we believe that his view of this relationship was too straightforward; he thought that the structure of long cycles (K-waves) was similar to the structure of medium-term J-cycles (see also Румянцева, 2003: 19). Note that Schumpeter, when developing his theory of cycles with different characteristic periods, based his thinking on the principle of a single cause and multiplicity of effects of that single cause (Аврамов, 1992: 67); this does not appear to be quite correct despite some heuristic value of the respective principle. Long-term processes are likely to be caused by factors that are different from the ones causing short-term processes (see, e.g., Korotayev, Malkov, & Khaltourina, 2006a: 105–111). Below we will demonstrate that the factors generating K-waves are inherent within the expanding reproduction of the economy; however, the shorter-term impulses generating J-cycles produce some ordering of the K-waves.

We believe we need a more profound study of the relationship between these two types of cycles, and we think that the study of the interaction between J-cycles and K-waves is capable of shedding light on the reasons of the relative stability of the

---

[24] As regards the underlying causes, one can identify mono-causal and multi-causal approaches; the latter with more or less success can be combined into one or another paradigm synthesis. For the criticism of mono-causal approaches see, e.g., Румянцева, 2003: 50.

[25] Concept of long waves and the 'normal' business cycle theory exist and develop relatively independently. Experts on the theory of the business cycle with minimal exceptions try to ignore the existence of long waves, and K-wave students make little use of the 'conventional' business cycle theory (Полетаев и Савельева, 1993: 11–12).

characteristic period of the K-waves and their phases. It does not appear to be possible to explain completely this periodicity with exogenous factors—such as the alteration of technological or population generations. It appears necessary to look for such economic and social processes that are capable of supporting the abovementioned rhythm. From our point of view, the only real factor that is able to give Kondratieff waves their respective rhythm is contributed by the Juglar cycles. In addition to the study of the organic links between K-waves and J-cycles, it appears absolutely necessary to research the links between those two types of cycles and certain world-system processes.

Some Preliminary Conclusions

The analysis of the K-wave manifestation and alteration demonstrates quite convincingly that, notwithstanding a considerable variety of explanations of K-waves, proponents of all the respective theories are partly right. However, each of those theories has a rather limited range of application. Thus, in order to achieve a more adequate understanding of the nature of the K-waves and their driving forces, we need a profound synthesis of various theories.[26] The situation here is somehow analogous to the one attested in the theory of medium-range cycles. Essentially, proponents of most approaches are right, but the general understanding may only be worked out through a synthetic theory (see, e.g., Haberler, 1964 [1937]). Note, by the way, that more theories have been proposed to account for the J-cycles than for K-waves (in particular psychological factors are hardly taken into account in the latter case,[27] though such factors are very important for an adequate understanding of the alteration of phases of K-waves).

We have based ourselves our thinking on the following approaches to the study of endogenous factors: innovation-based and investment-based approaches, as well as on those approaches that pay most attention to such factors as capital depreciation, decline of profit rates, and the alteration of technological paradigms. We have also taken into account such approaches that pay special attention to exogenous factors: influence of warfare and the expansion of an external resource base, as well as monetary theories. However, those theories are only used by us within certain limits determined by our general approaches. It also appears necessary to take into account the point that we only consider K-waves in their economic dimension, ignoring civilizational, cultural and other manifestations of K-waves, but also taking into account the full spectrum of factors of K-wave dynamics (including political, legal, and social factors).

---

[26] Such a task is mentioned from time to time by the K-wave students (see, e.g., Лазуренко, 1992; Меньшиков и Клименко, 1989).

[27] For more details on those factors see, e.g., Grinin, Korotayev, & Malkov, 2010; Haberler, 1964 [1937]; Гринин, 2009г.

It appears necessary to emphasize again that a very important component of our theory that allows us to integrate various approaches is the reliance on the organic link between K-waves and J-cycles.

Below we will present our answers to a few questions that are important with regard to the analysis of K-waves.

1. **Are there endogenous factors that generate the alteration of upswings and downswings?**

    The very alteration of economic downswings and upswings is connected with the need of the industrial economy to expand; this expansion, however, inevitably meets serious obstacles. One may speak about the alteration of two developmental trends: (1) the prevalence of qualitative innovation development (creation of new technologies); (2) the prevalence of quantitative development — implying a wide introduction/diffusion of innovations (see, e.g., Korotayev, Zinkina, & Bogevolnov, 2011). Both tendencies are simultaneously present in economic systems; however, in some periods one of these tendencies prevails, whereas in the other periods the other tendency does (see, e.g., Grinin, 2006, 2007a, 2007b; Grinin 2012a; Grinin L.E., Grinin A. L. 2016; Гринин, 2003, 2006а, 2006б, 2009д, 2010а, 2012б, 2013а; Korotayev, 2005, 2006, 2007a, 2007б; Korotayev & Grinin, 2012, Коротаев и Гринин, 2012; Korotayev, Malkov, & Khaltourina, 2006a, 2006b; Perez, 2002, 2010, 2011a; Перес, 2011; Гринин и Коротаев, 2010). Innovation (qualitative) processes are connected with periods of emergence and approbation of new technologies of various types (production technologies, financial technologies, and social technologies — including technologies of counter-crisis management). Quantitative processes are connected with such periods when such technologies diffuse widely — up to the exhaustion of their potential. For those countries that follow World System leaders the process of wide diffusion of technologies is virtually equivalent to the process of catch-up modernization. At the World System level, the analysis of processes of such a modernization (as we will see further) may play an important role in the explanation of the length of particular A-phases.

    Periods of predominantly qualitative development determine a potential possibility of the B-phase realization, whereas periods of predominantly qualitative development determine a potential possibility of the A-phase realization. Qualitative changes (having shown their advantages) tend to expand/diffuse. After new technologies become habitual, after they come to the saturation level, they then lose their impulse for further diffusion (see, e.g., Perez, 2002, 2010, 2011, 2012; Перес, 2011; see also Акаев, Румянцева et al., 2011); for a new acceleration, the global economic system needs a transition from extensive (quantitative) development to a new period of innovative qualitative development. As is well known, this leads to changes of technological paradigms, but also to changes of financial styles, relationships in the framework of the world trade and so on (see, e.g., Grinin & Korotayev, 2010b; Пантин и Лапкин, 2006; Лазуренко, 1992; Кондратьев, 2002; Korotayev, Zinkina, & Bogevolnov, 2011; Меньшиков, Клименко, 1989; Румянцева, 2003; Schumpeter, 1939; Гринин, 2010а, 2012б).

Thus, prolonged processes of innovation generation and diffusion, of the change of technological paradigms, as well as changing models of international relations and economic regulation provide long-term impulses toward the acceleration or deceleration of the growth of production, sales, prices, and so on. However, the above described scheme only implies the possibility of alteration of upswings and downswings, but it does not imply that such an alteration should be regular/periodic. The mechanism that generates a relatively regular periodic temporal rhythm of phase alteration is established through the alteration of J-cycle clusters (see below). Thus, the Kondratieff wave dynamics are generated by a complex set of various factors and causes that acquire a particular directionality through a synthesis of long-term impulses, due to J-cycle rhythm, as well as various reactions of economic actors. That is why we cannot agree with Sergey Glaziev who believes that the basis of the K-wave dynamics is created by the life cycles of technological paradigms, whereas 'at the surface of economic phenomena these appear as long cycles of economic conjuncture' (Глазьев, 2009: 26). This appears to be an approach in spirit similar to that of a Hegel—Marx' set of 'essences and their epiphenomena' that not only strips K-waves of their specificity—it reduces them to one causal factor only while ignoring a number of other such factors that are of no less importance.

As regards exogenous factors (for example, wars), they amplify certain (e.g., inflationary) impulses (that may trigger process change). However, it is important to understand that at the World System level it does not really make sense to distinguish between endogenous and exogenous factors (except, of course, certain natural [from seismic to cosmic[28]] ones). To their full extent both K-waves and J-cycles are traced at the World System level. We can hardly find any single society where those waves and cycles are perfectly traced throughout all 200 years of industrial development. And if we analyze K-waves at the World System level, then we have to interpret all the relevant social and economic processes as endogenous. In other words, at the World System level we should rather speak about endogenous factors of various orders of magnitude (except, as has been already mentioned, some natural factors).

2. **Which factors determine the relative temporal stability of the length of K-waves and their A- and B-phases?**

The K-waves' length and relative regularity of the alteration of their phases is determined by J-cycle clusters. An A-cluster may consist of two to four upswing J-cycles (though most frequently their number is three); a B-cluster may consist of two or three downswing J-cycles (though most frequently their number is two). During the K-wave A-phase fast economic expansion leads inevitably to the necessity of societal change; as a result, a B-phase starts. But, the possibilities of societal transformation lag behind the demands of the economy, that is why periods of such a restructuring correspond to periods of more difficult development, that is, to K-wave downswings. Below we will discuss this point in more detail. It makes sense to pay attention to the point that cyclical crises are attributes of medium term crises only (Fig. 3.2).

---

[28] E.g., solar activity.

Clusters of Juglar Cycles and Stable Duration of K-waves and Their Phases

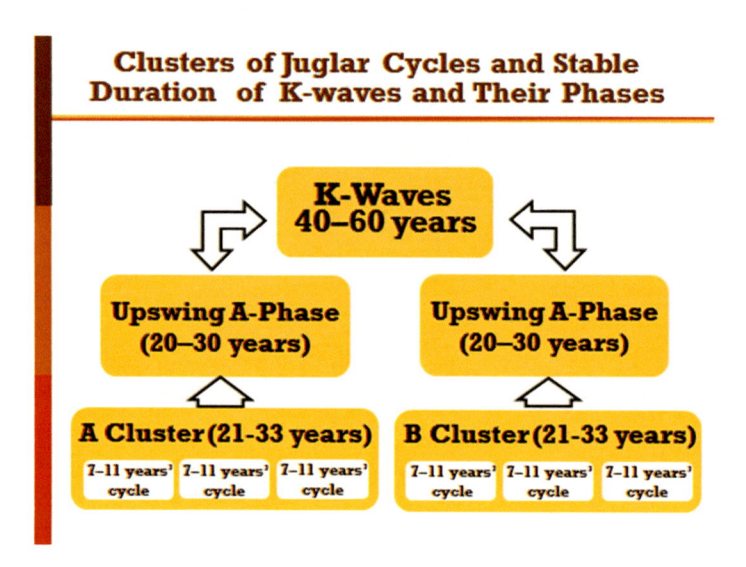

K-Waves 40–60 years

- **Upswing A-Phase (20–30 years)**
  - **A Cluster (21-33 years)**
    - 7–11 years' cycle
    - 7–11 years' cycle
    - 7–11 years' cycle
- **Upswing A-Phase (20–30 years)**
  - **B Cluster (21-33 years)**
    - 7–11 years' cycle
    - 7–11 years' cycle
    - 7–11 years' cycle

Fig. 3.2 Clusters of Juglar cycles

3. **Why and how do the main K-wave dynamics characteristics change?**

   This is a result of the development of the world economy, the transition to new conditions, and is a result of the World System transformation. In the metallic standard epoch, prices were the best K-wave indicators (they are visible there till now when the prices of key commodities expressed in grams of gold [e.g., Гринин, Коротаев и Цирель, 2011]); later they became more visible in some indicators of economic growth.

4. **Which endogenous mechanisms account for the alteration of long-term inflation/deflation trends?**

   Those trends are embedded in the nature of the industrial economy itself (whereas wars, discoveries of new rich deposits of precious metals and other exogenous factors of this sort may amplify additionally inflationary trends). The trends toward expansion and growth tend to lead to increasing resource limitations and—hence—inflation. However, with metal money, the growth rates of the productivity of labor and the potential to produce goods start to outstrip the growth rates of the monetary funds (effective demand). Money becomes more expensive and profits tend to decrease. This leads to the search for new ways to increase production, and one of such ways is to reduce costs. The latter leads to the further growth of the volume of produced goods against the background of the reduction of their prices. *Thus, the tendency toward economic expansion generates both inflationary and deflationary trends.* Businessmen look actively for specific opportunities to increase profit rates and to fight deflation. Such opportunities are usually found (though in no way automatically) through market expansion (export) and/or the creation/diffusion of new financial technologies. To counteract deflation effectively a rather wide diffusion of financial technologies is necessary. This increases the availability of money and—consequently—effective demand (at the level of both individual societies and the World System as a whole). However, with the exhaustion of the potential for new technologies to expand, the deflationary trend strengthens again. By the way since 2011 we can see such phenomenon when deflationary trend is growing.[29]

5. **Is it possible to speak about the decrease of the characteristic period of the K-waves? And, if yes, what is the mechanism of this decrease?**

It appears appropriate to mention that in the nineteenth and twentieth centuries the characteristic period of the J-cycles decreased from 11 to 7–9 years. This was accompanied by the decrease of the characteristic period of K-waves from 60 to 45–50 years. Thus, some decrease of the K-wave period appears to be observed. However, this change of the length of the K-waves is rather complex (some explanations for this phenomenon will be suggested below).

There are some quite well grounded hypotheses regarding a significant shortening of the periods of the fourth and fifth K-waves in comparison with those K-waves that preceded the 2nd World War, suggesting that *the lengths of phases and waves depend generally on the speed of reaction of social systems.* In the 1970s and the 1980s in the USA and Europe (especially in the UK) some new radical decisions were made that helped respective societies to move faster from the downswing trough. It appears important to note that in some respects those decisions contributed to the emergence and development of *new technologies (and—in particular—new financial technologies).*

It is important to note that states and other actors spend enormous efforts in order to prolong the prosperous period and to shorten the depressive period. Against this background it is hardly surprising that this is precisely the B-phase (and not the A-phase) whose length is shortening. We believe that this is a much simpler and more adequate explanation for the shortening of the B-phase of the

---

[29] It is worth to remember, that after the Second World War and especially, starting from the 1960s, the inflation became the main problem which persisted even in the 1970s at the B-phase of the fourth K-wave when one observed a serious decline in Western economy. During the economic downturn, prices usually fall or at least do not rise; meanwhile, at that period the prices grew against the background of economic decline, thus giving rise to a new dangerous phenomenon called 'stagflation'. In short, the deflation was forgotten as something remote and as a historical archaism. There appeared theories of secular inflation, organically inherent in current economy based on paper money (not dependent on gold) and on central banks which make credits of their own will. In the 1980s, the fight against inflation required great efforts. Against this background, Japan was a strange and difficult to explain exception, as after the crisis of the 1990s (caused by the burst of the housing bubble) it began to suffer from deflation. The year of 1994 turned critical in this regard. After the Second World War, this was the first case when a developed economy suffered from the consumer deflation. First this seemed to be a specific feature of the Japanese economy. However, the deflation began to pose a serious threat for the European countries and the USA after the end of the first phase of the global financial-economic crisis in 2010. At present the deflation trends continue to gain their strength and proliferate to some other countries. We think that this may be regarded as a certain return of those tendencies that were described by Kondratieff (i.e., inflation tendencies at A-phases, and deflation at B-phases of K-waves [see Grinin & Korotayev, 2014d for more detail]).

fourth K-wave in comparison with the explanation proposed by Pantin and Lapkin (Пантин и Лапкин, 2006: 289–303).[30]

6. Is there any relationship between K-waves and warfare?

Before the First World War a particular background of wars was observed during both K-wave phases. However, during A-phases warfare frequency was increased due to the intensification of World System modernization processes. The point is that accelerating modernization generates strains within states and between them, which tends to lead to the increase in warfare frequency.

An explanation of the J-cycle characteristic period. Thus, the temporal rhythm of changes of K-wave phases is connected with the J-cycle characteristic period. But what determines the length of the J-cycle itself?

There is no clear explanation as to why the characteristic period of the Juglar cycle is between 7 and 11 years. We suggest that the minimum and maximum length of the J-cycle stems from rather natural circumstances. If we take a cycle consisting of four phases, even with an average length of each phase around a year the cycle period will be about 4 years (however, it should be taken into account that each phase consists of at least two sub-phases). Of course, within K-wave A-phases the phases of recession, depression, and recovery may last 1 year each (whereas the recession may last even <1 year), though depression and recovery phases may last for 2 and even more years each. On the other hand, the upswing phase of the J-cycle can hardly last for only 1 year, as a 1 year long upswing can barely generate the economic overheating.

In order for a downswing to transform into a boom a period of fast growth should continue for at least three years. The first 2 years of expansion tend to go on the basis of the engaging of existing capacities as well as the realization of the changes made during the recession and depression. Two years of expansion make businessmen confident that the economic situation is permanently improving. They begin to invest more actively, credit expands, and the prices of resources start growing. However, in order that development might reach a limit beyond which an easy economic growth becomes impossible, a rather significant increase in GDP should be observed,[31] which normally needs not less than 4 years even with rather fast growth

---

[30] The gist of their approach is that there are two different types of upward and downward phases of long waves and long waves themselves constitute half of a longer cycle, which consists of two Kondratieff waves and leads to a radical change in technological and institutional foundations of the economy and the international division of labor. According to Pantin and Lapkin, duration of the downswing phase of long waves with the transition from one complete evolutionary cycle to another is reduced by an average of 12 years, while the duration of the upswing phase of Kondratieff waves is kept roughly constant (about 24 years). The very same shortening of evolutionary cycles of world development is due, in their opinion, to the general acceleration of social development. Indeed, one would expect that the acceleration of the rate of development will reduce the duration of Kondratieff waves, but the logic of these authors is not clear — why does the length of some phases decline? And why do the others remain stable (whereas the shortening should rather be manifested proportionally)?

[31] No less than 30–50 %, whereas in emergent markets the growth may be twofold, or even threefold.

rates. This time is necessary for the 'bubbles' to form, for prices to reach record levels, and for credit expansion to experience overloading. In any case, 4–5 years of expansion (+3–4 years for the other phases) yields together at least 7–9 years. However, in favorable conditions the expansion may continue to even 7 or 8 years. The empirical data on the J-cycle lengths are discussed further in this chapter.

Juglar Cycles as Structural Elements of the K-Waves

How Many J-Cycles Are There per a K-Wave Phase? An Analysis of Empirical Data

> 'Economists use a broad modeling approach based on the use of so-called stylized facts. This is achieved through the simplification of a real situation by abstracting it from concrete historical fluctuations, which allows one to identify the most significant features in the economic dynamics of the system. Such stylized facts include the statement that the large cycle consists of six medium-range Juglar cycles. The duration of the industrial cycle of this type almost always (this is also a stylized fact) falls within the range of 7–11 years. Accordingly, the total duration of the big cycle can range from 42 to 66 years, which is roughly consistent with observations from the beginning of the industrial revolution in the UK, as well as with the assertion that the average length of a long wave is half a century. It is also argued that a long cycle consists of approximately equal halves: the rising and falling waves of economic conditions. Thus, every half contains three Juglar cycles' (Клинов, 2008: 64).

In our verbal model of the relationship between K-waves and J-cycles (as in our spectral analysis [Korotayev & Tsirel, 2010; Гринин, Коротаев и Цирель, 2011: Ch. 2] and our mathematical model of the J-cycle [Гринин, Малков и Коротаев 2010б; Grinin, Korotayev, & Malkov, 2010]) we were bound to use stylized facts mentioned by Vilenin Klinov. Now we will try to find out how much those stylized facts correspond to the empirical data. We will pay a special attention to the following 'stylized facts': (a) each K-wave consists of 6 J-cycles; (b) the length of the A-phase of each K-wave is equal to the length of its B-phase; (c) each A-phase consists of three J-cycles, and each B-phase also consists of 3 J-cycles.

First, consider the general picture of the correlation between Juglar cycles and Kondratieff waves (see Table 3.1 and Figs. 3.3 and 3.4):

At this point it appears reasonable to return to the consideration of the general dynamics of the annual world GDP growth rates in 1945–2007 (see Fig. 3.5):

This diagram indicates rather clearly an ambiguous position of the nineteenth J-cycle (1979/1982–1990/3). Following a number of K-wave students, we have included it above as part of the fifth K-wave A-phase. However, due to the patently transitional character of this cycle, we do not see sufficient grounds to exclude the possibility of its inclusion into the K-wave B-phase. In addition, the diagram suggests that the 1967–1974 period (the eighteenth J-cycle) can be considered to be a part of both A-phase and B-phase of the fourth K-wave. In this case, we get a different picture of the correlation between K-waves and J-cycles (see Table 3.2 and Figs. 3.6 and 3.7).

Juglar Cycles as Structural Elements of the K-Waves

Table 3.1 Correlation between Juglar cycles and Kondratieff waves (the first version)

Serial numbers of K-waves	Long waves' phases and their dates	Serial numbers and dates of J-cycles	Number of J-cycles per the respective K-wave phase
I	B (downswing): 1817–1847	J1: 1817–1825	3
		J2: 1825–1836/7	
		J3: 1836/7–1847	
II	A (upswing): 1847–1873	J4: 1847–1857	3
		J5: 1857–1866	
		J6: 1866–1873	
	B (downswing): 1873–1890/3	J7: 1873–1882	2
		J8: 1882–1890/3	
III	A(upswing): 1890–1929/33	J9: 1890/3–1900/3	4
		J10: 1900/3–1907	
		J11: 1907–1920	
		J12: 1920–1929/33	
	B(downswing): 1929/33–1948/9	J13: 1929/33–1937/8	2
		J14: 1937/8–1948/9	
IV	A(upswing): 1948/9–1966/7	J15: 1948/9–1957/8	2[a]
		J16: 1957/8–1966/7	
	B(downswing): 1966/7–1979/82	J17: 1966/7–1974/5	2
		J18: 1974/5–1979/82	
V	A(upswing): 1979/82–2008/10	J19: 1979/82–1990/3	3
		J20: 1990/3–2001/2	
		J21: 2001/2–2008/10	

[a]However, it is possible to single out in this phase three shorter (rather than two longer) J-cycles: 1947–1954; 1954–1961 (whose course was somehow interrupted by the 1957 crisis); 1962–1967. The general length of the phase—20 years—allows to speak about three short J-cycles. Such a vague cyclical dynamics was produced by an active Keynesian interference in the cycles, as well as by the difference in the course of the cycles in Europe and the USA (for more details see Grinin and Korotayev 2010b)

We believe that our analysis allows us to make the following preliminary conclusions (Figs. 3.10 and 3.11).

1. First of all, we see that the actual lengths of K-waves, as well as their A- and B-phases do not correspond fully to the 'stylized facts'; in addition, there are significant variations both in the absolute lengths, and the number of J-cycles that fit into them. In the framework of the first version the same number of J-cycles in the A-phase and B-phase within a K-wave is observed in only one case out of three, and in two cases the number of J-cycles in the A-phase exceeds the number of J-cycles in the B-phase. Within the second version the number of A-phase J-cycles exceeds the number of B-phase cycles in all the three cases. At the same time, taking into account what has been said in the note to Table 3.1, the number of A-phase J-cycles may exceed the number of B-phase cycles in all three cases in the first version as well. Based on these conclusions, we graphi-

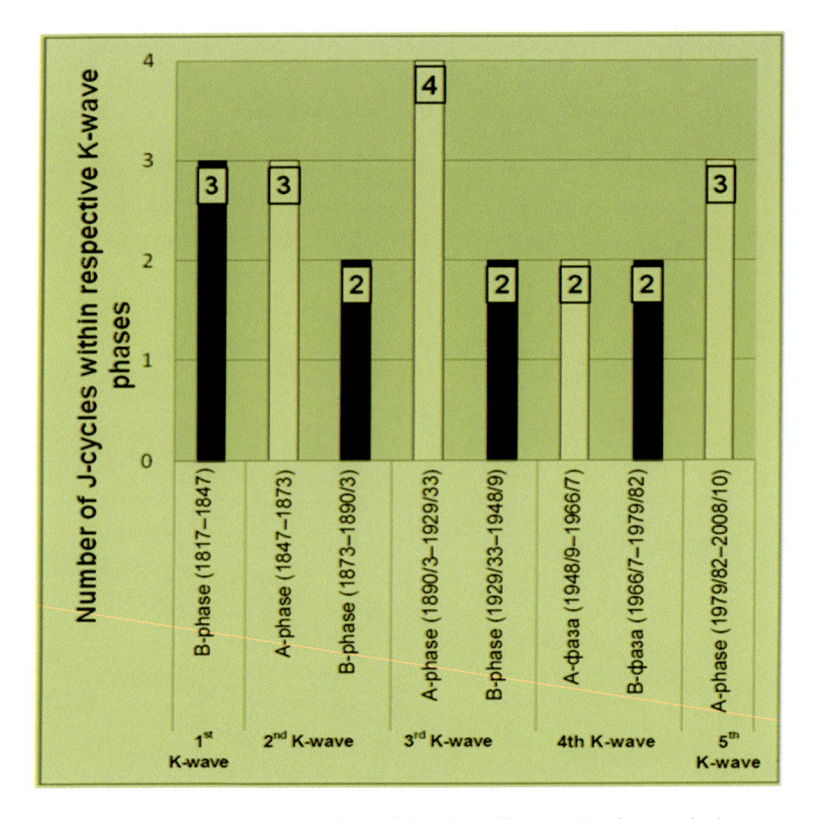

Fig. 3.3 Correlation between Juglar cycles and Kondratieff waves (the first version)

cally represent two versions of the relationship between the J-cycles and K-waves in Figs. 3.8 and 3.9 at the end of this chapter): one with equal numbers of J-cycles in the A- and B-phases (Fig. 3.8), whereas in Fig. 3.9 this number is unequal (three A-phase J-cycles versus two B-phase J-cycles).

2. Note that in both cases we observe the tendency that we have already discussed above, the tendency toward the reduction of the absolute temporal duration of B -phases. In this chapter we suggest a possible explanation for this phenomenon. With respect to the A-phase this reduction does not appear to be observed in a comparably clear way (and we will suggest our explanation for this phenomenon too). Thus, as we shall see below, due to the deliberate action of economic agents upon the Juglar dynamics, the duration of A-phases tends to be longer than the duration of the B-cycles (irrespective of how we count this duration — in years, or in Juglars).

   In general, for both versions for four A-phases we find 12 J-cycles, whereas for four B-phases we only find 9 J-cycles.

3. Much has been written about the absolute duration of K-waves over the years (see above), so we will not dwell on this issue here. But if we use 'Juglar' as a unit of measurement of the length of K-waves, we must note that this length fluctuates

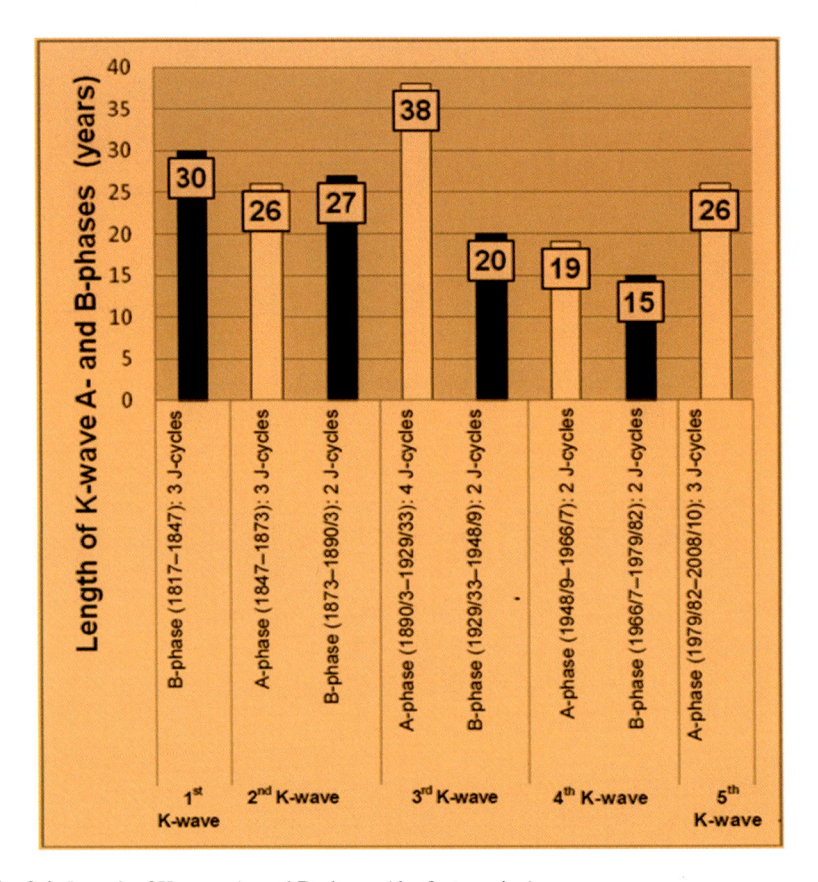

Fig. 3.4 Length of K-wave A- and B-phases (the first version)

between 4 and 6 'Juglars'. On average, if 21 'Juglars' are divided into four waves (three full wave and two 'halves'), then one has on average 5.25 'Juglar' per one K-wave (note that with the second version of the estimate of the fourth K-wave A-phase duration, we will get, on average, 5.5 'Juglars' per one K-wave).

However—and this is crucial to the theory presented in this chapter—whatever the duration of the phases, in any case, we see an integral number of J-cycles in any K-wave. This shows that the deep and tangible connection between J-cycles and K-waves is observed on the 'essential' rather than phenomenological level.

4. Thus, the idea of measuring the duration of the K-phase waves not only in years, but also in 'Juglars' has a very specific meaning, as the number of 'Juglar' in different waves and phases respectively ranges from 4 to 6 and from 2 to 4 (see, e.g., Figs. 3.6 and 3.7 above). In this case, 'economic time begins to be measured not in years, but in cycles' (Аврамов, 1992: 64).

Thus, depending on the chosen periodization, the number of 'Juglars' in the same K-wave and the same phase of the wave varies. For example, according to Version 1 the fourth K-wave includes four 'Juglars'; according to Version 2 it consists of five 'Juglars'. Accordingly, the A-phase of the fifth K-wave includes

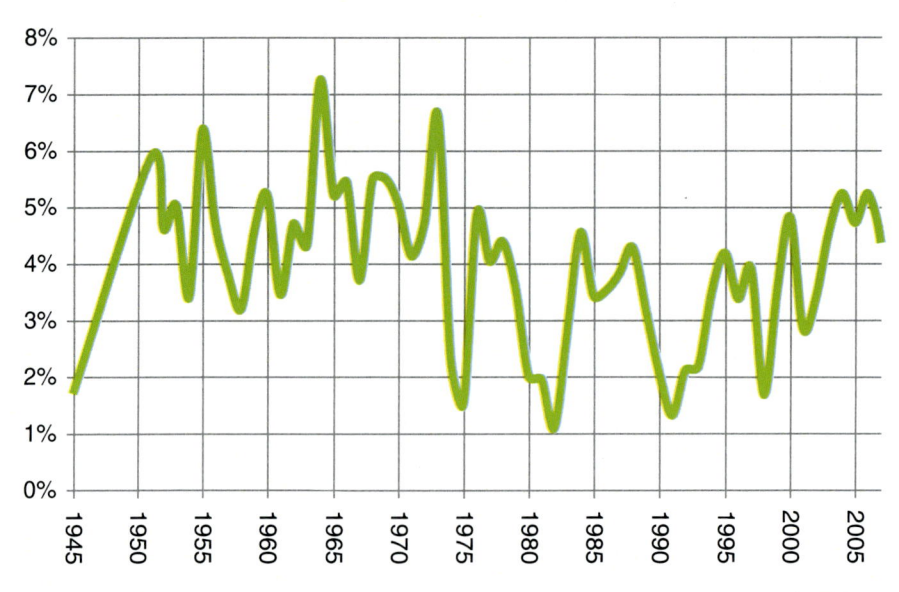

Fig. 3.5 Dynamics of the annual world GDP growth rates (%), 1945–2007. *Sources:* (Maddison, 2010; World Bank, 2016)

Table 3.2 Correlation between Juglar cycles and Kondratieff waves (the second version)

Serial numbers of K-waves	Long waves' phases and their dates	Serial numbers and dates of J-cycles	Number of J-cycles per the respective K-wave phase
I	B (downswing): 1817–1847	J1: 1817–1825	3
		J2: 1825–1836/7	
		J3: 1836/7–1847	
II	A (upswing): 1847–1873	J4: 1847–1857	3
		J5: 1857–1866	
		J6: 1866–1873	
	B (downswing): 1873–1890/3	J7: 1873–1882	2
		J8: 1882–1890/3	
III	A (upswing): 1890–1929/33	J9: 1890/3–1900/3	4
		J10: 1900/3–1907	
		J11: 1907–1920	
		J12: 1920–1929/33	
	B (downswing): 1929/33–1948/9	J13: 1929/33–1937/8	2
		J14: 1937/8–1948/9	
IV	A (upswing): 1948/9–1966/7	J15: 1948/9–1957/8	3 (or 4[a])
		J16: 1957/8–1966/7	
		J17: 1966/7–1974/5	
	B (downswing): 1974/5–1990/3	J18: 1974/5–1979/82	2
		J19: 1979/82–1990/3	
V	A (upswing): 1990/3–2008/10	J20: 1990/3–2001/2	2
		J21: 2001/2–2008/10	

[a]See the note to the first version of this table

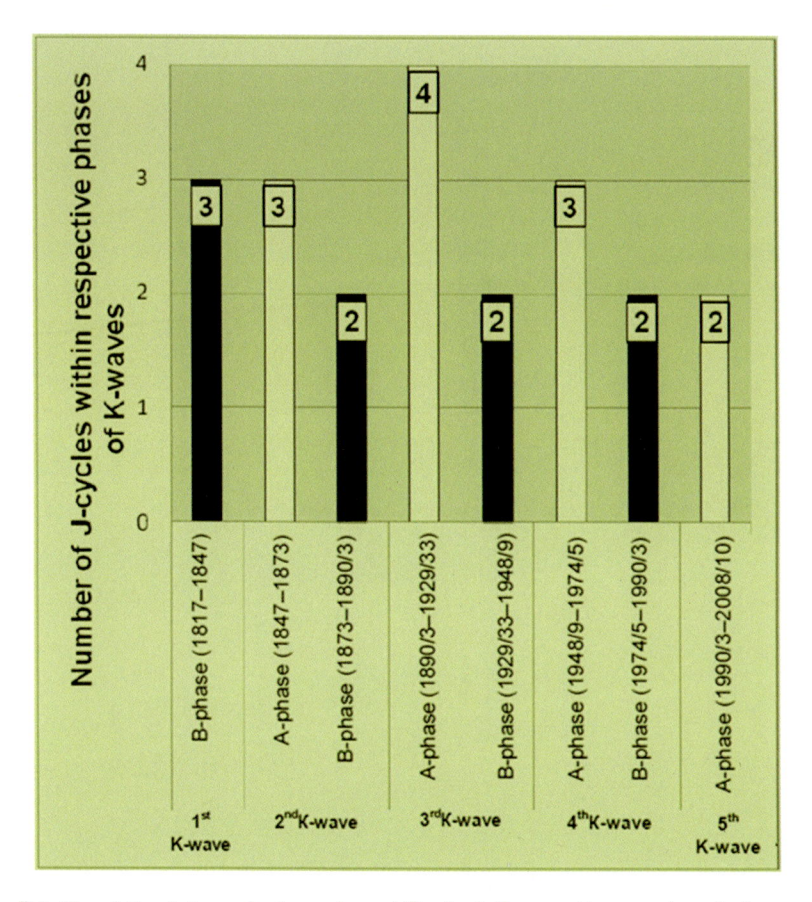

Fig. 3.6 Correlation between Juglar cycles and Kondratieff waves (the second version)

either three or two 'Juglars'. And the latter is very essential for the development of economic forecasts, as we shall see below.

When you add an electron to an atom (or take an electron from it), this atom undergoes a substantial change (it becomes a positively or negatively charged ion instead of the neutral atom). In a similar way, the elongation/contraction of A- or B-phase by one Juglar cycle leads to significant changes in the economy and economic moods, the tone of economic theories, as well as to the intensification in search of anti-crisis measures.

5. Kondratieff's conclusion that 'during the rise of the long waves, years of prosperity are more numerous, whereas years of depression predominate during the downswing' (1935: 111) may be augmented with the conclusion that, generally, at the position of the K-wave B-phases J-cycles are longer than at the A-phases. In particular, the calculation shows that at the position of an A-phase the average duration of one J-cycle is about 9–9.1 years (and if we add an additional cycle to the A-phase of the fourth K-wave, this duration will be equal to about 8.3 years), while the average duration of one J-cycle at the B-phase is about 10.2–10.3 years. We

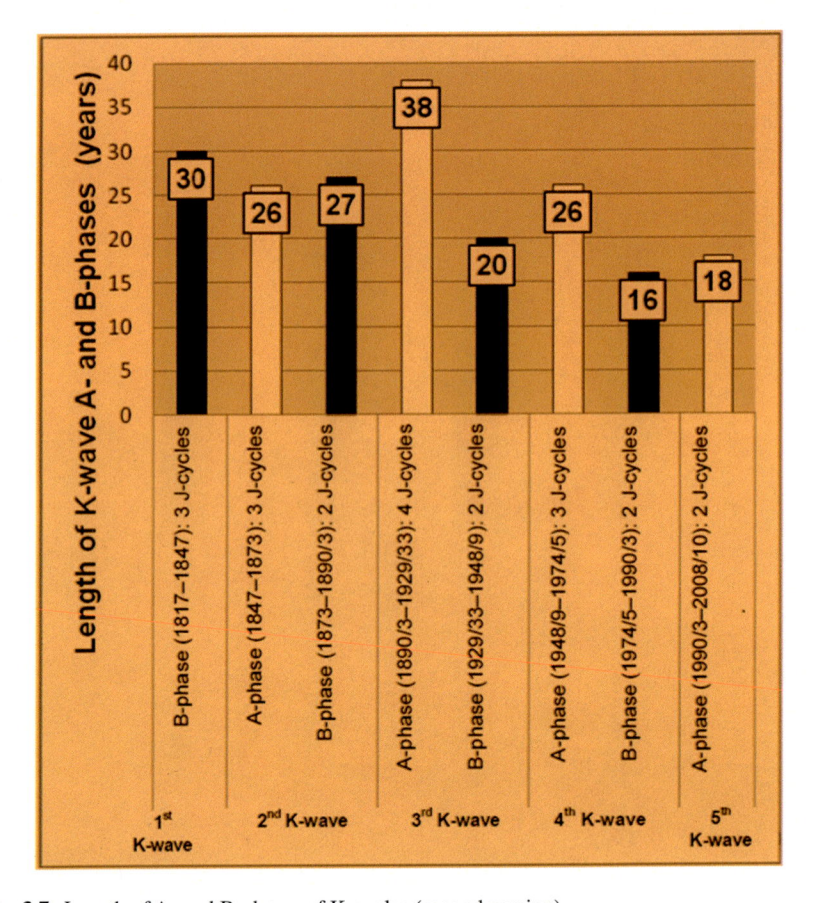

Fig. 3.7 Length of A- and B-phases of K-cycles (second version)

attribute this to the following circumstances: (a) within B-cluster J-cycles we observe the lengthening of recession and depression phases in comparison with A-clusters, and (b) in the A-cluster J-cycles one observes so powerful expansion phases, that sub-phases of overheating, acute crisis and recession phases progress very quickly, within a rather short period of time.

6. The forecast of K-waves' development in the next decades may change substantially depending on what version of the periodization of the fifth K-wave will be chosen. For example, in Chap. 2 of one of our monographs (Гринин, Коротаев и Цирель, 2011) we offered two versions of wave dynamics forecasts for the forthcoming 20 years. Note that in both cases we base our reasoning on the assumption that the A-phase of the fifth K-wave must be longer than its B-phase. In any case, the A-phase of the fourth K-wave corresponds to three J-cycles, whereas its B-phase is most likely to consist of two 'Juglars'.

We find the first version to be more probable; it suggests that the A-phase of the fourth K-wave ended with the start of the global crisis in 2008, when the

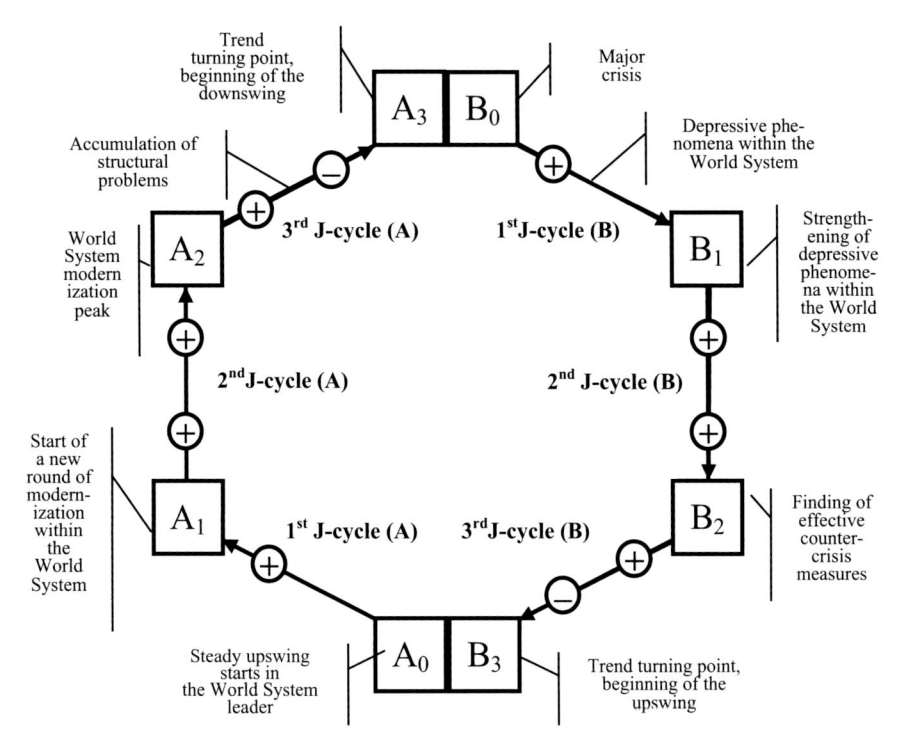

Fig. 3.8 Correlation between Kondratieff waves and Juglar cycles. Version 1

B-phase started. In this case—taking into account the active search throughout the World System for effective anti-crisis measures—the duration of the B-phase should not be more than two 'Juglars', and it is very likely that the duration of J-cycles within the cluster should not be very long. We should also take into account the tendency for the duration of B-phases to decrease. But at the same time, a B-phase shall not be less than two 'Juglars', whereas, as we have seen, short J-cycles are less typical for B-phases than for A-phases. Therefore, we can suggest a tentative forecast that the present B-phase of the fifth K-wave will have a duration of 14–18 years (see also our forecast about the date of the beginning of the sixth K-wave, which we expect to start in the 2020s).

7. The presence of more than one version of periodization and forecasts should not be surprising—taking into account the extreme narrowness of the apparent empirical basis. Indeed, one can talk reliably about Juglar cycles only starting from the first clear Juglar cycle of 1817–1825. Therefore, to date, we can only talk about three full K-waves and two 'halves', in which the interaction between Juglar and Kondratieff dynamics has been clearly observed, which does not meet the minimum requirements for regular analysis of cyclic processes (Аврамов, 1992: 72; Гринин и Коротаев, 2013а). In his paper published in 1992, Avramov

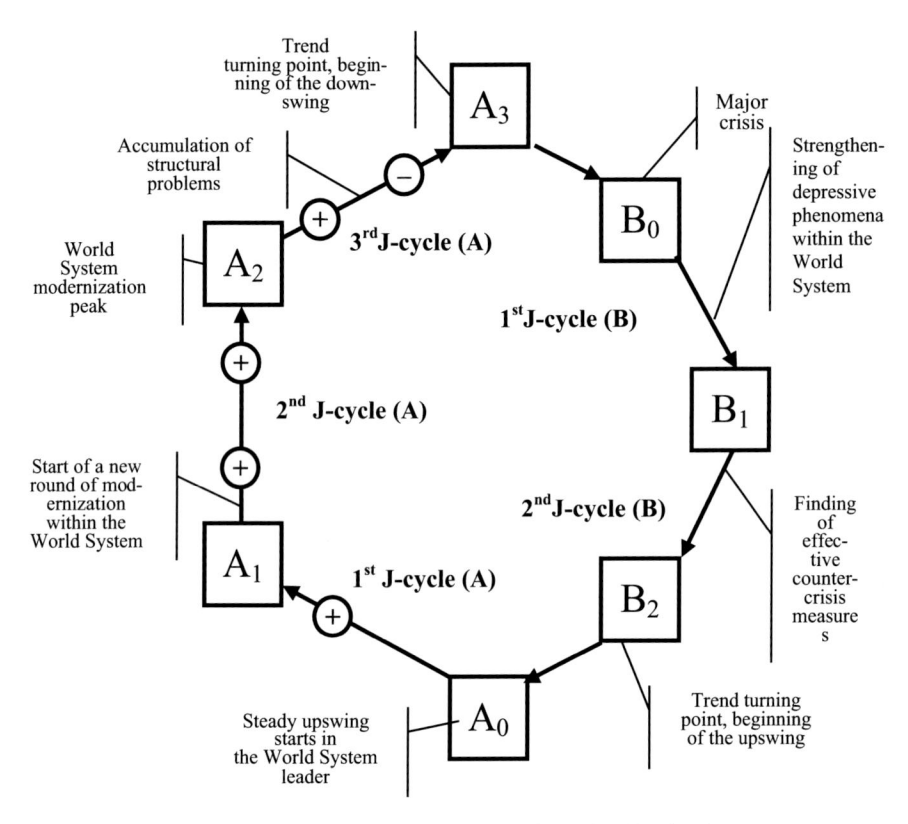

Fig. 3.9 Correlation between Kondratieff waves and Juglar cycles. Version 2

maintained that within the relative chronology of the theories of his day, the stage of development of long-wave theory could be compared with the situation in medium-term cycles theory in the 1870s (*Ibid.*). With the passage of time, the theory of K-waves approached the level of development of the theory of medium-term cycles at the time of the first edition of Tugan-Baranovsky's classical volume in 1894; however, Tugan-Baranovsky himself said at that time about the theory of medium-term cycles that it was 'the least studied subject in the economic literature' (Туган-Барановский, 1894: 377).

Verbal Model of K-Waves

General Outline

The main 'intrigue' of the K-wave phenomenon is a relatively regular periodization of the change from K-wave upswings to K-wave downswings, and vice versa. Our general ideas that allow us to understand better the mechanism of changing trends can be spelled out as follows:

1. Both trends (upward and downward) are present in the modern economy at the same time (so periods when there is no qualitative or quantitative development at all, are extremely rare; it is that one hardly finds cases of overall growth without any indication of stagnant sectors at all); but at every phase one of those trends predominates.
2. The trend's change is largely initiated by the trend's exhaustion, that is, the weakening of one trend paves the way for the strengthening of the next.
3. In other words, one can observe an evident negative feedback between the trends, which strengthens with each new medium-term cycle (until the trend does not change), since the nature and results of each J-cycle is a signal for a particular type of action of active participants in the process (from individual entrepreneurs to whole states and supranational organizations). Rising prices and profit margins, as well as high demand cumulatively lead to the expansion of production. The falling rate of profit, the reduction of the growth rates, etc. lead to a reduction in investment and the search for new innovative solutions.
4. The nature of the trend depends largely on the type of action chosen by the majority of participants in the process.
5. The relatively regular characteristic period of the K-wave phase alteration is determined by the relative stable characteristic period of the J-cycles (7–11 years), whereas J-cycle clusters (that mostly include three J-cycles each) tend to last somewhere in the range between 20 and 30 years. We would also add that, in relation to the theory of generations, 10 years is not a period that is long enough to significantly alter the generation of businessmen (and especially politicians) so that more proactive and less cautious entrepreneurs could appear. Two or three J-cycles (7–11 years each) are just sufficient to renew the generation of businessmen.
6. The only exception is constituted by the upswing (A-) phase of the First K-wave (the late 1780s—the early 1790s—1810–1817, as it was generated mostly by external [military] factors—more on that below. However, the First K-wave B-phase started with the first J-cycle (approximately 1815/1818–1825) that ended the first large-scale cyclical crisis in 1825.

Thus, the alteration of upswings and downswings is inherent in the properties of the industrial and post-industrial economy that seeks to expand, but is impeded by all sorts of obstacles, and the rather regular duration of K-wave upswing and downswing phases is connected with the time frames of the J-cycle length.

Notes on Dynamics

As we have already mentioned above, in modern economic systems the periods of predominantly qualitative (innovative) development are followed by periods of mainly quantitative development and vice versa. However, it is important to note that such a development occurs with sufficient frequency not within a single country, but only in the framework of the World System as a whole (but in some periods, it can also be observed in the core states of the World System). In addition, each such pulsation is associated with the expansion of the World System and with the changes of its configuration. This leads to a change in the economic and political relations within the boundaries of the World System. The mechanism of a rather fast impulse propagation within the framework of the World System and relatively synchronous change of development vectors are associated with the increasingly close interaction of economies and societies through a variety of financial and other links.

Secondly, by themselves the alteration of innovation and modernization trends may not have sufficiently clear time limits. Modernization trends within the World System cannot arise from the investments and implementation of major innovations in different countries, because the timing and modalities of these processes are very different, and investments themselves cannot be synchronized. To repeat: **the timing and the relative accuracy of the K-wave phase alternation are determined by the nature of the J-cycle clusters.** During a K-wave upswing one can observe a rapid expansion, which inevitably requires significant changes in society.[32] However, such changes lag far behind in time from their immediate objective need (due to the time required for the emergence of awareness of the problem, its discussion, the search and decision-making involved in finding a solution, implementation of solutions in practice, etc.) Such a delay is one of the important reasons why after the upward phase we tend to observe a period of more difficult ('downswing') development (B-cluster of J- cycles). During the struggle with crisis-depressive phenomena, economic actors are searching for ways to overcome these difficult phenomena. As a result, in some society a social innovation emerges, which then begins to be applied not only in this society but also in many others. Then new upward momentum in some societies creates conditions for transition to a new A-phase upswing. But the wide (i.e. in many societies) awareness of the benefits of such a social innovation does not happen immediately, but around the second J-cycle of a new A-phase.

The emergence of a variety of technical and social innovations and their successful testing lead to a new round of extensive World System growth. **This is a very important fact, which draws little attention, but it is the *expansion* of modernization that enhances the momentum of the A-phase.** Expansion of modernization (combined with technological and social innovations) leads to the expansion and reconfiguration of the World System, which creates the need for a change in relations within the World System. Results of the extended modernization become visible in 10–15 years. By this time, prices can reach very high values; many large 'bubbles' emerge in the economy under the influence of excessive demand for resources. However, the momentum of modernization loses its original strength. In a situation of prolonged overheating of the economy, such a slowdown leads to various kinds of difficulties and increased global competition, the bursting of bubbles, and Juglar crises. Finally, we see the transition to a B-cluster of J-cycles (and to a B-phase of the following K-wave).

---

[32] This was noticed already by Simon Kuznets (1966).

We also note that, as a result of the development of each J-cycle cluster one can observe the change of generations of businessmen, their approach to doing business, the attitude to the different parameters, etc. Thus, again, the idea of the, influence of generational change on the alteration of K-wave phases may also find its place in the synthetic theory of the K-waves.

The Main Principles for the Development of the K-Wave Model

So, to summarize, the alteration of the K-wave upswings and downswings is explained by the following points:

(a) Both trends (upward and downward) are always present, which, incidentally, can be clearly seen in the continuous alternation of J-cycle phases of rise and recession;
(b) periodically some trend is amplified at the expense of another at the level of both medium length cycles and long waves;
(c) the development of every trend is initially enhanced by some sort of positive feedback;
(d) but the strengthening of this trend eventually leads to its weakening and the strengthening of a countertrend;
(e) in other words, the phase change mechanism is defined by the switching time associated with negative feedback, which leads to the increase in strength of the countertrend;
(f) thus, there is a time lag that is essential for the generation of cyclical dynamics;
(g) the nature of medium-term cycles and their phases are the most important signals to business and society, defining the mode of their strategy;
(h) more active (in the B-phase) or less active (during the A-phase) innovative-reforming activities are the most important factor affecting the occurrence of negative feedback, and the latter ultimately leads to a change in the phase of K-waves.

Phase Alteration in the K-Wave Model

When the A-phase (upward trend) begins, this puts into action a positive feedback effect in the form of investment, growth in demand (reinforcing the rise in prices and GDP) and other activity that warms up the economy. This positive relationship operates at the level of individual companies and intersocietal contacts (trade, financial flows, etc.). Further one observes a new level of positive feedback — the World System level — due to the fact that in the World System the modernization process accelerates as a whole under the influence of growth and success thanks to the emergence at the B-phase of a system of technical, financial and social innovations. This leads to a temporary acceleration of positive feedback and a delay of the appearance of negative feedback. This lag (taking into account the point that World System modernization is a fairly lengthy process) can be about 10–20 years. But when modernization is on the wane, negative feedback mechanisms start being felt as a reaction to excessive overheating of the preceding period: reducing demand, causing falling prices, falling profit margins, and a decrease of investment activity, etc. As a result, the downward trend begins to dominate, and a new B-phase starts.

With the start of a B-phase a certain positive feedback mechanism begins working, as over some period of time one can observe the strengthening of the process by which within the World System more and more economic agents and even whole countries begin to experience difficulties and to change their strategies (to reduce investments, to reduce costs, not to pay debts, etc.). In other words, there is a natural chain reaction of negative momentum transfer through the World System. Further, this positive feedback is strengthened and stretched in time due to the fact that the necessary changes in the societies involved were not made in due time (in phase A), and most importantly—due to the fact that the emergence and launch of necessary social (and other) innovations requires quite a long time.

This lag is also estimated to be about 10–20 years (taking into account the need to change policy, to enact laws, etc.). One should keep in mind that periodically occurring temporary improvements (in expansion phases of J-cycles), paradoxically, hinder the process of change in society. Finally, after the introduction of such social innovations (which generally add up to the overall system with other types of innovation: technical, financial, etc.), and after they begin to show their effectiveness, a negative feedback starts to be felt, which leads to a decrease in negative trends and a strengthening of the upward trend. And as these phenomena emerge at least within one or a few societies of the World System, the upward momentum of these trends becomes distributed throughout the whole world. The A-phase begins, which accelerates positive feedback due to the introduction of sets of innovations, which again leads to an extension of the World System or to the growth of its complexity.

This system of relationships is graphically represented at the end of this chapter in Figs. 3.8 and 3.9.

Relationships between K-Waves and J-Cycles

K-Waves and J-Cycle Clusters

J-Cycle Clusterization

As has already been mentioned, the most mysterious moment in K-waves is their relatively stable duration (as well as the relatively stable duration of their phases—respectively, 40–60 years and 20–30 years). None of the theories has been able to explain this phenomenon satisfactorily, i.e. to show such economic or social factors within which such a rhythm would be present naturally enough. In our opinion, the only real factor that can set the pace of a certain duration of Kondratieff waves and their phases is the Juglar cycle. We would like to underline again that the J-cycles appear in the ontological sense more real than K-waves, hence these are J-cycles that should be considered as basic structural units, creating in the totality of their processes K-waves and their phases (and not vice versa).

In the analysis of such a relationship between J-cycles and K-waves it is necessary to take into account the point that in addition to general model properties of J-cycles one can identify more common properties for groups of nearby J-cycles. These properties are derived not only from their greatest historical proximity, but also from the fact that they have a general trend, as well as from the fact that the nature of their crisis-depressive phases and phases of growth and prosperity has certain properties in common.

Thus, J-cycles can be seen not just as structural units of the same type, but as a more complex system that represents a single chain/cluster of two, three or more J-cycles possessing within the cluster additional common features.

It appears necessary to emphasize that: (a) such clusters of J-cycles tend to have a duration of roughly 20–30 years (assuming that the cycle is 7–11 years, then three cycles in duration constitute 21–33 years), which correspond to average lengths of K-wave phases; (b) an organic link between the J-cycles and K-waves is particularly supported by the fact that the phase boundaries of Kondratieff waves (as well as boundaries of particular waves themselves) in many theories practically coincide with the boundaries of certain medium-term cycles and crises.[33]

The character of J-cycle clusters correlates with the character of K-wave phases. Of course, this cannot be accidental; actually, this is accounted for by certain mechanisms of reaction of particular societies and of the World System to J-cycles.[34] Incidentally, it appears necessary to note that the ratio between the extreme values of the duration periods of K-waves (40–60 years) and J-cycles (7–11) is very similar: 7: 11 ~= 0.64 ~ 40: 60 = 0.66.

---

[33] Initially long waves were considered as combinations of a few adjacent medium-term business cycles (Burns & Mitchell, 1946; Delbeke, 1987; van Duijn, 1983; van der Zwan, 1980). These were still regarded as a sort of rather mechanical combination, whereas the idea that adjacent J-cycles could form a real system was expressed very rarely and was not developed in any significant way.

[34] Some researchers speak about a tight connection between Kuznets cycles and K-waves (see, e.g., Акаев, Румянцева et al., 2011; Румянцева, 2003). We do not exclude the possibility that such a connection does exist. However, Kuznets swings have been detected mostly in the USA (see Abramovitz, 1961: 230; Hansen, 1951; Kuznets, 1958; see also Акаев, Румянцева et al., 2011: 91), whereas the J-cycles may be traced in all the main countries of the World System. In addition, Kuznets cycles are much less pronounced and do not have so dramatic crisis phase; that is why there is some sense in the prevalent tendency to denote them as 'swings', rather than as 'cycles'.

On the Correlation between J-Cycles and K-Wave Phases

As was already established by Kondratieff, within upswing phases of K-waves J-cycles are characterized by stronger expansions and weaker depressions, whereas within K-wave downswings a contrary pattern is observed.

Nikolay Kondratieff himself addressed the analysis by Arthur Spiethoff (Кондратьев, 2002: 380). Below is Spiethoff's table (Table 3.3). The other researchers' analysis proves Kondratieff's assertions concerning the proportions between the number of depressive and growth years at different phases of K-waves. In particular, William Mitchell (1913), (see also: Burns & Mitchell, 1946: 438) concluded that within the long-term inflationary trends (i.e., at the A-phase of the K-wave), the phases of growth and depression in Juglar cycles with respect to the USA are in the ratio 2.7: 1, and in the periods of prolonged deflation (i.e., at the B-phase of the K-wave) the ratio is only 0.85: 1. Alvin Hansen, who used to be rather skeptical of the K-waves theories, nevertheless, found that for the period from 1872 to 1920 (i.e., second–third K-wave) during the upward rise in prices (at the A-phase), an average duration of depression was two years, and at the downtrend (the B-phase) it was 5.3 years. And conversely, the respective rises at the A-phase were by 1.8 times longer than at the B-phase (Хансен, 1959: 115–116). We present these calculations in Tables 3.3 and 3.4.

Modern data on characteristics of upswings and recessions for the 1919–1994 period confirm the presence of this regularity — the lengthening of expansion phases during K-wave upswings and the lengthening of recession phases during K-wave downswings (for details see Румянцева, 2003: 25).

Thus, we can speak of two types of chain-clusters of J-cycles characterized by specific boom-depression patterns: (1) at upswing phases of K-waves J-cycle depressions are less pronounced, and J-cycle expansions are more durable; (2) at downswing phases of K-waves J-cycle depressions are more pronounced, and J-cycle expansions are less intense and prolonged. Accordingly, the first type of J-cycle chain-clusters can be called 'A-clusters', whereas the second type can be denoted as 'B-clusters'.

Table 3.3 The correlation between the years of upswing and depression at the A- and B-phases according to Spiethoff

Periods	Upswing years	Depressive years
The downswing of the long cycle from 1822 to 1843	9	12
The upswing of the long cycle from 1843 to 1874	21	10
The downswing of the long cycle from 1874 to 1895	6	15
The upswing of the long cycle from 1895 to 1912	15	4

Table 3.4 The correlation between the duration of upswing and depression phases according to some economists

Economist	A-phase	B-phase
A. Spiethoff	2.5:1	0.6:1
W. Mitchell	2.7:1	0.85:1
A. Hansen	3:1	0.75:1

As has already been mentioned, the relationship between K-waves and J-cycles has not been studied sufficiently. Recall that Kondratieff pointed out that J-cycles are sort of interwoven within K-waves and depend on the latter. In particular, he wrote, 'The long waves belong really to the same complex dynamic process in which the intermediate cycles [i.e. J-cycles.—*Authors.*] of the capitalistic economy with their principal phases of upswing and depression run their course. These intermediate cycles, however, secure a certain character from the very existence of the long waves. Our investigation demonstrates that during the rise of the long waves, years of prosperity are more numerous, whereas years of depression predominate during the downswing' (Kondratieff, 1935: 111).

However, it seems that the relationship between K-waves and J-cycles is not only significantly deeper and more complex, but—most importantly—the causal relationship between them in general looks different. **Hence, Kondratieff was not quite correct when he contended that the nature of J-cycles depended on the nature of the respective K-wave phases; the actual situation seems to be simply the opposite—this is the nature of the respective J-cycle clusters that largely determines the nature of the respective K-wave phases.**

This view on the causal relationship between the two types of cycles stems from the fact that Juglar cycles are more observable empirically than K-waves, which, in the words of Maevsky (Маевский, 1992: 58), 'appear as a kind of surreal force that cannot be perceived directly'. The factors that produce J-cycles are also more clear and better described. Moreover, the presence of these factors has been confirmed "experimentally", because more than half a century of economic regulation in many countries has proved that the course of Juglar cycles can be influenced by certain measures of economic policy, that this course can be modified, and in some cases the critical phase of those cycles can even be avoided. In the meantime, any successful attempts to influence consciously the course of Kondratieff waves do not appear to be known.[35]

General Causes and Mechanisms of Economic Cycles

J-cycles and K-waves arise from the general properties of the industrial economy—the ability of expanded reproduction (on this feature see, e.g., Abramovitz, 1961; Gellner, 1983; Grinin, 2006, 2007а, 2007b; Полетаев и Савельева, 1993; Kuznets, 1966; Гринин, 2003, 2009д; Гринин и Коротаев, 2010). Economic growth cannot go on constantly and continuously; therefore, slowdowns are

---

[35] Note that reality of medium-term cycles is recognized by many (though still not all) economists that is expressed in the fact that in most textbooks on macroeconomics these cycles are discussed in special chapters or sections (see, e.g., Мэнкью, 1994: Chap. 14; Сакс и Ларрен, 1996: Chap. 17; Abel & Bernanke, 2008: Chap. 8), whereas reality of long Kondratieff cycles recognized by minority of economists (and—consequently—references to them in Economics textbooks are either absent or very scarce).

inevitable; and those slowdowns can only be overcome through qualitative changes. Thus, the constant expansion and development imply that the structure within whose framework this development takes place, at times should be substantially modified. In particular, such changes should occur as a result of technological revolutions (see, e.g., Grinin & Grinin, 2015a; Perez, 2002, 2010, 2011, 2012; Гринин, 2003, 2009д, 2012б). But such a change, as a rule, lags behind the more dynamic economic (technological) component underlying expanded economic growth. Therefore, this change occurs in the form of more or less severe crises that, in fact, generate cyclical fluctuations.

There are certain important (and not random) similarities between J-cycles and K-waves in terms of their 'structure' as regards some cyclical factors and certain properties of cyclical processes. The understanding of those similarities must be able to further clarify the mechanisms of interaction between those different cycles. There are also important similarities both in terms of the nature and mechanisms of transmission of impulses (leading to the generation of J-cycles and K-waves) from one country to another within the framework of the World System. Both cycles never occur only within a particular society, they always extend beyond individual societies and are somehow connected with the world-system processes. This is all the more important that J-cycles (especially J-crises) always tend to become global, or at least that J-cycles take place simultaneously in a number of societies. Thus, through J-cycle ups and downs embedded within, the World System momentum of growth and decline is transmitted very quickly and fairly synchronously. But, of course, for the K-wave dynamics Juglar cycles within the World System leaders are of special importance.

Mechanism of Influence of J-Cycles on the Temporal Rhythm of K-Wave Alteration

Emergence and Resolution of Societal Structural Crisis within A- and B-Clusters of J-Cycles

How can medium-term cycles affect the dynamics of upward and downward phases of long cycles?

The mechanism of change in K-wave phase structure, specifically the relationship of its A-phase with respect to its dependence on J-cycles looks like this (see also the end of this chapter, Figs. 3.8 and 3.9). More severe in their manifestations of crises-depressive phases of J-cycles at a downswing, K-wave B-phases inevitably require from societies deeper and more radical changes, not only in technical and technological aspects, but also in social, legal, political, ideological, and cultural aspects, as well as in the field of international relations and world-system links. Otherwise, a society will not be able to overcome the negative effects of economic crisis and come out of depression.

Only a profound change in many different areas of society, as well as new approaches to the regulation of the economy will eventually allow the society to make the transition and to have a significant expansion.[36] Previously this has already been discussed. The cluster structure of two J-cycles (see Fig. 3.9) can be schematically represented as follows: first cycle—awareness of the difficulties and search for counter-depression and reformist measures, the second cycle—the introduction of anti-crisis measures and their first results. With three cycles the following pattern can be identified (see Fig. 3.8): the first cycle—awareness of the difficulties, the second—the search for counter-depression and reformist measures and their application, and the third cycle—the time required to develop the result.

Ultimately the struggle with depressions, conducted changes, as well as introduced innovative technologies will lead to the replacement of a J-cycle B-cluster with an A-cluster (and, thus, to the transition from a K-wave downswing to a K-wave upswing).

As a result, there is a transition to a new system of relations, which opens the possibility for economies to develop in the coming decades without exhibiting such strong crisis manifestations.[37] However, since further development proceeds in a relatively soft way, the need for reforming and modernizing relations weakens. Accordingly, the society experiences insufficient changes compared with those that are necessary to re-start rapid growth, even though any cycle is associated with an increase in structural economic, social, political and other problems. And if they are not resolved, this will lead to the amplification of negative trends, as a result of which rapid economic growth becomes impossible, or there are internal and international problems leading to various new crises. Within about three J-cycles the potential for free growth is exhausted, and problems will accumulate. Next there is a powerful crisis, triggering a more or less protracted depression. As a result, an upswing A-cluster of J-cycles is replaced with a downswing B-cluster that corresponds to the K-wave B-phase.

Thus, it is through the medium-term economic cycles in the downward phase of the K-wave that conditions are being prepared for the transition to the K-wave upswing. The stronger the crises, the weaker the expansions, and the more intense the structural changes. And in turn, less painful crisis-depressive phases of J-cycles at K-wave upswings causes them to turn into downswing phases. That's why the most severe crises occur at the turning points from the K-wave upswings to the K-wave downswings (in particular, the crisis of 1847, 1873, 1929, 1973, as well as the current global crisis that started in 2008).

So, in the upswing phase, when there is a more intensive growth, cyclical crises resemble a kind of 'stumbling when scooting', when excessive speed leads to inevitable stops and kickbacks. However, within A-clusters J-cycles are less related to each other; they are rather more similar to isolated events. These are crisis of growth, during

---

[36] Recall that Americans and Europeans had to carry out very deep reforms during and especially after the Great Depression of the late 1920s and 1930s.
[37] Menshikov and Klimenko (Меньшиков и Клименко, 1989) use the following metaphor—they say that 'society changes its skin' while going through a Kondratieff wave.

which structural problems within societies (and in general within the World System) accumulate. At the downward phases of the K-wave, crises are very different. They are much more closely related to each other, either directly, so that the next crisis is a sort of continuation of the first (e.g., the crisis of 1937 was a sort of continuation of the previous crisis that started in 1929), or they go against a common negative background (e.g., the cycles of the 1875–1895 period went against the background of a protracted agrarian crisis, and the J-cycle crises of 1971–1982 period went against the background of currency, commodity and energy crises). This is explained by the fact that such crises are structural in nature, as they resolve complex structural problems that were accumulated in the previous upswing period. Moreover, military, political or revolutionary crises (as well as world wars) fit rather well in those downward phases, as those crises act as components of a general world-system crisis that make people change the relationship structure within the World System. In short, **these are structural crises that lead to structural changes** (Figs. 3.10 and 3.11).

Table 3.5 Number of days of sessions of the US Congress corresponding to different K-waves and their phases

K-wave serial number	K-wave phase	K-wave phase datings[a]	Corresponding periods of Congress sessions[b]	Overall number of session days	Average number of session days per year
I	A: upswing	1789–1817	1794–1822 (29 years)	4263	147
	B: downswing	1818–1847	1823–1852 (30 years)	4931	164,4
II	A: upswing	1848–1873	1853–1878 (26 years)	4820	185,4
	B: downswing	1874–1893	1879–1898 (20 years)	3904	195,2
III	A: upswing	1894–1929	1899–1934 (36 years)	7242	201,2
	B: downswing	1930–1948	1935–1953 (19 years)	5475	288
IV	A: upswing	1949–1968	1954–1973 (20 years)	5737	287
	B: downswing	1969–1982	1974–1987 (14 years)	4495	321
V	A: upswing	1983–2006[c]	1988–2006[d] (19 years)	6077	320[e]
	B: downswing				?

Source: Sessions of Congress, 1st–110th Congresses, 1789–2007. URL: http://www.llsdc.org/attachments/wysiwyg/544/Sess-Congress.pdf
[a]The dates in this column do not take into account versions of the starts and ends of various phases mentioned in Table 3.5
[b]Taking the 5-year lag into account (see above)
[c]In this phase we took the period preceding the 2007–2010 crisis
[d]Within this phase we have taken the period preceding the start of the crisis
[e]Which is less than in the B-phase of the fourth K-wave. We can forecast that during the B-phase of the fifth K-wave the average number of the US Congress sessions per year will be higher

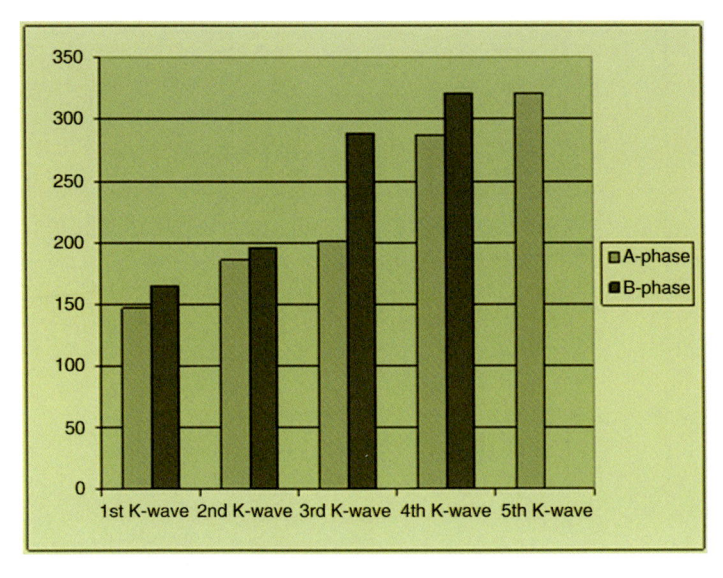

[Bar chart showing A-phase and B-phase values for 1st through 5th K-waves, with values ranging from about 150 to 325 on a 0-350 scale]

Fig. 3.10 Correlation between K-wave phases and average number of the US Congress session days per year (taking the 5-year lag into account, version 1). *Note.* The point that the average number of session days per year at B-phases is higher than at A-phases is more visible as regards the third and fourth K-waves (rather than the first and the second). It appears necessary to note the following in this respect: (1) The situation reflects the fact that since the late nineteenth century governments started paying much more attention to economic problems than earlier. (2) As regards the second wave, one should take into account that its B-phase was rather peaceful, whereas its A-phase includes the periods of the Civil War and Reconstruction of the South when the Congress had to work more intensively. If we only consider the peaceful part of the K-wave A-phase, the distribution of the US Congress session time looks as follows: *1853–1861*—1480 days of the US Congress sessions in 9 years (on average 164.4 days per year); *1870–1878*—1600 days of the US Congress sessions in 9 years (on average 177.8 days per year. Thus, altogether for all the peaceful years of the second K-wave A-phase—on average 171.1 days per year, which is substantially less than 195.2 days per year attested for the second K-wave B-phase; *1862–1869* (war-and-reconstruction period)—1740 days of the US Congress sessions in 8 years (on average 217.5 days per year). As we see a higher level of average annual US Congress sessions at the second K-wave A-phase is connected with this difficult period of the USA history. As regards the third K-wave, war periods are found there at both A- and B-phases. A graphic picture of this pattern is presented in Fig. 3.11

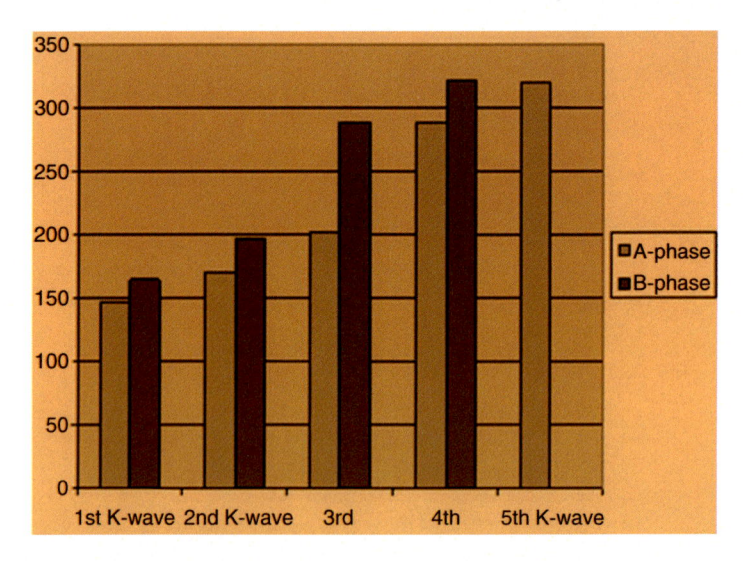

Fig. 3.11 Average annual number of days of the US Congress sessions in their relationship with K-waves and their phases (taking the 5-year lag into account, version 2: taking into consideration the 2nd K-wave A-phase). *Note.* Figure displays the relationship between the number of the US Congress sessions at the A-phases and B-phases of K-waves with the elimination of the war-and-reconstruction years (1862–1869). Here it is especially visible that within all the documented K-waves the respective society paid more attention to necessary changes during the downswing B-phases

Additional Notes

An Example of More Active Social Activities During K-Wave B-Phases in Comparison with K-Wave A-Phases

To illustrate the idea that in the economically prosperous K-wave A-phase periods societies tend to change less than in the period of crisis in depressive phases, we analyze the average annual number of days of meetings of the U.S. Congress since 1790 to the present (see Table 3.5 and Figs. 3.10 and 3.11). At the same time we have moved the origin period for meetings' calculations for each phase by 5 years as this can be estimated as the average minimum time required for an adequate understanding of the situation (i.e., datings for column 4 lag behind the respective datings for column 3 by 5 years).

Social Innovations as a Factor of K-Wave Interphase Transitions at the Level of Individual Societies, the Level of Intersocietal Interactions, and the World System Level

It appears rather important to emphasize that, though the change of K-wave phases is connected with the exhaustion of the potential of respective technological paradigms,[38] its immediate factors include first of all behavior of particular economic agents (including the state institutions), which is very tightly connected with psychological sets of businessmen and political elites. When development accelerates at the A-phase, this stimulates additional investment activities. In contrast, during depressions society is actively seeking opportunities to minimize losses, and to re-introduce an accelerating growth trend. During the past two centuries more and more forces joined the agents of economic development in their attempts to re-start upswings; and these included government, state and interstate agencies, education institutions, ideology, science, etc. These are the activities of all those forces that lead to the eventual end of the downswing and the start of a new upswing.[39]

It appears possible here to expand Schumpeter's idea (Schumpeter, 1939; Шумпетер, 1982) regarding innovators as well as the notion of creative destruction; many economists like this idea, but they do not appear to apply it always in a sufficient way. In fact, in the downswing phase innovators associated with all kinds of social activities have more chances to implement their innovations: politicians who promise to solve economic problems, reformers, legislators, scientists, etc. also have more chances to implement their innovations. The ideas that begin to be discussed and implemented could be expressed over a significant period of time and limited experiments could be carried out much earlier (or in other countries), but it is during these times of difficulties when clusters of reform and change appear. And the solution for these difficulties can be found — ceteris paribus — in those societies where depressive manifestations of crisis are stronger. Ultimately innovative changes begin to work, to spread and to have effect, in particular they contribute to the diffusion of financial and technological innovations (in other words, a **new innovative synthesis** emerges). *Thus, we should talk about innovations and innovators of all kinds, including social innovators and innovations.* In this respect, effective counter-crisis methods will begin to spread, and, like technological innovations, they may be borrowed by modernizing societies but with a significant delay, but also in a completely finished form. The more widespread this reforming is, the more opportunities for there to be economic growth and the longer can be the upswing. In particular, this explains economic successes in several post-World

---

[38] In the widest possible sense of this notion, i.e. the one that includes financial, social, cultural, and political technologies.

[39] It appears necessary to note that social innovations are not always found, or they may turn out not to be quite effective, or blind-alley innovations emerge (e.g., in Nazi Germany); in these cases crises could be especially destructive — and not only economically (as these was, for example, observed in the case of World War II).

War II European countries and Japan (economic 'miracles') in the 1950s and 1960s, as well as some of the modern achievements of China actively using a whole arsenal of counter-cyclical measures developed in Western countries. At the same time, taking into account the point that the Chinese leadership has more opportunities to effectively pursue such policies than the governments of the countries with full market economies status, the results of counter-cyclical policies in China are very impressive indeed.

Time lags. Intensification of modernization processes within the World System. But the emergence of a major social innovation (effective in combating new manifestations of depression) may not be a quick thing. Therefore, although a collision with difficulties initially often causes active, significant anti-crisis actions, even so they do not lead to profound changes. That is, a considerable time must elapse before a new innovative system starts working. This may take up to ten years or even more. In the meantime, on the one hand, during the B-phase social innovations lag behind, because they are only beginning to be implemented sometime after the first third of the B-phase (or even later), and can be completely implemented only during the second third of it (or later). And on the other hand—in fact, social innovations produce their real effect toward the end of the B-phase. However, early in the A-phase social innovations get implemented fully. As a result, when the upswing is already underway, the inertia of social change further accelerates the A-phase. Conversely, at the beginning of a downward phase we deal with yet another sort of inertia when society is not ready to change, which, accordingly, further aggravates the B-phase.

Within the B-cluster of three J-cycles one can observe the emergence of a set of technological, financial, and social innovations, which leads to an accelerated modernization of the semi-periphery, that in itself is due to faster growth and increased demand (including state demand), which accelerates the A-phase upswing.[40] Gradually these innovations add up into a system, which is picked up by 'catching up' societies. This further explains the inertia of the upswing: in the first J-cycle of the A-phase one can see belated reforms that would have to be carried out in the B-phase, while during the second J-cycle imitation reforms may be carried out.

Thus, the successful implementation of anti-crisis social innovations in advanced countries during the B-phase and the transition to the following A-phase is a signal for many 'catching up'/ modernizing countries. This is amplified by a certain excess of capitals in the core countries of the World System, as in a B-phase context those capitals are not in enough demand. Modernizing countries are beginning to implement not only technical and economic but also social technologies. This leads to both a more powerful process of modernization in the World System in the A-phase than in the B-phase, and to a more rapid growth of economically active parts of the World System, but also to a more rapid spread of impulses throughout

---

[40] It appears appropriate to note that many social innovations/counter-crisis technologies emerge not in the central societies of the World System but in those societies that aspire to become central.

the World System. All together this creates a new situation in the World System, which is very sensitive to the exhaustion of the potency to develop. Therefore, the crisis, which eventually captures the World System center, has an impact to some extent on every aspect of the World System at once.

Additional note on the diffusion of technologies. During the A-phase a more active modernization of peripheral countries is usually connected with the adoption of such technologies that can hardly be characterized as the most advanced. Rather, these are technologies of the previous wave. Thus, the most advanced technologies remain in the leading countries. But the core technologies of the previous generation are moved from advanced countries (as this was observed, e.g., in the 1990s). Such outsourcing has disadvantages (structural unemployment, etc.), but it also has some pluses, since it clears the advanced countries physically from the old technologies (this is also a kind of innovation at the level of the World System). If such technologies remain and are artificially supported by the state, the leaders start losing their leading positions (as this happened to Britain with her textile and coal industries).

What Limits the Length of the K-Wave A-Phases?

Economists have long pondered over the question, *why prosperity does not last indefinitely*? (Mitchell, 1913: 452; see also Hansen, 1951). And in the early twentieth century they suggested that prosperity and decline should be explained by the processes occurring regularly within the economy itself (Mitchell, 1913: 452–468). We also maintain that growth, although it is an essential feature of the industrial and post-industrial economy, does not occur automatically, but requires sustained efforts.[41] The faster the economic growth, the more effort is required, and thus at some point the system confronts the law of diminishing returns, that is, for each new point of growth more effort is required. Ultimately because of this effect of diminishing returns the increase in economic growth cannot be infinite.

However, the question arises, why is the upswing momentum limited to a certain period? Above we have explained the reasons for such time constraints. This section will discuss aspects of these new restrictions, and additionally shows some aspects of the relationship between K-waves and J-cycles.

The reasons that the A-phase does not last, as a rule, more than three or four J-cycles are connected to the following points:

- to the exhaustion of resources or growth factors (that are necessary to ensure upswing dynamics);

---

[41] Internal impulse to the growth is created by the desire of businessmen to increase their profits, as well as by the desire of population to increase the standard of living and consumption.

- to the inflated optimism about the prospects for business growth, which is also reflected in the excessive increase in the value of assets;
- to the emergence of long depression pauses in those J-cycles that are situated at the border of upswing and downswing phases of K-waves, which leads to changes of business development strategies.

In this case the first two points in K-waves and J-cycles are substantially similar, and the last point is specific only for long-term processes, that is, for K-waves. The latter point is part of what can be called the *factor of duration of recessive-depressive phases of J-cycles*. In our opinion, it is very important for understanding the causes of the shifts from K-wave upswings to downswings. The fact is that if crisis pauses are brief, they generally do not dramatically change business strategy vectors in the direction of growth and investment. However, during prolonged crisis-depressive phases of J-cycles business strategies can be truly reversed.

Let us now consider these reasons in detail.

Exhaustion of Growth Factors

The weakening of upswing phases is due to the exhaustion of available resources (factors promoting growth) in the broadest sense of the word. We believe that during an A-phase a much more rapid consumption of resources for growth (outstripping their creation) takes place. As a result, after some time, the resources are exhausted, and the upward movement of the economy inevitably slows down and stops (as, in the conditions of a certain level of technology, resources are always limited). Accordingly, during B-phases the accumulation of potential resources runs ahead of their consumption.

Note that here we speak about 'resources' in the widest possible sense of this word — that is about technological, financial, innovational, social, demographic (and so on) resources both at the societal level and at the level of the World System.

In particular, important resources are needed to continue the recovery; they include new business technologies (including financial technologies), expansion of markets, removal of obstacles for exchange, trade, export, and easy movement of capital; free capitals themselves; unsatisfied effective demand for some important goods and services; a number of important unimplemented innovations, etc. Finally, this is the willingness of states to invest and support business processes. Within the framework of the World System these are societies that are ready to modernize, etc.

During A-phases resource consumption rates tend to be higher than resource accumulation rates due to a rather simple reason: the main focus of business is attracted by the expansion of production, investment and so on, which, by definition, implies a rather high rate of resource consumption (note that these also include credit resources).[42]

For the emergence of additional powerful impulses qualitative changes are required. For these kinds of qualitative changes society needs major restructuring and the involvement of new resources that will not happen automatically, but will require considerable time.

Thus, A-phase (upswing) gives place to B-phase (downswing); during B-phase one can observe not only the systemic restructuring, but also the accumulation of many resources, including both innovations (e.g., Schumpeter, 1934, 1939) and such conventional resources as uninvested capitals.[43]

It is important to understand that after a long period of weak growth, interrupted by crises and depressions (i.e., after the B-phase), the momentum to accelerate a new K- wave can take place only in the presence of large amounts of resources and growth factors. Synchronism in the rise of a new K-wave is achieved, because *a certain set of resources is required for it*, and because one innovation in one area may lead to innovations in other areas; on the other hand, free capital contributes to the acceleration of modernization, whereas the development of modernization constantly requires new capitals, and so on.

The immediate impetus to the growth of a K-wave is given, as already mentioned, at the recovery stage of one of the J-cycles, and the mechanism for the transition from depression to recovery has been already described many times (see, e.g., Hansen, 1951; Mitchell, 1927). Thus, the mechanism has a great similarity to the transition from growth to slow down and new growth within J-cycles and K-waves. This mechanism is associated with the rapid depletion of resources in the period of growth and boom, leading to a rapid increase in their prices, and then the accumulation of resources during the recession, until finally the abundance of resources will not push the economy to a new upsurge. However, the acceleration of the K-wave A-phase (in contrast to the transition from a depression phase to a phase of recovery within the J-cycle) requires qualitatively different resources: technological and social innovations, new modernizing societies, new technologies, etc.

---

[42] It reminds accelerated mining operations during the boom without intensive investment in exploration. Accordingly, the amount of proven reserves decreases.

[43] For example, Tugan-Baranovsky (Туган-Барановский, 2008 [1913]) connected economic upswing impulses precisely with this factor.

Excessive Business Optimism about the Prospects for Growth and the Revaluation of Assets

Many projects and investments, which are carried out in the growth phases of J-cycle, are designed to be carried out during rather long periods of time. As has been already stated, if the recessive depressive phases are short, the processes of investment and growth do not lose momentum, no—that is very important—psychological confidence. As a result, with a short recessive pause various projects get suspended much less frequently.

As we have seen, short recessions are typical for K-wave upswing phases when growth factors (resources) have not been exhausted yet.

However, after the first (and even more so after the second) relatively favorable J-cycle (with short phases of recession and depression) one can observe in business and society the growth of optimism (the desire and courage to invest profitably), which is in opposition with the diminishing growth resources.

In the A-phase, the revaluation of assets (stocks, real estate, commodities, etc.) is also associated with a lengthy economic growth and bullish price trend, which leads to excessive demand for some resources, large scale speculation and the emergence of 'bubbles'. Dramatic overestimation of the value of assets is connected with the increasing demand for resources and the growth of unjustified assumptions that asset prices will rise further. In fact, the situation is evolving in a pyramid-like way (whereas the 'pyramid' is becoming more and more unstable every month). Below we will see that it is at the moment of the greatest depletion of resources (and at the same time the greatest weakening of growth potential—with both occurring by the end of the last J-cycle of the A-phase) that unreasonable optimism among the businessmen about the future growth in asset prices is peaking.[44]

It is clear that, as a result of the collapse, asset revaluation occurs with a minus sign (which is especially noticeable during the acute phase of the crisis).

The Long Depression Pause Emerging within Border J-Cycles and the Change of Development Strategy

As we have seen, the duration of a recessive-depressive phases of J-cycles is important for understanding the dynamics of K-wave phase changes. Meanwhile, after two (sometimes three) J-cycles in which these phases have been short, in the third (sometimes fourth) A-phase J-cycle the duration of the recessive-depressive

---

[44] For example, Hansen (1951) demonstrates in a rather convincing way that during the Great Depression it became perfectly clear how completely resources of new construction had been used, which was one of the drivers of the rise in the 1920s. But the peak of the construction was achieved long before 1929, about 1925–1926. High demand for the construction of real estate at this time is explained by the fact that during the First World War, civil construction was almost entirely frozen.

period qualitatively increases. Thus, the respective J-cycle becomes a landmark between the A- and B-phases of the respective K-wave.

An increase in the recessive-depressive phases is due to the coincidence of extreme values of divergent trends. On the one hand, the value of assets and the level of revaluation reach their peaks, and the optimism of businessmen and society as a whole is at an apogee; on the other hand—the amount of resources available for growth (growth factors) reaches a minimum value.

Simultaneously, in society and in the economy there are too many unresolved issues. As a result, the recession acquires a very large scale, and attempts to overcome the crisis and continue to grow do not work out. And as there are not enough resources to resume the upward movement, there is an insufficient momentum to continue the A-phase upswing.

Prolongation of the recession and depression phases leads inevitably to changes in business and social strategies.[45] Of course, there is a significant difference between a crisis that continues for a few months, and a depression that continues for several years. It is necessary for society to adapt to the new situation, and hence to reduce costs and volumes, while starting to rebuild business and seeking new ways for its development. Projects are suspended, investment declines, demand falls, prices (at least on revalued assets) are also falling, capitals are not invested, etc. Thus, there is a feedback loop: the longer the recessive period, the less investment, and vice versa—the less investment, the longer the recession will not end. Then a new rise may start, but it will be of a different type (which is characteristic of J-cycles in the downward phase). To maintain an upward trend after a fairly prolonged period of stagnation and depression a society needs an appropriate big enough momentum that cannot appear from nowhere (especially without the presence of effective anti-crisis social innovations).

Thus, the question about the reasons for a particular duration of the K-wave A-phase is largely related to the question of the causes of sudden lengthening of crisis-depressive phases of J-cycles (at the end of the A-cluster of those cycles). And this is undoubtedly further demonstrates the close connection between the K-waves and J-cycles.

It is also clear why during the B-phase the economy cannot gain earlier momentum. Firstly, it takes time to develop counter-crisis measures. Secondly, it is necessary to accumulate a sufficient amount of growth factors, including breakthrough technological innovations. Thirdly, you need a push to change the business strategy. Thus, a feedback loop gets established: weak expansions—inactive strategy—lack of investment—no impulses for a strong recovery—weak expansions, and so on. And this feedback loop may operate for a quite long period of time.

---

[45] On the society's strategy and its search for counter-crisis social innovations see above.

The World System Dimension

Modernization and World-System Socioeconomic Crises

Tensions of intensive modernization; relationship of the K-wave A-phases to semi-peripheral economic and social crises, as well as wars of certain types.

During K-wave upswings peripheral and semi-peripheral economic and political crises occur more frequently. Recall that already Kondratieff (1935: 111) noted that 'it is during the period of the rise of the long waves, i.e., during the period of high tension in the expansion of economic forces, that, as a rule, the most disastrous and extensive wars and revolutions occur'.

This point requires further explanation. The fact that (a) semi-peripheral modernizing countries tend to borrow social innovations rather quickly; (b) but often they do not have a sufficient basis for the 'digestion' of such innovations (and social innovation can be for them altogether alien). The result is what can be called a 'crises of modernization', which is expressed not only in economic crises, but also in the revolutions and even wars.[46] The Asian crisis of 1997 was largely such a modernization crisis. Revolutions of the early twentieth century can also be considered as such crises.

As for the wars, of course, not all, but some of them may well be attributed to a reaction to the rapid modernization, as well as to manifestations of the restructuring of the World System. In particular, major wars were connected with the formation of large nation-states in Europe in the 1850s–1870s (Italy, Germany). The war factor will be discussed in more detail below.

World-System Crises and Obstacles for the Emergence of the World-System Innovations. World-System Innovations and Their Delays

The increase in World System modernization (combined with technological and social innovations) leads to the expansion and reconfiguration of the World System, that after some time creates the need for a change in relations within the World System. If the latter is delayed, then crises emerge, and those crises cannot be overcome within individual countries and through individual social innovations. In this case, the World System confronts a series of deep crises (as was observed in the period between 1914 and 1945).

---

[46] They become even more dangerous if coincide with rapid population growth that is so characteristic of the period of the escape from the Malthusian trap (for more details on the modernization crises see Grinin, 2012c; Korotayev, Zinkina, Kobzeva et al., 2011; Коротаев, Халтурина, Малков et al., 2010; Коротаев, Халтурина, Кобзева et al., 2011; Korotayev, Malkov, & Grinin, 2014; Гринин, 2011; Гринин et al., 2009).

Thus, the development of the World System and modification of K-waves are closely interdependent. Accordingly, some phases of K-waves appear as special, with regard to exiting from a crisis at some stage of a given K-wave, since world-system solutions are necessary, and consequently such innovations may be delayed. In particular, during the third wave (1890–1940s) one could observe a profound transformation of the World System, so its downswing phase crises acquired a military-political form and generally were the most pronounced.

Already in the early twentieth century the World System encompassed, in fact, the entire Globe. Innovations at the level of individual countries were not sufficient (partly because of very strong protectionism, military and colonial rivalries). There were also very different political regimes. Hence, the further development required new world-systemic innovations in relations between the countries. However, at the world-system level the traditional ways of solving conflicts and problems were still operating and new ones had a hard time gaining prominence. As a result, the restructuring of the World System was brought about by traditional military and revolutionary methods.

Only after the First World War did it become apparent that it is necessary to look for new innovative solutions at the World System level. But this was not reached immediately, since there was no generally accepted model or supranational bodies, and there were large differences between metropolises and colonies. As a result, some countries tried to counteract the crisis phenomena that are characteristic for the World System as its whole in their own ways. At some stage there was a major contradiction: on the one hand, the interactions became very dense and more interdependent, and on the other—clashes between participants became sharper, some development models and social innovations (that were used by some states) were dangerous to others. As a result, crises became more and more acute. Ultimately, the world-system contradictions escalated into the huge Second World War. Only in this way did the world community finally manage to establish the leading model of development and common patterns of behavior in world markets at least in the main part of the World System, and in some major countries—in order to conduct the necessary social changes that are important for economic development around the world. In this way, war gradually ceased to be the leading form of restructuring the World System.

Today the situation is rather similar to the one that was observed in the early twentieth century. A serious reconfiguration of the World System is forthcoming, which implies a number of significant world-system innovations in the near future. However, the nature of those innovations is not yet clear. This may lead to the prolongation of depressive processes and to the aggravation of crisis phenomena (needless to mention that the military forms of searching for such innovations should be excluded nowadays).

How Does the K-Wave Synchronicity in the World System Emerge?

To some extent, it reminds one of growth-generating mechanisms in national economies, where growth points emerge, and those growth points—if they are powerful—pull the whole economy with them. On the other hand, we observe here the emergence of such states that act as locomotives creating momentum for all. To a certain extent this is reflected in the theory of leading sectors and leading economies as applied to the World System (Modelski, 1987; Modelski and Thompson, 1996; Rasler and Thompson, 1994; Rennstich, 2002; Thompson, 1990, 2000). A leading sector leads a respective national economy, whereas the respective leading economy leads the world economy. It is important, however, that new counter-crisis technologies emerge, which are also gradually adopted; finally, states develop some common solutions that may evolve into the World System solutions. Downswing signals are transmitted in a similar way.

The mechanism of relatively rapid momentum transfer from certain World System zones to its other areas is determined by the mechanisms associated with World System economic relations; these are rising/falling world trade (including the effect of changes in import/export duties); movement of global capital (and the formation of its new centers); currency (gold) fluctuations; export/import of technology (patents); international agreements; fluctuations in the prices of raw materials, fuel, food and other commodities. Regardless of whether this transfer was due to growth in certain countries, these mechanisms may well be changing the trends in development in the World System periphery or semi-periphery, if they have been already changed in the World System core.

If we take the transmission of impulses from the leading countries to the less developed or less actively developing ones throughout the extent of a given K-wave, the connection with J-cycles becomes more visible. During the period of one J-cycle (7–11 years), the advantages of new technologies, organizational arrangements, and other achievements (that have appeared in the leading country or countries) become more obvious. The second cycle starts the process of modernization with great intensity in a large number of countries. The third cycle extends the process of modernization, but at this level there are already difficulties associated with the complexity of sharing as well as a fall in the rate of profit, and—very importantly—especially in the transformation of institutions and relationships both within individual countries and across the World System.

General Characteristics of K-Wave Evolution, Factors, Mechanisms, and Indicators

How and Why Do the Main K-Wave Dynamics Indicators Change?

General Direction of Changes

We have examined how K-waves and J-cycles interact. Let us now see how and why the main K-wave dynamics indicators change during this process.

As has already been mentioned above, Kondratieff himself and many researchers after him believed that the main indicators of the upswing/downswing dynamics within the K-waves are associated with directions of price trends. But in recent decades this role is actually played by the relative GDP growth rate dynamics (Mandel, 1975, 1980, see also: Bieshaar & Kleinknecht, 1984; Kuczynski, 1980; Полетаев и Савельева, 1993; Kleinknecht, 1987). Some researchers use other indicators up to the class struggle indices.

This inconsistency adds complexity to the measurement of K-wave amplitude and periodicity: how can we talk about the long process of K-wave alteration, if the figures are different, and sometimes these figures are in opposition? K-waves in price dynamics have the most recognized empirical support (see, e.g. Berry, 1991; Cleary & Hobbs, 1983; Gordon, 1978: 24; Van Ewijk, 1982, etc.). But the logic of K-waves in price dynamics disappeared after the Second World War, as in this period, prices tend to rise even during downswing phases.[47]

At the moment, attempts to detect K-wave dynamics in the global GDP (and similar indicators) have yielded rather conflicting results. In particular, empirical tests of some researchers did not confirm the presence of K-waves in world industrial dynamics (see, e.g.: Chase-Dunn & Grimes, 1995: 407–409; Van der Zwan, 1980: 192–197). One of the main reasons is, of course, insufficient data on the pace of economic growth in earlier periods, but more importantly, that the data that do exist, cannot demonstrate the existence of global long-wave oscillations until the middle of the nineteenth century (see, e.g., Полетаев и Савельева, 1993: 221; Korotayev & Tsirel, 2010). We can assume that this is not accidental, as rising prices and GDP growth in certain periods can occur not quite in phase (see below our analysis of the causes of price trends and changing trends in the increases/decreases of profit rates). Similarly, there are some doubts that K-waves can be traced in the dynamics of the global GDP in the period up to 1870, though in this period K-waves appear to have been present in the economic macrodynamics of the West (Grinin & Korotayev, 2010b: 240; Korotayev & Tsirel, 2010; Коротаев и Цирель, 2010а, 2010б).

Nevertheless, our analysis of the dynamics of K-waves for over two hundred years suggests that within this apparent incompatibility one may still trace some

---

[47] However, it is possible that it will remain, if we measure the current prices in the prices of gold.

organic link, if we assume that the factors that define K-wave phases change (at least, according to their importance) in a natural way. K-waves change their manifestations in connection with the development of industrial production, as well as with the expansion of the World System and the interconnectedness of World System links. In addition, the role of the state grows. It is worth noting that J. J. van Duijn puts forward a very plausible hypothesis that long waves in economic growth emerged in the second half of nineteenth century replacing long waves in price movements (van Duijn, 1983: 91).

If we accept the idea of natural changes in the K-wave factors, it allows us to move to an organic synthesis of all the major theories explaining K-waves through monetary, technological, investment, external and military factors. Note that during the A-phase of the first K-wave the upward trend in prices was produced primarily by the war (in fact, it lasted for more than 20 years—from 1792 to 1815) and the continental blockade policy. But then from that point we observe a gradual transition from exogenous factors generating long waves to endogenous trends related to innovation, large investments and the alteration of technological paradigms.

This also accounts for contradictions of the upswing and downswing phases of the first K-wave connected with the transition from one type of reason that determine price fluctuations, to another—namely the replacement of purely external factors with a symbiosis of internal factors associated with the growth of labor productivity and external factors. This may explain the meaning of a rather strange assertion that the phase associated with endless Napoleonic wars is declared upward, and the next phase (associated with the industrial revolution, the most powerful economic restructuring and a huge increase in productivity) is declared to be downward.

But of course, that such a change of the driving forces of long-term trends could not be either rapid or complete. During the downward phase of the first K-wave, changes were really strong in only one country (Britain), and this could not completely change the trend toward lower prices in Europe, which was also caused by a very rapid increase in labor productivity that reduced the production costs of manufactured products. But already the next K-wave was caused not only by external factors (wars and expansion of gold production), but also by a change in the global trading system (the transition to the principles of free trade). This eliminated the narrowness of foreign markets and led to powerful investments in many different countries. We also note the emergence of a more complex system of industry (heavy and light) and the creation of new transport and information and communication technologies (railroads and telegraph).

On the one hand, the transition to the second K-wave A-phase precisely in the early 1850s was to a certain extent a contingency, since it coincided with the discovery of gold deposits in California and Australia, which gave a powerful upward momentum to the A-phase of that K-wave. If we take the period between 1814 and 1847, then we would not have been surprised if this phase had started, say, in 1842 and a long upswing had begun at that time. This upswing actually started and, in particular, due to the expectations of demand on the part of the Chinese market, so that there was even an acute shortage of workers (see, e.g., Туган-Барановский, 2008 [1913]: 122), but the famine of 1845–1846 suspended it.[48] And during this time, opportunities for new growth had improved.

Note that the rise has large enough reserves to become really long depending on the conditions that it is accompanied by the expansion of the World System's core (and, hence, semi-periphery's catch-up).

It seems that the price changes as the main K-wave indicator started to be replaced by fluctuations in economic growth rates sometime in the early twentieth century. This, in particular, is reflected in the competition between Britain and Germany. Finally, this all became clear after the First World War and the postwar crisis of 1920, and it is no accident that in the period preceding the Great Depression prices barely rose (see Гринин и Коротаев, 2010: 123–125; Хаберлер, 2008: 9–10, 28 for more detail), which even was a cause of some forecast errors. Such a radical change in oscillation factors coincided (but not coincidentally): (a) with an almost complete expansion of the World System, (b) with the change of its leader, (c) with the weakening of the gold standard, and (d) with the fact that the industry, including heavy industry, began to play a decisive role in the pace and direction of economic growth.

Change of the Role of the State

During the nineteenth century the role of the state changed significantly: it stopped being neutral, as states became more and more interested in high economic growth rates (some states showed interest in the development of trade and industry quite long ago, in particular, parliamentary commissions in England analyzed reasons for the decline of industry during the 1825 crisis, see e.g., Туган-Барановский, 2008 [1913]). Prior to this, states at best cared for maintaining the stability of the currency and government securities and also partly for the construction of communications. We should also note the state's role in the development of military technology and military orders. Starting from the Great Depression economic growth became one of the main concerns of the state.

---

[48] This is evidenced, e.g., by the following fact: in 1845–1847 the share of food in the British import grew from 3 to 50 % (Трахтенберг, 1963: 155).

Chapter 4
From Kondratieff Cycles to Akamatsu Waves? A New Center-Periphery Perspective on Long Cycles

Preliminary Remarks

In this chapter we would like to continue discussing the fact that Kondratieff long cycles should be considered in the framework of the center-periphery structure of the global economy (see *Chap. 2* above) already in respect of manifestation at the country's level. It is obvious that on this level such long waves in every country and epoch would be rather diverse as regards the length of waves as well as their strength and apparency.

Already the Japanese economist Kaname Akamatsu, who was a great admirer of Kondratieff, hinted at the connection between "national" and international center-periphery structure cycles (for some biographic detail on Akamatsu see *Appendix A*). His most well-known tribute to Kondratieff (Akamatsu, 1961) specifically links the rise and decline of the global peripheries to the larger Kondratieff cycle. His contribution, which is hardly ever mentioned nowadays in the framework of K-cycle research, is the starting point of our analysis in this chapter.

Analyzing the data on convergence and divergence of real incomes of the countries of the world in the international system, it appears that mostly they do not exhibit linear upward movements of the poorer nations to catch up with the richer countries, but rather that there are strong cyclical upward and downward swings, which we call henceforth "Akamatsu cycles".[1]

Akamatsu cycles may be defined as cycles (with a period ranging from 20 to 60 years) connected with convergence and divergence of core and periphery of the World System and explaining cyclical upward and downward swings (at global and national levels) in the movements of the periphery countries to catch up with the richer ones.

---

[1] A special analysis turns out to be necessary to detect the trends of Great Convergence (in the recent decades) and Great Divergence (in the preceding period) pushing there way through these complex oscillations (see Grinin & Korotayev, 2015a).

In fact, these "Akamatsu cycles", analyzed here on the basis of the well-known Maddison data series are even stronger and seem to be more devastating than the national, 50–60 years Kondratieff waves. This leads us to the discovery of what might be termed a "double-Tsunami wave structure" of economic cycles.

It is important to use the most relevant and accurate data for such a research question. Our Maddison data are for the following countries: Argentina; Australia; Austria; Belgium; Brazil; Canada; Chile; Colombia; Denmark; Finland; France; Germany; Greece; India; Indonesia; Italy; Japan; Netherlands; New Zealand; Norway; Peru; Portugal; Russia; Spain; Sri Lanka; Sweden; Switzerland; UK; Uruguay; USA; and Venezuela (available at http://www.ggdc.net/maddison/maddison-project/data.htm). They present a fairly comprehensive picture of the world in terms of continents (with the salient exception of Africa), cultures, global trade and global production over the last 130 years, and currently make up approximately 40.8 % of global population and 57.8 % of global purchasing power.

In the framework of our re-analysis, to be theoretically founded in the present chapter and *Appendix B*, we will find new empirical evidence on the existence of such Akamatsu cycles of around 20 years length or less in Australia; Chile; Denmark; Germany; Norway; Spain; Sweden; Switzerland; and Uruguay. Akamatsu cycles of around 30–40 years length were found in Belgium; Brazil; Canada; Denmark; Finland; France; Germany; Greece; India; Indonesia; Japan; Netherlands; New Zealand; Norway; Peru; Portugal; Sri Lanka; Sweden; Switzerland; and the UK. Akamatsu cycles of around 60 years length were found in Colombia and Russia.

Our re-analysis of standard world industrial production growth data since 1741 as well as standard global conflict data since 1495, all presented in *Appendix B*, cautiously support the earlier contentions of world-system research with evidence tested by spectral analysis and auto-correlation analysis.

In the present chapter, we will concentrate on what this "dual" or even "triple" structure of cycles—global ups and downs, national ups and downs, and ups and downs in the relative position of countries in the global economy—mean for the future of the analysis of international economic relations.

Our re-analysis of these entire sets of questions in the present chapter also sheds some light on the question why cycles (Kondratieff or Akamatsu) in some countries are shorter or longer than in other countries. We also try to show why in some countries Akamatsu cycles seem to have priority, while in the other countries the Kondratieff cycle seems to have priority.

Our analyses show one single, overriding, and strong tendency: richer and more resilient countries of the center with well-established social safety net, and appropriate efforts to develop mechanisms of what Amin so aptly called "auto centered development" (Amin, 1994) tend to have shorter cycles, while the peripheries with long-run tendencies to suffer from a lack of sustainable development are characterized by longer cycles (though since the late 1980s this pattern has been altered substantially by the mounting Great Diveregence processes [Grinin & Korotayev, 2015a]).

Richer, more resilient countries also tend to be characterized by the priority of the Akamatsu wave over the Kondratieff wave. The United States, Germany, France, and the Netherlands are the four nations, singled out in this work, to show our case.

Our analytical research program, to be presented in this chapter and *Appendix B*, also aims to be a fairly comprehensive test of the hypotheses about Kondratieff and Kuznets cycles (Devezas, 2006; Solomou, 2008a, 2008b) as well as to link the issue of long cycles with the issue of economic convergence and divergence. The matter is that the startling discovery which one makes upon closer inspection of the trajectories of economic convergence in the 31 countries with the newly available Maddison data set since the nineteenth century (Bolt & van Zanden, 2013) is that there are very strong cyclical ups and downs of the relative convergence of these countries in relationship to the real GDP per capita at the world level and in the capitalist system's leading economies, such as the United Kingdom and the United States of America, and not just in their own "national" growth rates and national economic cycles.

There is also a long-run trend with a turning point for many countries taking place in the recent decades. We think that the most important message for future world-systems research from the present chapter and *Appendix B* is the realization that convergence processes in many nations of the world are discontinuous and have a salient cyclical component. Several semi-peripheries in Asia, Africa and Latin America are ascending nowadays at the expense of the sharp downward trend in the European Southern periphery. But the rightward indented S-curve of income convergence and divergence now also affects the European center.

Background

The recent crisis of the semi-peripheries in Europe's South and in Ireland, recently referred to in the economics profession as the "PIIGS countries" (*P*ortugal, *I*reland, *I*taly, *G*reece, *S*pain, see, for differing perspectives on this issue Baglioni & Cherubini, 2010; De Grauwe and Ji, 2012; Erber, 2013; Hadjimichalis, 2011; Noren, 2011; Richardson, 2011; Wind, 2011) makes an analysis of the convergence or divergence of periphery and semi-periphery countries all the more relevant.

The background to the present chapter and *Appendix B* is thus the recent severe recession on the European continent and in several other regions of the world economy.

Our freely available documentation, made available at https://www.academia.edu/3742045/Korotayev_Grinin_Tausch_Economic_Cycles_Crises_and_the_Global_Periphery_Springer_2016_-_Supporting_online_materials further underlines this case, with similar materials for all the 31 countries, covered by the Maddison data set.

From Kondratieff Waves to Akamatsu "Flying Geese" Model

So, in this chapter, we try to establish the relationship between the economic cycle and the cycle of income convergence in the World System: indeed, this way an unexpected Kondratieff revival might be happening again, via the important link between the theory of global income convergence, best captured by the works of the late Italian American world-system researcher Giovanni Arrighi and the Japanese economist Kaname Akamatsu.

Since Akamatsu's contributions appeared much earlier than Arrighi's, let us primarily mention Akamatsu, and we will deal later on with Arrighi's contribution.

In Akamatsu's theory, there are important links between his *"flying geese" (Gankō Keitairon)* model and Kondratieff's ideas. This *"flying geese"* model was first proposed in a far-reaching and long tribute to Kondratieff's theory published internationally in 1961, but it was originally published in imperial Japan already in 1937 (shortly before the onset of the Second World War). It specifically links the rise and decline of the global peripheries to the larger Kondratieff cycle. The very essence of the *"flying geese"* and the K-cycle is that the two processes are intractably linked together, and that one cannot separate the two.

Now let us briefly relate the basic connection between Akamatsu's theory and the contribution by Kondratieff.

The clearest link to his own theory is then the following quotation, which also refers to an article written by Akamatsu in Japanese in 1937, where he already established the statistical pattern of "flying geese" in Japanese import substitution:

> *"In the foregoing pages, I have discussed how innovations in advanced industrial nations bring about differentiation of the world economy and cause expansion and liberalization of international trade; how these innovations are at length diffused to other industrial nations, resulting in uniformization of the world economy and leading to stagnation of international trade and protective policies; and how new innovations arise from this stage. I have shown how the international economy has grown by describing structural waves. Nevertheless, in the process by which underdeveloped countries which have not yet reached the level of industrial nations grow, a somewhat different pattern is found. I call this the 'wild-geese-flying pattern' of economic growth, which is a literal translation of a term coined in Japanese [...] Wild-geese are said to come to Japan in autumn from Siberia and again back to north before spring, flying in inverse V shapes, each of which overlaps to some extent [...]" (Akamatsu, 1937/1961: 205–206).*

Figure 4.1 describes the original scheme, as it was presented by Akamatsu in his publications, all referring to the sequence of development stages along Kondratieff cycles. We have adapted the graph for the purpose of the present chapter:

Akamatsu's new input into the Kondratieff cycle debate is that he puts the "differentiation" of the world economy into the center of his theoretical developments (Akamatsu, 1961, 1962). The differentiation of the world economy leads to the rapid diffusion of new techniques to rising industrial nations, which starts with the import of new commodities by these nations. In time, techniques and capital goods are imported as well, and homogenous industries are being established. According to Akamatsu, the uniformization of both industry and agriculture gave

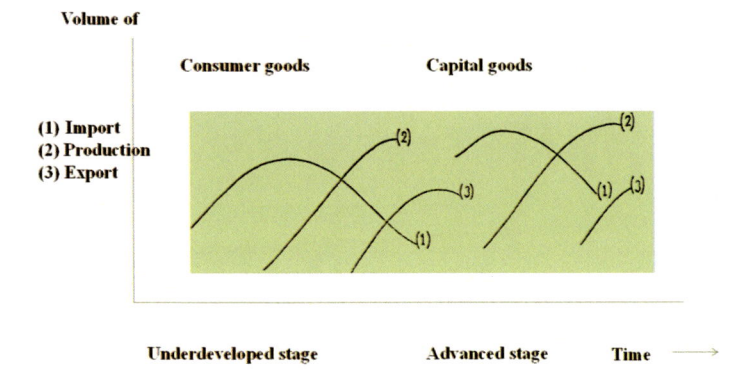

Fig. 4.1 The Akamatsu model of flying geese. (*Source*: our own adaption from Akamatsu, 1961: 206)

rise to the fierce and conflictive competition between Europe, the United States and Japan in the last quarter of the nineteenth century. When an innovation occurs in some industry in an advanced nation, investment is concentrated there, causing a rise in the trade cycle. Innovation leads to an increase in exports, and the nation's prosperity creates and increases the import of raw materials and foodstuffs. Akamatsu sees a counter-movement in other parts of the world, centered on the rising production of gold, which, according to him, leads to an increase in effective demand and further stimulates exports of the innovating nation. In that way, world production and trade expand, prices increase and a world-wide rise in the long-term trade cycle results (see Arrighi, Silver, & Brewer, 2003; Kasahara, 2004; Krasilshchikov, 2014; Ozawa, 2004, 2013; Schroeppel & Nakajima, 2002).

Quite similarly to Kondratieff (1935: 111), for Akamatsu, innovations occur mainly at the end of an old and waning economic cycle, and are put into practice during the new emerging economic cycle. Akamatsu notes that innovation occurs first in an industry of an advanced industrial nation, investment is concentrated there, causing a rise in the trade cycle. Innovations increase exports. Increased prosperity, due to rising exports of the advanced nation, causes an increase in the import of raw materials and foodstuffs. Increased gold exports from other regions increase effective demand and further stimulate exports of the innovating nation.

However, innovations spread from the innovating nations to other nations, leading to the development of industries in those countries, with the result of a conflictive relationship with the industries of the innovating nation. Exports of the innovating nation become stagnant, and on the world level, there is a tendency towards overproduction, prices turn downwards, and the rates of growth of production and trade fall. That what later K-cycle research tended to call the upswing A-phase of the cycle will be according to Akamatsu a period of differentiation in the world economic structure, while the "falling period" (or B-phase of the cycle) will, Akamatsu argues, coincide with a process of uniformization in world economic structure. Figure 4.2 supports the contention by Akamatsu that the A-phases

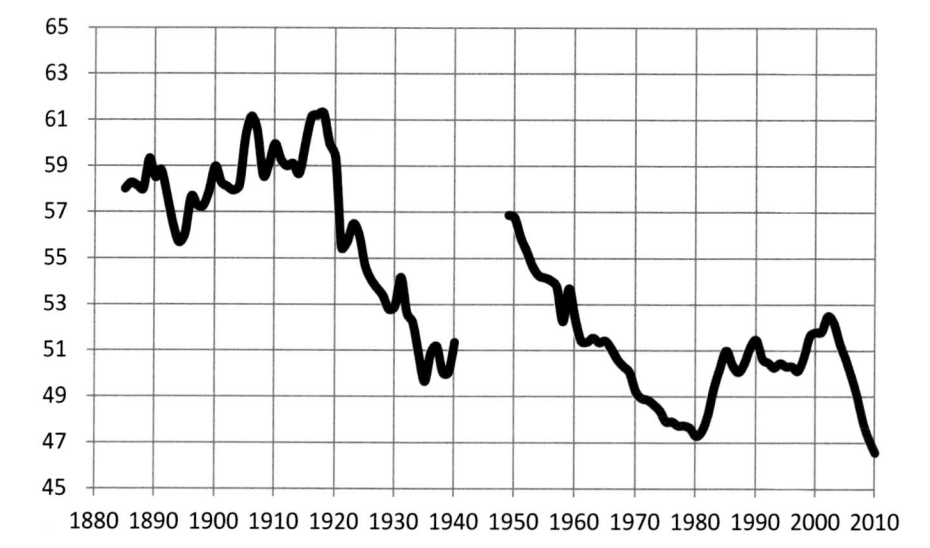

Fig. 4.2 The coefficient of variation of constant real world GDP per capita incomes in purchasing power parity rate according to Maddison's database (for 31 countries), 1885–2010. *Note*: our own compilations, based on Maddison's dataset (as documented in Bolt and van Zanden, 2013). Calculated from the original data with Microsoft EXCEL 2010

of long upswings in the world economy widen international inequalities,[2] while the B-phases of long decline reduce constant real international GDP per capita purchasing power differences:

In the nineteenth century, Akamatsu sees the following major tendencies at work:

- The innovations of the first wave of the Industrial Revolution and the respective differentiation in the world economy.
- The B-phase after the Napoleonic Wars brought about a re-uniformization.
- Uniformization especially of European agriculture, innovation in iron industry after 1850; England's position as a prime exporter of railroad materials and textiles. The discovery of gold in California and Australia increases global demand.
- The beginning of the decline around the time of the Franco-Prussian War 1870, rising mercantilism and imperialism.

For Akamatsu, imperialism with its tendencies to develop "complementary" economic structures instead of homogenization, together with its financial expenditures led towards the third expansion wave. New industries, such as the electric industry, and the automobile industry were born, and the center of the world economy shifted towards the United States of America. The third long-term wave began from the 1900s onwards, and again the spread of industrial innovations to other regions

---

[2] Note, however, that this does not appear relevant for the A-phase of the most recent, fifth, Kondratieff cycle (see, e.g., Grinin & Korotayev, 2014a, 2014b, 2015a; Korotayev, Zinkina, Bogevolnov, & Malkov, 2011a, 2011b, 2012; Korotayev & de Munck, 2013, 2014; Малков, Божевольнов и др., 2010; Малков, Коротаев, и Божевольнов, 2010; Коротаев, Халтурина и др., 2010; Гринин, 2013а).

and the accompanying uniformization of the world economy play a major role in the path towards a depression, which culminated in the 1930s. The depression of the 1930s was caused, Akamatsu argues, not only by uniformization, but also by the reduction of arms expenditures after World War I, the gold standard and the policies of deflation in force in the 1920s and early 1930s. Gold production showed a marked decrease during this era. High tariff policies, the world-wide race to depreciate the exchange rate after England's suspension of the gold standard in September 1931 additionally deepened the recession, giving rise in turn to control measures such as exchange control and quantitative restrictions on trade.

According to Akamatsu's analysis in 1961, the fourth wave started in 1933, with the aircraft industry and the synthetics industry as the leading new sectors. Going off gold, carrying out devaluations of currencies, i.e., raising the world price of gold, were additional elements in the new upswing. Military expenditures in addition increased effective demand. In contrast to the 1920s, Akamatsu thinks that successful policies were continued by the United States after 1945, now with atomic power, electronics, and innovations in consumer durables in the lead (Akamatsu, 1961). Development aid by America, and the strengthening of labor unions, the increase in military expenditures after the Korean War and the policies of full employment and social security all contributed towards the stability of the Post-War economic expansion. At the end of Akamatsu's lengthy analysis of the Kondratieff cycle in 1961, he expresses the hope that national and international economic policies will prevent the recurrence of a world depression like that of the 1930s.

For Akamatsu, the characteristic structure of the Center—Periphery relationship, which he more deeply analyzes also in his publication (Akamatsu, 1962), is characterized by the fact that the underdeveloped nation will export primary products and will import industrial goods for consumption (see Arrighi, Silver, & Brewer, 2003; Grinin & Korotayev, 2015a; Kasahara, 2004; Krasilshchikov, 2014; Ozawa, 2004, 2013; Schroeppel & Nakajima, 2002). However, the role of foreign capital received little attention in Akamatsu's theory, as he worked out his theory proceeding from the observations of the textile industry development in Japan (then still a developing rather than developed country) during the period of 40–50 years starting from the late nineteenth century. Later on, an underdeveloped nation will attempt to produce goods which were hitherto imported, first in the field of consumer goods, and later on in the area of capital goods. As the fourth stage of the process, the underdeveloped nation will attempt to export capital goods. There will be a tendency of "advanced" differentiation in the world economy, however, because the capital goods industries in advanced nations will still advance further, giving rise to "extreme differences of comparative costs". The wild-geese flying pattern includes three sub-patterns: the first is the sequence of imports—domestic production—exports. The second is the sequence from consumer goods to capital goods and from crude and simple articles to complex and refined articles. The third is the alignment from the advanced nations to backward nations according to their stages of growth (see Arrighi, Silver, & Brewer, 2003; Kasahara, 2004; Krasilshchikov, 2014; Ozawa, 2004, 2013; Schroeppel & Nakajima, 2002).

However, there is a darker and more somber nature of these cycles as well—the condition of discrepancy will be met, Akamatsu argues, by means of imports, leading to discrepancies in the balance of payments, and the pressure to increase exports of primary products to improve the balance. Discrepancies will also lead to a shift of production away from domestic industries in the underdeveloped country towards the export sector; leading, in the end, also to problems of excessive supply capacities in the underdeveloped country *et cetera* (see Arrighi, Silver, & Brewer, 2003; Kasahara, 2004; Krasilshchikov, 2014; Ozawa, 2004, 2013; Schroeppel & Nakajima, 2002).

At the end of the day, Akamatsu believes in a Hegelian dialectic between the three basic discrepancies, characterizing the process of development: the discrepancy of development, the cyclical discrepancy between the rich and the poor countries, and the structural discrepancy. At this stage however, Akamatsu does not formalize his arguments any further.[3]

Until now we concentrated on global level of working of Akamatsu cycles. Below we will move to analisys of their examples of national ups and downs—and ups and downs in the global relative position of countries.

In this chapter (as well as in *Appendix B*), we also test the crucial relationship of the Akamatsu cycles of convergence and the cross-correlation relationship between the Akamatsu cycle and the Kondratieff cycle. In Argentina, Austria, Italy, and Venezuela there are either clear linear overall convergences (Austria) or divergences (Argentina), and in Italy and in Venezuela, as well as in Russia, convergence had the shape of an inverted "U". Akamatsu cyclical oscillations are shortest in Spain, and longest in Russia. Cross correlation analysis also reveals that in Spain; Denmark; Finland; Australia; Greece; Netherlands; and Argentina there is a clear priority of the cyclical Akamatsu movements over the economic growth rates, while in the other countries of the 30 nations with available data the Kondratieff cycle determines the Akamatsu cycle. Only further research can clarify whether these differences are to be explained by the structure of exports, the role of raw material exports in the economic processes *et cetera*.

Our research also sheds some light on the question why cycles (Kondratieff or Akamatsu) in some countries are shorter or longer than in the other countries, and why in some countries, Akamatsu cycles seem to have priority, while in the other countries, the Kondratieff cycle seems to have priority.

The hypothesis, why there are such differences in cycle length between the various countries of the world, has to be found: a simple center—periphery or machinery exporter versus raw material exporter dychotomy does not apply, and also other factors, such as GDP per capita, or education also would not explain the difference alone. An interesting hypothesis could be the application of Bornschier's dependency theory, centered around penetration by transnational capital in the different economies of the

---

[3] The development of Japan between the 1950s and the 1980s, then new industrialized countries (Korea, Taiwan, etc.) and later China, Thailand, and Malaysia, in which the role of foreign capital and export sector had already become fundamentally different, allowed many Japanese and foreign scientists to expand and modernize Akamatsu's paradigm. They included the factors of FDI and TNC in their analyses and demonstrated in what way the technological and financial transfers promote economic progress in developing countries (Kojima, 2000; Ozawa, 1992, 2001, 2005, 2009, 2010; Shinohara, 1982; see also Ginzburg & Simonazzi, 2005; Ito, 2001; Korhonen, 1998; Kwan, 1994; Yamazawa, 1990).

world and the weakness or **strength of** *"national capital"* (Bornschier & Chase-Dunn, 1985; Tausch, 2010). By and large, the role of transnational capital in the countries with longer Kondratieff cycles seems to be historically more pronounced than in the countries with shorter cycles, and the strength or weakness of the national bourgeoisie seems to determine the shortness or length of cycles. Typical cases, supporting such an interpretation would be the short cycles in France, Germany, Japan, the Netherlands, and Switzerland versus the long cycles in Argentina, Canada, Chile, Greece, India, New Zealand, Spain and Russia.

Our following tables (Tables 4.1–4.3) and the supporting online maps (Map 16, Map 17, Map 18a, Map 18b) show to us the *differentia specifica* of the countries with longer Kondratieff cycles, Akamatsu cycles, the priority of the Akamatsu cycle over the Kondratieff cycle, and the long-term determination of the trend of the Akamatsu cycle by polynomial expressions of higher order (as shown in Electronic Appendix 5). For lack of comparative cross-national data since the 1880s, we used a freely available standard cross-national development studies dataset based on international standard international statistics. To make a long story short, all these analyses show one single, overriding, strong and un-directional tendency: richer and more resilient countries of the center with well-established social safety nets, and appropriate efforts to develop mechanisms of what Samir Amin so aptly called **"autocentered development"** tend to have **shorter cycles,** while the **peripheries** with long-run tendencies to suffer from a lack of sustain-

Table 4.1 Correlates of the maximum length of Kondratieff cycles

	Pearson corr. maximum length Kondratieff cycle	Slope maximum length Kondratieff cycle
Military expenditures per GDP	0.430	0.070
Carbon emissions per million US dollars GDP	0.373	5.516
Carbon emissions per capita	0.296	0.119
Tertiary enrollment	0.243	0.004
MNC PEN—stock of Inward FDI per GDP	0.228	0.184
Quintile share income difference between richest and poorest 20%	0.219	0.101
Net exports of ecological footprint gha. per person	0.214	0.049
Civil and political liberties violations	0.209	0.019
Avoiding net trade of ecological footprint gha. per person	–0.200	–0.243
Life expectancy (years)	–0.211	–0.078
Comparative price levels (US=1.00)	–0.216	–0.006
Population density	–0.218	–1.974
Social security expenditure per GDP average 1990s (ILO)	–0.239	–0.162
FPZ (free production zones) employment as % of total population	–0.303	–0.014

Table 4.2 Correlates of the maximum length of Akamatsu cycles

	Pearson corr. maximum length Akamatsu cycle	Slope maximum length Akamatsu cycle
Civil and political liberties violations	0.704	0.083
Combined failed states index	0.558	1.406
Carbon emissions per million US dollars GDP	0.509	10.136
Total unemployment rate of immigrants (both sexes)	0.489	0.134
Military expenditures per GDP	0.422	0.094
ln (number of people per mill inhabitants 1980–2000 killed by natural disasters per year + 1)	0.335	0.020
Comparative price levels (US = 1.00)	−0.320	−0.013
Social security expenditure per GDP average 1990s (ILO)	−0.352	−0.329
Economic growth in real terms pc. per annum, 1990–2005	−0.360	−0.037
Closing political gender gap	−0.360	−0.005
Human development index (HDI) value 2004	−0.379	−0.004
2000 Economic freedom score	−0.401	−0.328
Democracy measure	−0.437	−0.112
Overall 35 development index	−0.454	−0.004
Overall 35 development index, based on 7 dimensions	−0.455	−0.004
Female survival probability of surviving to age 65 female	−0.470	−0.345
Life expectancy (years)	−0.530	−0.277
Rule of law	−0.532	−0.054
Corruption avoidance measure	−0.538	−0.061

able development are characterized by **longer cycles**. Richer, more resilient countries tend to be characterized by the priority of the Akamatsu wave over the Kondratieff wave. With the plausible outlyers of two countries, where insurgents controlled a large part of the national territory for parts of the twentieth century, only countries of the center in addition could escape the high degree of statistical determination in their convergence trends over time since 1885. The United States, Germany, France, and the Netherlands are the four nations, singled out in our Electronic Appendix Map 18b. The two exceptions to this rule are quickly explained. One country is Greece, whose Maddison per capita income data might be not too reliable at any rate, and which suffered severe historical upheavals in the aftermath of the First World War right through to the end of the Greek Civil War in 1949. The other country is Colombia, which also suffered from large scale political violence to make historical income data hardly reliable (*"la violencia"*, 1948–58; Colombian guerrilla wars, 1964 to the present). It is still true that typical center countries exhibit a large R^2 in their convergence trends, analyzed in *Appendix B* and summarized in Electronic Appendix Map 18b. The United Kingdom,

Table 4.3 Correlates of the priority of the Akamatsu cycles over the Kondratieff cycles

	Pearson corr.
Life Satisfaction (0–10)	0.353
UNDP education index	0.342
Happy life years	0.339
Global tolerance index	0.338
Gender empowerment index value	0.328
Tertiary enrollment	0.307
Human development index (HDI) value 2004	0.298
Years of membership in EMU, 2010	0.279
Female survival probability of surviving to age 65 female	0.252
Overall 35 development index	0.245
Democracy measure	0.238
Closing of global gender gap overall score 2009	0.237
Closing political gender gap	0.234
Life expectancy (years)	0.233
Absolute latitude	0.225
Social security expenditure per GDP average 1990s (ILO)	0.224
Infant mortality 2005	−0.233
ln (number of people per mill inhabitants 1980–2000 killed by natural disasters per year + 1)	−0.240
Total unemployment rate of immigrants (both sexes)	−0.243
Combined Failed States Index	−0.275

Japan and Sweden (the latter two were still semi-peripheries by 1885) are such cases. But by and large, the tendency holds that only the United States, Germany, France, and the Netherlands present convergence trends which seem to be not too strongly affected by the time factor. In a sense, only their historical development exhibited a stronger "degree of freedom" from the tidal waves of the Akamatsu cycles.

All the other countries were characterized in their historical development by some variants of Akamatsu cycles.

Arrighi's Center-Periphery Model

Arrighi, Silver, and Brewer (2003) further developed these arguments, put forward by Akamatsu, and consciously linked their theoretical advances also with the models implied in the works of Raymond Vernon (1966, 1971), which specifies the life cycle of a product as defined by introduction, growth, maturity, saturation, and decline. Profit-oriented innovations (and their impact on competitive pressures) cluster in time, generating swings in the economy as a whole from long phases of predominating "prosperity" to long phases of predominating "depression". Arrighi already foresaw that they not only cluster in time, but that they also cluster in space.

There will be a spatial polarization of zones of predominating "prosperity" and zones of predominating "depression". Arrighi draws a specific parallel with Schumpeter's theory of innovations, Akamatsu's "flying geese" model (1961), and Raymond Vernon's "product cycle" model (1966). For Arrighi, Silver, and Brewer (2003), both models portray the diffusion of industrial innovations as a spatially structured process originating in the more "developed" (that is, wealthier) countries and gradually involving poorer, less "developed" countries. But, according to Arrighi, Silver, and Brewer (2003), the innovation process will be highly unequal, for it tends to begin in the wealthier countries. The residents of the countries where the innovation process starts have the best chances to win from this.

According to these authors, the process tends to begin in the wealthier countries because high incomes create a favorable environment for product innovations; high costs create a favorable environment for innovations in techniques; and cheap and abundant credit creates a favorable environment for financing these and all other kinds of innovations. Moreover, as innovators in wealthy countries reap abnormally high rewards relative to effort, over time the environment for innovations in these countries improves further, thereby generating a self-reinforcing "virtuous circle" of high incomes and innovations. The obverse side of this virtuous circle is a second tendency—the tendency, that is, for the poorer countries at the receiving end of the process to reap few, if any, of the benefits of the innovations. For Arrighi, Silver, and Brewer (2003), by the time the "new" products and techniques are adopted by the poorer countries, they tend to be subject to intense competition and no longer bring the high returns they did in the wealthier countries.

Equally, there is for Arrighi, Silver, and Brewer (2003) the destructive aspect of innovations in the tradition of Schumpeter at work. For them, poor countries are not necessarily more exposed than wealthy countries to the destructiveness of major innovations. Nevertheless, the greater mass and variety of resources that wealthy countries command nationally and globally will endow their residents with a far greater capacity to adjust socially and economically to disruptive strains and to move promptly from the activities that innovations make less rewarding to those they make more rewarding. As a result, even when they do not initiate the innovations, wealthy countries tend to be in an incomparably better position than poor and middle-income countries to reap their benefits and shift their costs and disruptions onto others. In short, opportunities for economic advance, as they present themselves successively to one country after another, do not constitute equivalent opportunities for all countries (Arrighi, Silver, & Brewer, 2003).[4]

Recent contributions in international social science have begun to approach these issues of the evolution of international convergence on the basis of the Maddison data since the 1870s, without, however, mentioning Akamatsu's eco-

---

[4] Note, however, that since the late 1980s this pattern has been modified in a dramatic way by the processes of the Great Convergence (see, e.g., Акаев, 2015; Amsden, 2004; Derviş, 2012; Grinin & Korotayev, 2014a, 2014b, 2015a; Korotayev, Zinkina, Bogevolnov, & Malkov, 2011a, 2011b, 2012; Korotayev & de Munck, 2013, 2014; Korotayev & Zinkina, 2014; Korotayev, Goldstone, & Zinkina, 2015; Мельянцев, 2009; Гринин, 2013a; Sala-i-Martin, 2006; Spence, 2011).

nomic framework, and without employing econometric time series analysis techniques (Rasler & Thompson, 2009; Reuveny & Thompson, 2008). Giovanni Arrighi also seems to have been very conscious about this problem as well, which is now hitting with the devastating force of a social tsunami his country of birth, Italy, and his world-system theory clearly distinguished between the centers, the semi-peripheries and the peripheries, and highlights the fact that some semi-peripheries rise while others stumble on their development paths (Arrighi, 1995; Arrighi, Silver, & Brewer, 2003).

Figure 4.3 symbolizes our own vision of the consequences of the Akamatsu cycle perspective for the analysis of global income convergence or divergence in the World System.

Starting with the usual IMF World Economic Outlook data, we immediately see that the share of the Western "triade" in global purchasing power has been reduced dramatically. Even in their wildest anti-Western dreams, opponents of the West would not have been able to imagine what has come true today—the tremendous reduction of Western economic power within only three decades (see Grinin & Korotayev, 2015a and Fig. 4.4 below):

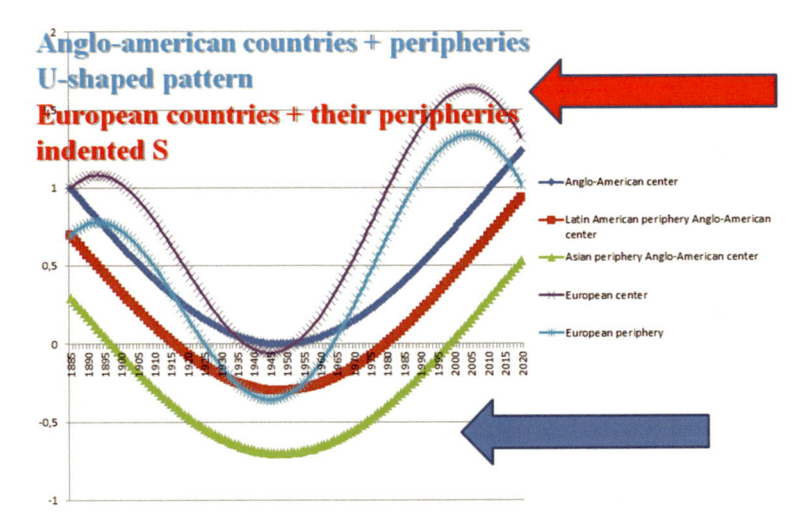

Fig. 4.3 Flying geese nations: stylized tendencies of GDP per capita as a % of average world GDP per capita (cyclical sine and cosine movements). *Source*: our own analytical perspectives on the statistical tendencies on the basis of the Maddison data, analyzed in this chapter (In the single quantitative long-wave study that did appear in the flagship journal of the Wallersteinean world-systems approach, the *Journal of World Systems Research*, Li, Xiao, and Zhu (2007), which is based on a global aggregate data analysis about movements of the Marxist concept of the rate of profit in the world economy, the authors came to the conclusion that between the mid-nineteenth century and 2005, in the UK and in the United States there were four long waves, and in Japan, since 1905, there were three such waves. The Euro-zone profit rate has, according to Li et al. (2007) tended to fall over the past four decades since 1963, and nearly halved between the early 1960s and the early 2000s. That would suggest a profit-rate related cycle of around 30–40 years duration.)

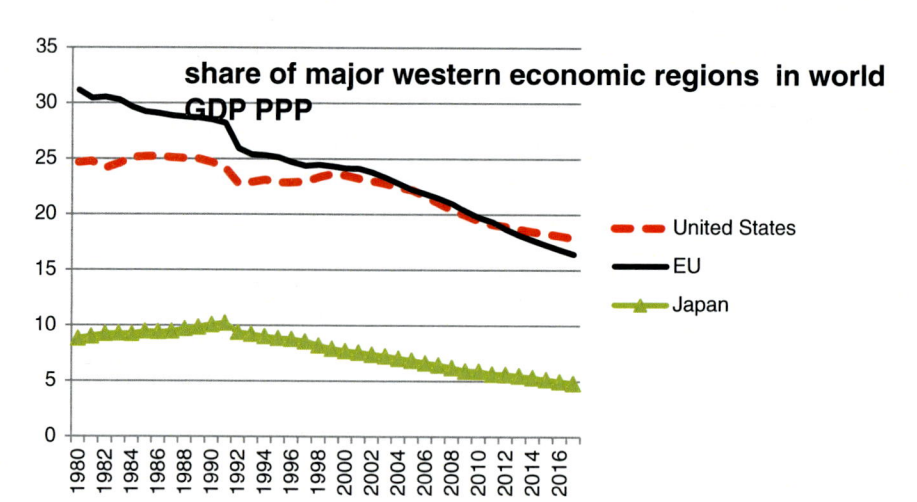

Fig. 4.4 The observed and projected decline of the share of the United States, the European Union and Japan in global purchasing power, 1980–2016. *Source*: our own calculations, based on IMF World Economic Outlook database, available at http://www.imf.org/external/pubs/ft/weo/2013/01/weodata/index.aspx. Microsoft EXCEL 2010 Graphs and Statistical Analyses

As Table 4.4 shows to us, the strong decline of real incomes in many countries in the periods 1929–1933 and 2007–2011 has not been universal, and the data rather suggest that crises are also times of major shifts in the relative position of countries in the global economy.[5] Table 4.4 underlines how dramatically different the experience of the European periphery is in comparison to the BRICS countries. And no one can say that social sciences did not voice warnings about these tendencies already three decades ago, as the very necessary re-reading of Seers, Schaffer, & Kiljunen (1979) as well as Seers, Vaitsos & Kiljunen (1980, 1982) will clearly suggest.

The severity of the Great Depression in the 1930s, which so deeply struck at North America, Poland, Austria and several but not all nations of Latin America, was not felt universally. Notably enough, several countries, starting from Scandinavia, the UK, several Latin American countries, Portugal, Turkey, Russia, China, India, Japan *et cetera* did relatively well and dived out from the depression in an often remarkable way. The three countries most seriously affected by the 1930s depression were Chile; Canada; and the United States; followed by Uruguay; Poland; Austria; Guatemala; Peru; Venezuela; Nicaragua; Czechoslovakia; Yugoslavia; Honduras; Mexico; Malaysia; Sri Lanka; Singapore; Indonesia; New Zealand; Netherlands; Germany; El Salvador; France; and Spain, where the real

---

[5]The freely available color maps (Online Electronic Appendix Maps 1–3) in our online electronic documentation accompanying this chapter (see https://www.academia.edu/3742045/Korotayev_Grinin_Tausch_Economic_Cycles_Crises_and_the_Global_Periphery_Springer_2016_-_Supporting_online_materials) visualize the information, contained in Table 4.4.

Table 4.4 Comparing the real GDP per capita declines in the two crashes, 1929–1933 and 2007–2011 in the countries of the World System with complete data

	Crash 1929–1933 in %	Crash 2007–2011 in %	Trend value linear regression crash 1929=>crash 2007	Residual (=how well a country survived the 2007 crisis judged by the crash in 1929)
China	3.02	41.60	3.23	38.37
India	−3.85	25.27	3.88	21.39
Uruguay	−28.52	24.67	6.20	18.46
Sri Lanka	−13.92	23.17	4.83	18,34
Peru	−18.34	23.25	5.24	18.00
Indonesia	−13.71	20.29	4.81	15.49
Ecuador	−3.03	13.47	3.80	9.68
Poland	−24.89	14.59	5.86	8.72
South Korea	11.54	10.39	2.42	7.97
Brazil	−5.36	11.76	4.02	7.74
Colombia	4.78	9.58	3.06	6.52
Philippines	−3.18	10.12	3.81	6.31
Turkey	10.63	7.85	2.51	5.34
Chile	−35.28	11.11	6.84	4.26
Malaysia	−14.39	8.97	4.87	4.10
Bulgaria	6.19	6.82	2.93	3.89
Singapore	−13.88	7.31	4.82	2.48
Russian Federation/USSR	7.72	4.98	2.78	2.20
Costa Rica	4.93	4.48	3.05	1.44
Serbia/Yugoslavia	−15.92	4.89	5.02	−0.12
South Africa	−4.94	3.27	3.98	−0.71
Romania	2.78	2.37	3.25	−0.88
Nicaragua	−16.80	4.15	5.10	−0.95
Australia	−8.00	3.27	4.27	−1.00
Germany	−12.22	3.50	4.67	−1.16
Sweden	−0.74	1.16	3.58	−2.43
Switzerland	−6.70	0.41	4.15	−3.74
Czech Republic/Czechoslovakia	−16.11	1.22	5.03	−3.81
Honduras	−15.81	0.29	5.01	−4.71
Austria	−23.41	0.79	5.72	−4.93
Guatemala	−21.05	0.46	5.50	−5.04
Belgium	−7.38	−1.32	4.21	−5.53
Portugal	7.58	−2.73	2.80	−5.53
Mexico	−14.57	−0.71	4.89	−5.60
El Salvador	−11.43	−1.15	4.59	−5.74
Netherlands	−12.88	−1.22	4.73	−5.95

(continued)

Table 4.4 (continued)

	Crash 1929– 1933 in %	Crash 2007– 2011 in %	Trend value linear regression crash 1929=>crash 2007	Residual (=how well a country survived the 2007 crisis judged by the crash in 1929)
Japan	4.74	−3.08	3.06	−6.15
Hungary	−4.12	−2.36	3.90	−6.26
France	−10.00	−2.12	4.46	−6.58
Venezuela	−17.37	−1.83	5.15	−6.98
Norway	4.34	−4.48	3.10	−7.58
Canada	−33.46	−1.14	6.67	−7.81
Finland	−0.55	−4.42	3.56	−7.99
Denmark	4.26	−5.76	3.11	−8.87
United States	−30.76	−2.63	6.42	−9.05
United Kingdom	−4.11	−5.19	3.90	−9.09
New Zealand	−13.04	−4.85	4.74	−9.59
Spain	−9.24	−5.52	4.38	−9.90
Italy	−7.67	−6.60	4.24	−10.84
Ireland	−0.85	−13.85	3.59	−17.44
Greece	2.26	−15.46	3.30	−18.76

Note: PPP GDP is gross domestic product converted to international dollars using purchasing power parity rates. An international dollar has the same purchasing power over GDP as the U.S. dollar has in the United States. GDP at purchaser's prices is the sum of gross value added by all resident producers in the economy plus any product taxes and minus any subsidies not included in the value of the products. It is calculated without making deductions for depreciation of fabricated assets or for depletion and degradation of natural resources. Data are in constant 2005 international dollars

purchasing power contraction in each case was 10 % or more. In Australia; Italy; Belgium; Switzerland; Brazil; South Africa; Hungary; United Kingdom; India; Philippines; Ecuador; Ireland; Sweden; and Finland the purchasing power contraction was less than 10 %.

The Great Depression resulted even in a slight or greater increase of real purchasing power per capita from 1929 to 1934 in the following countries of our sample: South Korea; Turkey; USSR; Portugal; Bulgaria; Costa Rica; Colombia; Japan; Norway; Denmark; China; Romania; and Greece. The results of these comparisons are to be seen from Table 4.4 and from Electronic Appendix Map 1.[6]

For China; India; Uruguay; Peru; Sri Lanka; Indonesia; Poland; Ecuador; Brazil; Chile; South Korea; Philippines; Colombia; Malaysia; Turkey; Singapore; Bulgaria; Russian Federation/USSR; Serbia/Yugoslavia; Costa Rica; Nicaragua; Germany;

---

[6] https://www.academia.edu/3742045/Korotayev_Grinin_Tausch_Economic_Cycles_Crises_and_the_Global_Periphery_Springer_2016_-_Supporting_online_materials.

South Africa; Australia; Romania; Czech Republic/Czechoslovakia; Sweden; Austria; Guatemala; Switzerland; and Honduras, the 2008/2011 crisis did not result in a real longer-term contraction of purchasing power per capita, while the tsunami of the depression swept most severely over the economic landscapes of Greece; Ireland; Italy; Denmark; Spain; United Kingdom; New Zealand; Norway; Finland; Japan; Portugal; United States; Hungary; France; Venezuela; Belgium; Netherlands; El Salvador; Canada; and Mexico. The results of these comparisons are to be seen from Table 4.4 and from Electronic Appendix Map 2.[7]

Now one might speculate on the "resilience" of certain types of economies and societies in times of crisis. Table 4.4 establishes a straightforward simple linear OLS regression relationship between the crisis performance in 1929 and in 2008. China; India; Uruguay; Sri Lanka; Peru; Indonesia; Ecuador; Poland; South Korea; Brazil; Colombia; Philippines; Turkey; Chile; Malaysia; Bulgaria; Singapore; Russian Federation/USSR; and Costa Rica did better—or sometimes far better— than what was to be expected from the effects of the crisis in 1929.

In 2008, Greece; Ireland; Italy; Spain; New Zealand; United Kingdom; United States; Denmark; Finland; Canada; Norway; Venezuela; France; Hungary; Japan; Netherlands; El Salvador; Mexico; Portugal; Belgium; Guatemala; Austria; Honduras; Czech Republic/Czechoslovakia; Switzerland; Sweden; Germany; Australia; Nicaragua; Romania; South Africa; and Serbia/Yugoslavia did suffer more than what would have been to be expected by the crisis performance in 1929. This indicates that the North Atlantic arena has become the focal point of the earthquake of economic transformations which currently affect the world economy.

The results of these comparisons are to be seen from Table 4.4 and from Electronic Appendix Map 3.[8]

Equally astonishing is the contemporary rise of the importance of the two BRICS countries, China and India, in the international system evidenced by their share in the world purchasing power today (Electronic Appendix Graph 4[9]see also (Gosh, Havlik, Ribero, & Urban, 2009; Havlik, Pindyuk, & Stoellinger, 2009).

Also, equally breathtaking is the decline of the Euro-area, which in the 1990s and early 2000s still hoped to become the world's leading economy by around 2010 (Electronic Appendix Graph 5[10]).

Today, not economic ascent, but rising unemployment is the hallmark of the Eurozone (Electronic Appendix Graph 6[11]).

---

[7] Ibidem.

[8] See https://www.academia.edu/3742045/Korotayev_Grinin_Tausch_Economic_Cycles_Crises_and_the_Global_Periphery_Springer_2016_-_Supporting_online_materials.

[9] Ibidem.

[10] Ibidem.

[11] Ibidem.

The Analysis of Economic Disasters and the Analysis of Economic Convergence

There is now some new light in international research on the hotly contested issue of economic convergence, so well-known from neo-classical contemporary economics (Barro & Ursúa, 2008; Jaeger & Springler, 2012; Mankiw, Romer, & Weil, 1992). In their truly remarkable article on all economic crashes and downturns since the mid-nineteenth century, based on their own version of the Maddison dataset, the neo-classical economists Barro and Ursúa (2008) open the way for a new long-term, structural research approach to the question of K-cycles in the international system. According to the "law of convergence," mentioned by Barro, *inter alia,* in Barro (2012), under certain conditions countries tend to eliminate gaps in levels of real per capita GDP at a rate around 2 % per year. Convergence at a 2 % rate implies that it takes 35 years for half of an initial gap to vanish and 115 years for 90 % of the gap to disappear (see also: Berthold & Kullas, 2009; Gennaioli, La Porta, Lopez-de-Silanes, & Shleifer, 2014). But as we will show in this chapter, the countries of the world experience—more often than not—dramatic implosions of their once so successful development path, as shown in Electronic Appendix Graph 7a to Electronic Appendix Graph 7f.[12] In this sense, a good part of the experience of the countries of the world rather looks like the contrary of Electronic Appendix Graph 7a, which shows the optimistic assumption of contemporary neoclassical economics.

Without mentioning the legacy of Kondratieff, Barro and Ursúa (2008) reach the conclusion that for their country samples starting at 1870, a peak-to-trough method to isolate economic crises, defined as cumulative declines in consumption or GDP of at least 10 %, yielded 95 crises for consumption and 152 for GDP in the World System, implying disaster probabilities of 3 % a year, with a mean size of 21–22 % declines and an average cycle durations of 32 years. This entirely mainstream, neoclassical approach thus opens up the way for a new approach to the whole question of Kondratieff cycles.

Latest advances in mainstream economic theory in the traditions of research, initiated by Barro and associates, like Gourio (2012), also seem to be well aware of the kind of causal processes, which for a long time have been at the center of the debates about K-cycles, although Gourio (2012) does not even mention the name of Kondratieff. For Gourio (2012), a disaster is a combination of permanent and transitory shocks to productivity, and a depreciation shock to capital, and shows that this simple approach allows replicating accurately the response of consumption to a disaster. An increase in the disaster probability affects the economy by lowering expectations, and by increasing risk. Because investors are risk averse, this higher risk leads, according to Gourio (2012), to higher risk premia, and has significant implications both for business cycles and for asset prices: stock prices fall, employment and output contract, and investment declines.

---

[12] Ibidem.

New Evidence on Economic Cycles in 31 Countries of the World System, the Discovery of the Akamatsu Cycle and the Relationship of the Akamatsu Perspective with Long-Run Tendencies of Inequality

In this section we will present the results of the analysis of the Maddison data and the cyclical fluctuations of the Akamatsu type whose methodology will be described in detail in *Appendix B*.

To present the original growth data or convergence data, the diagrams with the periodogram, the spectral density graphs, the autocorrelation plots and the rolling correlation plots would require for each of the 31 nations in the world 5 graphs for each country, that is to say 155 graphs for the Maddison economic growth data and 155 graphs for the Maddison convergence data, i.e. 310 graphs. We will concentrate in the following on the interpretation of the main results, and leave it to our readers to look at the supporting online materials[13] with further, more detailed graphs on the subject

Tables 4.5–4.7 now present the main results of our analysis of Maddison's dataset. Kondratieff cycles of around 60 years duration are most clearly visible in the periodograms for Argentina, Canada, and Russia. These periodograms and other econometric time series tests are available from *Appendix B* and as supporting online materials.[14]

We have also found evidence on the existence of longer cycles of more than 35 years in the following countries: Belgium, Chile, Greece, Netherlands, India, New Zealand, Spain, and USA—while for the other countries, the spectral density analysis results reported in Diebolt and Doliger (2006) could not be falsified.

In *Appendix B*, we will highlight some of the more general tendencies of the possible determinants of Kondratieff cycle and Akamatsu cycle length. At this stage of presentation, we only would like to present the simple "facts" of "proven cycle length", and it should suffice to say that maps in *Appendix B* highlight the most important geographical facts of cycle length, while Tables 4.7 and 4.8 show some of the cross-national characteristics of nations which could be tentatively regarded as drivers of Kondratieff and Akamatsu cycle length. Table 4.5 is now the "clinical" evidence about the simple fact of "proven" national Kondratieff cycle length in the 31 countries, for which such calculations were possible.

For the 31 nations trajectories, see our supporting online materials.[15]

In Table 4.6 we test the crucial relationships of the Akamatsu cycles and the cross-correlation relationship between the Akamatsu cycle and the Kondratieff cycle.

In Argentina, Austria, Italy, and Venezuela there are either clear linear overall convergences (Austria) or divergences (Argentina), and in Italy and in Venezuela,

---

[13] Ibidem.

[14] Ibidem.

[15] Ibidem. Online Appendices 4 and 5 as well as the numerous other background data, presented there highlight the Akamatsu cycles in 31 countries of the world economy since 1885.

Table 4.5 The Kondratieff cycles in the countries of the World System

	Cycle length (years) K-cycles, as suggested by the periodograms
Argentina	20 and 60
Australia	20 and 30
Austria	20
Belgium	20 and 38
Brazil	20 and 30
Canada	18 and 58
Chile	15 and 38
Colombia	20 and 30
Denmark	15 and 30
UK	15 and 30
Russia	18 and 22 and 58
Finland	25
France	18
Germany	14 and 22
Greece	15 and 25 and 40
Netherlands	20 and 40
India	25 and 40
Indonesia	20
Italy	18
Japan	15
New Zealand	20 and 40
Norway	18 and 30
Peru	20
Portugal	30
Spain	40
Sri Lanka	15
Sweden	16
Switzerland	16
Uruguay	20
USA	20 and 40
Venezuela	20

as well as in Russia, convergence had the shape of an inverted "U". Akamatsu cyclical oscillations are shortest in Spain, and longest in Russia, and the ascending order of implied Akamatsu cycle length is given by the following list of countries: Spain, Uruguay, Denmark, Norway, Sweden, Chile, Canada, Finland, Japan, New Zealand, Portugal, Australia, Germany, Switzerland, India, Indonesia, Belgium, Brazil, UK, France, Greece, Netherlands, Peru, Sri Lanka, Colombia, Russia.

Cross correlation analysis also reveals that in Spain, Denmark, Finland, Australia, Greece, Netherlands, and Argentina there is a clear priority of the cyclical Akamatsu movements over the economic growth rates, while in the other countries the Kondratieff cycle determines the Akamatsu cycle. Below we highlight some of the

Table 4.6 The length of the Akamatsu cycles and the relationship between the K-cycles and the Akamatsu cycles in 30 countries of the world

	Cycle length (years) of Akamatsu cycles, as suggested by the periodograms based on the original convergence data with the US	Time series cross-correlation analysis suggests the following causality
Argentina	No significant result	A->K
Australia	20 and 40	A->K
Austria	No significant result	K->A
Belgium	40	K->A
Brazil	40	K->A
Canada	30	K->A
Chile	25	K->A
Colombia	60	K->A
Denmark	20 and 30	A->K
UK	40	K->A
Russia	60	K->A
Finland	30	A->K
France	40	K->A
Germany	20 and 40	K->A
Greece	40	A->K
Netherlands	40	A->K
India	30 and 40	K->A
Indonesia	30 and 40	K->A
Italy	No significant result	K->A
Japan	30	K->A
New Zealand	30	K->A
Norway	20 and 30	K->A
Peru	40	K->A
Portugal	30	K->A
Spain	18	A->K
Sri Lanka	40	K->A
Sweden	20 and 30	K->A
Switzerland	25 and 40	K->A
Uruguay	20	K->A
Venezuela	No significant result	K->A

possible theoretical dimensions which explain why in some countries there seems to be a priority of the Kondratieff cycle, and why in other countries, there seems to be a priority of the Akamatsu cycle. *Appendix B* and supporting online Maps 17, 18a and Map 18b[16] further highlight these tendencies. Only further research can clarify whether these differences are to be explained by the structure of exports, the role of raw material exports in the economic processes and so on.

---

[16] See https://www.academia.edu/3742045/Korotayev_Grinin_Tausch_Economic_Cycles_Crises_and_the_Global_Periphery_Springer_2016_-_Supporting_online_materials.

Table 4.7 The Akamatsu cycle and convergence trends in the Kondratieff cycles, 1885–2010

	Cycle 1885–1913	Cycle 1914–1932	Cycle 1933–1953	Cycle 1954–1973	Cycle 1974–1992	Cycle 1993–2010
Argentina	0.267	−0.031	−0.860	−0.784	−0.460	0.878
Australia	−0.618	−0.859	−0.462	−0.888	0.714	0.549
Austria	0.499	0.316	0.418	0.972	0.791	0.602
Belgium	−0.853	0.340	−0.913	0.955	0.554	−0.579
Brazil	−0.878	0.145	0.813	0.858	−0.885	0.827
Canada	0.938	−0.674	0.822	0.713	−0.656	−0.886
Chile	0.482	−0.635	−0.523	−0.863	0.948	0.995
Colombia	−0.909	0.923	−0.847	0.122	−0.086	0.973
Denmark	0.926	0.451	−0.663	−0.875	0.267	−0.968
Finland	0.696	0.706	0.830	0.853	−0.256	0.333
France	0.169	0.591	−0.200	0.954	−0.703	−0.993
Germany	0.672	0.236	−0.257	0.523	−0.840	−0.823
Greece	−0.582	0.733	−0.815	0.951	−0.798	0.485
India	−0.742	−0.846	−0.968	−0.913	0.974	0.978
Indonesia	−0.908	−0.526	−0.950	0.778	0.789	0.948
Italy	−0.789	−0.243	0.545	0.973	0.244	−0.995
Japan	0.302	−0.091	−0.363	0.936	0.429	−0.943
Netherlands	−0.948	0.725	−0.665	0.355	0.910	−0.641
New Zealand	0.486	−0.903	0.308	−0.953	−0.798	−0.610
Norway	−0.121	0.412	0.842	0.804	0.884	−0.839
Peru	0.842	0.702	−0.460	−0.947	−0.780	0.963
Portugal	−0.819	0.316	−0.098	0.939	0.898	−0.965
Russia	0.298	0.103	0.908	−0.505	−0.951	0.977
Spain	−0.806	0.084	−0.496	0.956	0.953	−0.934
Sri Lanka	−0.214	−0.846	−0.981	−0.746	0.931	0.975
Sweden	0.939	0.559	0.883	−0.895	−0.769	0.716
Switzerland	0.838	0.045	−0.710	−0.947	−0.956	−0.462
UK	−0.662	−0.785	−0.928	−0.945	0.892	−0.622
Uruguay	−0.428	0.535	−0.117	−0.702	0.729	0.887
USA	0.730	−0.401	0.725	−0.783	0.791	−0.924
Venezuela	−0.866	0.930	0.918	−0.977	−0.921	0.682

In Austria, Belgium, Brazil, Canada, Chile, Colombia, France, Germany, India, Indonesia, Italy, Japan, New Zealand, Norway, Peru, Portugal, Russia, Sri Lanka, Sweden, Switzerland, UK, Uruguay, Venezuela there was a clear priority role of the Kondratieff cycle over the Akamatsu cycle. The following synopsis further highlights the length of the Akamatsu cycles.

Akamatsu cycles of around **20 years length or less** are found in the following countries: Australia, Chile, Denmark, Germany, Norway, Spain, Sweden, Switzerland, Uruguay.

Table 4.8 Effects of the Great Depression, 1929–1939 on the relative position of country per capita purchasing power per capita in relationship to the "world average"

	Correlation, convergence over time 1929–1939	Slope
Russia	0.971	2.064
Germany	0.898	2.704
Finland	0.884	1.875
Norway	0.847	1.620
New Zealand	0.839	3.238
Sweden	0.827	1.491
Japan	0.805	1.313
Colombia	0.756	0.662
Australia	0.721	1.768
Venezuela	0.698	1.983
Brazil	0.642	0.302
UK	0.640	1.170
Greece	0.435	0.516
Peru	0.329	0.320
Chile	0.129	0.386
Denmark	0.033	0.077
Portugal	–0.199	–0.240
USA	–0.330	–1.228
Austria	–0.335	–0.831
Italy	–0.410	–0.401
Canada	–0.464	–1.450
Uruguay	–0.634	–1.849
Belgium	–0.744	–1.512
India	–0.772	–0.418
France	–0.802	–1.260
Switzerland	–0.819	–4.496
Spain	–0.837	–3.529
Indonesia	–0.855	–0.368
Sri Lanka	–0.856	–0.605
Argentina	–0.871	–1.093
Netherlands	–0.892	–2.206

Akamatsu cycles of around **30–40 years** length are found in the following countries: Belgium, Brazil, Canada, Denmark, UK, Finland, France, Germany, Greece, Netherlands, India, Indonesia, Japan, New Zealand, Norway, Peru, Portugal, Sri Lanka, Sweden, Switzerland.

Akamatsu cycles of **around 60 years** length are found in Colombia and Russia.

No proof of an Akamatsu cycle with the methods used in this chapter (see *Appendix B*) are found with respect to Argentina, Austria, Italy, and Venezuela.

Table 4.6 further summarizes our evidence at this stage.

For the 31 nations trajectories, see our supporting online materials.[17]

Table 4.7 highlights another important consequence of our research for the study of the world-system dynamics. In that table, we highlight the "convergence paths" of the countries of the World System with available data in terms of their GDP per capita distance to the "world average".[18] Table 4.7 highlights the dramatic singularity of Keynesian postwar European reconstruction, and it also shows that since the 1990s, other mechanisms have set in, which clearly are to the detriment of countries of the European Union, and which benefit, among others, some countries of neoliberalism. It is even feasible that each period has its own "correct" economic theory, with Keynesian strategies being most successful in the postwar period.

Table 4.7 and Electronic Appendix Electronic Appendix Map 4 to Electronic Appendix Map 9[19] provide the more in depth-analysis of these strategically important questions. The following synopsis highlights the most successful nations (from our sample of 31 countries):

Post 1885 — top 5: Sweden, Canada, Denmark, Peru, Switzerland.
Post 1914 — top 5: Venezuela, Colombia, Greece, Netherlands, Finland.
Post 1933 — top 5: Venezuela, Russia, Sweden, Norway, Finland.
Post 1954 — top 5: Italy, Austria, Spain, Belgium, France.
Post 1974 — top 5: India, Spain, Chile, Sri Lanka, Netherlands.
Post 1993 — top 5: Chile, India, Russia, Sri Lanka, Colombia.

The information contained in Table 4.7 is also visible in a geographical fashion in Electronic Appendix Map 4 to Electronic Appendix Map 9,[20] which are intended to be geographical guiding posts in the changing landscapes of emerging and submerging nations along the Kondratieff cycles' A- and B-phases.

For the 31 nations trajectories see ibidem. Our interpretation, however, is characterized by the same general perspective of Kondratieff cycles and world-system analysis, but with Akamatsu it contends that the divergence process is stronger in the A-phase of the Kondratiev cycle than in the B-phase.[21] More important still, it can be shown that the World System is characterized over the last 130 years by the evolution and the ups and downs of two axes of power and its corresponding peripheries. The first Axis are the dominant English speaking powers, the United Kingdom (until the Great Depression 1929) and since then the United States of America. The relative wealth of this power center in comparison to the average of world society

---

[17] Ibidem.

[18] To be exact this is the average for those 31 countries that we study. In fact, this "world average" is considerably higher than the real world average, as our sample consists of almost exclusively high and middle income countries, and hardly includes any countries with the lowest per capita incomes. Indeed, the overwhelming majority of countries with the lowest per capita incomes are found now in tropical Africa, whereas our sample does not include any African countries at all.

[19] Ibidem.

[20] Ibidem.

[21] Note, however, that this does not appear relevant for the A-phase of the most recent, fifth, Kondratieff cycle because since the late 1980s this pattern has been modified in a dramatic way by the processes of the Great Convergence (see above).

can be best described in the shape of an "U"; also the main peripheries of this system in Latin America (the Southern Cone of Latin America) and in East and Southeast Asia (China, India, Sri Lanka) correspond to such a pattern. The second Axis is constituted by Germany and Japan, the main hegemonic contenders of the United States and the United Kingdom in the Second World War. The economic fate of this axis and Germany's main peripheries in Southern Europe, like Greece, Italy, Portugal and Spain, as well as the economic fate of its main trading partners in Europe, like Austria, Belgium, France, and the Netherlands, correspond somewhat to an "S" which is heavily indented towards the right. Europe had its chance, but its chance is waning.

True, there are countries which do not fit into that general pattern, like the slowly upward pointing but very fluctuating development path of Brazil, or the very clear convergence path of the Scandinavian nations Denmark, Finland, Norway, and Sweden, which also do not really fit unto this more general pattern of countries, whose convergence paths can be studied on the basis of available long-term real GDP in purchasing power parities time series. Also it should be emphasized that the four heavily raw material export dependent semi-peripheries, Colombia, Peru, Russia, and Venezuela, different as they may be, all correspond to an inverted "U" shaped ascent and decline in world society since the mid-1880s. Or should we rather say, upon inspecting the data that their development path in relation to the average of world society remotely resembles a small "m" followed by an inverted "U", to be followed again by a small "m"?

At this point, and confronted with the archaic and tectonic structure of the development of the World System since 1885 which inexorably shifts the dynamics away from the Eastern part of the Atlantic towards the countries of the Pacific and the Indian Ocean (see also the dramatic implications of our Maps 4–9, which attempt to illustrate this drama affecting Europe) one should also cautiously mention the debates started by the French economist Thomas Piketty (Piketty & Goldhammer, 2014) and his emphasis on inequality. Although we share Piketty's conviction that growing inequality is becoming a long-term development constraint of its own in many developed nations around the globe, most notably in Europe, we have decided to use the University of Texas Inequality Project (UTIP) annual data on GINI coefficients of household income inequality[22] instead of documenting maps of growing global inequality trends. In Piketty's data,[23] there are only a limited number of countries, apart from the intricate questions of the reliability and comparability of his long-term data.[24] Even if we attempt to standardize the sometimes changing measurement concepts within the Piketty country time series over time, the fact remains that the Piketty data—valuable as they may be for the question of income concentration at the very top of the social and economic pyramid—naturally are deficient in terms of country coverage. Our Maps 10–12, which highlight the global dramatic trend towards inequality-driven economic and political regimes from the mid-1970s

---

[22] http://utip.gov.utexas.edu/data.html.

[23] http://piketty.pse.ens.fr/fr/capitalisback.

[24] http://www.ft.com/cms/s/0/1e8c6814-e3fb-11e3-a73a-00144feabdc0.html.

onwards would be largely an empty space of countries without data if we were to attempt to work with the Piketty database and not the UTIP database instead.

Our methodology to arrive at the trend diagnosis is based on time series correlation analysis with the time axis for each of the countries of the World System for all the separate time periods 1963–1973; 1974–1992; and 1993–2008 (the time point where the data series ends) on the x-axis and the UTIP within country inequality GINI indices on the respective y-axis. The "Keynesian" postwar order showed only some patches of "blue" neoliberal rising inequality in the period 1963–1973, while most of the countries of the world still were characterized by the "red" consensus of declining inequality. Looking at our online maps, you will discover however that what was the exception in 1963–1973 in the United Kingdom, in Colombia, in Mexico, in the Netherlands, in India, Pakistan and in some African and other developing countries, became the global neoliberal "blue" rule of the game of rising inequality over time 1974–1992. Notable exceptions during this period are practically only Cuba (which had a prior communist revolution in 1959), Denmark, India (withdrawal of the emergency rule 1975–1977 on 21 March 1977), and Iran (Islamic Revolution in 1979). The University of Texas Inequality Project data for 1993–2008 also suggest that the "blue" neoliberal consensus of rising inequality governed large sections of our globe right through to the onset of the global economic crisis in 2007/2008.

In order not to overburden the presentations of our materials in the body of the text of this chapter, we have decided to present the competing and scarcely available Piketty data and their tendencies in Maps 19–24 of the Electronic Appendix[25] only, and not here in the text. Again, we have calculated linear time series correlations of the inequality indices, presented by Piketty on the y-axis, and the time axis for each nation of the World System with available data on the respective x-axis. In the online Appendix 13, we also show the 5 year moving averages and the polynomial trend of unweighted global averages of the share of the top income earners since the nineteenth century.[26] These figures point into the direction of a "wave" of rising inequality before the world depression of the 1930s and in the contemporary period since the mid-1970s. However, the pre-1945 data, on a country to country basis, raise several questions, like the one on obviously rising inequality in the United Kingdom, but falling inequality in Germany immediately before 1932. But the postwar period seems to confirm the rather robust hypothesis about the "red to blue shift" in global economic policy from egalitarian Keynesianism to inegalitarian neoliberalism since the middle of the 1970s. Also the World Bank data on 5 year moving averages and polynomial trend of unweighted global averages of GINI household inequality coefficients in the countries of the World System since 1963 to be seen in Appendix 13 emphasize this point, which is also clearly visible in our respective Piketty data Maps 23 and 24.[27]

---

[25] See https://www.academia.edu/3742045/Korotayev_Grinin_Tausch_Economic_Cycles_Crises_and_the_Global_Periphery_Springer_2016_-_Supporting_online_materials.
[26] Ibidem.
[27] Ibidem.

However, Electronic Appendix Map 19 and Electronic Appendix Map 22, as well as Electronic Appendix Map 11 and Electronic Appendix Map 12[28] raise an important question: several of the ascending nations, like Germany before 1914, Germany and Japan after 1954, as well as many ascending nations after 1974 and/or 1993 were or are characterized by rising inequality and not falling inequality, raising doubts about the direction of causality in the inequality ↔ stagnation nexus. A final answer to this interesting question cannot as yet be presented here, since we would have to present massive econometric time series evidence of the type.[29]

The Global Maps of Convergence During World Depressions

A very prominent consensus among "critical" development researchers influenced by dependency theories (Bernal, 1988; Cardoso & Faletto, 1971; Frank, 1967; Krasilshchikov, 2014) maintains that the industrialization of the Latin American semi-periphery in the phase of import substitution from the 1930s onwards coincided with what dependency theory calls "the weakness of the center" at the time of the Great Depression. Especially Andre Gunder Frank is prominent among the global social scientists to have developed a "metropolis/satellite" concept based on his original historical studies on Brazil, Chile and Mexico and the effects which the Great Depression had on the Latin American countries, published in his work (Frank, 1967), which in many ways revolutionized the debate on development and underdevelopment.

But as plausible as this reading of the history of Latin American industrialization in the 1930s and the political changes it was connected with may sound, it is important to look at the Maddison data in a more detailed way to draw some real conclusions.

And these conclusions rather support a reading of events, compatible with the theories of Kaname Akamatsu and Karl Polanyi, and less so with the "metropolis/satellite" concept of a world economy, based on an apparent zero-sum-game between the capitalist centers and the Latin American periphery at the time of the 1930s. Frank suggests throughout his seminal work (Frank, 1967) that the strength of the center caused the weakness of the periphery throughout much of history, and that the weakness of the center in the 1930s enabled the strengthening of the periphery and its industrialization. Looking at our comparative graph for Argentina, Brazil, Chile, France, the UK and the USA during the period 1918–1940 and 1995–2010[30] we could be at first sight rather inclined to say that the Frank hypothesis may be

---

[28] Ibidem.

[29] It presented in online Appendix 8 of this work (Cross Correlation Functions time series analysis for each country since the nineteenth century on the respective relationships between inequality and subsequent economic ascent or decline and on inequality and subsequent economic growth or stagnation).

[30] See https://www.academia.edu/3742045/Korotayev_Grinin_Tausch_Economic_Cycles_Crises_and_the_Global_Periphery_Springer_2016_-_Supporting_online_materials.

Table 4.9 Effects of the Great Depression, 2008 (time series: 2000–2010) on the relative position of country per capita purchasing power per capita in relationship to the "world average"

	Correlation, convergence over time 2000–2010	Slope
Chile	0.993	1.319
Russia	0.983	1.678
India	0.975	0.696
Colombia	0.958	0.577
Sri Lanka	0.949	0.767
Indonesia	0.949	0.560
Peru	0.943	0.901
Sweden	0.789	0.690
Brazil	0.771	0.344
Uruguay	0.754	1.442
Argentina	0.653	0.814
Greece	0.644	0.723
Australia	0.642	0.494
Venezuela	0.572	0.829
Austria	0.549	0.148
Finland	0.483	0.450
New Zealand	–0.328	–0.231
UK	–0.330	–0.286
Switzerland	–0.618	–0.392
Belgium	–0.669	–0.195
Netherlands	–0.735	–0.480
Norway	–0.779	–0.422
Canada	–0.838	–0.637
Spain	–0.847	–0.714
Germany	–0.865	–0.815
USA	–0.921	–1.444
Japan	–0.952	–1.062
Portugal	–0.968	–1.131
Denmark	–0.970	–1.510
Italy	–0.983	–1.910
France	–0.984	–1.200

perhaps more valid for today than for the time period for which it was originally developed, i.e. the explanation of Latin American industrialization during the Great Depression (see Electronic Appendix Graph 25).

Tables 4.8 and 4.9 now show the time series correlations 1929–1939 and 2000–2010. In descending order we are presented with the following facts based on time series correlations of the relative position of a country in the global hierarchy of per capita purchasing power:

Positive trend 1929–1939: Russia, Germany, Finland, Norway, New Zealand, Sweden, Japan, Colombia, Australia, Venezuela, Brazil, UK, Greece, Peru, Chile, and Denmark.

Positive trend 2000–2010: Chile, Russia, India, Colombia, Sri Lanka, Indonesia, Peru, Sweden, Brazil, Uruguay, Argentina, Greece, Australia, Venezuela, Austria, and Finland.

Negative trend 1929–1939: Netherlands, Argentina, Sri Lanka, Indonesia, Spain, Switzerland, France, India, Belgium, Uruguay, Canada, Italy, Austria, USA, Portugal.

Negative trend 2000–2010: France, Italy, Denmark, Portugal, Japan, USA, Germany, Spain, Canada, Norway, Netherlands, Belgium, Switzerland, UK, and New Zealand.

The center—periphery, or if you wish, metropolis—satellite concept would explain to us very well that Russia, Colombia, Venezuela, Brazil, Greece, Peru, and Chile could increase their relative positions in the world economy during the Great Depression, while the center countries Netherlands, Switzerland, France, Belgium, Canada, Austria, and the USA weakened in their respective positions.

But the metropolis—satellite concept cannot explain to us why the center countries Germany, Finland, Norway, New Zealand, Sweden, Japan, Australia, UK, and Denmark in fact strengthened, and not—as predicted by that theory—weakened in their position, while at the same time, some peripheries and semi-peripheries (Argentina, Sri Lanka, Indonesia, Spain, India, Uruguay, Italy, and Portugal) further lost in their position as evidenced by the negative time series correlational trend in their relative income over time during the Great Depression.

So the metropolis—satellite concept explains the convergence behavior during the Great Depression in 14 countries, i.e. 45 % of the 31 countries under scrutiny,[31] while for the other 17 countries (55 %)[32] it fails to do so. Rather, we are inclined to say that future research on the subject of the comparative effects of economic depressions, which cannot be treated here exhaustively, would do well to concentrate on Polanyian "New Deal" models in the successful center countries or Akamatsu-type "flying geese" industrializations in the successful semi-periphery and periphery models as an explanation. We also should emphasize that the trajectory of the 31 countries for the time period 2000–2010 only includes three crisis years, and that with currently emerging international data in the post 2008 period we will know much more about these processes in the not too distant future.

Conclusions

In this chapter we highlight the fact that Kondratieff long cycles are to be seen in the framework of the center—periphery structure of the global economy. We also highlight the long-run trends of international convergence and divergence, with a turning point

---

[31] Russia, Colombia, Venezuela, Brazil, Greece, Peru, Chile, Netherlands, Switzerland, France, Belgium, Canada, Austria, USA.

[32] Germany, Finland, Norway, New Zealand, Sweden, Japan, Australia, UK, Denmark, Argentina, Sri Lanka, Indonesia, Spain, India, Uruguay, Italy, Portugal.

for many countries taking place in the present decade. We discuss this subject in a prism of three models (Akamatsu "flying geese" model, Arrighi centre—periphery model, and Barro economic disasters and economic convergence theory). Our analisys supports our general idea that the gap between core and periphery of the World System is growing shorter. However this trend is far from linear upward movements of the poorer nations to catch up with the richer countries (as would have been to be expected by neo-classical economics), but rather that there are strong cycliclal upward and downward swings which are sometimes very dramatic.

In this respect it is worth also to mention such country as Russia. Measuring by Russian/USSR constant GDP per capita in real purchasing power parity as a percentage of global average constant GDP per capita in real purchasing power parity just shows how dramatic these long-term "Tsunami waves" of global convergence/divergence can be. Thus Russia fell two times within the time-span of 100 years from the comfortable position of the world's income middle class to the level of the world's lower class (Fig. 4.5):

In the present chapter, we have studied the question what this "dual" or even "triple" structure of cycles—global ups and downs, national ups and downs, and

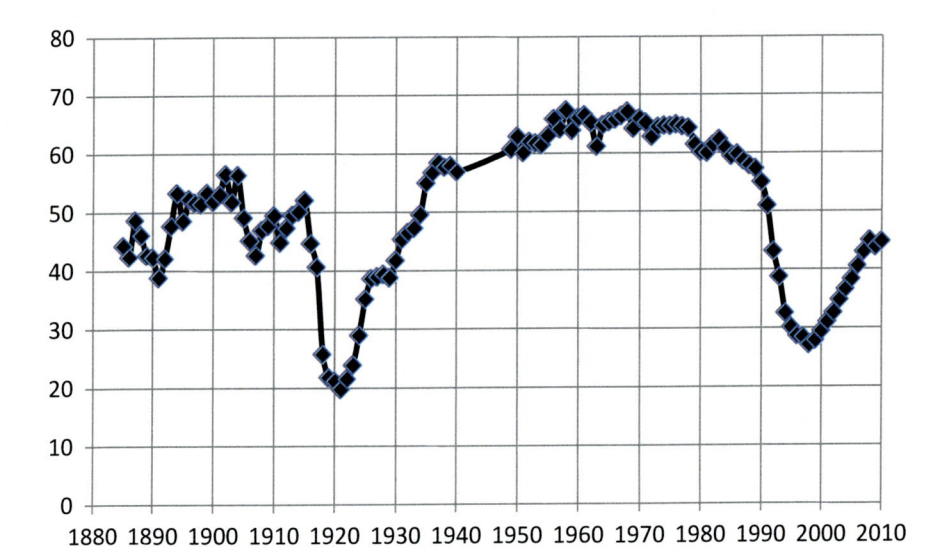

Fig. 4.5 Former USSR/Russian constant GDP per capita in real purchasing power parity as a % of "global average" constant GDP per capita in real purchasing power parity. Time series from 1885 to 2008. *Source*: our own compilations, based on the Maddison data sets, as documented in Bolt and van Zanden, 2013. Calculated from the original data with Microsoft EXCEL 2010. The time series of real GDP per capita is expressed in constant 1990 dollars for the following countries since 1885 (1942–1948 were omitted): Argentina; Australia; Austria; Belgium; Brazil; Canada; Chile; Colombia; Denmark; England/GB/UK; Former USSR/Russia; Finland; France; Germany; Greece; Holland/Netherlands; India; Indonesia (Java before 1880); Italy; Japan; New Zealand; Norway; Peru; Portugal; Spain; Sri Lanka; Sweden; Switzerland; Uruguay; USA; Venezuela. Source: http://www.ggdc.net/maddison/maddison-project/home.htm

ups and downs in the relative position of countries in the global economy—mean for the future of the analysis of international economic relations. We have also shed some light on the question why cycles (Kondratieff or Akamatsu) in some countries are shorter or longer than in other countries. We will provide additional explanations on some issues of this chapter in *Appendix B*.

Chapter 5
Kondratieff Waves and Technological Revolutions

In the present chapter, on the basis of the theory of production principles and production revolutions, we reveal the interrelation between K-waves and major technological breakthroughs in history and make forecasts about features of the sixth Kondratieff wave in the light of the theory of Cybernetic Revolution that, from our point of view, started in the 1950s.

Production Principles, Production Revolutions and K-Waves

According to our theory (Grinin, 2007a, 2007b, 2012b; Grinin & Grinin, 2013, 2014, 2015a, 2015b; Гринин А. и Гринин Л., 2013), the whole historical process can be most adequately divided into four large periods, on the basis of the change of major developmental stages of the world productive forces, which we call production principles. *The production principle is a concept which designates very large qualitative stages of development of the world productive forces in the historical process, whereas every new production principle surpasses the previous one in a fundamental way (in opportunities, scales, productivity, efficiency, product nomenclature,* etc.*).*

We single out four **production principles**:

1. Hunter-Gatherer.
2. Craft-Agrarian.
3. Trade-Industrial.
4. Scientific-Cybernetic.

This chapter has been prepared in cooperation with Anton Grinin. The research has been supported by the Russian Science Foundation (Project No. 15-18-30063).

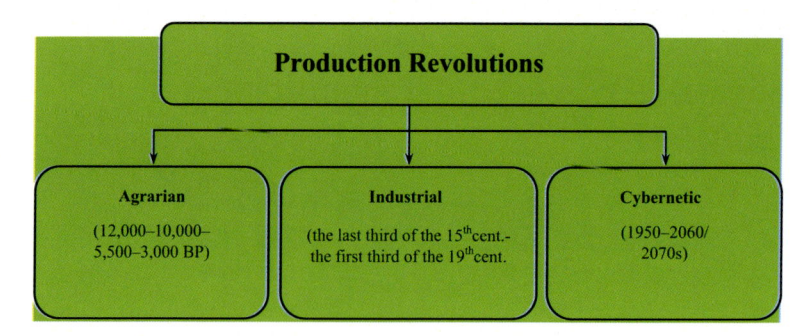

Fig. 5.1 Production revolutions in history

Among all various technological and production changes that took place in history the following three production revolutions had the most comprehensive and far-reaching consequences for society:

1. **Agrarian** or Neolithic Revolution. Its result is the transition to systematic production of food and, on this base, to the complex social division of labor. This revolution is also connected with the use of new power sources (animal power) and materials.
2. **Industrial** Revolution, which resulted in the main production being concentrated in industry and production being carried out by means of machines and division of labor mechanisms. Not only was manual labor replaced by machines, but also biological energy was replaced by water and steam power.
3. **Cybernetic** Revolution which has already led to the emergence of powerful information technologies, and in the future will stimulate transition to the wide use of self-regulating systems.

Each production revolution means the transition to a fundamentally new production system; the beginning of each production revolution marks the borders between corresponding production principles.

Structural Model of Production Revolutions

Within the proposed theory we suggest a fundamentally new idea that each production revolution has an internal cycle of the same type and, in our opinion, includes three phases: two *innovative* (initial and final) and one *modernization* phase (Grinin, 2006, 2007a, 2012a; Grinin L.E. & Grinin A.L., 2013, 2016; Grinin A.L. & Grinin L.E., 2015a, 2015b; Гринин Л.Е. и Гринин А.Л., 2013, 2015б; see Fig. 2). In the initial *innovative* phase, new advanced technologies emerge which eventually spread to other societies and territories. As a result of the final *innovative* phase of a production revolution the new production principle reaches its peak.

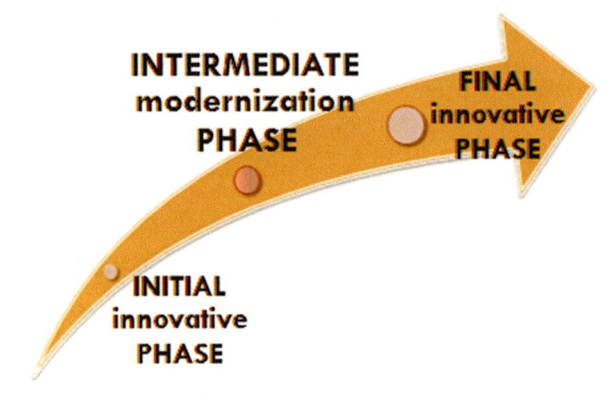

Fig. 5.2 Phases of production revolutions

Table 5.1 Phases of agrarian revolution

Phases	Type	Name	Dates	Changes
Initial	Innovative	Manual agriculture	12,000–9000 BP	Transition to primitive manual (hoe) agriculture and cattle-breeding
Intermediate	Modernization	Diffusion of agriculture	9000–5500 BP	Emergence of new domesticated plants and animals, development of complex agriculture, emergence of a complete set of agricultural instruments
Final	Innovative	Irrigated and plow agriculture	5500–3500 BP	Transition to irrigated agriculture or plow agriculture without irrigation

Between these phases there is the *modernization* phase—a long and very important period of distribution, enrichment, diversification of the production principle's new technologies (which appeared in the initial innovative phase) when conditions for a final innovative breakthrough are created.[1]

Thus, the cycle of each production revolution looks as follows: *the initial innovative phase* (emergence of a new revolutionizing production sector)—*the modernization phase* (diffusion, synthesis and improvement of new technologies)—*the final innovative phase* (when new technologies acquire their mature characteristics).

The Agrarian Revolution was a great breakthrough from hunter-gatherer production principle to farming (about its phases see Table 5.1).

---

[1] For example, in the modernization phase of the Agrarian Revolution local varieties of plants and breeds of animals (borrowed from other places) were created.

Table 5.2 Phases of industrial revolution

Phases	Type	Name of the phase	Dates	Changes
Initial	Innovative	Manufacturing	15th–16th centuries	Development of shipping, technology and mechanization on the basis of water engine, development of manufacture based on the division of labor and mechanization
Intermediate	Modernization	Diffusion of industrial enterprises	17th–early 18th centuries	Formation of complex industrial sector and capitalist economy, increase in mechanization and division of labor
Final	Innovative	Machinery	1730–1830s	Formation of sectors with the machine cycle of production using steam energy

The Industrial Revolution was a great breakthrough from craft-agrarian production principle to machine industry, marked by intentional search for and use of scientific and technological innovations in the production process[2] (about its phases see Table 5.2).

The Cybernetic Revolution is a great breakthrough from industrial production to the production and services based on the operation of self-regulating systems.

Its **initial** phase dates back to the 1950–1990s. The breakthroughs occurred in the spheres of automation, energy production, synthetic materials production, space technologies, exploration of space and sea, agriculture, and especially in the development of electronic control facilities, communication and information. We assume that the **final** phase will begin in the nearest decades, that is in the 2030s or a bit later, and will last until the 2070s.

We denote the initial phase of the Cybernetic Revolution as **a scientific-information** one, and the final—as **a phase of self-regulating systems**. So now we are in its modernization phase which will probably last until the 2030s. This intermediate phase is a period of rapid distribution and improvement of the innovations made at the previous phase (e.g., computers, Internet, cell phones, etc.). The technological and social conditions are also prepared for the future breakthrough. *We suppose that the final phase of the Cybernetic Revolution will lead to the emergence of many various self-regulating systems.*[3]

---

[2] For a detailed application of Production Revolution Theory to the analysis of the Industrial Revolution see our previous monograph in the present Springer series (Grinin & Korotayev, 2015a: 17–84).

[3] For more detail see Grinin, 2007a, 2007b, 2012a; Grinin L.E. & Grinin A.L., 2013, 2014, 2016; Grinin A.L. & Grinin L.E., 2015a, 2015b, 2015c; Гринин, 2006a, 2013a; Гринин А. и Гринин Л., 2013, 2015; Гринин Л. и Гринин А., 2015а, 2015б, 2015в.

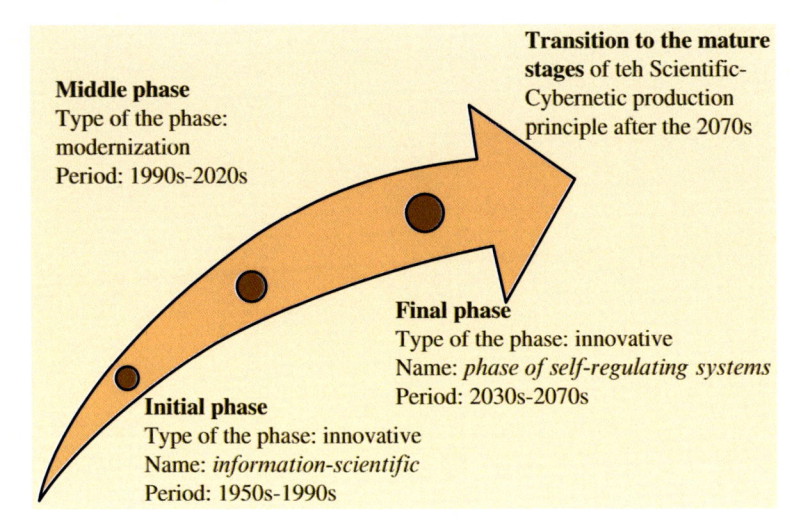

Fig. 5.3 The phases of the Cybernetic Revolution

Middle phase
Type of the phase: modernization
Period: 1990s-2020s

Transition to the mature stages of teh Scientific-Cybernetic production principle after the 2070s

Final phase
Type of the phase: innovative
Name: *phase of self-regulating systems*
Period: 2030s-2070s

Initial phase
Type of the phase: innovative
Name: *information-scientific*
Period: 1950s-1990s

The scheme of the Cybernetic Revolution is presented in Fig. 5.3.

The Structure of the Production Principle

Development of the production principle consists of a period of genesis, growth and maturity in the new forms, systems and paradigms related to the organization of economic management, which far surpass former modes of management in terms of their major parameters.

The principle of production is a six-phase cycle. Its first three stages correspond to three phases of the production revolution. The subsequent three (post-revolutionary) stages are a period of maximizing the potentials of the new forms of production in a structural, systemic, and spatial sense:

1. *The phase of the production revolution's beginning.* A new, not yet developed production principle emerges.
2. *The phase of primary modernization*—diffusion and strengthening of the production principle.
3. *The phase of completion of the production revolution.* The production principle acquires advanced characteristics.
   The last three phases of the production principle characterize its mature features.
4. *The phase of maturity and expansion of the production principle.* In this phase there occurs a wide geographical and sectoral diffusion of new technologies,

Table 5.3 Chronology of the production principle's phases

No	Production principle	1st phase	2nd phase	3rd phase	4th phase	5th phase	6th phase	Total production principle dates and duration
1.	Hunter-Gatherer	40,000–30,000 (38,000–28,000 BC) **10**	30,000–22,000 (28,000–20,000 BC) **8**	22,000–17,000 (20,000–15,000 BC) **5**	17,000–14,000 (15,000–12,000 BC) **3**	14,000–11,500 (12,000–9500 BC) **2.5**	11,500–10,000 (9500–8000 BC) **1.5**	40,000–10,000 (38,000–8000 BC) **30**
2.	Craft-agrarian	10,000–7300 (8000–5300 BC) **2.7**	7300–5000 (5300–3000 BC) **2.3**	5000–3500 (3000–1500 BC) **1.5**	3500–2200 (1500–200 BC) **1.3**	2200–1200 (200 BC –800 AD) **1.0**	800–1430 AD **0.6**	10,000–570 (8000 BC – 1430 AD) **9.4**
3.	Trade-industrial	1430–1600 **0.17**	1600–1730 **0.13**	1730–1830 **0.1**	1830–1890 **0.06**	1890–1929 **0.04**	1929–1955 **0.025**	1430–1955 **0.525**
4.	Scientific-cybernetic	1955–1995/2000 **0.04–0.045**	1995–2030/40 **0.035–0.04**	2030/40–2055/70 **0.025–0.03**	2055/70–2070/90 **0.015–0.02**	2070/90–2080/105 **0.01–0.015**	2080/2105–2090/2115 **0.01**	1955–2090/2115 **0.135–0.160**

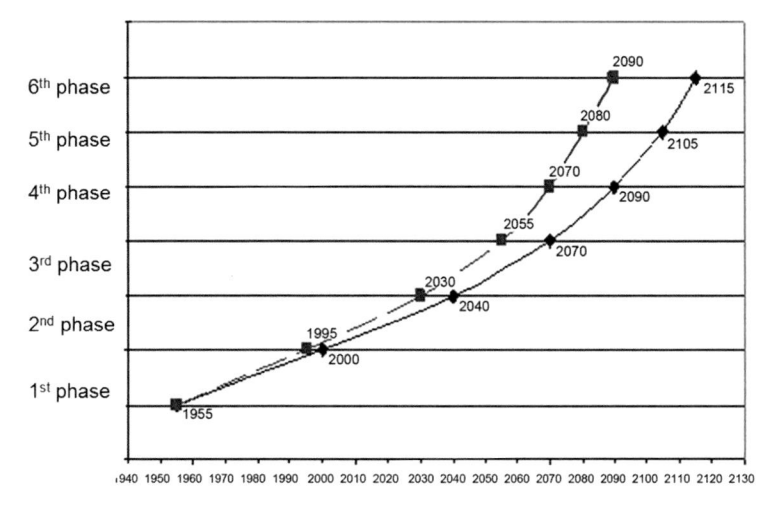

Fig. 5.4 Development of the scientific-cybernetic production principle. *Note:* The *dashed line* depicts one of the scenarios for the expected development of the scientific-cybernetic production principle and corresponds to the dates before the slash in the fifth column of Table 5.1

bringing the production principle to mature forms. A consequence of this phase is vast transformations in the social and economic spheres.

5. *The phase of absolute domination of the production principle.* The final victory of the production principle in the world yields an intensification of technologies, bringing opportunities to the limit of their 'reach,' beyond which crisis features appear.
6. *The stage of non-system phenomena, or a preparatory phase.* The intensification leads to emergence of non-system elements which prepare the birth of a new production principle. Under favorable conditions these elements form a system and in some societies the transition to a new production principle will begin and the cycle will repeat at a new level.

Note: Figures before the brackets—absolute scale (BP), figures in the brackets— BCE. Chronology in the table is simplified (for a more detailed chronology see Grinin, 2006, 2012а; Гринин, 2009д; Гринин и Коротаев, 2013б). The duration of phases (in 1000 years intervals) is marked by the bold-face type. Duration of phases of the scientific-cybernetic production principle is hypothetical. The duration of the scientific-cybernetic production principle is also given in Fig. 5.4

As is clear, the scientific-cybernetic production principle is at the beginning of its development. Only its first phase has been completed, and in the mid-1990s the second phase started up. The second phase is proceeding now and will last till the early 2030s. The third phase is likely to begin approximately in the 2030s or the 2040s. At this particular time the final phase of the Cybernetic Revolution should start. The end of the scientific-cybernetic production principle will fall in the early twenty-second century (for more details see Grinin, 2006).

The Industrial Production Principle Is a Cycle Consisting of K-Waves

We have established a close correlation between production principle cycles and Kondratieff cycles (for more details see Grinin L.E. & Grinin A.L., 2014, 2016; Гринин, 2012б, 2013а; Гринин Л.Е. и Гринин А.Л., 2015б). Taking into account that K-waves arose only with the emergence of a certain level of economic development, we can consider *K-waves as a specific mechanism connected with the emergence and development of the industrial-trade production principle* (see Chap. 1). Given that each new K-wave does not just repeat the wave motion, but is based on a new technological mode, *K-waves can be treated, to a certain extent, as phases of the development of the industrial production principle and the first phases of development of the scientific-cybernetic production principle.*

It has been shown that the first three K-waves are connected with the industrial production principle (Гринин, 2013а; Grinin L.E. & Grinin A.L., 2014, 2016; Гринин, 2012б). Special attention is paid to the correlation between the duration of the industrial production principle phases and the duration of K-wave phases. Certainly, there can be no direct duration equivalence of both K-waves and their phases, on the one hand, and the industrial production principle phases, on the other, due to the different duration of the industrial production principle phases. That is, within the principle of the production's cycle its phases differ in duration, but their duration proportions remain the same in each production principle. We have also found a more complex ratio according to which on average, one K-wave corresponds to one phase of the industrial production principle. In general, we found that three and a half waves coincide with three and a half phases of the industrial principle of production. It is clearly seen in Table 5.4. Such a correlation is not coincidental, as innovative development of the industrial production principle is realized through long Kondratieff cycles which are largely defined by large-scale innovations.

The Cybernetic Revolution, Scientific-Cybernetic Production Principle, the Fourth, Fifth and Sixth K-Waves

The Cybernetic Revolution

The production revolution which began in the 1950s and is still proceeding, has led to a powerful acceleration of scientific and technological progress. Taking into account expected changes in the next 50 years, this revolution deserves to be called **'Cybernetic'** (see our explanation below). The initial phase of this revolution (the 1950s—the 1990s) can be referred to as a **scientific-informational** as it was characterized by the transition to scientific methods of planning, forecasting, marketing, logistics, production managements, distribution and circulation of

Table 5.4 Periods of the industrial production principle and Kondratieff waves

Phases of industrial production principle	The third phase, 1730–1830 ≈**100 years**	The fourth phase, 1830–1890 ≈**60 years**	The fifth phase, 1890–1929 ≈**40 years**	The sixth phase, 1929–1955 ≈**25 years**	Total: ≈225 years, from 1760 **195 years**
The number of the K-wave	Zero (B-phase)/the first wave (A-phase), 1760–1817—about **60 years**	The end of the first wave/the second wave, 1817–1895— more than **75 years**	The third wave, the upward phase, 1895–1928— more than **35 years**	Third wave, the downward phase, 1929–1947— about **20 years**	About **190 years**
The phase of K-wave	B-phase of the zero wave, (we took as the beginning a zero K-wave in which the downward phase coincided with the beginning of the industrial revolution, i.e. the 1760s (as we know, it is downward phases that are especially rich in innovations) 1760–1787	The second half of the downward phase, 1817–1849	The upward phase, 1895–1928	The downward phase, 1929–1947	
The phase of K-wave	The upward phase, 1787–1817	The upward phase, 1849–1873			
The phase of K-wave		The downward phase, 1873–1895			

Note: for the sake of simplicity, we take specific years as dates for the beginning and the end of the periods

resources, and communication. The most radical changes took place in the sphere of informatics and information technologies. The final phase will begin approximately in the 2030s or the 2040s and will last until the 2070s. We called this phase a 'phase of self-regulating systems' (see below). Now we are in the intermediate (modernization) phase which will last until the 2030s (see Fig. 5.3). It is characterized by powerful improvements and the diffusion of innovations made at the initial phase in particular by a wide proliferation of easy-to-handle computers, means of communication, and the formation of a macro-sector of services

Table 5.5 The scientific-cybernetic production principle (initial phases) and Kondratieff waves

Phases of the scientific cybernetic production principle	The first phase (initial phase of the cybernetic revolution) 1955–1995 ≈**40 years**	The second phase (middle phase of the cybernetic revolution) 1995–the 2030s/2040s ≈**35–50 years**	The third phase (final phase of 'self-regulating systems' of the cybernetic revolution) the 2030s/2040s–2055/2070s ≈**25–40 years**	Total: ≈**100–120 years**
K-waves and their phases	The fourth wave, 1947–1982/1991 ≈**35–45 years**	The fifth wave, 1982/1991–the 2020s The beginning of the upward phase of the sixth wave (2020–2050s) ≈**30–40 years**	The sixth wave, 2020–2060/2070s. The end of the upward phase and downward phase (the latter ≈ 2050–2060/2070s) ≈**40–50 years**	About **110–120 years**
K-waves and their phases	Upward phase, 1947–1969/1974s	Downward phase of the fifth wave, 2007–2020s		
K-waves and their phases	Downward phase, 1969/1974–1982/1991	Upward phase of the sixth wave, 2020–2050s		
K-waves and their phases	The fifth wave, 1982/1991–2020s, upward phase, 1982/1991–2007			

among which information and financial services take center stage. At the same time the innovations necessary to start the final phase of the Cybernetic Revolution are being prepared.

Table 5.5 demonstrates the connection between three phases of the scientific-cybernetic production principle (which coincide with three phases of the Cybernetic Revolution) and three Kondratieff waves (the fourth, fifth and sixth). The correlation here is even stronger than between the first three K-waves and the industrial production principle phases, due to the shorter duration of the scientific-cybernetic production principle phases in comparison with those of the industrial production principle.[4]

Taking the theory of production principles into account, we have also revised the sequence of change of the major (leading) production sectors during the change of K-waves (Гринин, 2012б; Grinin L.E. & Grinin A.L., 2014, 2016).[5]

---

[4] The reason for the shorter duration is the general acceleration of historical development.
[5] While compiling this table we have taken into account ideas and works cohering with the theories which explain the nature and pulsation of K-waves by changing of technological systems and/or *techno-economic paradigms*: (Ayres, 2006; Dator, 2006; Dickson, 1983; Dosi, 1984; Freeman, 1987; Freeman & Louçã, 2001; Hirooka, 2006; Kleinknecht, 1981, 1987; Маевский, 1997;

Table 5.6 K-waves, technological modes and leading macrosectors

Kondratieff wave	Date	A new mode	Leading macrosector	Production principle and number of its phase
The first	1780–1840s	The textile industry	Factory (consumer) industry	Industrial, 3
The second	1840–1890s	Railway lines, coal, steel	Mining industry and primary heavy industry and transport	Industrial, 4
The third	1890–1940s	Electricity, chemical industry and heavy engineering	Secondary heavy industry and mechanic engineering	Industrial, 5/6
The fourth	1940-e – the early 1980s	Automobile manufacturing, manmade materials, electronics	General services	Industrial, 6, scientific-cybernetic, 1
The fifth	1980s–~2020	Micro-electronics, personal computers	Highly-qualified services	Scientific-cybernetic, 1/2
The sixth	2020/2030s–2050/2060s	**MANBRIC-technologies** (med-bio-nano-robo-info-cognitive)	Medical human services	Scientific-cybernetic, 2/3

Peculiarities of the Fourth K-Wave in Connection with the Beginning of the Cybernetic Revolution

The fourth K-wave (the second half of the 1940s–1980s) fell on the initial phase of the Cybernetic Revolution (see Table 2.2). The beginning of a new production revolution is a special period which is connected with the fast transition to more advanced technological components of economy. All accumulated innovations and a large number of new innovations generate a new system that has a real synergetic effect. It would appear reasonable that *an upward phase of the K-wave coinciding with the beginning of a production revolution can appear more powerful than A-phases of*

Mensch, 1979; Modelski & Thompson, 1996; Modelski, 2001, 2006; Tylecote, 1992; Глазьев, 1993; Яковец, 2001; Kleinknecht & van der Panne, 2006; Papenhausen, 2008; see also Лазуренко, 1992; Perez, 2002; Глазьев, 2009; Полтерович, 2009).

other K-waves (see, e.g., Figs. 2.5 and 2.8 in *Chap. 2* above).[6] That was the feature of the upswing A-phase of the fourth K-wave (1947–1974) which coincided with the scientific-information phase of the Cybernetic Revolution. As a result a denser than usual cluster of innovations (in comparison with the second, third and fifth waves) was formed during that period. All this also explains why in the 1950s and 1960s the economic growth rates of the World System were higher, than in the A-phases of the third and fifth K-waves. The downswing phase of the fourth K-wave (the 1970s–1980s) in its turn also fell on the last period of the initial phase of the Cybernetic Revolution. This explains in many respects why this downswing phase was shorter than those of the other K-waves.

The Fifth K-Wave and the Delay of the New Wave of Innovations

It was expected that the 1990s and the 2000s would bring a radically new wave of innovations, comparable in their revolutionary character with computer technologies, and therefore capable of creating a new technological mode. Those directions which had already appeared and those which are supposed to become the basis for the sixth K-wave were considered in position to make a breakthrough. However, it was the development and diversification of already existing digital electronic technologies and rapid development of financial technologies that became the basis for the fifth K-wave. Those innovations which were really created during the fifth K-wave as, for example, energy technologies, still have a small share in the general energy, and, above all, they have not developed properly. Some researchers believe that from 1970s up to the present is the time for the decelerating scientific and technological progress (see a discussion on this topic in Brener, 2006; see also Maddison, 2007). Polterovich (Полтерович, 2009) also offer the notion of a technological pause. But, in general, the mentioned technological delay is, in our opinion, insufficiently explained. We believe that taking features of the intermediate modernization phase of a production revolution (i.e., the second phase of the production principle) into account can help explain this. Functionally it is less innovative; rather during this phase earlier innovations become more widely spread and are improved. As regards the 1990s–2020s (the intermediate phase of the Cybernetic Revolution) the question is that the launch of a new innovative breakthrough demands that the developing countries reach the level of the developed ones, and the political component of the world catches up with the economic one; all this requires there to be changes in the structure of societies and global relations (see

---

[6] Therefore, it appears reasonable that the A-phase of the sixth K-wave can also make great progress, as it will coincide with the beginning of the Cybernetic Revolution final phase. Thus, the sixth wave will have a stronger manifestation than the fifth one. We will return to this point below.

Grinin & Korotayev, 2010b). Thus, the delayed *introduction of innovations of the new generation* is explained (Grinin et al., 2016), first, by the fact that the center cannot endlessly surpass the periphery in development, that is the gap between developed and developing countries cannot increase all the time. Secondly, the economy cannot constantly surpass the political and other components, as this causes very strong disproportions and deformations. And the appearance of new general-purpose technologies, certainly, would accelerate economic development and increase disparities. Thirdly, introduction and distribution of the new basic technologies do not occur naturally, but only within the appropriate socio-political environment (see Гринин, 2012б, 2013а; see also Perez, 2002). In order for basic innovations to be suitable for business, structural changes in political and social spheres are necessary, eventually promoting their synergy and wide implementation in the world of business.

Thus, the delay is caused by difficulties of changing political and social institutions on the regional and even global scale, and also (or, perhaps, first of all) within the international economic institutions. The latter can change only as a result of the strong political will of the main players, which is difficult to execute in the framework of the modern political institutions. These institutions rather can change under the conditions of depressive development (and probable aggravation of the foreign relations) compelling them to reorganize and dismantle conventional institutions that are unlikely to be changed under ordinary conditions due to a lack of courage and opportunities (for our vision of the future of the world order see Grinin & Korotayev, 2010b, 2015a; Grinin, Ilyin, & Andreev, 2016; Гринин, 2016).

The above explains as well the reasons of different rates of development between the center and periphery of the World System during the fifth K-wave (for more details see Гринин, 2013а; see also Grinin & Korotayev, 2010a, 2015a). The periphery was expected to catch up with the center due to the faster rates of its development and slowdown of the center development. However, one should not expect continuous crisis-free development of the periphery—a crisis will come later and probably in other forms (see about ups and downs on this way in *Chap. 4*). Without a slow-down of the development of the periphery and serious changes, full harmonization of the economic and political component will not happen. Consequently, it might be supposed that in the next decade (approximately by 2020–2025) the growth rates of the peripheral economies can also slow down, and internal problems will aggravate that and can stimulate structural changes in the peripheral countries, thus also increasing international tension. The world order has already begun to change, and it will continue to change over the next 10–20 years and some visible results of this change may appear by the start of the new K-wave. We have called this change "the World System reconfiguration" (see Grinin & Korotayev, 2012a, 2015a: 159–166; Гринин, Исаев и Коротаев, 2016). Thus, we suppose that in the next 10–15 years the world will face serious and painful changes. The World System reconfiguration processes further explain the reasons for the very turbulent processes observed in the recent years, as well as increased tensions in the last 2–3 years in the world (see the next chapter for more detail on the reconfiguration processes)

Characteristics of the Cybernetic Revolution

What Are Self-Regulating Systems and Why Are They So Important?

Self-regulating systems are systems that can regulate themselves, responding in a pre-programmed and intelligent way to the feedback from the environment. These are the systems that operate either with a small input from human or completely without human intervention. Today there are many self-regulating systems, for example, the artificial Earth satellites, pilotless planes, navigation systems laying the route for a driver, self-driving cars. Another good example is life-support systems (such as medical ventilation apparatus or artificial hearts). They can regulate a number of parameters, choose the most suitable mode of operation and detect critical situations. There are also special programs that determine the value of stocks and other securities, react to price changes, buy and sell them, carry out thousands of operations in a day and fix a profit. A great number of self-regulating systems have been created but they are mostly technical and informational systems (as robots or computer programs). During the final phase of the Cybernetic Revolution there will be a lot of self-regulating systems connected with biology and bionics, physiology and medicine, agriculture and environment. The number of such systems as well as their complexity and their autonomy will dramatically increase. These systems will also significantly reduce energy and resource consumption. Human life will become organized to a greater extent by such self-regulating systems (for example, by monitoring health, daily regimens, regulating or recommending levels of personal exertion, having control over the patients' condition, prevention of illegal actions, etc.).

Thus, we designate the modern revolution 'Cybernetic,' because its main sense is the wide creation and distribution of self-regulating autonomous systems. Cybernetics, as is well-known, is a science of regulatory systems. Its main principles are quite suitable for the description of self-regulating systems (see, e.g., Ashby, 1956; Beer, 1967, 1994; Foerster & Zopf, 1962; Теслер, 2004; Umpleby & Dent, 1999; Wiener, 1948).

As a result, the opportunity to control various natural, social and production processes without direct human intervention (that is impossible or extremely limited now) will increase. In the fourth phase (*of maturity and expansion*) of the scientific cybernetic production principle (the 2070s and 2080s) the achievements of the Cybernetic Revolution will become quite systemic and wide-scale in its final phase (for more detail see Гринин, 2006а).

Below we single out the most important characteristics of the Cybernetic Revolution. One can observe them today, but they will be realized in their mature and mass forms only in the future. These features are closely interconnected and corroborating each other (see Grinin A.L. & Grinin L.E., 2015a, 2015b, 2015c; Grinin L.E. & Grinin A.L., 2016; Гринин Л. Е. и Гринин А. Л., 2015а, 2015б, 2015в; Гринин А. и Гринин Л., 2013, 2015 for more detail).

Below we enumerate the most important characteristics and trends of the Cybernetic Revolution and its technologies. These features are closely interconnected and support each other.

The Most Important Characteristics and Trends of the Cybernetic Revolution

1. Increases in the amount of information and complications in the analysis of the systems (including the ability of systems for independent communication and interaction);
2. Sustainable development of the system of regulation and self-regulation;
3. Mass use of artificial materials which previously lacked the appropriate architectural properties;
4. Qualitatively increasing the controllability a) of systems and processes that vary in their constitution (including living material); and b) of new levels of managing the organization of matter (up to sub-atomic and using tiny particles as building blocks);
5. Miniaturization and microtization[7] as a trend of the constantly decreasing size of particles, mechanisms, electronic devices, implants, etc.;
6. Resource and energy saving in every sphere;
7. Individualization as one of the most important technological trends.
8. Implementation of smart technologies and a trend towards humanization of their functions (use of the common language, voice, etc.);
9. Control over human behaviour and activity to eliminate the negative influence of the so-called human factor.[8]

The Characteristics of the Technologies of the Cybernetic Revolution

1. The transformation and analysis of information as an essential part of technologies;
2. The increasing connection between the technological systems and environment;
3. A trend towards autonomation and automation of control is observed together with the increasing level of controllability and self-regulation of systems;
4. The capabilities of materials and technologies to adjust to different objectives and tasks (smart materials and technologies) as well as capabilities for *choosing optimal regimes in the context of certain goals and tasks*;
5. A large-scale synthesis of the materials and characteristics of the systems of different nature (e.g., of animate and inanimate nature).

---

[7] See: http://www.igi-global.com/dictionary/microtization/18587.
[8] For example, the control of human insufficient attention in order to prevent dangerous situations (e.g., in transport) as well as to prevent human beings from using means of high-risk when they are in an unlawful or incompetent state (e.g., not allowing a person to drive a motor vehicle while under the influence of alcohol or drugs).

6. The integration of machinery, equipment and hardware with technology (know-how and knowledge of the process) into a unified technical and technological system[9];
7. Self-regulating systems (see below) will become the major component of technological processes. That is the reason why the final (forthcoming) phase of the Cybernetic Revolution is (or should) be called **the epoch of self-regulating systems** (see above).

Various directions of development should generate a system cluster of innovations.[10]

Medicine as a Sphere of the Initial Technological Breakthrough and the Emergence of MANBRIC-technology Complex

It is worth remembering that the Industrial Revolution began in a rather narrow area of cotton textile manufacturing and was connected with the solution of quite concrete problems—at first, liquidation of the gap between spinning and weaving, and then, after increasing weavers' productivity, searching for ways to mechanize spinning. However, the solution of these narrow tasks caused an explosion of innovations conditioned by the existence of a large number of the major elements of machine production (including abundant mechanisms, primitive steam-engines, quite a high volume of coal production, etc.) which gave an impulse to the development of the Industrial Revolution. In a similar way, we assume that the Cybernetic Revolution will start first in a certain area.

Given the general vector of scientific achievements and technological development and taking into account that a future breakthrough area should be highly commercially attractive and have a wide market, we predict that the final phase (of self-regulating systems) of this revolution will begin somewhere at the intersection of medicine and a number of other technologies (we will provide reasons for this statement below and in *Chap. 6*). Certainly, it is almost impossible to predict the concrete course of innovations. However, the general vector of breakthrough can be defined as a rapid growth of *opportunities for correction or even modification of the human biological nature*. In other words, it will be possible to extend our opportuni-

---

[9] During the Industrial Epoch these elements existed separately: technologies were preserved on paper or in the engineer's minds. At present, thanks to informational and other technologies the technological constituent fulfils the managing function facilitating the path to the epoch of self-regulating systems.

[10] For example, resource and energy saving can be carried out via choosing optimal modes by the autonomous systems that fulfil specific goals and tasks and *vice versa*, the choice of an optimum mode will depend on the level of energy and materials consumption, and a consumer's budget. Or, the opportunities of self-regulation will allow choosing a particular decision for the variety of individual tasks, orders and requests (*e.g.*, with 3D printers and choosing of an individual program as the optimal one).

ties to alter a human body, perhaps, to some extent, its genome; to widen sharply our opportunities of minimally invasive influence and operations instead of the modern surgical ones; to use extensively means of cultivating separate biological materials, bodies or their parts and elements for regeneration and rehabilitation of an organism, and also artificial analogues of biological material (bodies, receptors), etc.

This will make it possible to *radically expand the opportunities to prolong life and improve its biological quality*. It will be the technologies intended for common use in the form of a mass market service. Certainly, it will take a rather long period (about two or three decades) from the first steps in that direction (in the 2030–2040s) to their common use.

The drivers of the final phase of the Cybernetic Revolution will be medical technologies, additive manufacturing (3D printers), nano- and bio-technologies, robotics, IT, cognitive sciences, which will together form a sophisticated system of self-regulating production. We can denote this complex as MANBRIC-technologies.[11] As is known, with respect to the sixth technological paradigm (known also as the sixth technological system or style) there is a widely used idea connected with the notion of NBIC[12]-technology (or NBIC-convergence) (see Акаев, 2012; Bainbridge & Roco, 2005; Dator, 2006; Ковальчук, 2011; Lynch, 2004). There are also some researchers (e.g., Jotterand, 2008) who see in this role another set of technological directions—GRAIN (Genomics, Robotics, Artificial Intelligence, Nano-technology). However, we believe that this set will be larger. And medical technologies will be its integrating part.

Thus, we maintain the following:

1. Medicine will be the first sphere to start the final phase of the Cybernetic Revolution, but, later on, self-regulating systems development will cover the most diverse areas of production, services and life.
2. We treat medicine in a broad sense, because it will include (and already actively includes) for its purposes a great number of other scientific branches: e.g., the use of robots in surgery and care of patients, information technologies in remote medical treatment, neural interfaces for treatment of mental illness and brain research; gene therapy and engineering, nanotechnologies for creation of artificial immunity and biochips which monitor organisms; new materials for growing artificial organs and many other things to become a powerful sector of economy.
3. The medical sphere has unique opportunities to combine the above mentioned technologies into a single system.
4. There are also some demographic and economic reasons why the phase of self-regulating systems will start in medicine:

---

[11] The order of the letters in the acronym does not reflect our understanding of the relative importance of areas of the complex. For example, biotechnologies will be more important than nanotechnologies, let alone additive manufacturing. The order is determined simply by the convenience of pronunciation.

[12] Nano-Bio-Info-Cogno.

- Increase in average life expectancy and population ageing will favor not only the growth of medical opportunities to maintain health, but also allow the extension of working age, as population ageing will be accompanied by shortages in the working-age population;
- People, in general, are always ready to spend money on health and beauty. However, the growth of the world middle class and the cultural standard of people implies much greater willingness and solvency in this terms;
- Medical corporations usually do not impede technological progress, but, on the contrary, are interested in it.

Thus, today medicine is a very important sector of the economy, and tomorrow it will become even more powerful.

In the present monograph we confined ourselves to a short description of the spheres which represent a new, in a broad sense, medical system or realm of medicine, creating a complex of technologies and their application with other perspective directions.

In the next chapter we will consider the future development of medical technologies in connection with the global ageing.[13]

---

[13] It should be noted that Leo Nefiodow has been writing about health as the leading technology of the sixth Kondratieff wave for a long time (Nefiodow, 1996; Nefiodow & Nefiodow, 2014a, 2014b). He explains that health is much more than medicine and includes mental, psychosocial, environmental and spiritual aspects. He believes that medicine covers only a small part of the health problems we face today. We agree that health is more than medicine. However, we regard medicine as the most important business sphere connected with health care (note that the overwhelming majority of researchers in the health area work with medical technology). We also agree with Nefiodow that business and profit far from always serve people. But we do not know any power beside medical business which has opportunities (in co-operation with such state agencies as the National Institutes of Health in the USA) to finance research and development in this area, to elaborate new ways to fight mortal diseases, to invest in prolongation of life expectancy. In Nefiodow's opinion, health area covers not only psychotherapeutic, psychological and psychiatric services, but also numerous measures of health improvement that, using his terms, will reduce social entropy. The problems with this argument, based on reducing social entropy (e.g., corruption, small and large crime, drug addiction, lack of moral guide, divorces, violence, etc.), is that social entropy (as Nefiodow himself points out) has always existed in society. Social changes can be really extremely important for the creation of starting conditions for a long-term upswing in reducing social entropy (see Grinin L. & Grinin A. 2014 for more detail). However, it is production and/or commercial technologies that represent the driving force of the K-Wave upswing phases. There is one more important point. The Nefiodows believe that it is biotechnologies that will become an integrating core of the new technological system. However, we suppose that the leading role of biotechnologies will be, first of all, in their possibility to solve the major medical problems. That is why it makes sense to speak about medical technologies as the core of a new technological paradigm. Besides, we forecast a more important role of nanotechnology than the Nefiodows do (Nefiodow & Nefiodow, 2014b: Chap. 2). Nanotechnologies will be of great importance in terms of the development of bio- and medical technologies (they are supposed to play a crucial role in the fight against cancer; at the same time nanotechnologies will play a crucial role in other spheres too, in particular in energy and resource saving).

Chapter 6
Afterword: New Kondratieff Wave and Forthcoming Global Social Transformation

This final chapter analyzes some aspects of the population ageing and its important consequences for particular societies and the whole World System with respect to the new K-wave and the technologies that characterize it. The population ageing is important for both the World System core and many countries of the global periphery and it has turned into a global issue. In the forthcoming decades the ageing of the populations is likely to become one of the most important social processes influencing the future society characteristics and the direction of technological development.

On the basis of this analysis, we can conclude that the future technological breakthrough is likely to take place in the 2030s (which we define as the final phase of the Cybernetic Revolution). In the 2020s and 2030s we will expect the upswing of the forthcoming sixth Kondratieff wave, which will introduce the sixth technological paradigm (system). All those revolutionary technological changes will be connected, first of all, with breakthroughs in medicine and related technologies. We also present our ideas about the financial instruments that can help to solve the problem of pension provision for an increasing elderly population in the developed countries. We think that a more purposeful use of pension funds' assets together with the allocation of funds (with necessary guarantees of the latter) into education and upgrading skills of young people in the World System periphery, perhaps, can partially solve the indicated problem in the developed states.

Human capital is one of the most important drivers of economic development whose contribution to the growth of production and innovations is constantly increasing. According to the OECD definition, *human capital* is 'knowledge, skills, competencies and attributes embodied in individuals that facilitate the creation of personal, social and economic well-being' (OECD, 2001: 18; see also Капелюшников, 2012: 6–7). Human capital is central to debates about welfare, education, health care, and retirement. However, we think that the latter (i.e., retirement) is less frequently debated than it should be. Meanwhile, in the West the rapid ageing of the population

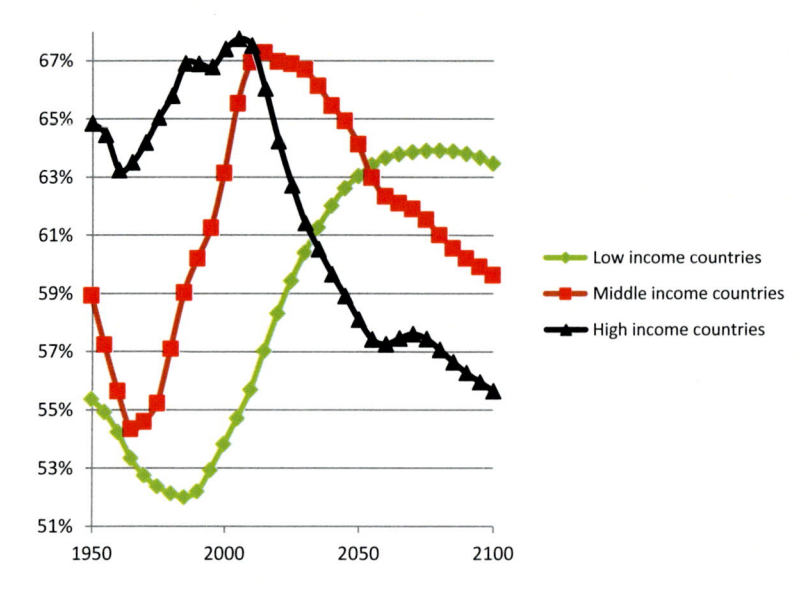

Fig. 6.1 The dynamics of the working age population percentage in the total population, 1950–2015, according to the UN medium forecast to 2100. (*Source*: UN Population Division, 2016)

actually devalues the national human capital in every developed country. There are certain reasons for expecting that if the ageing generation is not substituted by a more numerous generation of young professionals, the share of the elderly population will increase and the human capital is likely to decline.

Thus, while the human capital as well as its contribution to the economic development is significantly larger in the core of the World System than in the global periphery, the situation is different in respect of the demographic structure of human capital. The global periphery's situation is significantly better at this point, and this can increasingly contribute to the economic competition between the World System's core and its periphery. We should also take into consideration the fact that the generation of highly educated pensioners in the countries of the core has increased the demands on society and they play a more active political role than the generation of uneducated 'old men' in the global periphery. While the World System's core has apparently depleted its demographic dividend, many countries of the global periphery, in fact, are only in the process of its accumulation. And consequently, in this context they can get the most important advantage in the coming decades (see Fig. 6.1).

This also confirms the idea of growing convergence between the developed and developing countries that we adhere to, as the current differences in the demographic structure and potentialities of the demographic dividend will contribute to the fact that at least in the next two decades the developing countries' growth rates will be on average higher than those of the developed countries, although this process can proceed with certain interruptions (see *Chaps. 4* and *5*).[1]

---

[1] See also Grinin & Korotayev, 2014a, 2014b, 2015a; Коротаев и Божевольнов, 2010; Korotayev & de Munck, 2013, 2014; Коротаев и Халтурина, 2009; Korotayev & Zinkina, 2014; Korotayev,

Problems of Population Ageing and Their Possible Solutions

The ageing population (and an increasing number of disabled people) as well as the change of the age structure (see Figs. 6.2, 6.3, 6.4, and 6.5) alongside with forthcoming progress in medicine, innovation technologies, and increasing life expectancy in the developed countries will bring great problems associated with (a) the scarcity of labor resources; and (b) problems of pension support for the older population.

In some countries they are already today rather acute, but they are to become much more pressing.

As shown above, an especially rapid global increase in the number of age persons above retirement-age is expected to come in the next 20 years—their number will actually double during a short historical period, thus it will increase by almost 600 million and the total number will considerably exceed a billion.

However, a massive acceleration will be observed in particular of people aged 80 years or more. While by 2050 the number of persons of retirement age will approximately double, the number of elderly people aged 80 years or more will practically quadruple, and in comparison with 1950 their number by 2075 will increase almost by 50 times (see Fig. 6.5):

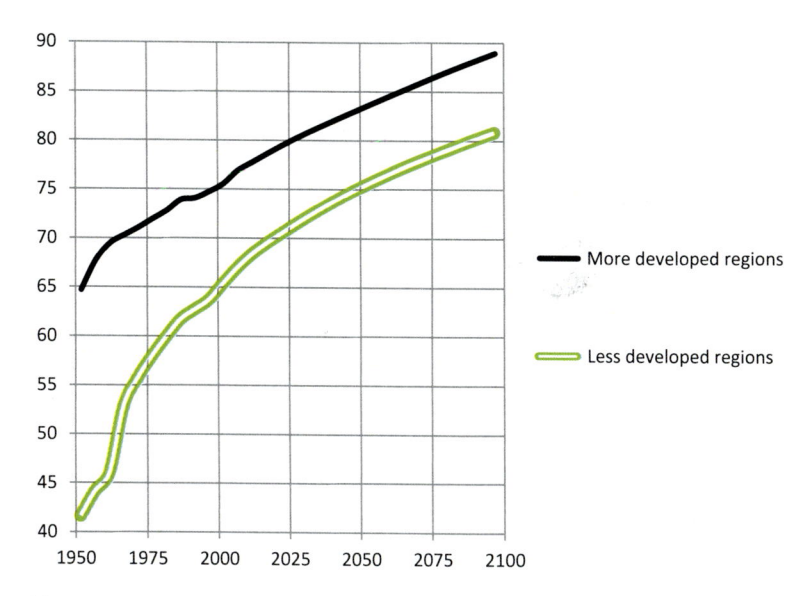

Fig. 6.2 Dynamics of the life expectancy at birth (years) in the World System core and global periphery, 1950–2015, the UN medium forecast to 2050. (*Source*: UN Population Division 2015)

Goldstone, & Zinkina, 2015; Коротаев, Малков et al., 2010; Коротаев, Халтурина, Малков et al., 2010; Korotayev, Zinkina et al., 2011a, 2011b, 2012; Малков, Коротаев и Божевольнов, 2010; Малков, Божевольнов, Халтурина et al., 2010; Халтурина и Коротаев, 2010; Гринин, 2013б, 2013в, 2013г, 2014, 2015; Zinkina et al., 2014.

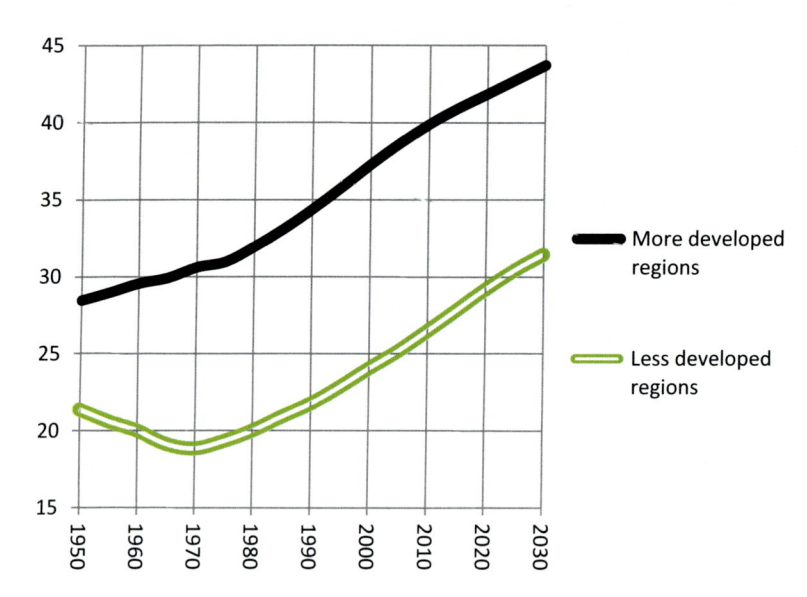

Fig. 6.3 Dynamics of the median age of population (years) in the World System core and global periphery, 1950–2015, with the medium forecast of the UN till 2030. (*Source*: UN Population Division, 2016). We would like to remind the reader that if the median age of population of a given country equals, for example, 40 years, it means that half of the population of this country is younger than 40 years, and the other one is older

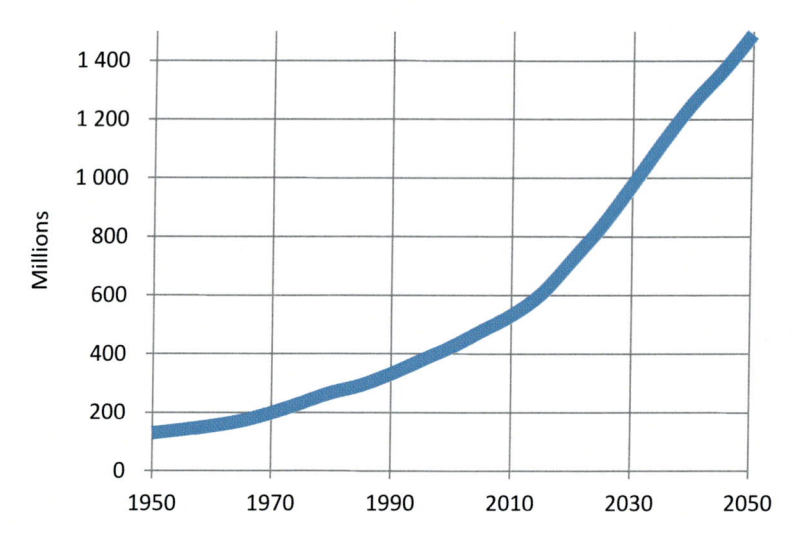

Fig. 6.4 Increasing number of persons of retirement age (over 65), 1950–2015, with the UN medium forecast till 2050. (*Source*: UN Population Division, 2016)

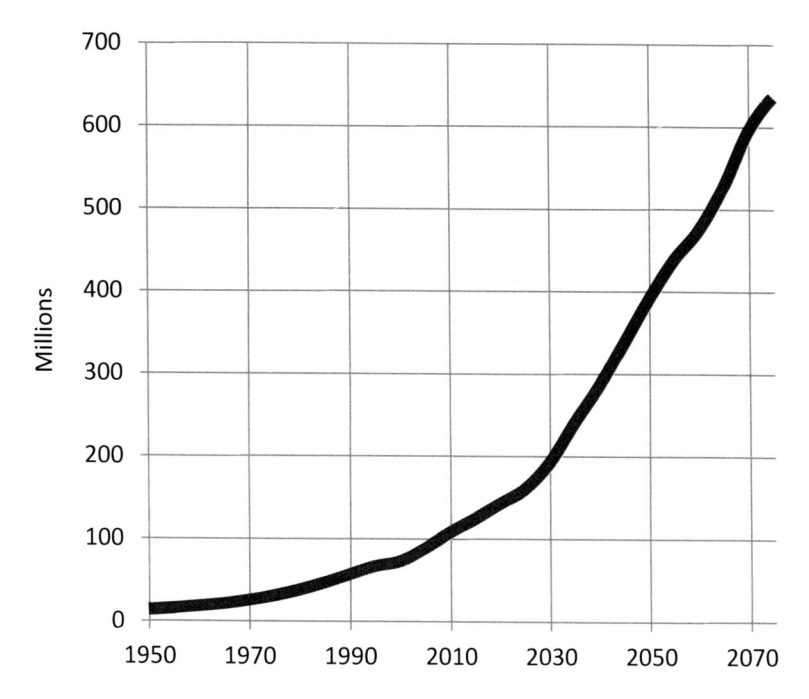

Fig. 6.5 Increase of global number of elderly people (aged 80 years+), 1950–2015, with the UN average forecast till 2075. (*Source*: UN Population Division, 2016)

The countries of the Global North will face particular difficulties in the next 20–30 years due to a rapid increase in the number of people above retirement-age, a development that is accompanied by an accelerated reduction of the active working age population, and in 20 years the number of the former will exceed the number of the latter (see Fig. 6.6).

As one can notice, the ratio of older people to working age adults will increase. This will lead very likely to a decline in living standards and to increasing tensions between generations.

One should keep in mind that the older population will form a major part of voters, thus urging politicians to take them into more seriously into account. Besides, the highly educated generation of pensioners in the core of the World System has certain demanding social requirements and they are more politically active than the generation of uneducated old people in the global periphery. The transition to such a sort of gerontocracy also poses many other threats to a society and to its homogeneity because older people are more apt to conservatism and are less inclined to purchase expensive products, novelties and property, and this may reduce the focus on innovation and lead to considerable change of the contemporary economic model based on the expansion of consumerism. In particular, the ageing population is in Japan one of the reasons of the current deflationary trend (for more details see Гринин и Коротаев, 2014в, 2015б).

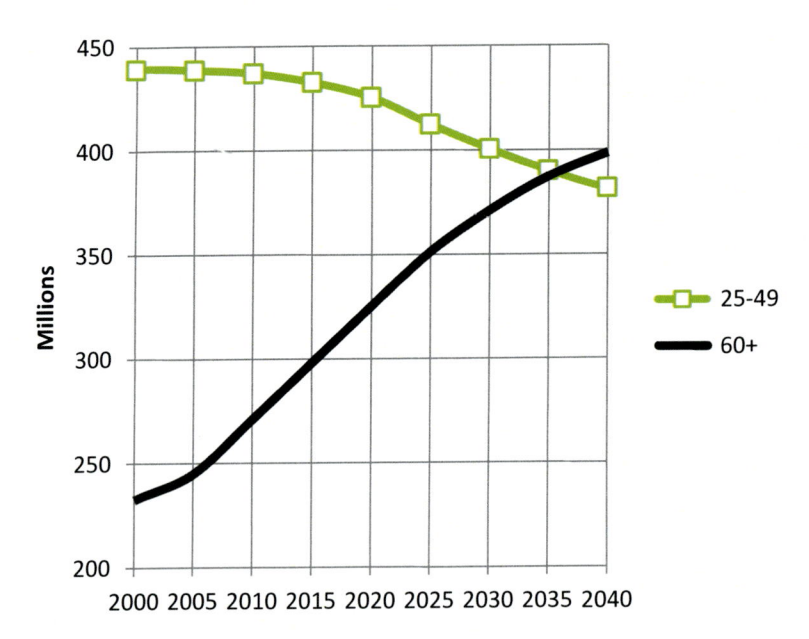

Fig. 6.6 Dynamics of active working-age (25–49 years) population and number of persons of retirement age (aged over 60) in the World System core (More developed countries/regions according to the UN classification), in millions, 2000–2015, with the medium forecast of the UN for the period till 2040. *Source:* (UN Population Division, 2016)

In theoretical terms, it is possible to distinguish the following possibilities as candidates for solving the specified problems (here we suppose that all those solutions will be applied, while none of them can solve the problem comprehensively):

1. To increase the number of immigrants in the developed countries. Still the opportunities of this pattern are to a large extent depleted and besides, it leads to the erosion of the society's major ethno-cultural basis (today we face serious challenges in this direction).
2. To raise the retirement age and the real physical and mental potential of elderly people together with active rehabilitation of the disabled people through new medical technologies (see *Chap. 5* above; for more detail see Grinin A.L. & Grinin L.E., 2015a; Grinin L.E. & Grinin A.L., 2016; Гринин Л. и Гринин А., 2015а, 2015б, 2015в). Against the background of the forthcoming revolution in medical and rehabilitating technologies this looks like an important (although insufficient) resource.
3. The development of labor-saving technologies, in particular robot techniques for nursing, as well as elder and disabled people care (see Ibidem). This will allow a partial reduction of expenses for care and different services, but it can hardly bring a complete solution of the problem of scarce resources.
4. Finally, the development of the financial system opens another path to the solution of problems with the pension system. The population ageing is directly related to the financial system not only within national systems, but within the

global financial system as well. Due to the increasing number of retirees the pension savings have become not simply important, but essential to a certain extent. Besides, we should note that, on the one hand, today pension and other social funds are not isolated only within a framework of national system, but make an important component of the world finance in the long run. On the other hand, stable pension system substantially depends on the stable and efficient global financial system, even to a greater extent than on the national one.

In the present chapter we will first consider interconnected directions 2 and 3 in the solution of the problem of global population ageing and then we will pass to consideration of the fourth (financial) way.

Global Population Ageing and the Sixth Technological Paradigm

As we have already explained in the previous chapter, the Cybernetic Revolution is a great breakthrough from industrial production to production and services based on the operation of self-regulating systems. Let us recollect that its **initial** phase dates back to the 1950–1990s. The breakthrough occurred in different spheres (see *Chap. 5*), especially in automation, in development of electronic control facilities, in communication and information technologies. We assume that the **final** phase will begin in the nearest decades, that is in the 2030s or a bit later, and will last until the 2070s. It *will lead to the emergence of many various self-regulating systems* (for more detail see Grinin & Grinin, 2015b; Гринин, 2006а, 2009д, 2012б, 2013а; Гринин А. и Гринин Л., 2013, 2015; Гринин Л. и Гринин А., 2015а, 2015в). We assume that this technological breakthrough will be at first connected with a breakthrough in the field of new medical (and related) technologies. And just the increasing process of population ageing (as we will show below) will become one of the most important reasons of development of the final phase of the Cybernetic Revolution.

This phase, according to our forecasts, will be imposed on the sixth Kondratieff wave (which will probably last from the 2020s to the 2060s). Therefore, the sixth technological paradigm (known also as technological system or style) will be connected with major transformations of the Cybernetic Revolution. As we have mentioned in the previous chapter, the widespread ideas that the basis of the sixth technological paradigm will be formed by the NBIC technologies (or NBIC-convergence), which are nano-bio-information and cognitive technologies (see Акаев, 2010, 2011; Dator, 2006; Lynch, 2004; Прайд и Коротаев, 2008; see also Fukuyama, 2002) are only partially true. We believe that the basis of the sixth technological paradigm will be significantly wider. We named (see *Chap. 5* above) the system of innovative technologies of the sixth K-wave and the final phase of the Cybernetic Revolution with an acronym MANBRIC (i.e. *medical, additive-, nano-, bio-, robo-, info-, and cogno-technologies).* They will become the leading areas in which technological trends develop *and will create a complex system of self-regulated production.* It makes sense to speak about medical sphere as the central element of the new technological system. Medicine more than any other field provides unique opportunities for merging all these new technologies into a single system. Besides, a number of demographic and economic reasons explain why in particular in medicine the transition to the new technological paradigm should start (see also *Chap. 5*).

This will be supported by particularly an advantageous situation developing by 2030 in economy, demography, culture, a standard of living, etc.—these will define a huge need for scientific and technological breakthrough. By *advantageous* situation we do not mean that everything will be perfectly good in the economy; just on the contrary, everything will be not as good as it could be. Advantageous conditions will be created because reserves and resources for prolonging previous trends will be exhausted, and at the same time the requirements of currently developed and developing societies will increase. Consequently, one will search for developmental new patterns.

Let us describe the background.

- By this time the problem of an ageing population will be completely obvious (for more detail see the previous section). Moreover, this issue can become fatal for democracies in developed countries (because the main electorate will be represented by elderly cohorts, and also the generation gap will increase; see also Fukuyama, 2002). In addition, the problem of population ageing will become more acute in a number of developing countries, for example, in China and even in India to a certain extent (about ageing in Asia see Park & Shin, 2015).
- Pension payments will become a pressing problem (as the number of retirees per an employee will increase) and at the same time the scarcity of labor resources will increase, which is already felt strongly in a number of countries including Russia (for more detail see Arkhangelsky et al., 2015; Архангельский et al., 2014; Grinin & Korotayev, 2010b, 2015b; Коротаев и Божевольнов, 2012; Коротаев, Халтурина, и Божевольнов, 2011; Коротаев, Зинькина et al., 2015; Гринин и Коротаев, 2015б).[2] Thus, *the problem of scarce labor and pension contributions will have to be solved in such a way that people physically could work for ten, fifteen and even more years (certainly here we can also face a number of social problems)*. This also implies the disabled people's adaptation for fuller involvement into labor processes made possible by new technical and technological means and achievements in medicine (see Гринин Л. и Гринин А., 2015б for more detail).
- Simultaneously, by this time, the birth rate in many developing countries will significantly drop (for example, such developing countries as China, Iran, or Thailand already experience below-replacement fertility). Therefore, the respective governments will begin (and some of them have already started) worrying generally not about the problem of restriction of population growth, but about promotion of population growth and the health of the population.
- About 10 % of the GDP (and in a number of developed countries even more than 10 %, as, for example, in the USA—17 % [calculated on the basis of World Bank,

---

[2] About the influence of ageing on growth rates see Goldstone, 2015; Park & Shin, 2015.

2016 data]) stems from medical services. The ageing population will contribute to a significant increase of the volume.[3]
- The development in the Third World countries leads to the growth of a vast stratum of the middle class, while poverty and illiteracy are reduced. As a result, the emphasis of these countries' efforts will shift from the elimination of unbearable living conditions to the improvement of the quality of life, health care, etc. Thus, large opportunities open up for the development of medicine which will get additional funds.

So by the 2030s, the number of middle-aged and elderly people will increase; economy will desperately need additional labor resources while the state will be interested in increasing the working ability of elderly people, whereas the population of wealthy and educated people will grow in a rather significant way. In other words, the unique conditions for the stimulation of business, science and the state to make a breakthrough in the field of medicine will emerge, and *just these unique conditions are necessary to start the innovative phase of revolution!*

It is extremely important to note that *enormous financial resources will be accumulated for the technological breakthrough, such as: the pension money of which the volume will increase at high rates; spending of governments on medical and social needs; growing expenses of the ageing population on health (related) services, and also on health services obtained by a growing world middle-class. All this can provide initial large investments, an appeal of high investment of respective venture projects and long-term high demand for innovative products, thus a full set of favorable conditions for a powerful technological breakthrough will become available.*

In the context of the problem of an ageing population we will consider some characteristics of the global financial system.

The Crisis and the Characteristics of the Financial System

The 2008 crisis and subsequent years aggravated both financial and economic, as well as some global social problems. One of the most important problems among them is the problem of secure social guarantees for the rapidly ageing population of the core of the World System. In each country the security of these guarantees is connected with stability of the world financial system.

Let us recollect some important reasons of the global financial economic crisis:

---

[3] Some studies find that health care costs of patients aged 75–84 years are almost twice as large as the costs of 65–74 years old patients; and the expenses on patients of the 85+ age group increase by more than three times in comparison with the latter (Alemayehu & Warner, 2004; Fuchs, 1998). The cost of home care and short-term stay in the hospital also to a large degree depends on the patients' age (Liang et al., 1996).

- Random and extremely rapid development of new financial centers and financial flows;
- Non-transparency of many financial instruments, which led to the actual concealment of risks and their global underestimation;
- An excessive level of public debt in many countries of the World System's core and the global periphery combined with ineffective use of credits.

As has already been mentioned above in *Chap. 3*, modern financial instruments are fundamentally deleterious and only cause diverse troubles and that they are only beneficial to financiers and speculators. Thus, it would hardly be an exaggeration to maintain that the global crisis, as well as other events, demonstrated, in an especially salient way, the necessity for major changes of the system of regulation of international economic activities and the movements of world financial flows.

Nevertheless, we believe that it is reasonable to speak not only about the negative role of the world financial flows. On the whole, new financial technologies decrease the risks in a rather effective way and expand opportunities to attract and accumulate enormous capitals, involve actors, and penetrate markets.

The positive effects of the new financial technologies consist of the following:

1. A powerful expansion of the range of financial instruments and products, which leads to the expanding opportunities to choose the most convenient financial instrument.
2. The standardization of financial instruments and products provides a considerable time-saving for those who use financial instruments; it makes it possible to purchase financial securities without a detailed analysis of particular stocks; this leads to an increase in the number of participants by an order of magnitude.
3. The institutionalization of the ways to minimize different individual and corporate risks. Some financial innovations and new regulations help to minimize both the individual/corporate risks of unfulfilled deals, decreasing prices, and also of bankruptcies in the framework of some stock markets.
4. The increase in the number of participants and centers for the trade of financial instruments. Modern financial instruments have made it possible to include a great number of people via various special programs, mediators, and structures.

We also suppose that new financial technologies and the modern financial sector have also got such important positive functions as the 'insurance' of social guaranties at the global scale. The matter is that the rejection of the gold standard resulted in the shift of the function of the protection of savings from an 'independent' guarantor (i.e., precious metals) to the state. However, there was no state left for the capital owners to entirely rely on as on a perfectly secure guarantor.

The absence of secure guarantees **is especially important in terms of the ways to preserve pension and other social funds**.

The sharp increase in the quantity of capitals, the necessity to protect them against consequences of inflation and to find their profitable application are objectively pushing the financial market actors towards searching for new forms of financial activities. Generally, the faster the movements and transformations of financial objects are, the better is the preservation of capitals.

Another important point is the distribution of risks on the global scale. We observe growing opportunities to distribute risks among a larger number of participants and countries, to transform a relatively small number of initial financial objects into a very large number of financial products. This makes it possible to achieve the maximum diversification by allowing people to choose convenient forms of financial products and to change them whenever necessary.

The next point is the growth of financial specialization (including various forms of deposit insurance) that supports diversification and the possibilities for expansion.

Pensioners and Pension Funds

In 2010, there was one pensioner per four working-age adults, whereas in 2025, according to the forecasts of the UN Population Division there will be less than three working-age adults per pensioner in the developed countries, and there exist even more pessimistic forecasts (see Fig. 6.7; see also the first section of this chapter). This cannot but cause alarm. Who will fill the pension funds in the future? Who will fulfill the social obligations with respect to hundreds of millions of elderly voters?

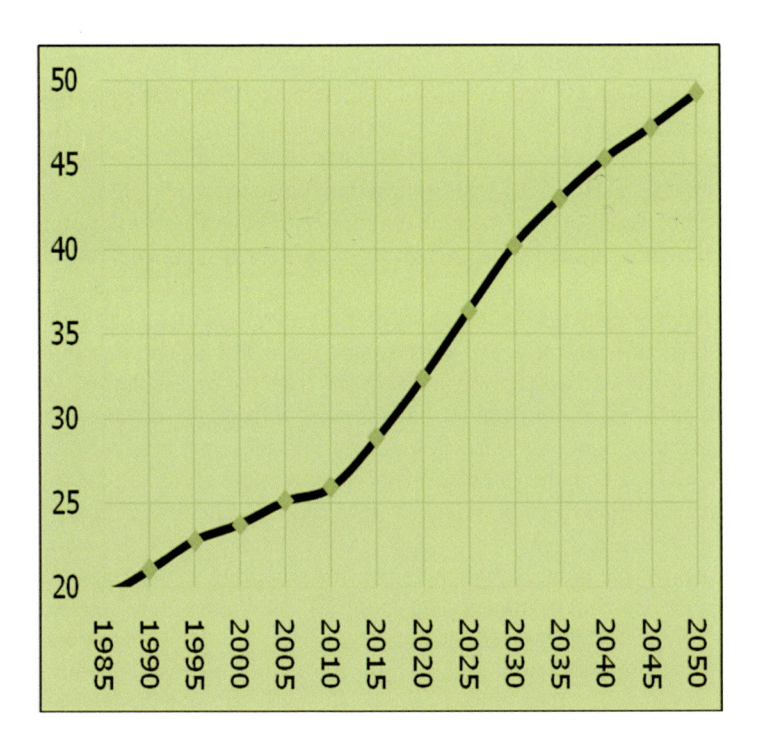

Fig. 6.7 Dynamics of number of pensioners aged 65 and older, per 100 working age adults aged 25–64 years in the World System core, 1985–2050 with medium forecast of UN for the period till 2050. (*Source*: UN Population Division, 2016)

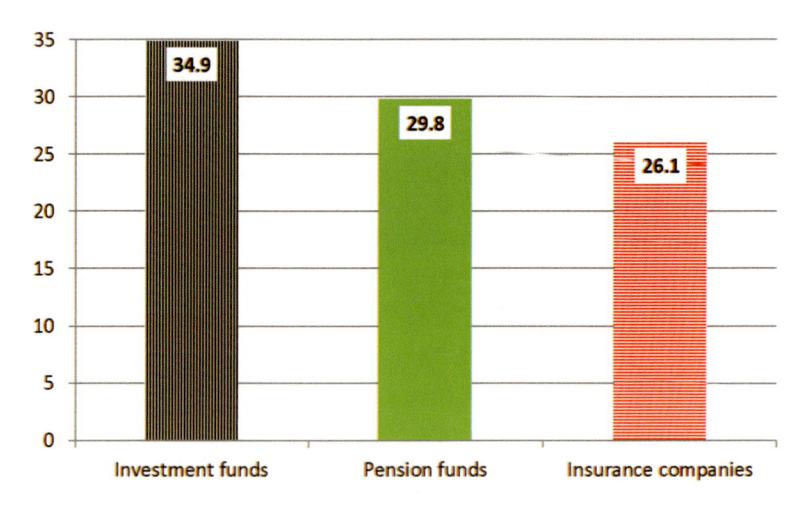

Fig. 6.8 Amounts of capital accumulated in the countries of OECD by 2013 by the main types of institutional investors (in trillions US dollars). (*Source:* OECD, 2014b: 7)

Here one should take into account that most pension funds are concentrated not in the state pension funds, but in thousands of private (non-state) pension funds (OECD, 2014b) that rather actively search for the most secure and profitable investments. The amounts of money concentrated in pension and other funds are enormous: dozens trillion US dollars (see, e.g., Штефан, 2008; OECD, 2014a, 2014b, 2015; see also Fig. 6.8).

In 2012, the accumulations in pension funds of the OECD countries amounted 77.1 % of their GDP, but in 2013 this indicator mounted to 84.2 % (OECD, 2014b: 7).

Meanwhile, we observe in the global periphery a huge number of young adults; and it is extremely difficult to provide all of them with jobs and education (see Fig. 6.9).

It is difficult or even impossible to solve this task without integrating the peripheral economies fully and as active partners into the World System economy as well as without diffusion of capitals and technologies from the core of the World System; in its turn, such integration cannot be achieved without the development of the world financial system. The situation favors this in some respects because the number of pensioners in the global periphery is still relatively small, the social obligations with respect to them are relatively few, and only after a significant period of time the problem of the pensioners' support will become acute in those countries.

Consequently, the point is to include pension and other social funds into strategies aiming on boosting the developing countries' economies more actively.[4] It will assist the latter to provide jobs and education for the young people at present and will multiply the funds in the future. In this case under certain agreements between

---

[4] It is worth noting that they already participate in this process. Thus, in the large private retirement funds surveyed in 2014 by OECD staff, an average of 36.6 % of all capital were invested abroad (OECD, 2014a: 15), whereas more than a half of the surveyed large pension funds invested a part of their capitals in developing economies (OECD, 2014a: 13, 31, 43).

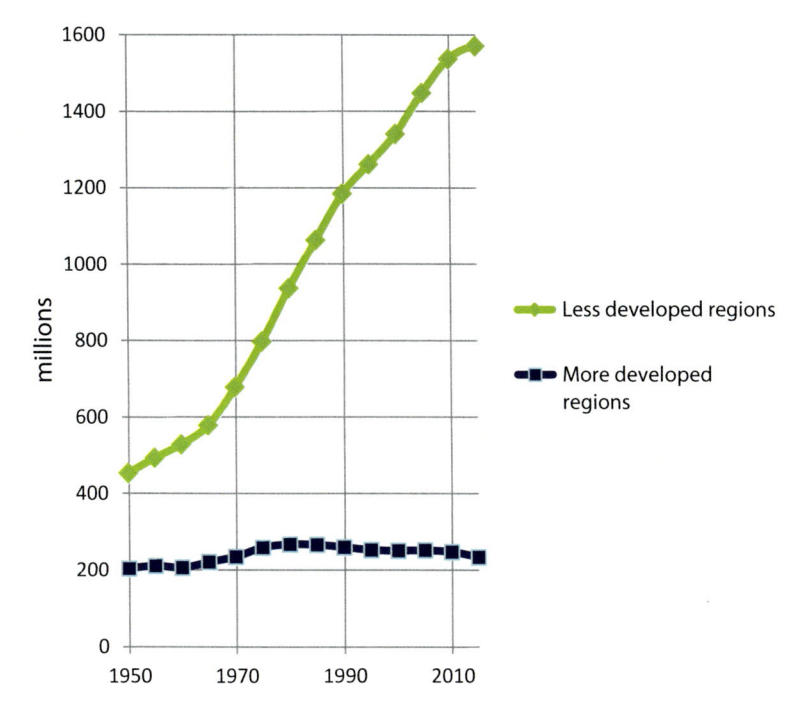

Fig. 6.9 Young population (aged 15–29 years old) of more and less developed regions, mlns, 1950–2015. (*Source*: UN Population Division, 2016)

developed and developing countries it will be possible to achieve a situation when the rising economies will allocate some assets to support the growing layer of older people in the West, the latter will act in this case as a rentier (recently Joseph Stiglitz has expressed similar ideas Stiglitz, 2015).

Then, there will be no need in the direct migration of millions of young people from the Third World to the First one; thus, there could emerge a sort of solidarity between different generations of the global world. Of course, such a system will demand considerable measures with respect to security and reliability of such investments. But at the same time, it would provide a certain convergence of different countries' interests.

Reflexions on a Possible Global Pension System

Thus, we may say that:

- The participation of pension and insurance funds in financial operations leads to the globalization of the social sphere.
- The countries that lack capital, but have large cohorts of young people, are more and more involved in a very important (though not quite apparent) process of

supporting the older population in the West through the unification of the world financial system, its standardization, and the search for ways to make it more fair and socially oriented.
- Modern financial assets and flows became global and international; a considerable amount of money circulates within this system (though, of course, not all its participants make equal profits).
- At the same time, one should realize that a considerable part of the circulating money comes from social funds (in particular from the pension ones) and their loss can lead to disasters — the consequences are difficult to predict.
- Safe management of the global capital (in addition to its obvious economic and social merits) assures the safe future for the elderly and those who needs social protection.
- Therefore, the problem of institutional support of financial globalization becomes more and more important.

Let us indicate some key points which clarify the opportunities and difficulties of the suggested scheme; besides, let us outline some of the most important institutional decisions which could help this scheme to function in practice.

First. The pension monies play a certain role in the financial system and depend on well-being and normal functioning of the latter. Money from pension funds is still one of the major systemic components of national and world financial systems. Actually, this means that these are just pension funds that remain one of the leading traders buying government bonds, and also actively buying shares and other securities at stock markets. While the conservative investment policy of pension funds is quite reasonable in general, at the same time it makes them as well as many other subsystems of the financial system highly dependent on the manipulations of the Central Bank, rating agencies and other actors. Particularly, the income of pension funds has considerably decreased in recent years due to deflationary tendencies (see Grinin & Korotayev, 2014d, Гринин и Коротаев, 2015б) and low rates on the government debt securities (as the government pays low interests rates to pension funds on the most reliable debt bonds).

Second. The permanent crisis in the financial system is able to radically undermine the solidity of pension funds. The latter have actively invested in securities; therefore, the cost of their assets largely depends on the price of securities. On the one hand, the governmental authorities and financial speculators wish to manipulate this cost and its artificial high price (e.g., the so-called buyback transaction of the securities by firms), and on the other hand, in case of crisis the assets' slump can be quite serious. For example, while in 2007 the asset value of US pension funds amounted to 78.0 % of the American GDP, during the crisis in 2008 it dropped to 59.6 % of GDP. The situation returned to pre-crisis level only in 2013 (OECD, 2015: Funded Pensions Indicators: Occupational pension funds' assets as a per cent of GDP); in other words, pension contributions have become entirely dependent on the economic situation. Therefore, we need some mechanisms of preserving accumulations, including the opportunity to lean on the world financial system.

Third. As we have said earlier, today the secure preservation of the value of accumulated funds depends on the speed of their circulation. However, finances do not exist by themselves, they can hardly break for a long time from the productive foundation and have to rely on real production (the increasing separation of the financial system from production is one of the main problems of the current situation which is largely supported by the monetarist doctrine). Thus, we face the necessity of driving the finances (and pension money) beyond national borders. Especially at present, since the production is rather actively moved to the global periphery. Therefore, no wonder that many pension funds invest into emerging markets to increase their income (OECD, 2014a: 15). Only few funds do not invest in foreign assets, while some, on the contrary, invest a large amount of their capital abroad (Ibidem). Certainly, the foreign investments do not always imply investments into countries of the global periphery. Nevertheless, some investment is made there, and thus, the proposed scheme already functions in a certain way. But we can face several serious problems. First, this is most often 'short', in fact, speculative money, whereas generally these are long-term investments can serve as real source of economic development and income. Second, this money is almost the first to leave the emerging markets because of their volatility (not least connected with the policy of FRS and ECB) and fully justified conservatism of pension funds; and this also increases the volatility. Third, the emerging markets certainly offer less guarantees than the developed ones, and therefore, the cautiousness of the funds is fully justified.

Fourth. For an effective functioning of the proposed scheme some high-level agreements are necessary. Here various forms could be used, for example, investment of money of pension funds in the assets of the largest international financial institutions as the IMF, WB, ADB, etc. These investments would be non-voting, but there the money would be much more secure, and special obligations could guarantee that these funds would be allocated to increase the level of education and qualification of young people in the global periphery.

It would be quite reasonable to develop some global organizations for the sake of cooperation between pension and other funds, as well as establishing common insurance funds that will make it possible to support countries in case of a crisis. It would be possible to establish an International Pension Fund or something that can guarantee financial transfers so that the assets of the 'older' population of some countries could help to raise the economy in the countries with a 'young' population, thus accumulating funds for donor countries for the future. Some specific arrangements between countries with certain guarantees for safety of funds would seem rather appropriate. In brief, there could be many options. But the main problem is that despite the fast population ageing, the versions of global solution for the problem are barely considered.

The Russian philosopher, Alexander Zinoviev, deported to Germany in the 1970s, quite accurately described the Western society as a society of monetary totalitarianism (Зиновьев, 2003) where the mechanism, realizing and preserving it, had reached enormous scales and had become one of the most important pillars of the society. This mechanism was established during the period of the gold standard and after its discontinuation the scale of the financial sector has grown tremendously, spreading all over the world. In fact, a new huge sector of financial services emerged which in some countries amounts to 25–30 % of the GDP. But the importance of this sector will increase in almost all countries, and will also involve their most important social functions.

Hence, the issue of the institutional support of the financial globalization becomes more and more important. We can speak about an extraordinary importance of the reliability and controllability of this system. Changes should include the increasing coordination between governments and unified international legislation which regulates financial activities and movements. Besides, one should take into account that today the developed countries generally get more benefits from this system and constantly use it to solve their national issues (thus, affecting the whole world) and they use it also willingly as a means to influence other countries' economies.

We suppose that important guarantees for the future Western pensioners will consist in the development pattern of the global economy which should transform into a single organism. Thus, the global financial system would become strong but will be used neither to get the global periphery under control nor as a means to collapse the economies of the Third World countries, nor as a means of unwarranted sanctions and suppression of societies and regimes which the West considers uneasy. There should occur some transformations in the global financial system that would take into account the growing economies' interests and thus allow the global periphery to more actively use the social funds accumulated by the World System core. And at the same time, this will prevent certain governments from expropriating the invested funds.

Changing Global Order and the World System Reconfiguration

Actually, the world needs a new system of financial-economic regulation at the global scale. However, such a global regulation cannot emerge from nowhere. It can be realized only in the fight against the crisis-depressive phenomena, and as a result of the reconfiguration of the World System, as both its result and as one of its drivers.

Globalization over the last three or four decades has produced a significant impact on the system of the world order (see Grinin, Ilyin, & Andreev, 2016; Гринин, 2015, 2016). First it destroyed the world order that had emerged after World War II. Furthermore, globalization has contributed to the establishment of a total hegemony of the US and the West in general; but subsequently it began to change the balance of economic power in the world in favor of the global periphery (see Акаев, 2015; Садовничий и др., 2014; Grinin & Korotayev, 2015a, 2015b; Коротаев, 2013, 2014, 2015а, 2015б, 2015в; Коротаев, Малков, Божевольнов и Халтурина, 2010; Korotayev & de Munck, 2013, 2014; Коротаев и Халтурина, 2009; Korotayev & Zinkina, 2014; Korotayev, Goldstone, & Zinkina, 2015; Korotayev, Zinkina, Kobzeva, Bogevolnov et al., 2011, 2012; Малков, Божевольнов et al., 2010; Малков, Коротаев и Божевольнов, 2010; Гринин, 2013б, 2013в; Zinkina, Malkov, & Korotayev, 2014).

Changes in the global economic balance of power sooner or later entail changing the world order, but this transformation will take quite a long time and is likely associated with increased tensions and conflicts (see below).

Our assumptions about the principles of the new world order are based on the following findings (see Grinin, 2011, 2012a, 2012b; Grinin & Korotayev, 2010b,

2015a; Grinin, Ilyin, & Andreev, 2016; Гринин, 2009a, 2015, 2016; see also Kissinger, 1994, 2001, 2014, 2015). Firstly, the US cannot be replaced by any new hegemon that would have the same set of leadership roles that the United States have today. Second, the weakening of the leadership capabilities of the United States is inevitable and will become more and more noticeable in the forthcoming years. However, the US will possess a number of advantages for quite a long time (see, e.g., Bremmer, 2015; Zakaria, 2008). Thirdly, the world is to some extent interested in a sort of soft US leadership, but not in the USA dictatorship, whose mission is to undermine the power of the opponents by any possible means. Fourthly, for the transition to the new world order the global community will have to search for new principles and conditions, to create precedents and desired combinations (Grinin, Ilyin, & Andreev, 2016; Гринин, 2016). Therefore, the search will be difficult and long. Fifthly, the movement to the new world order is likely to involve a temporary increase of turbulence and conflict, as well as competition between different versions of the new world order.

Why is the growth of disorder at the transition phase more likely than a soft transition? First of all, the transition to a new world order requires wisdom on the part of the administration of all the states, but, especially, the US administration. Wisdom has always been a scarce quality within the political elite. However, there are deeper reasons. A radical change in the balance of economic power in the world, which we mentioned above, creates objective conditions for a revision of the world order. However, it does not entail the automatic change in the military-political balance. For this purpose, as already mentioned in *Chap. 5*, it is required, "pulling up" the political component of global development (political globalization) to the economic component. We have denoted the inevitable narrowing of the gap between economic and political globalization as "the World System reconfiguration" (see the previous chapter, as well as Grinin & Korotayev, 2012a, 2012b, 2015a; Гринин, 2012б; Гринин, Исаев, и Коротаев, 2016).

The main vectors of this reconfiguration are the weakening of the old center of the World System (the US and the West), the simultaneous strengthening of the positions of a number of peripheral countries and the increasing role of developing countries in general. It should be borne in mind that the catch-up of political dimension to economic globalization occurs in spurts and implies more or less acute political and geopolitical crises in various regions. We consider the crises and turmoil in the Middle East and Ukraine, precisely as such geopolitical "reconfiguration crises" that demand changes in the world order. At the same time, emergence of powerful and probably sudden crises in different societies or regions becomes more probable. Their unpredictability may be akin to the one of a major earthquake. And, continuing the geological comparison, it should be noted that just as the tectonic shifts take place under the most mobile of the crust and on the boundary of tectonic plates, this sort if reconfiguration crises also arise in regions and societies that are the least stable and that are situated at the junction of "geopolitical plates". Both the Middle East and Ukraine belong to such regions. Therefore it can be assumed that very significant changes will occur in the peripheral countries, which, metaphorically speaking, lie at the intersection of "geopolitical plates". Among other such regions one may name the Caucasus and Central Asia, Western China (Tibet and Xinjiang), West Africa (at the intersection of Islamic and Tropical Africa), some regions of South America. These are quite unstable regions, which already manifested some symptoms of reconfiguration crises or such crises may occur there in the near (but this, of course, does not mean that they will occur their inevitably). But crises can occur in places that seemed quite stable at the outset.

Once Again about the Sixth K-wave and Cybernetic Revolution

In conclusion of this chapter and the present monograph in general, we find it appropriate to return to our forecasts on the future of the sixth K-wave and the overall future of Kondratieff waves.

So the sixth K-wave will probably begin approximately in the 2020s. Meanwhile the final phase of the Cybernetic Revolution has to begin later, at least, in the 2030s or 2040s. Thus, we suppose, that a new technological paradigm will not develop in a necessary form even by the 2020s (thus, the innovative pause will take longer than expected — see *Chap. 5*). However, it should be kept in mind that the beginning of the K-wave upswing phase is never directly caused by new technologies. This beginning is synchronized with the start of the medium-term business cycle's upswing. And the upswing takes place as a result of the levelling of proportions in economy, the accumulation of resources and other impulses that improve demand and conjuncture. One should remember, that the beginning of the second K-wave was connected with the discovery of gold deposits in California and Australia, the third wave with the increase in prices for wheat, the fourth one with the post-war reconstruction, the fifth one with the economic reforms in the UK and the USA, as well as oil price shocks. And then, given an upswing, a new technological paradigm (which could not completely — if at all — realize its potential) facilitates overcoming of cyclic crises and allows further growth.

Consequently, some conjunctural events will also stimulate an upward impulse of the sixth K-wave. And, for example, the rapid growth of the underdeveloped world regions (such as Tropical Africa, the Islamic East, and some Latin American countries) or new financial and organizational technologies can become a primary impulse. Naturally, there will also appear some technical and technological innovations which, however, will not form a new paradigm yet. Besides, we suppose that financial technologies have not finished yet its expansion in the world. If we can modify and secure them somehow, they will be able to spread into various regions which underuse them now. One should not forget that large-scale application of such technologies demands essential changes in legal and other systems, which is absolutely necessary for developmental levelling in the world. Taking into account a delay of the new generation of technologies, the period of the 2020s may resemble the 1980s. In other words, it will be neither a recession, nor a real upswing, but rather somehow accelerated development (with stronger development in some regions and continuous depression in others—see Figs. 2.8; 2.13; 2.14 in *Chap. 2*).

Then, given the favorable conditions as they had been mentioned above, during this wave the final phase of the Cybernetic Revolution will begin. In such a situation it is possible to assume that the sixth K-wave's A-phase (the 2020–2050s) will have much stronger manifestation and last longer than that of the fifth one due to more dense combination of technological generations. And since the Cybernetic Revolution will evolve, the sixth K-wave's downward B-phase (2050—the 2060/2070s), is expected to be not so depressive, as those during the third or fifth waves. In general, during this K-wave (2020—the 2060/2070s) the Scientific and Information Revolution will come to an end, and the scientific and cybernetic production principle will acquire its mature shape.

There Is Another Scenario

The final phase of the Cybernetic Revolution can begin later—not in the 2030s, but in the 2040s. In this case the A-phase of the sixth wave will terminate much before the beginning of the final phase of the Cybernetic Revolution; therefore, it will not be based on fundamentally new technologies and will not become so powerful as is supposed in the previous scenario. The final phase of the Cybernetic Revolution in this case will coincide with the B-phase of the sixth wave (as it was the case with the zero wave during the Industrial Revolution, 1760–1787—see *Chaps. 1* and *5*) and at the A-phase of the seventh wave. In this case the emergence of the seventh wave is highly possible. The B-phase of the sixth wave should be rather short due to the emergence of a new generation of technologies, and the A-phase of the seventh wave could be rather long and powerful.

The End of the Cybernetic Revolution and Possible Disappearance of K-Waves

The sixth K-wave (about 2020—the 2060/2070s), like the first K-wave, will proceed generally during completion of the production revolution (see *Chap. 5*). However, there is an important difference. During the first K-wave the duration of the one phase of the industrial production principle significantly exceeded the duration of the whole K-wave. But now one phase of the K-wave will exceed the duration of one phase of production principle. This alone should essentially modify the course of the sixth K-wave; the seventh wave will be feebly expressed or will not occur at all (on the possibility of the other scenario see above). Such a forecast is based also on the fact that the end of the Cybernetic Revolution and distribution of its results will promote integration of the World System and a considerable growth of influence of new universal regulation mechanisms. It is quite reasonable, taking into account the fact that the forthcoming final phase of the revolution will be the revolution in the regulation of systems. Thus, the management of the economy should reach a new level. *K-waves appeared at a certain phase of global evolution and they are likely to disappear at its certain phase.*

Appendix A: Biographies of Nikolay Kondratieff and Kaname Akamatsu[1]

Nikolay D. Kondratieff

Nikolay Dmitrievich Kondratieff was born on the 17th March, 1892 in the village of Galuevskaya, Kostroma Governorate, into a peasant family.[2] He was the eldest among ten other children of his parents. After he had finished his primary school, Nikolay entered a teachers training seminary where he befriended Pitirim Sorokin (who later became a world-famous sociologist as well as a founder of the Sociology Department in the Harvard University). This friendship continued throughout their life; in addition, until Sorokin's emigration they were tied together by political activities. During the First Russian Revolution (1905–1907) Nikolay joined the Party of Socialists-Revolutionaries, with which he remained connected for many years; he became deeply involved in revolutionary activities. As a result he was expelled from the seminary and had to go to Ukraine, where he continued his education. In 1908 he decided to study in Saint Petersburg and in 1910 he entered the Department of Economics of the University Faculty of Law. Nikolay attended classes of such brilliant scholars as Mikhail Tugan-Baranovsky, Maksim Kovalevsky, Leon Petrazycki and others; he continued contacts with them long after the graduation. Nikolay soon started his own research and in 1912–1914, while still being a student, he published more than 20 articles, reviews and other works. In 1915 he graduated from the University with a diploma of the First Grade. The same year he published his first monograph which was met with positive reviews in the academic

---

[1] This appendix has been prepared with support of the Russian Foundation for the Humanities (Project No. 14-02-00330).

[2] Depicting Kondratieff's biography hereinafter we use the following works: Симонов и Фигуровская, 1991, Симонов и Фигуровская, 1993; Яковец, 2002; Благих, 1993, 1994; Ефимкин, 1991; Горбунов и Шутов, 1994; Абалкин, 1992. We have used also 'Letters of N. D. Kondratieff to E. D. Kondratieffa (1932–1938)' (Кондратьев, 1991б [1932–1938]); Curriculum vitae of N. D. Kondratieff (*Idem* 1991a) and other materials.

press. The talented graduate was left to work in the University. In the same time he worked as the Head of Statistics Department of the Petrograd Zemgor.[3]

During all those years Nikolay continued to be actively involved in illegal revolutionary activities; in the revolutionary underground he got to know a number of future imminent politicians, including the ones belonging to the Bolshevik Party. It is not surprising that since the first days of the February Revolution Kondratieff took an active part in those stormy events as a member of the Party of Socialists-Revolutionaries. The year 1917 was the peak of his political carrier. In October 1917 at the age of 25 he became a Deputy Minister of Supply in the Provisional Government of Alexander Kerensky. However, he occupied this position just for a few days. Everything changed with the Bolshevik Revolution of October 1917. After it Kondratieff continued his political activities for some time, but he finally stopped taking any active part in politics after the dissolution of the All Russian Constituent Assembly in January 1918. He moved to Moscow where he served as an economist in various state departments, combining this activity with teaching.

1918 was a tragic year; it was a turning point in the Russian history. Kondratieff hardly published any academic research that year.[4] On the other hand, he established contacts with a number of well-known economists (Alexander Chayanov, the founder of modern Peasant Studies, was one of them). Chayanov invited Kondratieff to head the Laboratory of Agrarian Conjuncture in the Institute of Agrarian Economics and Politics that he organized in 1919. In October 1920 the Macroeconomic Conjuncture Institute was established on the basis of the laboratory and Kondratieff was appointed its director. He also continued his teaching activities. In the early 1920s the Bolsheviks abandoned their policy of so-called Military Communism (which implied a direct coercive extraction of resources from peasant households) and introduced the New Economic Policy (NEP); in connection with this the Soviet authorities employed Kondratieff for work over the identification of the optimum norms of peasant taxation, and later over the 5-year plan of agricultural development. He also studied the issues of cereal crop prices and trade and entered the civil service as the Head of the Administration for Agrarian Economy and Policy of the People's Commissariat (= Ministry) of Agriculture.

In the early 1920s Kondratieff was arrested for the first time after October 1917. That was a grim signal, revealing the real attitude of the Communist power toward such intellectuals as Kondratieff. However, this imprisonment had no serious consequences, and Kondratieff apparently considered it as a mere mistake. There were evident grounds to think so. His carrier went up; in 1924 he was even allowed to undertake a long trip abroad together with his wife. He visited Germany, Britain, Canada, and the USA. It was during this trip that he met for the last time his old friend Pitirim Sorokin; Pitirim suggested that Kondratieff could get a position as

---

[3] Zemgor (*Земгор* or *Объединённый комитет Земского союза и Союза городов*; literally *United Committee of the Union of Zemstvos and the Union of Towns*) was a Russian organization created in 1915 to help the government in World War I effort.

[4] In 1918 he published only two politically motivated texts. One of them had a rather symptomatic title—'On the Way to Famine' (Кондратьев, 1918a), the other's title was 'The Year of Revolution from an Economic Point of View' (*Ibid.*).

departmental head in one of the American universities. Yet, Kondratieff declined this offer, as he believed that his place was in Russia. Though Kondratieff made a number of successful forecasts, he could not forecast his own fate …

In the 6-year period between 1922 and 1928 all main works of Kondratieff containing really new ideas appeared. A renowned scholar of Kondratieff's life and research, Yuri Yakovets notes: 'his market analysis, his system of indexes, his academic research paved new ways of deep economic analysis, it got a wide recognition both in our country and abroad' (Яковец, 2002a, p. 711).

Among his rather numerous publications we would single out the following: *The World Economy and Its Conjunctures During and After the War* (Кондратьев, 1922); a book on Tugan-Baranovsky (Кондратьев, 1923); the article 'Concepts of Economic Statics, Dynamics and Conjuncture' (Кондратьев, 1924); the article 'Long Cycles of Economic Conjuncture' (Кондратьев, 1925); the report 'World Economy, 1919–1925: Current State and Main Development Trends' (Кондратьев, 1926в) and his seminal article 'The Problem of Foresight' (Кондратьев, 1926б); finally, he published also the article 'Critical Notes on the Plan of National Economic Development' (Кондратьев, 1927) and a separate issue of *Long Cycles of Economic Conjuncture* (Кондратьев, 1928, based on the materials of 1926 discussion, see below).[5] Kondratieff's views on long waves (as well as on other problems) faced rather tough criticism on the part of Soviet economists. He noted himself in one of his letters from the prison to his wife that his publications 'provoked storms' (Кондратьев, 1991б [1932–1938], p. 541).

The year 1926 was marked with a famous discussion on the issue of 'big cycles' where a number of prominent Soviet economists acted as Kondratieff's opponents.[6] This discussion marked a sharp turn in Kondratieff's academic carrier and influenced definitively his fate. Kondratieff's presentation *The Long Cycles of Economic Conjuncture* (Большие циклы конъюнктуры) as well as his final word contained the essence of his views on the nature and mechanisms of the long wave dynamics. Kondratieff's ideas were confronted with a sharp critique on the part of his opponents. Note that this critique could be only partly explained by the toughening political and ideological pressure in the country. It was also explained by the unusualness of some Kondratieff's ideas, as well as by some rather complex techniques applied by Kondratieff in order to detect long waves in the dynamics of various indexes. Indeed, in certain respects Kondratieff's methodology was not quite perfect, and in certain aspects criticism of his opponents was quite objective. However, as happened quite often in the history of science, the opponents failed to see wider perspectives beyond smaller defects. The arguments of Kondratieff's opponents did not shake his position; till the end of his life he was sure about the importance of his forecasts. There was a certain irony in the fact that he could see the confirmation of some of his ideas while already being in prison. In 1934 he wrote in one of the letters to his wife: 'I try to follow the course of the world economic development (as

---

[5] A considerable number of Kondratieff's works have been translated into English (see, *e.g.*, Kondratieff, 1935, 1984, 1998, 2004).

[6] This discussion was organized in February 1926 in the Institute of Economics of the Russian Association of Social Science Institutes with Dmitry Oparin as Kondratieff's principal opponent (for more detail see Гринин и Коротаев 2014а, 2014б; Grinin, Devezas, & Korotayev 2012).

much as I can get relevant data from the press), and I think that some of my ideas and forecasts that are based on them have been successfully tested and joined the fund of recognized facts...' (Кондратьев, 1991б [1932–1938], p. 546).

Kondratieff's analysis concentrated on value-dominated statistical series, that is, money, production, trade and wages. They do not move necessarily with the same periodicity as other driving factors of the economy, but they provide a 'thermometer' to measure the 'heat' of economy (prices), which move in phase with other series and essentially reflect the underlying forces in a capitalist economy, rising and falling with supply and demand. In other words, Kondratieff's ideas that a capitalist economy is subjected to periodic fluctuations did not please in any way the communist economists, for it implied that the economic crisis which then approached (and worsened in the 1930s) would be just another provisional oscillation of the capitalist economy, and not its ultimate demise as the Bolsheviks theorists wanted to see. This was the true origin of the contradiction between Kondratieff and his opponents, and Kondratieff refused to deny his ideas, as they were based on very robust empirical evidence.

The present short biographic sketch is not an appropriate place to analyze Kondratieff's ideas in any detail—this has already been done elsewhere—starting from the works of Schumpeter (1939) and Kuznets (1940). Kondratieff published his research on a rather wide range of topics. However, in the history of the world economic thought he will remain above all as the economist that launched the theory of long economic cycles (with a characteristic period of 40–60 years) that manifest themselves in a number of very important economic and physical indicators.

Though many contradictions still exist regarding the details and regularity of these long-term fluctuations of the global economy, it is hard to deny the fact that these fluctuations have happened all along the last two centuries, or even in earlier periods. Kondratieff was, perhaps, wrong in certain respects, and some of the eliminations that he applied to his graphs in order to demonstrate the presence of the long waves are far from being fully justified, his main discovery remains intact.

Copernicus believed that the orbits of the planets around the Sun have round shapes; later Johannes Kepler demonstrated that the shape of those orbits was elliptical. However, this did not make Copernicus' discovery less revolutionary. The redshift velocity has turned out to be much higher than was believed by Edwin Hubble, but this does not undermine the validity of Hubble's law and the birth of the idea of the Big Bang. Kondratieff launched the seeds of today's burgeoning evolutionary economics that permeates the general conception of the World System as a self-organizing complex system that moves forwards at the edge of chaos, out of equilibrium, subjected to typical limit-cycle oscillations. Kondratieff could not have imagined this 'complexity' that arose from the fluctuations that he detected, as well as Copernicus could not have imagined Newton's law that governed the regularity of the planetary movements that he had detected, or Hubble could not have imagined todays 'dark matter' theory that was developed to explain the apparently never ending expansion of the universe that he has once detected.

The year 1927 was actually the last real year of the New Economic Policy in the USSR. 1928 marked the end of the period of rather limited economic freedom and it is correlated with the catastrophic shrinking of the minimum creative freedom that was still left for the intellectuals, including the possibility to travel abroad, to have contacts with foreign scientists, to get published abroad. It was within these rather limited possibilities that the world happened to know about Kondratieff long wave theory, for he managed to publish a number of his works in European languages within the narrow 'opportunity window' open to him at that time—first of all, 'Die langen Wellen der Konjunktur' in *Archiv für Sozialwissenschaft und Sozialpolitik* (1926, pp. 573–609).

Stalin and the new clique of the Bolshevik leaders headed to the most rapid industrialization and militarization. Such a forced industrialization could only be carried out through a radical increase in the gross fixed capital formation, through the acquisition of huge amounts of modern machinery and industrial equipment. In order to do this Stalin needed enormous sums of hard currency, and to get this currency it was necessary to radically increase volumes of wheat exports. Wheat was also necessary to supply basic needs for the fast-growing urban population (including the fast-growing 'working class'). The Soviets/Stalin refused to buy wheat from peasants at normal prices, whereas it was impossible (and actually suicidal) for peasants to sell wheat at prices lower than standard market prices. This created a sort of deadlock for the Bolsheviks.

In order to escape from it they headed to the coercive expropriation of the "peasants' land" to transform them into a sort of state's slaves. Peasants were forced to enter 'collective farms' that had to sell agricultural products at a token price. The radical transition in this direction began in the fall of 1929. However, this was preceded by fierce battles within the Communist Party leadership, which, naturally, involved a significant part of the expert community of that time. The aim of that struggle was not only to determine the course of the further movement of the country; this was also a struggle for power—and so it was extremely fierce. Kondratieff was one of its victims—in addition to, say, numerous other economists who did not want to become Stalin's academic slaves whose academic reputation was supposed to be used in order to strengthen the authority of the Soviet power to perform total coercion over the people.

Such economists then became an obstacle with all their ideas about the stimulation of peasants' economic initiative, optimum (not forced!) industrialization, decreasing the burden of taxation, and so on. Efficient hard working farmers were called kulaks—this word denoted the 'class enemy' in the countryside. In 1927 the ideas of Kondratieff and his colleagues were proclaimed 'Kulak Party Manifesto' (this was the title of an article published by one of the Bolshevik leaders, Zinoviev, in the *Bolshevik* Magazine). Kondratieff felt an ice breath of execution, for it was evident that his political position could cost him freedom and even life.

In 1928, Stalin, Molotov, and Kaganovich crashed the so-called 'Right-Wing Faction' within the Soviet Communist Party (headed by such veteran party comrades as Bukharin, Rykov and others); independently minded agrarian economists and sociologists were repressed simultaneously. On May 1, 1928, Kondratieff was fired from the Conjuncture Institute, and the institute itself was closed down soon afterwards. Kondratieff continued his formal academic research for 2 more years, but he had already fallen into disgrace with the Soviet authorities, and he could hardly publish anything. One could imagine his psychological distress, all those feeling of oppressive clouds that were thickening over him. However, still greater sufferings were awaiting him. The year 1929 became known in the official Soviet historiography as 'the year of the great turn', or 'the year of the great break'. Millions of peasants were coerced to join collective farms, they were robbed of their lands and livestock; hundreds of thousands of the most efficient farmers (kulaks) were stripped of all their possessions and evicted to inhospitable areas of Siberia, European North, and Kazakhstan, where a very high proportion of them starved to death. The 'collectivization' led to catastrophic failures in the Russian agriculture and wide-spread famine, but Stalin's administration tried to maneuver. They tried to avoid social explosions and to blame the others for Stalinists' failures. It was necessary to invent such enemies to be blamed. One of such invented enemies was the so-called 'Labor Peasant Party' that never existed in reality but was fabricated by the Joint State Political Directorate (Soviet secret services). Almost all the independently minded agrarian economists and sociologists were accused of being active members of this fictitious party and arrested. Nikolay Kondratieff was one of them—he was arrested in June 1930. The trial of the 'kulak-professors' was finished in 1932 and Kondratieff was sentenced to eight years of prison. He was imprisoned in Suzdal, in a building of one of Suzdal monasteries that was turned into a political prison (called at that time 'political isolator').

During all his years in prison Kondratieff continued to work (as far as this was possible) on his book that was published (many decades afterwards) under the title "Main Issues of Statics and Dynamics in Economics" ("Основные проблемы экономической статики и динамики" [Кондратьев, 1991а]). However, Kondratieff's health and moral conditions deteriorated very fast; his letters provide the best evidence on this point. In late 1932 he wrote (one cannot exclude, however, that the text was somehow influenced by his fear of censorship): 'The Suzdal Political Prison makes an impression of a rather well-organized and civilized custodial' (Кондратьев, 1991б [1932–1938], p. 535). However, two years later the contents of his messages changed in a rather significant way. Kondratieff still tried to keep up, but quite often he was in despair. For example, he wrote: 'It is impossible to do anything really serious in prison' (Кондратьев, 1991б [1932–1938], p. 546). 'This is a place where the human life and thought is the most devalued value' (Ibidem). However, when despair went, he continued to work. Yet, terrible conditions and isolation took their toll. Kondratieff's health deteriorated, he felt physical weakness that decreased dramatically his capacity for intellectual work. The prison regime became tougher and tougher, and nutrition worsened. However, the psychological desire to work remained and Kondratieff continued his struggle; he still hoped to get amnesty or a reduction of sentence.

In 1937 he spent a few months in the prison hospital; doctors detected four serious diseases; in addition his sight weakened dramatically. As a result, he felt neither energy nor desire to continue his studies (Кондратьев, 1991б [1932–1938], p. 558). All the remaining forces were spent in order to struggle with diseases. 'The mood is very and very upset and strained... There is something wrong with my head. Continuing weakness... From time to time I feel attacks of enormous depression, despair, and disease', – he wrote in July 1938 (Кондратьев, 1991б [1932–1938], p. 560). But even in such a condition he continued to read. Reading, as he wrote, 'no doubt counteracts the disease' (Ibidem, p. 561).

While he was suffering and struggling with his illness in Stalin's political prison, while the dissemination of Kondratieff's ideas was strictly prohibited in Russia, his ideas still started the life of their own. In 1929 Wesley Mitchell in a new edition of his Business Cycles allotted quite a few pages to the discussion of Kondratieff's work on long wave dynamics (Mitchell, 1927, pp. 231–235); Mitchell's discussion was positive and the author came to the conclusion that Kondratieff's work had opened promising perspectives for future research (Ibidem, p. 234). In late 1934 Kondratieff's morale was greatly supported when he happened to read a part of Fisher's article dedicated to the analysis of his ideas. In 1935 a short version of his article 'The Long Wave in Economic Life' was published in English in the Review of Economics and Statistics (Kondratieff, 1935). Joseph Schumpeter, a famous Austrian-American economist, got rather interested in Kondratieff's theory and this had especially important consequences to the posterity.

Mikhail Bulgakov, a famous Russian writer and Kondratieff's contemporary (whose fate was also rather tragic) wrote in those years: 'Manuscripts do not burn'. He meant that really creative works can never be entirely silenced, and that really creative ideas should become known sooner or later (note that Bulgakov's novel containing the above-mentioned phrase was published only a few decades after it had been written, well after Bulgakov's death). Just in that very period when Kondratieff felt 'the inexorable advent' of his fate (Кондратьев, 1991б [1932–1938], p. 541) and despair from the sense that all his efforts had been dissipated pointlessly (Кондратьев, 1991б [1932–1938], p. 560), his ideas started to acquire immortality. It is interesting to note that the rather terrifying atmosphere of those years contributed to the positive reception of Kondratieff's long cycle theory. The world was quaking with economic crises, depressions, unemployment, stock exchange crashes and their concomitants. There was a need of new ideas and theories that could explain the unusually long depressions and stagnations. That was the time when a new economic science formed by such great economists as Keynes, Kuznets, and Schumpeter. Kondratieff's theory took its place among these new emerging ideas.

In the USSR the state terror reached its apogee. In 1937 and 1938 thousands of talented intellectuals, artists, writers, and scientists were executed or tormented to death. Special measures were taken with respect to those who were already in prison, who were about to go out of prison. Nobody really intended to give them freedom. Instead, authorities tried to invent new cases, new accusations resulting in death sentences — they were usually announced as 'ten years in prison without the right of correspondence', but the convicted people were executed almost immediately after the announcement of their sentences, whereas his or her relatives for ten poignant years still hoped to see the prisoner alive. On September 17, 1938, Nikolay Kondratieff was sentenced precisely to 'ten years in prison without the right of correspondence'. That meant: he was shot by a firing squad the same day.

This was the end of the life of political prisoner Kondratieff, but the life of scientist Kondratieff entered its new phase. In 1937 in Japan Kaname Akamatsu published an article that developed some of Kondratieff's ideas (see below for more detail). In 1939 Joseph Schumpeter published his famous Business Cycles (Schumpeter, 1939). In this monograph the economic long waves were denoted as 'Kondratieff cycles'. No doubt that Schumpeter's work influenced the posthumous interest in Kondratieff's life and ideas in a rather significant way. That time (the 1930s) was an epoch of great interest in the study of economic cycles. But for almost three decades, the issue of the Kondratieff long wave in economics remained in a kind of limbo, probably obfuscated, ironically, by the grand economic expansion and ebullience of the 1950s and 1960s forecast by the self same Kondratieff wave. It was not until the 1970s that a revival of long waves emerged, mainly due to the systematic works of Gerhard Mensch (1979), Ernest Mandel (1980), Jay Forrester (1978, 1981), and a research team at IIASA (International Institute for Applied Systems Analysis, Laxenburg) led by the physicist Cesare Marchetti (see, e.g., Marchetti, 1983). It is very curious to note that the interest in the phenomenon of economic long waves seems to move itself as long waves, as demonstrated by Devezas and Corredine (2001)—these authors have measured two long waves in publications on long waves, a first one centrated in 1927, and a second one centrated in 1986, exactly 59 years after the first burst of publications.

Only in the 1980s K-waves started being discussed in Kondratieff's homeland. In 1987 Kondratieff was formally 'rehabilitated' (together with all the other his colleagues of him who were sentenced in the framework of the case of the 'Labor Peasant Party'). One could observe then a wave of publications of Kondratieff's works as well as publications about him and his ideas going through the country (Кондратьев, 1988, 1991а, 1993б, 1993а; Меньшиков и Клименко, 1989; Полетаев и Савельев, 1993; see also a special issue of the *Voprosy ekonomiki* Journal [No 10, 1992]). His ideas received a new impulse.

Kaname Akamatsu

Kaname Akamatsu was a contemporary of Nikolay Kondratieff, only 4 years younger than he. So they observed many of the same economic and political events—though from different angles of the World System. However due to the fact that Kondratieff started his scientific carrier quite early and that his theory was published in English and German, it happened that Akamatsu became a follower of Kondratieff. The latter was slowly dying in the Suzdal prison while his ideas were finding new supporters. It seems deeply symbolic that a year before Kondratieff's death the famous work of Akamatsu in Japanese was published and that a year after Kondratieff's death Schumpeter published his book in which long cycles received the name of Kondratieff.

So there was a great admirer of Nikolay Kondratieff in distant Japan. What do we know about him? How long was the "pilgrimage"[7] of the son of an impoverished

---

[7] The term *"pilgrimage"* might be allowed here, because Akamatsu himself used it in his essay, which was published after his death 1974 in the year 1975; see the bibliographical reference contained

Appendix A: Biographies of Nikolay Kondratieff and Kaname Akamatsu   189

rice retailer from the southern Japanese island of Kyushu to his intellectual encounter with the great Kondratieff, at a time when Nikolai Dmitriyevich already suffered in the cold of the Gulag, and when Akamatsu, a critical spirit, well familiar with European philosophy and economics, especially with Marx, had to work under the stifling intellectual atmosphere of expansionist and imperial Japan which already started its policies of occupation in Asia?

Kondratieff cycle research must be grateful to Korhonen (1994) who presented some biographical facts about this important[8] follower of Kondratieff, whose life, very much like Kondratieff's own life, was not free from bitter experiences. So Kaname Akamatsu was born in 1896 into a very poor family in what was then the poorest part of the Japanese archipelago. As Korhonen could establish from documents only accessible in the Japanese language, Kaname was so poor that during his student days at Kobe he *"wore the same clothing for four years until they turned to rags and a friend replaced them, which aroused in Akamatsu an interest in Marxism"* (Korhonen, 1994, p. 93). Besides Marxism, Akamatsu studied mainstream economics, and became interested in German philosophy, especially in the work of Nietzsche, Schopenhauer and Kant. He became a University teacher, and in 1924 he went to Germany to continue his studies there. In early 1926 Akamatsu left Heidelberg and, as Korhonen shows, *"travelled to London to pay his respects at the grave of Karl Marx. He was shocked to find it neglected; indeed, he even had trouble locating it"* (Korhonen, 1994, p. 94). Respect for the ancestors is one of the deepest layers of Japanese culture, and the visit to Highgate Cemetery must have deeply impressed the researcher, who was now 30 years old. He had a chance to visit later on during his foreign trip the Harvard Bureau of Economic Statistics in Boston in the same year, studying the new approaches in empirical and statistical economic research; a visit, which should radically change his scientific approach. After his return to Nagoya, Akamatsu began to study empirically the mechanisms of import substitution and the history and development of the Japanese woolen and cotton textile industry. Akamatsu's statistical investigations established, as Korhonen shows, a pattern of economic development in one product category after the other.

From there on, a process of the ladder of success set in, which was not without dangers and not without perils and temptations of its own. While Kondratieff had the bad luck that the powerful political elite in the person of Joseph Stalin himself

---

in Schroeppel and Nakajima (2002). The bibliographical reference would be: Akamatsu K. 1975. *Gakumon henro [Academic pilgrimage].* In: Kojima, Kiyoshi et al. (Eds.). (1975). *Gakumon henro. Akamatsu Kaname sensei tsuit ronshu [Academic pilgrimage. Commemorating volume on Professor Akamatsu Kaname].* Tokyo: Sekai Keizai Kenkyu Kyokai, pp. 1–68.

[8] As Ozawa (2013) correctly remarks, it is the only Japan-born economic theory that has so far been well recognized outside Japan: *"The 'flying-geese (FG)' theory of economic development is now known the world over, having gained some respectability in the academia and wide popularity in the media— especially against the backdrop of a series of catch-up economic successes across Asia during the last few decades of the 20th century. The speech made by Saburo Okita (1914–1993), former Japanese Foreign Minister, referring to the theory at the fourth Pacific Economic Cooperation Conference in Seoul in 1985, made policymakers and the mass media aware of it. It is the only Japan-born theory that has so far been well recognized outside Japan. It is also accepted as a major doctrine of catch-up development strategy, along with the 'big-push' theory and the 'import substitution' approach"* (Ozawa, 2013, p. 2).

contradicted his theories, it was Akamatsu's bad luck that Imperial Japan fully endorsed his theories and even used it as a justification of its expansionist and brutal policy of occupation in many Asian countries to an extent unforeseen and not wished by Akamatsu. In 1939 Akamatsu became professor at the Tokyo University of Economics; in 1940 he was elevated to the post of Director of Research in the East Asian Economic Research Centre. In 1943 Akamatsu was finally conscripted into the military and was placed under military command and sent to Singapore to direct research on the economy of Southeast Asia under Japanese rule. As Korhonen states:

> "The flying geese theory had meanwhile become part of Japanese war propaganda aimed at nations of the Greater East Asian Co-prosperity Sphere as a way of lending intellectual legitimacy to Japanese claims of bringing freedom, development and prosperity to the nations of Asia. It seems that Akamatsu himself did not write such papers, but confined himself as much as possible to the academic field as a scholar. In his autobiography he recalls that in this respect life was easier in Singapore than in Tokyo. If he had stayed in Tokyo he would probably have been drafted to write propaganda for the war effort, whereas in Singapore he was able to concentrate relatively freely on research. It is true that Akamatsu was a nationalist, and once the nation had chosen a warlike course he contributed to the war effort, even though as a scholar he was well aware of the economic realities in respect to Japan's ability to win the war. On the other hand, Akamatsu seems to have had nothing against the principle that Asia should free itself from Western colonialism. He travelled around the area and became acquainted with Malay and Indonesian leaders such as Sukarno and Hatta" (Korhonen, 1994, p. 94).

In 1946, Akamatsu was even interrogated as a possible war criminal, but partly because of his troubles with the authorities in the context of his doctoral dissertation, where some of his words were interpreted by his censors as being respectless against the Emperor himself in person, and which were considered to be subversive in 1943, charges against him were dropped.

In 1953, Akamatsu became the Dean of the Faculty of Economics at Hitosubashi University, and could finish many additional works and could peacefully retire from his job at the University. Today, there is a vast debate on the flying geese model or FGM, as it is sometimes being referred to, which can also be evidenced by the fact that none the less than over 700 articles in "Google scholar" refer to Akamatsu 1961.[9]

---

[9] The union catalogue of all Japanese research libraries—the so-called CINII books catalogue - lists today under his author name at the address http://ci.nii.ac.jp/author/DA0263825X?count=200 &sortorder=2 none the less than 71 works, and only two of them are listed in Western languages; his essay in 1961 and his 1924 essay for the German Philosophical magazine *"Archiv für Geschichte der Philosophie und Soziologie 38/1–4, 1928 (Neue Folge 31)"*, which appeared under the title *"Wie ist das vernünftige Sollen und die Wissenschaft des Sollens bei Hegel möglich? Zur Kritik der Rickertschen Abhandlung "Über idealistische Politik als Wissenschaft"*, in 1924. One of the few major academic libraries in the world, where this essay is available today, is Fordham University in New York City, one of the leading Jesuit Universities in America. It is truly notable that Akamatsu could publish an original article in one of the leading German language journals of philosophy, written in German, on a central issue of German philosophy at the time. The *Stanford Encyclopedia of Philosophy* dedicates a lengthy article on Heinrich Rickert, a liberal German philosopher, on whom Akamatsu's essay was centered; available at http://plato.stanford.edu/archives/win2013/entries/heinrich-rickert/.

Appendix B: The Results of Spectral Analysis and Application of Other Statistical Approaches to the Study of Cycles with Different Lengths

In *Chapter 2* above we have already discussed the issue of the detection of the K-waves in the global GDP dynamics with spectral analysis methods. In this appendix we will continue this discussion in a wider perspective involving other variables and other cycles. In addition, in *Chapters 2* and *4*, we presented some thoughts on the relationship between cycles of the national economies and cycles of global convergence and divergence. In the present appendix, we will now provide empirical tests about these contentions. It will be based on a variety of standard econometric techniques, and aims to be a fairly comprehensive test of the hypotheses about Kondratieff long cycles in the framework of the center-periphery structure of the global economy.

Methodology and Data

Our historical time series data for 31 countries since 1885 are exclusively based on Angus Maddison's data (see Maddison, 2003, 2007) in the updated version by Bolt and van Zanden (2013; see also our electronic online documentation, accompanying this appendix[10]). The 31 countries with complete data since 1885 are Argentina; Australia; Austria; Belgium; Brazil; Canada; Chile; Colombia; Denmark; Finland; France; Germany; Greece; India; Indonesia; Italy; Japan; Netherlands; New Zealand; Norway; Peru; Portugal; Russia; Spain; Sri Lanka; Sweden; Switzerland; UK; Uruguay; USA; and Venezuela. These countries make up approximately 40.8 % of global population and 57.8 % of global purchasing power. The supporting online materials[11] further highlight our freely available data.

---

[10] See https://www.academia.edu/3742045/Korotayev_Grinin_Tausch_Economic_Cycles_Crises_and_the_Global_Periphery_Springer_2016_-_Supporting_online_materials.

[11] See Ibidem.

Our data for world industrial production growth are an extension of the materials, first presented by Goldstein (1988), updated by Tausch and Ghymers (2007), relying on UNIDO data on world-wide industrial production growth from the mid-1970s to the turn of the millennium, now updated by open access figures from the United States Central Intelligence Agency.

Our figures on major power wars were first presented by Goldstein (1988), updated by PRIO data (major power wars) until 2002 (Tausch & Ghymers, 2007). The Online Appendices further highlight our freely available data. Readers can download the most important data and also hundreds of spectral density graphs, rolling correlations and regressions, autocorrelation analyses at the level of the World System and at the level of the 31 analyzed countries.[12]

Our research endeavor made ample use of the considerable opportunities offered by Microsoft EXCEL 2010 for calculating long rows of percentage changes, relative ascent and decline, and rolling regressions and correlations over long distances of time. Rolling regressions and correlations as a methodology were discussed, among others, in Perman and Tavera (2005), Smith and Taylor (2001), and Tang (2010). At a glance, our data are based on the sources described below in Box 1.

Flagship essays written by professional economists, using advanced econometric techniques of time-series analysis have come to very divergent and often negative assessments on the existence and relevance of "*long cycles*" of economics, let alone global politics. Some essays, using advanced econometric methods, standing out in the literature have been written by Diebolt (2012), Diebolt and Doliger (2006), Diebolt and Escudier (2002), Silverberg (2006), and van Ewijk (1982)—thus echoing the early criticism against the long 40–60 year Kondratieff cycle, in Garvy (1943) and Kuznets (1940). Even authors from the econometric research tradition, originally sympathetic to the general notion of Kondratieff cycles, deny the existence of such fluctuations in the real economy, and rather talk about long swings of prices—like Berry, Kim, and Baker (2001), de Groot and Franses (2008), Haustein and Neuwirth (1982), and Van Ewijk (1982)—and hence prefer to talk about price cycles and not cycles of the real economy. The essay by Haustein and Neuwirth (1982) is particularly interesting and also—in a way—is typical for the econometric mainstream results on the issue: spectral analysis was applied to long-time series of industrial production, energy consumption, inventions, innovations, and patents in order to reveal quantitative regularities in their behavior and/or in their interdependence.

Spectral analysis is a statistical approach for analyzing stationary time series data in which the series is decomposed into cyclical or periodic components indexed by the frequency of repetition. Spectral analysis falls within the frequency domain approach to time series analysis. The spectral density function plays the central role and it summarizes the contributions of cyclical components to the variation of a stationary time series (Diebold, Kilian, & Nerlove, 2010; Vogelsang, 2008). Our supporting online materials[13] contain a non-mathematical primer on spectral analysis with many results from various simulated long cycles of different durations, and

---

[12] At the website https://www.academia.edu/3742045/Korotayev_Grinin_Tausch_Economic_Cycles_Crises_and_the_Global_Periphery_Springer_2016_-_Supporting_online_materials.

[13] Ibidem.

with results for different types of stronger or weaker "nested" cycles in the more overall swings in the recent research tradition of Devezas (2012, pp. 160–163). Another primer on spectral analysis can be found at the end of this appendix.

> **Box 1: The data sources IMF World Economic Outlook Database:** http://www.imf.org/external/pubs/ft/weo/2014/01/weodata/index.aspx
>
> **Inequality:** Estimated Household Income Inequality Data Set (EHII)—is a global dataset, derived from the econometric relationship between UTIP-UNIDO, other conditioning variables, and the World Bank's Deininger & Squire data set http://utip.gov.utexas.edu/data.html
>
> **Maddison time series data:** Bolt and Van Zanden (2013). The First Update of the Maddison Project; Re-Estimating Growth Before 1820, Maddison Project Working Paper 4 http://www.ggdc.net/maddison/maddison-project/abstract.htm?id=4
>
> **Top Income data:** http://piketty.pse.ens.fr/fr/capitalisback
>
> **War cycle since 1495 Data:** Goldstein, J. S. (1988). *Long cycles: Prosperity and war in the modern age*. New Haven: Yale University Press. and—after 1945—PRIO Oslo, see: Tausch A., & Ghymers Ch. (2007). *From the 'Washington' towards a 'Vienna Consensus'? A quantitative analysis on globalization, development and global governance*. Hauppauge, NY: Nova Science Publishers.
>
> **World Bank data:** http://data.worldbank.org/indicator
>
> **World industrial production growth since 1750:** Data: http://www.hichemkaroui.com/?p=2383; for the period after 1998: http://www.ereport.ru/en/stat.php?razdel=country&count=world&table=ipecia&time=2

Haustein and Neuwirth (1982) make an attempt to identify logistics within those time series. According to them, in the long cycle of 50–53 years, no significant autocorrelation could be detected. Logistics exist only in three special periods for innovations and inventions. Nondominant long cycles do appear in the interaction between innovations, production, patents, and energy consumption. The investigation shed light on the causal structure of the innovation system. In particular, it revealed a significant influence of industrial production on patents with a lag of 9 years. But this, certainly, is not what adherents of the K-cycle hypothesis would have hoped for. As Berry, Kim, and Baker state in their 2001 essay:

"One of the troubling characteristics of the long-wave literature is the equation of 56-year long waves (which Kondratieff explicitly associated with financial indicators) with waves of economic growth. This is wrong. As we teach our students in introductory economics, growth and development are different. It is the clusters of innovation that produce economic development that are associated with the long downwave, per Schumpeter, but the pulses of infrastructure building, capital outlays, and economic growth that flow from these innovation clusters come with the 18-year rhythms of the building cycle. Much of the confusion in the long-wave literature arises from this confusion of the rhythms of inflation and growth, and of the concepts of economic growth and economic development" (Berry, Kim, & Baker, 2001).

In turn, flagship empirical analyses, using advanced econometric techniques, including, but not exclusively, spectral analysis in favor of parts or the totality of Kondratieff's contentions (i.e. 40–60 year swings in prices and the "real economy") are represented by Bornschier (1996), Devezas (2010, 2012), Devezas and Corredine (2001), Forrester (1977), Goldstein (1987, 1988, 2006), Korotayev and Tsirel (2010; see also Коротаев и Цирель, 2010а, 2010б); Grinin, Korotayev, and Tsirel (Гринин, Коротаев и Цирель, 2011), Metz (2011), Sterman (1985, 1986), Tausch and Ghymers (2007), and Tausch and Jourdon (2011). A somewhat surprising turn of evidence is found in the essay published by Weber (1981), which maintains a cycle of themes and values in advanced societies. De Groot and Franses, in their analysis of the dynamics of national product, industrial production, employment, consumer prices, wages, interest rates, population, and stock market indicators for the USA, the UK and the Netherlands since the 19th century, however sympathetic the authors might have been to the notion of the K-cycle, come to the conclusion that in the USA there is a 40 year significant fluctuation of employment and a 60 year fluctuation of prices and interest rates, but not of GDP or industrial production. In the UK, the situation is similar, and also in the Netherlands. A Kondratieff cycle—their essay suggests—is rather a cycle of employment, interest rates, and perhaps wages, but certainly not an economic growth cycle per se (de Groot & Franses, 2008).

Rainer Metz comes up with a similar, rather pessimistic conclusion in his 2011 essay:

> "Besides these methodological implications, our results also have strong substantial implications. First of all it is noted that regular long waves of the Kondratieff type in UK GDP do not exist if outliers are modelled correctly. GDP movement in the UK displays a trend with a variable mean growth rate, a fairly irregular business cycle with a period of about 11 years and several infrequently occurring exogenous shocks with persistent as well as transitory effects. Obviously long-run growth follows a smooth trend with a variable mean growth rate (slope). The shocks causing this slope show long-term up- and downswings but without any regularity. This offers interesting perspectives for future research. First of all, such analysis should be extended to long-run GDP series for other countries. Second, the analysis should be extended to series other than GDP and also to series covering the pre-industrial period. If the results obtained in this article for UK GDP are then confirmed, we strongly recommend that 'long waves' should not be considered as oscillating trend cycles but as a kind of growth dynamics without any regularity and analyse them in the framework of (unified) growth theory." (Metz, 2011, p. 235)

In view of the often bitter controversies surrounding the idea of longer 40–60 year cycles, we have decided to re-assess the entire evidence, as far as it is possible, today, as the neat North American English saying goes, "*from scratch*", and using a plurality of different methods. As is well-known, the initiator of modern historical real purchasing power per capita statistics, Professor Angus Maddison, never believed himself even for a second in the existence of Kondratieff cycles (Devezas, 2012; Maddison, 2007).

To make matters worse, there is as well widespread disagreement even among members of the economics profession on the appropriate advanced quantitative methods to be used. A typical case in question is the already mentioned technique of spectral analysis, which for many was THE method par excellence to study long cycles just a few years ago. As Nathaniel Beck, a methodologist working in the field of political science, maintained still in 1991 with quite a strong dose of polemics against the mainstream of K-cycle-researchers:

> *"Why don't analysts of cycles always use spectral analysis? After all, it is exactly the technique designed to decompose a stationary series into its cyclic components, and its statistical properties are excellent. I think the prime fault of spectral analysis is that it usually fails to find long social cycles. My own feeling is that this is shooting the messenger, but such practice is not unknown."* (Beck, 1991)

The temptation to use this method, now that it is universally available in the IBM-SPSS standard statistical software, implemented at many Universities around the world, is great; and it is even greater because the IBM-SPSS software just requires you to enter the original data and to get the results by simply clicking the proper pre-installed windows.

But econometricians nowadays disagree on the continued appropriateness of this very methodology of spectral analysis as the adequate methodology to analyze data, testing the Kondratieff hypotheses:

> *"Spectral analysis thus involves a regularity of movements that is not verified and which, in addition, is not essential in affirming that they exist. In fact, the spectral analysis method cannot truly prove or refute the existence of socioeconomic cycles."* (Diebolt, 2012, p. 122)

Rainer Metz, another prominent theoretician of the art of econometric time series analysis, reaches in his 2011 article (Metz, 2011) the discomforting conclusion that no K-cycle in production exists, while in his book in 2008 (Metz, 2008) he was still more optimistic, with the troughs in world industrial production growth given in 1820, 1880, and 1955 (smoothed component, long waves, Figure 4.3, Figure 4.4 and Figure 4.5, pp. 165–166, Metz, 2008). Various filtering techniques and the (non)-elimination of the data for mining then, in 2008, did not change his final and resounding verdict on page 196 of his 2008 book that K-cycles in the real economy indeed exist; with tests provided not only at the level of the world economy, but also at the level of Danish, French, German, Italian, Swedish, UK, and US data. But in 2011, the very same researcher, Rainer Metz, reaches a more pessimistic verdict on the validity of the K-cycle hypotheses.

Our own humble approach will be very "down to earth". We first re-analyze the existence of world economic and political cycles and then proceed to show the results of different time series analyses for the 31 countries with fairly complete Maddison data since the middle of the 1880s, i.e. Argentina; Australia; Austria; Belgium; Brazil; Canada; Chile; Colombia; Denmark; England/GB/UK; F. USSR/Russia; Finland; France; Germany; Greece; Holland/ Netherlands; India; Indonesia (Java before 1880); Italy; Japan; New Zealand; Norway; Peru; Portugal; Spain; Sri Lanka; Sweden; Switzerland; Uruguay; USA; and Venezuela.[14]

The true nature of the K-cycle will be only revealed by looking at the patterns of ascent and decline in the world economy over a long time period **at the same time.**

---

[14] See https://www.academia.edu/3742045/Korotayev_Grinin_Tausch_Economic_Cycles_Crises_and_the_Global_Periphery_Springer_2016_-_Supporting_online_materials.

So we will evaluate with a plurality of quantitative techniques the evolution of the real income gap of the 30/31 countries mentioned in relation to the "world average", in relation to the highest and lowest income country in each year between 1885 and 2010 and in relation to the dominant country of the capitalist world economy, i.e. the United States of America; and alternately, the United Kingdom, and also with a UNDP type income index and in comparison to the "world average" per capita purchasing power. Thus we tested very exhaustively the hypothesis whether there is a "Kondratieff cycle" of convergence or divergence in the countries of the World System, by applying spectral analysis, autocorrelation analysis and rolling regression/correlation analysis to these convergence data as well.

Just as Camm *et al.* (1996), in their path-breaking medical analysis of heart rate variability, and Genzel and Cesarsky (2000), in their astronomical analysis of extragalactic results from the infrared space observatory (two randomly chosen high-impact articles from medicine and astronomy), we use a very common standard mathematical-statistical procedure (spectral analysis), and we do not hesitate to use an entire array of other necessary statistical tests as well to assess the simple contention: are these deep crises in the capitalist world really a recurrent phenomenon, and is there at least the hope of some light at the end of the tunnel? Or are these lights, as the bitter Irish joke has it, only the headlamps of an approaching train? **Or are the French econometricians Diebolt/Escudier correct in their very harshly formulated assumption that the long-term economic cycles of 40–60 years duration are comparable to the monster of *"Loch Ness"* and that they never existed nor do they exist (Diebolt & Escudier, 2002)?**

Another methodological aspect can be mentioned only briefly: the question of filters in time series analysis. As the already mentioned renown German econometrician and economic historian Rainer Metz explained recently (Metz, 2011), there are three unresolved questions in the entire debate: First, what are valid indicators for the long-wave phenomenon? Second, what time period should be analyzed? Third, are long waves to be conceived as cycles around the trend or oscillations of the trend itself? Most of the traditional approaches to long waves, Metz (2011) argues, see them as regular 40- to 60-year cycles oscillating around a non-periodic secular trend and superimposed by shorter oscillations such as Juglar and Kitchin cycles. Only this conception of long waves—introduced by Kondratieff and supported by Schumpeter—allows a statistical proof of the assumed regularity of long waves. But it requires:

> *"[...] a statistical apparatus that can isolate such oscillations in historical time series from other cycles, from the trend and from irregular oscillations, which belong neither to the trend nor to cyclical oscillations. Another possibility for formalising long waves is to see them as an endogenous part of the secular movement itself."* (Metz, 2011)

But regarding such efforts, the great Polish political economist Michal Kalecki once remarked already back in 1968:

> *"The contemporary theory of growth of capitalist economies tends to consider this problem in terms of a moving equilibrium, which is frequently not checked for stability, rather than adopting an approach similar to that applied in the theory of business cycles. The latter consists of establishing two relations: one based on the impact of the effective demand*

generated by investment upon profits and the national income; and the other showing the determination of investment decisions by, broadly speaking, the level and the rate of change of economic activity. […] In fact, the long-run trend is but a slowly changing component of a chain of short-period situations; it has no independent entity, and the two basic relations mentioned above should be formulated in such a way as to yield the trend cum business-cycle phenomenon. It is true that the task is incomparably more difficult than in the case of another abstraction, that of the 'pure business cycle' and, as will be seen below, the results of such an inquiry are less 'mechanistic'. This, however, is no excuse for dropping this approach, which seems to me the only key to the realistic analysis of the dynamics of a capitalist economy." (Kalecki 1968a, 1968b)

The issue of filtering the data series requires therefore some further comments. Diebolt and Doliger (2006) recommend using the so-called Hodrick and Prescott filter (Hodrick & Prescott, 1997) to apply to the data series before spectral analysis is being performed, because:

"[…] in such a way it is possible a priori to consider that the spectrum of the filtered series is more representative." (Diebolt & Doliger, 2006, p. 41)

However, another authoritative recent source in time series methodology, Cogley (2008), comes out against using such filters, a reason, why we altogether abandoned this procedure in favor of the more simple and easily understandable Maddison time series data transformation into annual straightforward percentage growth rates. **In addition to the methodological simplicity of this approach, it is also certain that political decision makers are primarily interested in annual GDP per capita growth rates, and not in filtered time series as such. Cogley (2008) correctly emphasizes that economic models are by definition incomplete representations of reality.** To relate business cycle models to data, empirical macroeconomists frequently filter the untransformed GDP per capita *et cetera* data prior to analysis to remove the growth component. Cogley (2008) mentions that until the 1980s, the most common way to do that was to estimate and subtract a deterministic linear trend. The desire to model permanent shocks in macroeconomic time series led

"to the development of a variety of stochastic de-trending methods. […] Another popular way to measure business cycles involves application of band-pass and high-pass filters. […] In the business cycle literature, the work of Hodrick and Prescott (1997) and Baxter and King (1999) has been especially influential. […] While data filters are very popular, there is some controversy about whether they represent appealing definitions of the business cycle. For one, there is a disconnect between the theory and macroeconomic applications, for the theory applies to stationary random processes and applications involve non-stationary variables. […] In practice, of course, measured cycles are not perfectly predictable because actual filters only approximate the ideal. But this means that innovations in measured cycles are due solely to approximation errors in the filter, not to something intrinsic in the concept. The better the approximation, the closer the measures are to determinism. How to square this deterministic vision with stochastic general equilibrium models is not obvious. […] Business cycle modellers also frequently abstract from trends. […] Contrary to intuition, trend-specification errors spread throughout the frequency domain and are not quarantined to low frequencies. That difference explains why the promising results on seasonality do not carry over to trend filtering. […] Finally, some economists question whether filter-based measures capture an important feature of business cycles. […] Trend reversion is a defining characteristic of the business cycle. […] Expected growth should be higher than average at the trough of a recession because agents can look forward

to a period of catching up to compensate for past output losses. By the same token, expected growth should be lower than average at the peak of an expansion. [...] Data filters are not for everyone. They are certainly convenient for constructing rough and ready measures of the business cycle, and they produce nice pictures when applied to US data. But some economists worry about the spurious cycle problem, especially in applications to business cycle models where the existence and properties of business cycles are points to be established." (Cogley, 2008)

Obviously the leading experts in econometrics, whose expertise has been consulted for the aims of this appendix, seem to agree nowadays that no *"single shot"* best method to test the relevance of Kondratieff's claims about a 40-60 year economic cycle exists (see especially Diebolt, 2012; Diebolt & Doliger, 2006; Metz, 2008, 2011; in contrast to the earlier optimism about the relevance of tests of autocorrelation and spectral density analysis, inherent in Beck, 1991). **In this appendix we arrive at a conclusion that a *"forensic approach"* to long cycles, based on the application of several tests at once is perhaps more appropriate than the search for a rejection or confirmation of the K-cycle hypothesis by a single econometric method.**

Since the foundations of the application of all the methods in question to real existing time series of economic variables across time in several countries—especially spectral analysis, once considered being the best single approach—are nowadays questioned, such an application of a plurality of tests, ranging from tests of autocorrelation via periodograms from spectral analysis and the analysis of spectral density to the *"poor man's"* time series analysis methodology of *"rolling regressions"* and *"rolling correlations"* will be applied, not to forget the simple, straight-forward visual inspection of the initial data series in question.

Since the political class across the world is interested in concrete, tangible and easily readable results, we have chosen to opt for a straightforward additional choice, which will meet perhaps with criticism from the econometric time series analysis community:

- Reproducing the periodograms spectral density and the spectral density analysis graphs in terms of periods and not frequencies without any logarithmic transformations to make the time periods of the cycles more visible to the general public reading this appendix.

But our choice of a plurality of methods, based on autocorrelations, spectral analysis, and "rolling regressions"/"rolling correlations" is based on a vast number of studies in the field of time-series methodology, consulted for this appendix (Abadir & Talmain, 2002; Babetskii, Komarek, & Komarkova, 2007; Bartlett, 1946; Beck, 1991; Bloomfield, 1976; Box & Jenkins, 1976; Chu & Freund, 1996; Clark & West, 2006; Collard, 1999; Cryer, 1986; Dempster, 1969; Dittmar, Gavin, & Kydland, 2005; Fuller, 1976; Junttila, 2001; Komarkova & Komarek 2007; Louçã & Reijnders, 1999; Quenouville, 1949; Silverberg, 2006; Zivot & Wang, 2006).

Our appendix is based on the standard IBM-SPSS-21 time series analysis tools, and all the used methods and their mathematical algorithms are fully documented to the international public by IBM (2014). For that reason, we refrain from reproducing the mathematical formula, which interested readers might easily download from the freely available IBM internet documentation (2014) (if they are not very familiar with the respective mathematical formula anyway).

- As to **correlations**, we used the standard Pearson-Bravais correlation coefficients (Blalock, 1972; Dziuban & Shirkey, 1974; Harman, 1976; Rummel, 1970). *"Rolling"* **regressions and correlations** are quite a powerful and straightforward instrument of the analysis of time-series and became more popular in recent times in the framework of financial market trend analysis and the necessity to have easily interpretable and reliable instruments of analysis at hand (Perman & Tavera, 2005; Smith & Taylor, 2001; Tang, 2010; Zivot & Wang, 2006, furthermore: Cook, 1977; Dempster, 1969; Velleman & Welsch, 1981). Throughout this work, we use 25 year (Kondratieff cycles, 2×25 years=50 years) and 75 year periods (war cycles, 2×75 years=150 years) for the moving time window of regression/correlation analysis. We also used shorter windows to reproduce the Barro, the Kuznets and the real estate cycles.
- Our analyses of **autocorrelation** and **cross-correlation** are based on the standard **IBM-SPSS ACF** and **CCF algorithm**, which are based on Bartlett (1946), Box and Jenkins (1976), Cryer (1986), and Quenouville (1949) (**autocorrelation**) and Box and Jenkins (1976) (**cross-correlation**). Our graphs allow also for the inspection of longer time series. In presenting the graphs, we also took care of the better visibility of the significant results.
- The **IBM-SPSS spectral density routine**, which is based on the methodological developments, presented by Bloomfield (1976) and Fuller (1976) was performed by using the IBM-SPSS default options; the chosen window was most of the time the Tuckey-Hamming window with three periods. We also tested the validity of our main results with longer windows as well. As we demonstrate however in our non-mathematical primer on spectral density analysis, available in our appendix and at https://www.academia.edu/3742045/Korotayev_Grinin_Tausch_Economic_Cycles_Crises_and_the_Global_Periphery_Springer_2016_-_Supporting_online_materials, longer windows seem to distort the results even of simulated time series, where *ex definitione* we really know the length of the oscillations already beforehand, and they do not really help us to discover the real periodicity of the oscillations in question, especially when we are confronted with the already mentioned "Devezas" paradox of longer cycles and "nested" shorter cycles, presented by Devezas (2012, p. 161). We use both the standard IBM-SPSS periodograms and the spectral density graphs (Diebolt, 2012).

Results on the Level of World Industrial Production Growth Since 1740–2011

Our results on the level of the world economy are a resounding "yes" for the hypotheses voiced by Kondratieff, but with several additional qualifications and extensions.

Kondratieff was right in analyzing a 54 year cycle of the real economy, but there are other important cycles too; some of them very well known to social science research, others perhaps still more to be explored.

On the level of industrial production growth in the world economy, there—parallel to the Kondratieff cycle, a 140 year "logistic" cycle, first analyzed by Immanuel Wallerstein; and in addition, there is evidence on a new 36 year disaster cycle, correctly predicted by the neoclassical contemporary economist Robert Barro (see in *Chapter 4*).

As regards shorter cycles, there is also evidence—although somewhat weaker than expected—for a 22–23 year Kuznets cycle and the shorter, well-known real estate cycles, Juglar cycles and Kitchin cycles. Electronic Appendix Graph 8 portrays the original data series from 1741 to 2011, and Electronic Appendix Electronic Appendix Graph 9 the result of our "rolling correlation" exercise.[15]

Electronic Appendix Graph 10 and Electronic Appendix Electronic Appendix Graph 11[16] reproduce the main results of the spectral analysis of the cyclical movements in the original, untransformed data. The Kuznets cycle, the Barro cycle, the Kondratieff cycle and the Wallerstein logistic cycle are all confirmed in their existence. Thus spectral density analysis of the untransformed global data suggests that on the world level, there are all the cycles at work which have been discussed for decades now in economic research.

Autocorrelation analysis also supports this contention (Electronic Appendix Graph 12). This analysis is centered around the autocorrelation analysis residual plot (ACF autocorrelation plot), showing coefficients and upper and lower bounds of confidence per number of lags.[17]

Electronic Appendix Graph 13 draws the attention of our readers to a type of cycle, really neglected in empirical K-wave research: the Wallerstein logistic cycle, whose shape suggests that the current crisis heralds the beginning of a trough along the oscillations of this cycle. In terms of its statistical qualities, this cycle is about equal in strength to the Kondratieff-cycle. There is strong reason to believe that the Wallerstein cycle is closely connected to the issue of leadership in the international system. The period from the end of the Napoleonic Wars to the Great Depression in the 1930s was the period of the British dominance in the world economy, while the US hegemony evolved as a result of World War II and seems to be declining.[18]

In Electronic Appendix (4),[19] we also document our results based on a 5-year moving averages research design, based on the original data. The 5 year moving averages design should serve to replicate the results, achieved earlier by us (Korotayev & Tsirel, 2010), where we also used such 5-year moving averages. **This exercise neatly reproduces our results mentioned above. The Kuznets, Barro, Kondratieff and Wallerstein cycles re-appear in the periodogram for that**

---

[15] See https://www.academia.edu/3742045/Korotayev_Grinin_Tausch_Economic_Cycles_Crises_and_the_Global_Periphery_Springer_2016_-_Supporting_online_materials.

[16] Ibidem.

[17] Ibidem.

[18] Ibidem.

[19] Ibidem.

research design (see also our periodogram for the periods 0–70 years with a wider spread); while there is also a confirmation of our hypothesis about the Kuznets, Barro, Kondratieff and Wallerstein cycles in the spectral density graphs under the assumption of a window (Tukey-Hamming) of three periods. The strength of the Wallerstein cycle is again shown to be considerable. In the following, we will test the validity of another major contention of contemporary K-cycle research, the assertion of war cycles, made tremendously popular internationally by the works of Goldstein (1985, 1987, 1988, 1991, 2006); although Goldstein in one of his later major works (Goldstein, 2011) distances himself from the certain determinism which might have been evident in the international reception of his earlier work. And he now believes that humanity can be at the brink of abolishing war.

Results on the Level of Major Power Wars in the World System Since 1495

Our data about major power war in the global system, as we stated, are an extension of Goldstein's (1988) dataset about battle fatalities from major power wars (i.e. the five current permanent members of the UN Security Council + Germany) from 1495 onwards. From 1946 onwards, we used the PRIO, Oslo data, reported by Tausch and Ghymers (2007), since the Goldstein data stop in 1975, while the PRIO/Tausch/Ghymers data cover the period between 1946 and 2002. To make the battle fatality rates comparable over time and to correct for the advances of international weapons technologies as well as practices of general conscription since the French Revolution, which all caused an exponential increase of annual battle fatalities from major power wars in the 20th century, we decided to calculate the fourth root of this variable. Interested readers will find, however, similar other results at their disposal as well, which are based on the original untransformed annual major power wars battle fatalities data series, and on a series which is based on the tenth root of the battle fatalities variable. Our chosen transformation properly highlights the intensity of earlier terrible wars in human history, like the Thirty Years War and the War of Spanish Succession, and makes a comparison to the destructive character of the wars of the 20th century more feasible than other mathematical transformations of the war intensity variable. War intensity under the formulation of the fourth root does not have a rising or falling trend over the time axis and thus better allows to analyze the real fluctuations of war intensity over time:

1. **Untransformed war intensity:** $y = 0.4165x - 32.636$
   $R^2 = 0.0487$
2. **Fourth root war intensity:** $y = 0.0002x + 1.7307$
   $R^2 = 0.0005$
3. **Tenth root war intensity:** $y = -0.0007x + 1.2304$
   $R^2 = 0.0273$

We also analyze the connection between the 75-year rolling correlation trend of the war cycle and the 75-year rolling correlation trend of the Wallerstein economic cycle. Our econometric time series data, based on cross-correlation (CCF) reveal no significant direct connection between the war variable (the fourth root of battle fatalities from major power wars) and the global economic variable (annual growth of world industrial production, see also Electronic Appendix Graph 14[20]).

Electronic Appendix Graph 15[21] shows the results from the rolling correlation analysis of the untransformed battle fatalities rate in history since the end of the Middle Ages, again showing—as Goldstein, 1988, so correctly emphasized—the peaks of the international conflagrations in the Thirty Years War, the French wars of the 18th century, the Napoleonic Wars, and the German quest for global dominance, 1914–1945 as well as the evolution of the postwar order with the Korean and Vietnam Wars.

Electronic Appendix Graph 16a and Electronic Appendix Graph 16b reproduce the time series plots, whereas Electronic Appendix Graph 17 and Electronic Appendix Graph 18 reproduce the results of the spectral analysis procedure, based on the 4th root of the intensity of warfare variable. Our data clearly support the hypothesis of longer waves of wars in the international system, which is part and parcel of contemporary world-system research (our own calculations from the data set *"Kondratieff cycles and war cycles"* is contained in https://www.academia.edu/3742045/Korotayev_Grinin_Tausch_Economic_Cycles_Crises_and_the_Global_Periphery_Springer_2016_-_Supporting_online_materials). As to the documentation, see also: Tausch and Ghymers (2007). Spectral analysis clearly reveals a 160 year cycle of global warfare, which was already evident in the earlier research by Goldstein (1985, 1987, 1988, 1991, 2006) on the subject. The *"illusion of cycles"* type of literature, initiated by Beck (1991) thus has to be refuted.

New Insights into the Kondratieff Cycle Dating Game

Our research also sheds lights on the necessary reformulation of Kondratieff cycle dating schemes and the assessment of the current crisis, which began in 2007. As we show in Electronic Appendix Graph 19,[22] there is some reason to hypothesize that the current crisis might not be a Kondratieff cycle trough (which hit the world economy in the late 1980s, culminating in the disintegration of Communist rule in Eastern Europe and the end of the Soviet Union), but a downswing phase of the 140 year Wallerstein cycle:

In the Great Depression starting in 1929, ALL cycle troughs coincided, while in the crisis of 2007, such an occurrence of ALL the cyclical troughs at once is just not the case. This is the main reason why the current crisis is far from being the *"final*

---

[20] Ibidem.
[21] Ibidem.
[22] See Ibidem.

crisis of capitalism", and why social science today can learn a lot from Kondratieff's stubborn resistance to similar conceptions advanced at the time of the Great Depression.

Note that in Electronic Appendix Graph 20a,[23] we used the following rolling correlation windows: 8 = 16–18 year real estate cycle[24]; 11 = 22 year Kuznets cycle; 18 = 36 year Barro cycle; 27 = 54 year Kondratieff cycle; 70 = 140 year Wallerstein cycle.

Another interesting point to be mentioned here is what social science can offer to the policy makers at the level of the G-7, the G-20, the European Union, the OECD, the Eurasian Economic Union and other institutions of democratic global governance in terms of the lessons one can draw about the most successful and the least successful strategies to confront the crises in 1929 and 2007.[25]

Exits from the Crisis

The four countries with the most consistent and stable convergence path in human history did practice many policy receipts, which are a *"forbidden medicine"* for neoliberal economics—the Scandinavian social Keynesian models Norway, Finland, Sweden and Denmark, combining a fair amount of social spending, investment in human capital, free trade, and a political partnership between wage labor and capital, tending towards wage rises in tandem with the growth of productivity. Their historical progress to stable democracy, humanism and well-being is really unparalleled. They all started out belonging to the lower half of purchasing power per capita in the world, and they all belong now to the highest 1/3 of countries.

The systematic comparison of the effects of the 2007 crisis (purchasing power per capita in 2010 as compared to purchasing power per capita in 1995) show to us that Japan, Italy, Denmark, France and Germany are the biggest losers, while Finland, Russia, Sweden, Chile and Uruguay were the biggest winners (Electronic Appendix Graph 21[26]).

In the following, we will also try to draw some conclusions into our insights about hegemonial contenders and their structural positions in the world economy, then, during the Great Depression, and nowadays. By comparing their historical trajectories, we of course would not like to commit the error of *"the poverty of historicism"* (Popper, 1961). On the contrary, we would simply like to draw our readers' attention to the various Scyllas and Charybdis, which nations might face emerging from crises and previous non-democratic political systems on their possible transition path towards a socio-liberal, open society and full-scale democracy.

---

[23] See Ibidem.

[24] http://www.cato.org/publications/commentary/great-18year-real-estate-cycle.

[25] See https://www.academia.edu/3742045/Korotayev_Grinin_Tausch_Economic_Cycles_Crises_and_the_Global_Periphery_Springer_2016_-_Supporting_online_materials.

[26] See Ibidem.

Predictions About the Hegemonial Contenders and the Global Hegemons in the 21st Century

Electronic Appendix Graph 22[27] shows the striking parallels between the global order in the six decades before 1940 (i.e. 1885–1940) and before 2010. Both Germany and Russia experienced a considerable decline during the world crisis of the 1920s (Germany-Weimar Republic) and the 1980s and early 1990s (Russia today), and both countries find another, formerly very poor and rising hegemonial contender among the nations of the international system on their side (Electronic Appendix Graph 22[28]).

Not only the possible hegemonial contenders (Germany and Japan prior to World War II; Russia and China in the contemporary period) have many world economic characteristics in common; also the hegemons (UK before 1940; the US before the crisis of 2007) were on comparable global trajectories: both experienced a history of sharp hegemonial decline (in the UK interrupted by the temporary rally during World War I). And both nations managed to have a hegemonial temporary recovery associated with the names of the UK-Prime Ministers Stanley Baldwin and Ramsey MacDonald, and the US-Presidents Ronald Reagan, George H. W. Bush and William J. Clinton (Electronic Appendix Graph 23).

Implications for Russia

So should Russia follow the footsteps of the Weimar Republic and the later hegemonial challenge against the West, or try to find a "Scandinavian path"? Given the limitations of book publication space, it would not be possible to present here the details of the debates among the Marxist classics of the early 20th century on the proper development strategies to follow. As has been shown already in Tausch and Prager (1992), the European social democrats, above all the Austrian Otto Bauer and the Swede Ernst Wigforss, were correct in emphasizing a path of slow and fundamental democratic reforms, while Lenin, from the very start, harshly criticized the social democrats, overlooking the powerful societal tradeoffs between reforms and economic growth, and political stability. Not only that: while agricultural and educational reform, an army, based on general conscription and democratic control, social security, public health *et cetera* are all mighty drivers of economic growth in a democratic and free society, the European social democrats of the early 20th century were also very correct in emphasizing the long-term limitations of unlimited state power, with Otto Bauer clearly predicting, already in 1920, the subsequent state terror under Bolshevik power in Russia.

---

[27] See Ibidem.
[28] See Ibidem.

Graphs 27a and 27b[29] show the dramatic truth of these predictions and debates in the history of the 20th century then to follow. Without debating the twisted turns of political history in Europe since the 1930s (Scandinavia) and since 1945 (Austria), social democratic reform ideas in the spirit of Polanyi's *"Great Transformation"* all gained ground in these countries and decidedly influenced the growth of a social welfare state, social partnership between wage labor and capital, and a strong state sector, which together assured the spectacular growth and ascent in world society right through to the early 1980s, and in some countries even beyond. At the same time, and starting from the post-World-War I recession, which was as deep in Russia as in the other countries, Russia's path towards state socialism initially led to an improvement of 45 % vis-à-vis the global average until the mid-1960s. Thus the net gains in world-systemic position as compared to the times before the transformation were then about equal in size in both Russia and in the European social partnership models, but the models in the framework of a bourgeois liberal democracy **were far more resilient against the world economic and political changes, which set in in the late 1970s**. It has to be emphasized as well that the temporary relative decline of the world-systemic position suffered by Finland and Sweden in the late 1980s and early 1990s is also connected with the crisis in the USSR/Russia, which was an important market for the export oriented industries in the Scandinavian countries at that time. In the direct comparison between the USSR/Russia on the one hand and Austria and Finland on the other hand, the results couldn't be more dramatic. Lenin's strategy brought about a net gain of around 45 % in the world-system position, to be wiped out again almost completely in the final phase of the collapse of communism, while the resilience of the social partnership model in Finland and Austria brought about an almost uninterrupted net gain of around 50–60 % in per capita purchasing power as compared to the 'world average' (see Electronic Appendix Graph 24[30]).

For Russia, after having suffered so much damage in all the cataclysms of its history over the last 100 years, it would be important to remember that the most successful postwar political economic strategies (see also Schulmeister, 2013; Tausch & Prager, 1992) were all defined by

(a) net real wage increases in the rhythm of economic growth;
(b) net interest rates slightly below the rate of economic growth;
(c) a strong mixed economy;
(d) a strong presence of the organized interests of wage labor, capital, and agriculture in a democratic decision making processes.

---

[29] See Ibidem.
[30] See Ibidem.

The New Global Maps of Convergence During the Current World Depression

What are the conclusions of the present appendix for the post-crisis years? From the viewpoint of this appendix, the Maddison datasets suffer from two major deficits: the relatively small number of countries, and the fact that the data series ends in 2010. The World Bank, meanwhile, offers a data series on gross national income (GNI) in purchasing power parties (PPP) at current international dollars from 1990 to today for most of the countries and territories of the world economy.[31] With the help of this data series, we hope to be able to answer questions which are unanswered when a researcher uses the Maddison data base.

The "medical diagnosis" about the acute state of economic and social health of the North Atlantic Arena, especially its Western European part, is again emerging from this kind of analysis. In terms of the average world GNI per capita in PPP, the engine of world growth, more than ever before, has shifted towards the China/India region, while Western Europe is facing a sharp decline of its growth perspectives in both the longer term (1990–2013) as well as in the medium term (2007–2013). The diagnosis only can be that the state of health of the patient has gravely deteriorated and that the situation has become really threatening. The uniformity of the downward trend in growth perspectives for the entire North Atlantic arena, especially after 2007, is really frightening and suggests basically questioning the underlying economic paradigm which governed the political economy of the region since the late 1970s and the early 1980s (Maps 13–15[32]).

In the following, we will highlight very briefly some further tendencies emerging from the systematic analysis of the Maddison and the World Bank datasets.

Some Unexpected Further Conclusions from the Analysis of Convergence Paths

Electronic Appendix Map 14[33] does not stand alone in its verdict that overall and underlying growth tendencies for the countries of the Indian Ocean arena, or if you wish to say as well, the house of Islam, the *Dar al Islam,* are not as pessimistic as so many people seem to pretend. The upturn of many periphery and semi-periphery countries in the 1980s and beyond (see also Appendix 7[34]) corresponds to the closer inspection of the convergence path of the majority of the Muslim countries.

---

[31] http://data.worldbank.org/indicator/NY.GNP.MKTP.PP.CD.
[32] See https://www.academia.edu/3742045/Korotayev_Grinin_Tausch_Economic_Cycles_Crises_and_the_Global_Periphery_Springer_2016_-_Supporting_online_materials.
[33] See Ibidem.
[34] See Ibidem.

Our online Appendix 6[35] highlights consequently the fact that all the international debate about poverty as the main cause of instability and terrorism in the Middle East region notwithstanding it is clear that during the last decades the majority of Muslim countries with available data are now on a positive convergence track again, making good some of the terrain which many of them lost especially in the 1960s and 1970s.

We also should highlight the fact that there are general tendencies at work which merit our attention, and which will be discussed in the context of Scheme 1 below.

Discussion

We of course very much appreciate the already existing research results, presented in the framework of world-system scholarship and in the framework of other theoretical traditions on long cycles of economics and politics. Studies confirming or claiming to confirm the basic tenets of the world-systems approach in the tradition of Kondratieff (1925, 1926, 1928, 1935), Schumpeter (1939) and Wallerstein (2000) about 40–60 year cycles of economics and even longer cycles of global wars were presented, among others, by Bornschier (1996); Devezas (2006, 2010, 2012); Devezas and Corredine (2001); Forrester (1977); Goldstein (1985, 1987, 1988, 1991, 2006); Husson and Louça (2012); Korotayev and Grinin (2012); Korotayev and Tsirel (2010); Louçã (1997); Louçã and Reijnders (1999); Mandel (1995); Marchetti (1980, 2006); Metz (2008); O'Hara (1994, 2001, 2005); Perez (1983); Sterman (1985, 1986); Tausch and Ghymers, 2007; Tausch and Jourdon (2011); and Thompson and Zuk (1982).

The readers of this book in particular are probably well acquainted with the results of these studies. And yet, to be honest, these advances in the direction of confirming the long cycle hypotheses nowadays face up to a formidable and technically often very advanced phalanx of competing studies, which question the very existence of longer cycles in international economics and politics altogether, or at least restrict the relevance of K-cycles to the movements of prices, and not the movements of the "real economy"; thus partially or completely falsifying a core concept of the entire world-system approach (Berry, Kim, & Baker, 2001; de Groot & Franses, 2008; Diebolt, 2012; Diebolt & Doliger, 2006; Diebolt & Escudier, 2002; Garvy, 1943; Haustein & Neuwirth, 1982; Kuznets, 1940, 1966; Metz, 2011; Van Ewijk, 1982).

The parallel world-system research hypothesis about cycles of global warfare was also fundamentally questioned in research, using advanced time-series analysis techniques (Beck, 1991; Silverberg, 2006). And we should recall, as has been re-stated recently by Robinson (2011), these long cycles are of a central and not only peripheral conceptual and theoretical importance for the entire paradigm of the world-system approach, especially Wallerstein's (Wallerstein, 2000).

---

[35] See Ibidem.

Our re-analysis of the entire issue of global cycles and national cycles as well as cycles of global convergence and divergence has revealed that Kondratieff cycles exist, but that there are other types of cycles as well in the global economy, among them two cycles hitherto virtually neglected in quantitative research on the subject—the 36 year Barro cycle and the 140 year Wallerstein cycle. For the first time in the literature, we also tried to analyze in a more systematic fashion the cycles of convergence and divergence.

There is strong reason to believe that the Wallerstein cycle is closely connected to the issue of leadership in the international system. The period from the end of the Napoleonic Wars to the Great Depression in the 1930s was the period of British dominance in the world economy, while the US hegemony evolved as a result of World War II and seems to be declining. Major world economic depressions have such a Tsunami force that they destabilize the entire international system as well. As has already been mentioned above, our results indicate peaks of international political conflagrations in the Thirty Years War, the French wars of the 18th century, the Napoleonic Wars, and the German quest for global dominance (1914–1945) and the evolution of the postwar order with the Korean and Vietnam Wars.

The main results of our analysis of Maddison's dataset at the national cycle level indicate that Kondratieff cycles of around 60 years duration are most clearly visible in Argentina, Canada, and Russia. We also found evidence on the existence of longer cycles of more than 35 years in Belgium; Chile; Greece; Netherlands; India; New Zealand; Spain; and USA; while for the other countries of the Maddison data set, the spectral density analysis results reported by Diebolt and Doliger (2006) could not be falsified.

A reasonable hypothesis, why there are such differences in cycle length between the various countries of the world has to be found: an interesting hypothesis could be the application of Bornschier's dependency theory, centered around penetration by transnational capital in the different economies of the world and the weakness or strength of "national capital" (Bornschier & Chase-Dunn, 1985; Tausch, 2010). By and large, the role of transnational capital in the countries with longer cycles seems to be historically more pronounced than in the countries with shorter cycles, and the strength of the national bourgeoisie seems to determine the shortness of cycles. Typical cases, supporting such an interpretation would be France, Germany, Japan, the Netherlands, and Switzerland versus Argentina, Canada, Chile, Greece, India, New Zealand, Spain and Russia.

We highlight the dramatic singularity of Keynesian postwar European reconstruction, and we also show that since the 1990s, other mechanisms have set in, which clearly are to the detriment of countries of the European Union and which currently benefit, among others, some countries of neoliberalism. Our K-cycle analysis suggests that Portugal, Italy and Spain are the Maddison sample countries most seriously affected by the current downturn.

Being conscious about the limitations of this appendix both in terms of the estimates used from the Maddison data set as well as the econometric techniques applied, we hope to have shown clearly nevertheless that some of the foundations of the current world-system research, i.e. the discourse about "long cycles" is not a discourse about a non-existing monster in Scotland. Both the re-analysis of world industrial production growth data since 1741 as well as the global conflict data since 1495 cautiously support the earlier contentions of world-system research with evidence, tested by spectral analysis and auto-correlation analysis. In addition, we could show that the world economy can be neatly separated into the Anglo-Saxon capitalist center and its peripheries in Latin America and Asia on the one hand, whose position in terms of 'world average' purchasing power since 1885 resembles an U-shaped curve, while the former contenders for global hegemony during World War II, Germany and Japan, the other European center countries and their European Southern periphery converged with and diverged from "world average" purchasing power in the shape of a right-ward, indented "S". The raw material export dependent peripheries/semi-peripheries, which all converged/diverged in the shape of a small letter "w", as well as the trajectory of the slightly upward pointing larger oscillations of Brazil should not distract as from the fact that the majorities of countries under scrutiny here either correspond to the "U" or the indented "S".

Our data and analyses (see also Maps 25 and 26[36]) finally underline how today an "Anglo-Saxon" capitalist model, tending towards inequality, at least partially takes advantage of world economic circumstances, and is at least partially well compatible with world economic growth. Map 1, which in a way contradicts Piketty's well-known analysis, shows that for several European countries, some countries of the Southern Cone of Latin America, some countries in Africa but especially in Iran, India and China, higher inequality had a 3-year time lagged positive effect on rates of economic growth.

In an earlier section of this appendix, we already highlighted that in view of our results there could be some new light in international research on the hotly contested issue of economic convergence, so well-known from neo-classical contemporary economics (Barro & Ursúa, 2008; Jaeger & Springler, 2012; Mankiw, Romer, & Weil 1992). We already said (in Chapter 4) that according to the "*law of convergence*," mentioned by Barro, *inter alia,* in Barro (2012), under certain circumstances countries tend to eliminate gaps in levels of real per capita GDP at a rate around 2 % per year. A convergence at a 2 % rate implies that it takes 35 years for half of an initial gap to vanish and 115 years for 90 % of the gap to disappear (see also: Berthold & Kullas, 2009; Gennaioli, La Porta, Lopez-de-Silanes, & Shleifer 2014). Electronic Appendix Graph 26a now portrays on the basis of World Bank data[37] the convergence paths as they should have happened in the countries whose per capita income was below the "world average" since 1963. Electronic Appendix Graph 26b re-iterates the "medical diagnosis" which we already established in our contribution on the basis of the Maddison dataset, this time with the World Bank data since 1963: there is lots of divergence in the World System, and many nations stumble on their way, whereas the Great Divergence of the recent decades (Grinin & Korotayev 2015a) is far from a perfectly smooth process.

---

[36] See https://www.academia.edu/3742045/Korotayev_Grinin_Tausch_Economic_Cycles_Crises_and_the_Global_Periphery_Springer_2016_-_Supporting_online_materials.

[37] http://data.worldbank.org/indicator/NY.GDP.PCAP.CD.

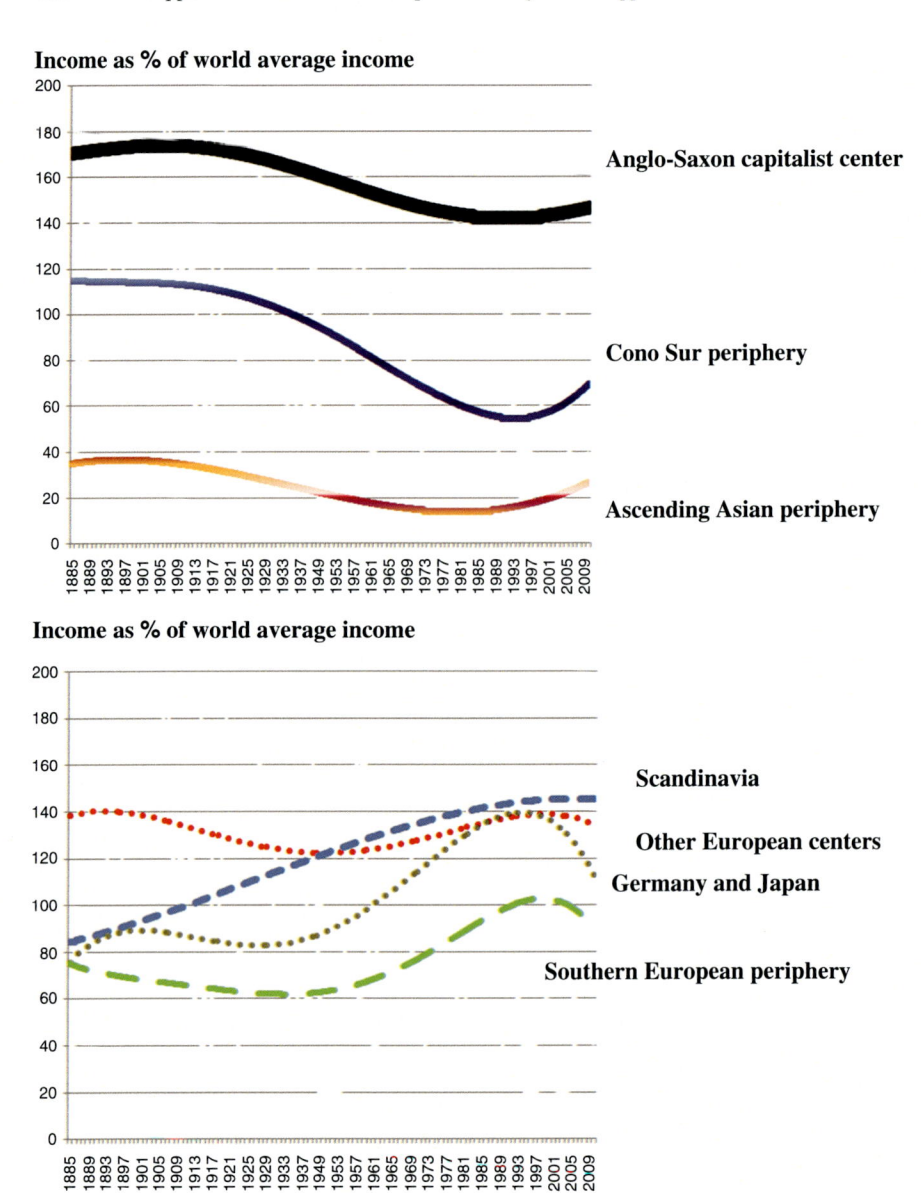

Scheme 1 The empirics of the Akamatsu trajectory of flying geese nations – a summary of the results of this study

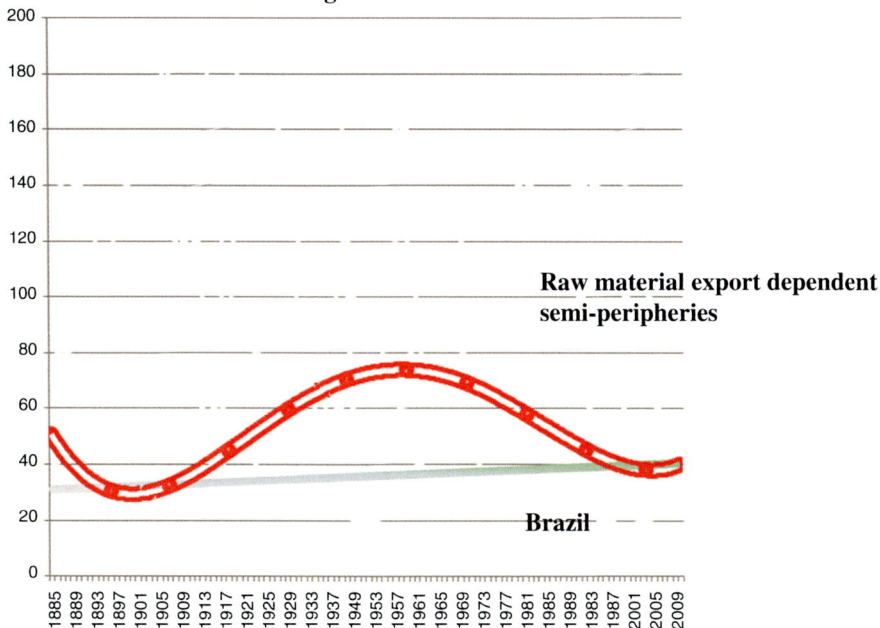

Appendix B: The Results of Spectral Analysis and Application of Other Statistical... 211

Income as % of world average income

Raw material export dependent semi-peripheries

Brazil

Scheme 1 (continued)

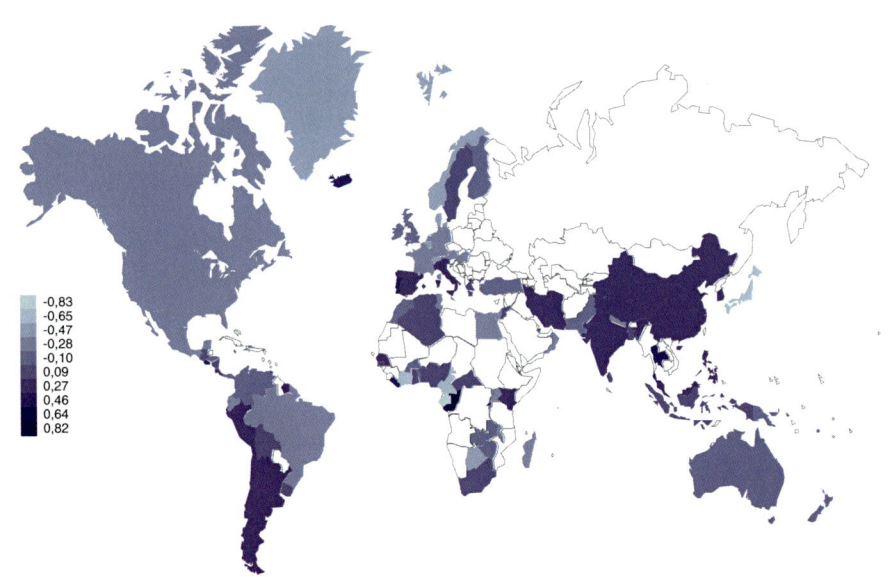

source: our own calculations and http://www.clearlyandsimply.com/clearly_and_simply/2009/06/choropleth-maps-with-excel.html

Map 1 The time-lagged effects of the GINI Income Inequality (3 years time lag, UTIP-data) on economic growth (World Bank Data) from 1963 onwards

Many countries of the world experienced dramatic implosions of their once successful development path. In this sense, a good part of the experience of the countries of the world also after 1963 rather looks like the contrary of Electronic Appendix Graph 26a. In order to bring some light into what might appear at first sight to be the chaos of Electronic Appendix Graph 26b, we attempt to present Graphs 26c and 26d, which summarize in an analytical fashion the underlying tendencies of the world economy since 1963.[38]

On the basis of three standard statistical measures of the average—the median, the geometrical mean, and the average proper, we can show that the standard "normal" average country whose per capita income in 1963 was below the "world average", experienced the following typical trajectory of a further declining relative per capita income until the mid-1990s, only to recover then from the low level below 20 % of the "world average"[39] (Electronic Appendix Graph 26c). Electronic Appendix Graph 26d shows the trajectory of the "standard" "normal" average country whose per capita income in 1963 was above the "world average". Relative to the "world average", the incomes in the richer countries increased only to implode somewhat at the very end of the half a century period 1963–2013.

Conclusions

Our re-analysis of the entire issue of global cycles and national cycles as well as cycles of global convergence and divergence revealed that Kondratieff cycles exist, but that there are other types of cycles as well in the global economy, among them two cycles hitherto virtually neglected in quantitative research on the subject – the 36 year Barro cycle and the 140 year Wallerstein cycle.

For the first time in the literature, we also tried to analyze in a more systematic fashion the cycles of convergence and divergence.

So, our results on the level of the world economy are to be interpreted as a resounding "yes" for the hypotheses voiced by Kondratieff, but with several additional qualifications and extensions. Kondratieff was right in analyzing a 54 year cycle of the real economy as well, but there are other important cycles too; some of them arevery well known to social science research, others perhaps are still more to be explored. On the level of industrial production growth in the world

---

[38] See https://www.academia.edu/3742045/Korotayev_Grinin_Tausch_Economic_Cycles_Crises_and_the_Global_Periphery_Springer_2016_-_Supporting_online_materials.

[39] It appears appropriate to remind the readers at this point that this is the average for those 31 countries that we study. In fact, this "world average" is considerably higher than the real world average, as our sample consists of almost exclusively high and middle income countries, and hardly includes any countries with the lowest per capita incomes. Indeed, the overwhelming majority of countries with the lowest per capita incomes are found now in tropical Africa, whereas our sample does not include any African countries at all.

economy, there is—parallel to the Kondratieff cycle—a 140 year "logistic" cycle, first analyzed by Immanuel Wallerstein; and in addition, there is the newly discovered 36 year disaster cycle, correctly predicted by the neoclassical contemporary economist Robert Barro. For sure, there is also evidence—although somewhat weaker than expected—for a 22–23 year Kuznets cycle and the shorter, well-known Juglar cycles and Kitchin cycles. We achieved our results with the untransformed data at our disposal, but also with 5-year moving average transformations of the original data, which wielded the same results. There is strong reason to believe that the Wallerstein cycle is closely connected to the issue of leadership in the international system.

In this appendix, we also tested the crucial relationship of the Akamatsu cycles of convergence and the cross correlation relationship between the Akamatsu cycle and the Kondratieff cycle. We think that the most important message for future world-systems research is the realization that divergence and convergence processes[40] in most nations of the world have a very strong cyclical component.

A Primer on Spectral Analysis and Time Series Analysis

All Calculations: SPSS 21 and EXCEL 2010, Innsbruck University

Simulating long cycles

If we want to understand the statistical methods used in this analysis, it is best to start with **simulated** cycles and to see which results they produce. So the simulated sinus-waves are:

---

[40] See Grinin and Korotayev (2015a) for more detail.

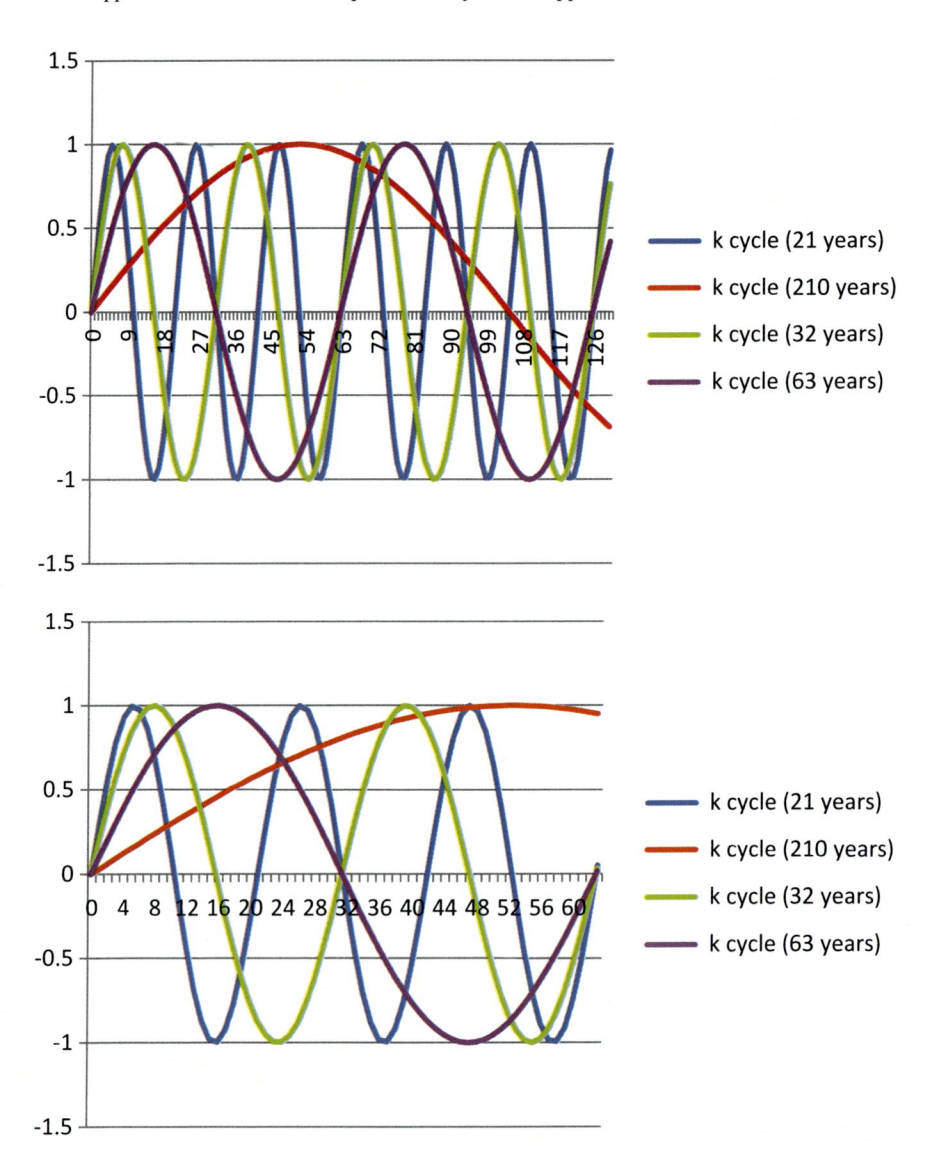

214　Appendix B: The Results of Spectral Analysis and Application of Other Statistical...

63 year cycle: =SIN(time point*0,1)

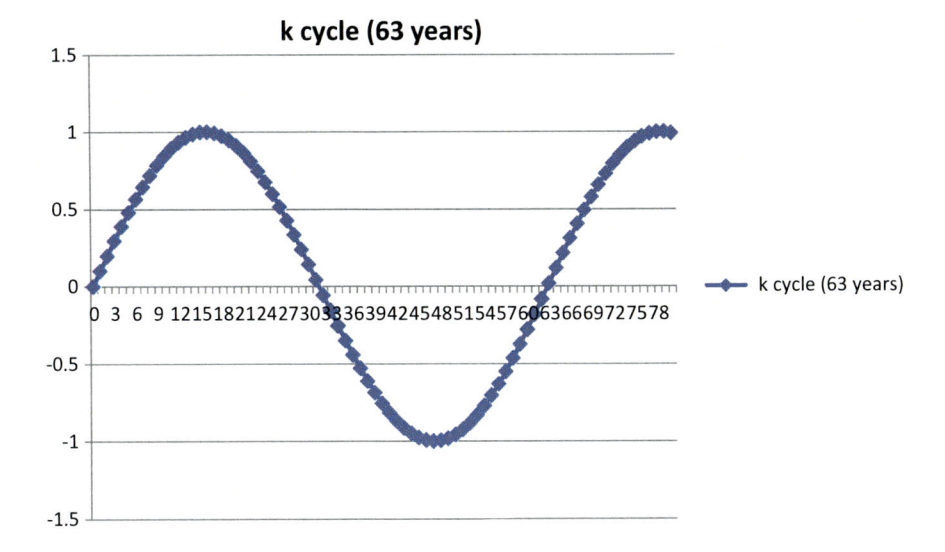

k cycle (63 years)

A Kondratieff cycle of 63 years duration will yield very clear-cut and easily identifiable results with our chosen statistical methods:

This is the way how the SPSS spectral analysis period diagram would look like if there is a real 63 year economic cycle

Plot of the periodogram

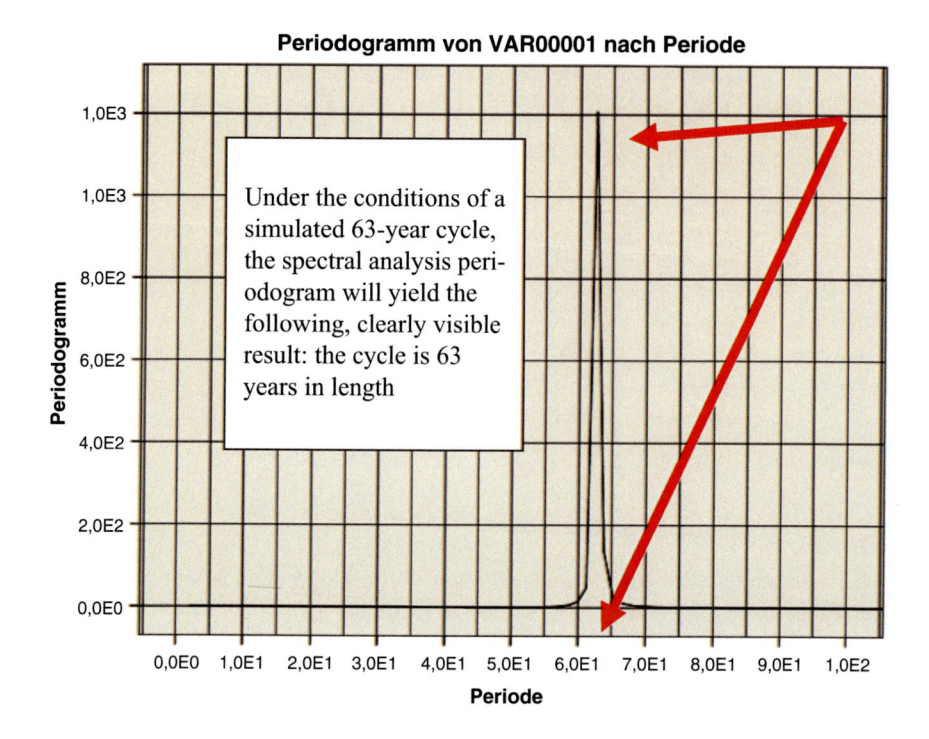

Periodogramm von VAR00001 nach Periode

Under the conditions of a simulated 63-year cycle, the spectral analysis periodogram will yield the following, clearly visible result: the cycle is 63 years in length

Appendix B: The Results of Spectral Analysis and Application of Other Statistical... 217

This is the way how the SPSS spectral analysis—spectral density diagram could look like if there is a real 63 year economic cycle (window of 11 periods)

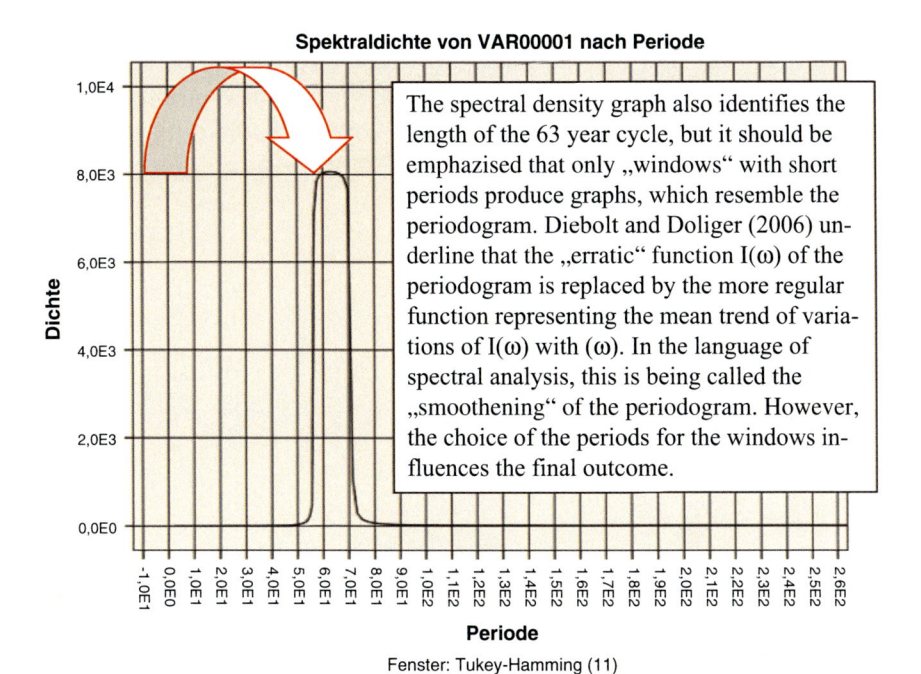

Spektraldichte von VAR00001 nach Periode

The spectral density graph also identifies the length of the 63 year cycle, but it should be emphazised that only „windows" with short periods produce graphs, which resemble the periodogram. Diebolt and Doliger (2006) underline that the „erratic" function $I(\omega)$ of the periodogram is replaced by the more regular function representing the mean trend of variations of $I(\omega)$ with (ω). In the language of spectral analysis, this is being called the „smoothening" of the periodogram. However, the choice of the periods for the windows influences the final outcome.

Fenster: Tukey-Hamming (11)

The ample methodological literature on the subject specifies:

"Although, for a stationary, nonlinearly deterministic process, the periodogram ordinates are asymptotically unbiased estimates of the spectral densities at the corresponding frequencies, they are not consistent estimates; moreover, the correlation between adjacent periodogram ordinates tends to zero with increasing sample size. The result is that the periodogram presents a jagged appearance which is increasingly difficult to interpret as more data become available. In order to obtain consistent estimates of the spectral density function at specific frequencies, it is common practice to weight the periodogram ordinates over the frequency range or to form weighted averages of the autocovariances at different lags. [...] The weights are called a 'spectral window'. Essentially the idea is to reduce the variance of the estimate of an average spectral density around a particular frequency by averaging periodogram ordinates which are asymptotically unbiased and independently distributed estimates of the corresponding ordinates of the spectral density function. [...]

218 Appendix B: The Results of Spectral Analysis and Application of Other Statistical...

Naturally the sampling properties of the spectral estimates depend on the nature of the 'window' used to obtain consistency [...] Regardless of the choice of window, the 'bandwidth' used in constructing the window must decrease at a suitable rate as the sample size grows. In the spectral window approach, this means that the window width must decrease at a slower rate than the sample size." (Diebold, Kilian, & Nerlove, 2010)

This is the way how the SPSS autocorrelation diagram should look like if there is a real 63 year economic cycle—tested with the SPSS routine "autocorrelation" using the option of possible lags of up to 100 years

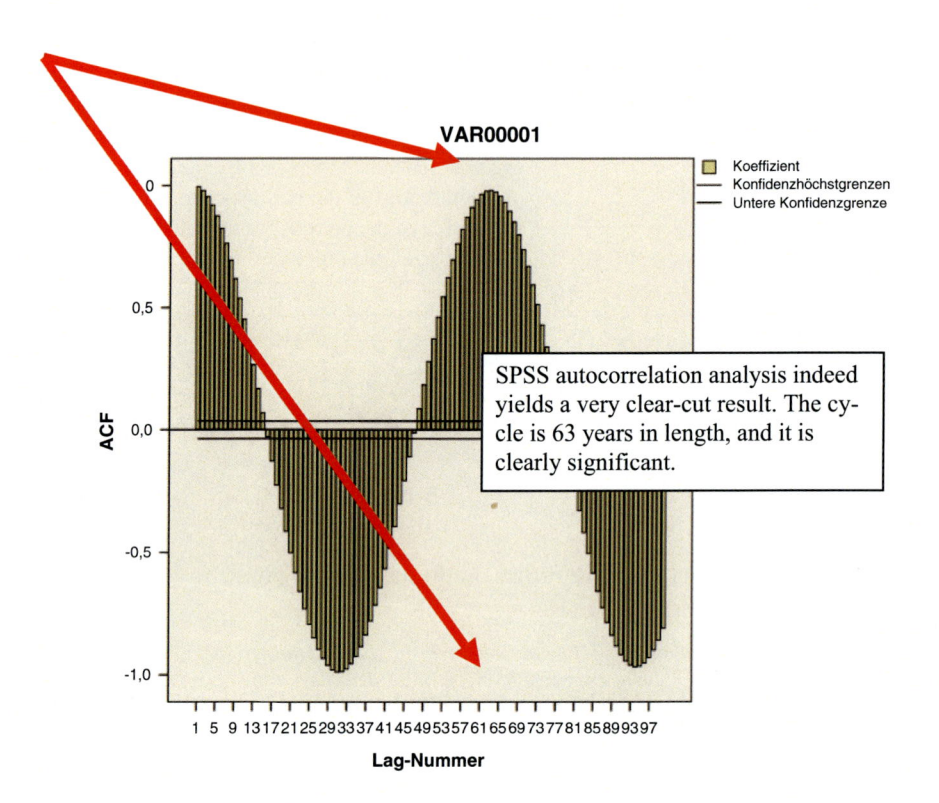

SPSS autocorrelation analysis indeed yields a very clear-cut result. The cycle is 63 years in length, and it is clearly significant.

Appendix B: The Results of Spectral Analysis and Application of Other Statistical... 219

But in the real world, there are no single-size sinus waves of long-term development patterns. Devezas, 2012 has suggested that there are "nested" shorter cycles in the larger Kondratieff waves.

A simple simulation of such a series with the EXCEL program could look like the following:

Series 1=SIN(time axis*0,1)
Series 2=SIN(time axis*0,6)
Combined series=Series 1 + ((Series 2)/3)

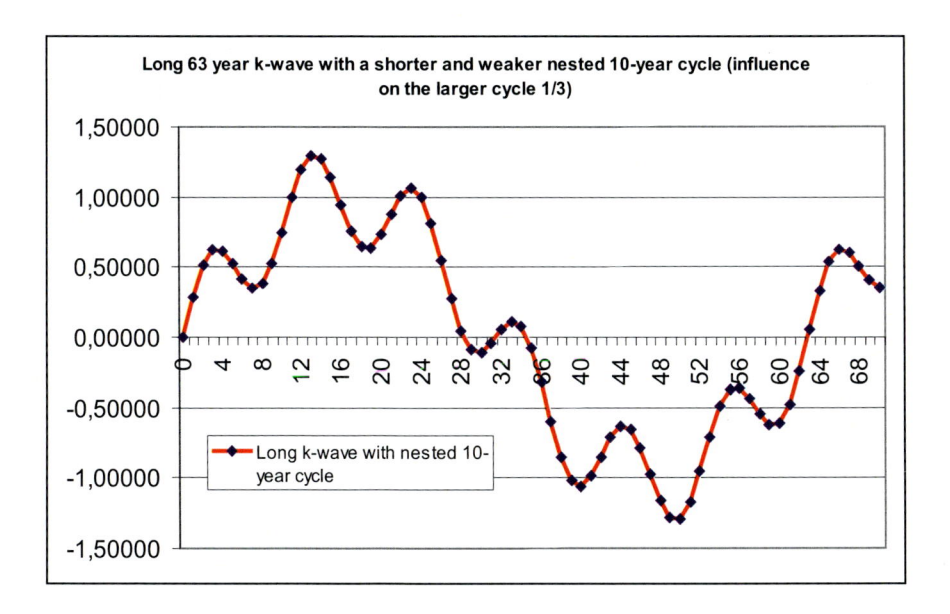

Long 63 year k-wave with a shorter and weaker nested 10-year cycle (influence on the larger cycle 1/3)

— Long k-wave with nested 10-year cycle

220   Appendix B: The Results of Spectral Analysis and Application of Other Statistical...

The SPSS time-series plot for the entire cyclical movements over two decades. This graph looks very identical to the title graph of the *Kondratieff Waves Almanac 2012* and the Devezas (2012) graph on page 161:

The Devezas graph:

Our simulated cycle:

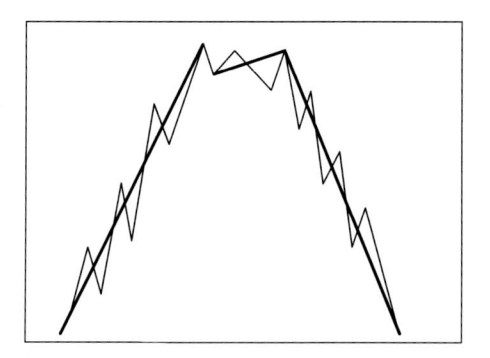

The simulated cycle—200 years observation

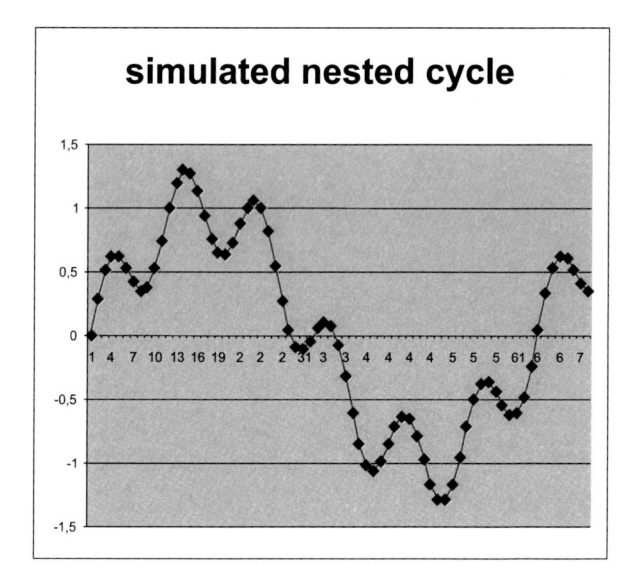

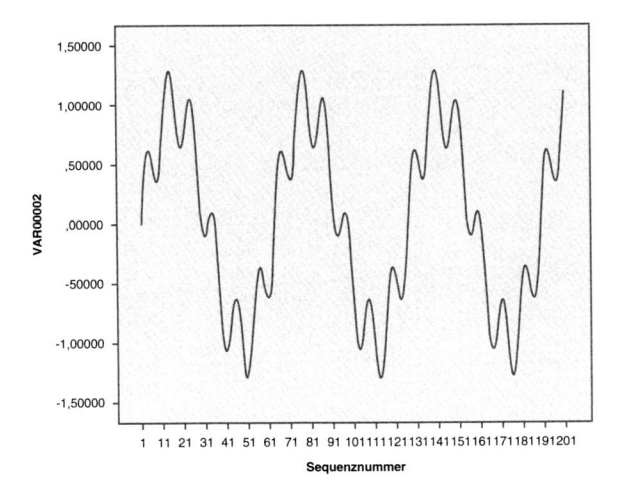

Appendix B: The Results of Spectral Analysis and Application of Other Statistical... 221

For such a simulated series, the spectral periodogram clearly discerns the simulated short cycle and the long cycle and thus clearly qualifies itself as the prime instrument for reaching verdicts about cycle existence and cycle length. Please note that the simulation assumed that the long cycle has a much bigger weight than the short cycle. The periodogram and also the analysis of autocorrelation clearly identify these two different weights (long cycle = weight 1; short cycle = weight 1/3)

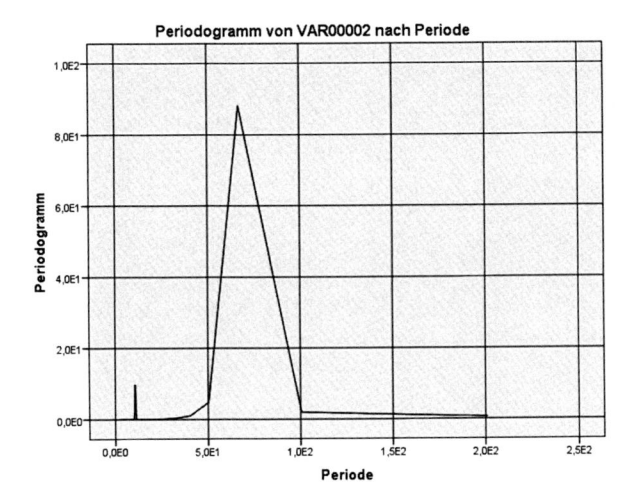

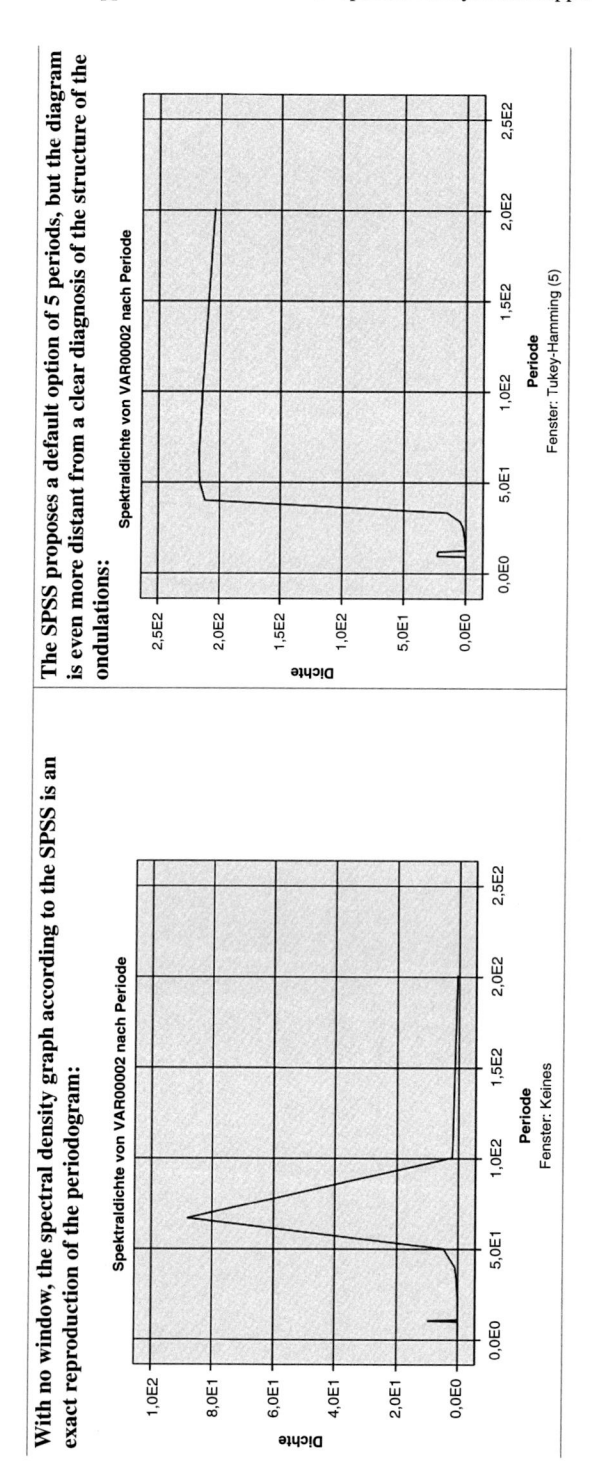

With no window, the spectral density graph according to the SPSS is an exact reproduction of the periodogram:

Spektraldichte von VAR00002 nach Periode

Dichte / Periode
Fenster: Keines

The SPSS proposes a default option of 5 periods, but the diagram is even more distant from a clear diagnosis of the structure of the ondulations:

Spektraldichte von VAR00002 nach Periode

Dichte / Periode
Fenster: Tukey-Hamming (5)

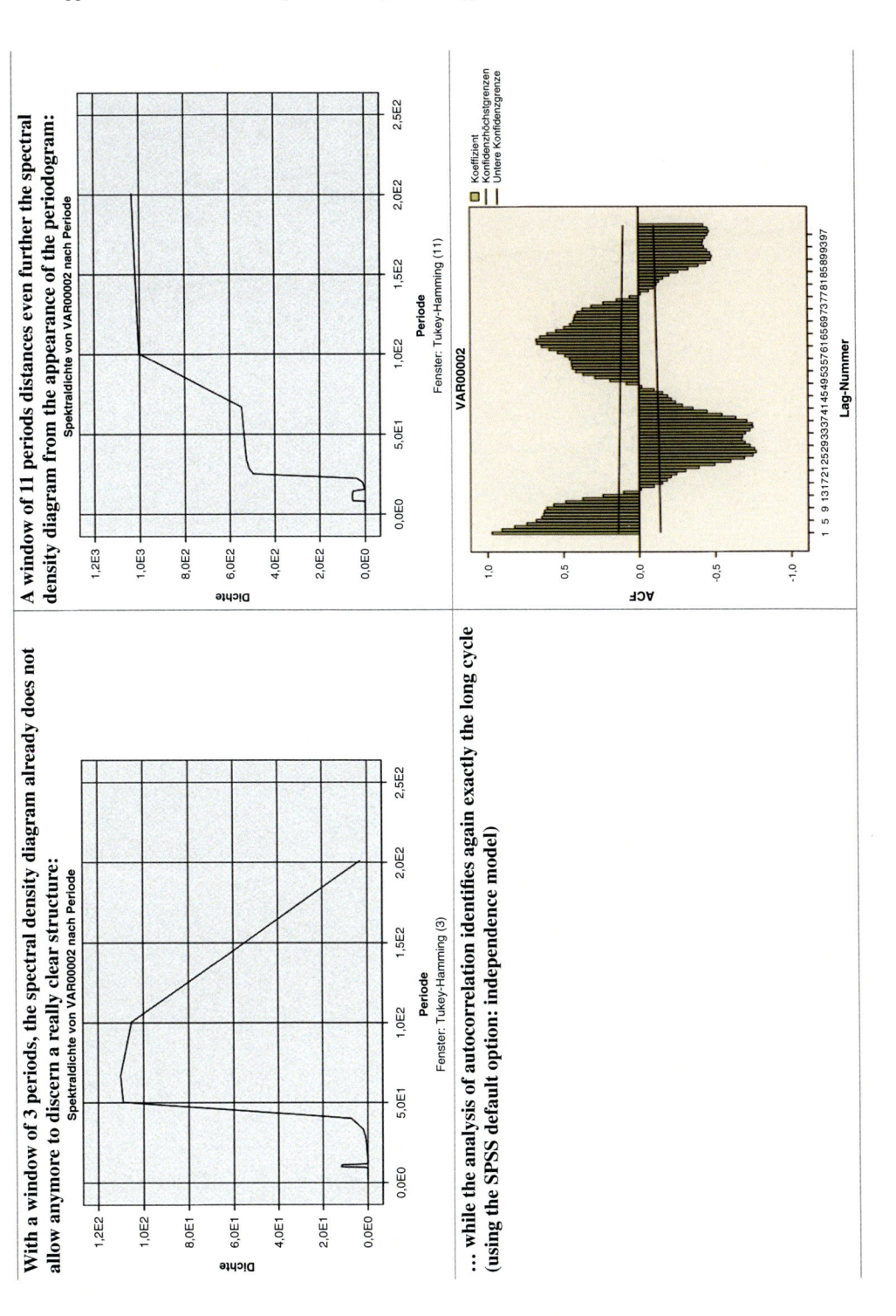

Appendix B: The Results of Spectral Analysis and Application of Other Statistical...

With a window of 3 periods, the spectral density diagram already does not allow anymore to discern a really clear structure:

A window of 11 periods distances even further the spectral density diagram from the appearance of the periodogram:

... while the analysis of autocorrelation identifies again exactly the long cycle (using the SPSS default option: independence model)

An even more pessimistic variant of events could assume that the "long cycles" are a tendency, while the shorter cycles are real cycles

Series 1=SIN(time axis*0,1)
Series 2=SIN(time axis*0,6)
Combined series=Series 1 + (Series 2)*1,5

Appendix B: The Results of Spectral Analysis and Application of Other Statistical... 225

The simulated time series could look like the following:

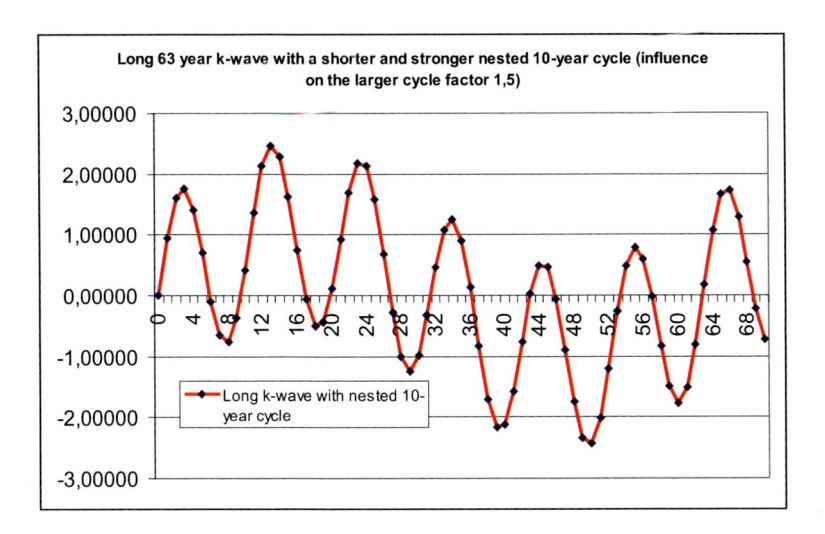

The entire simulated 63 year swing time series with 10-year shorter cycles looks like the following:

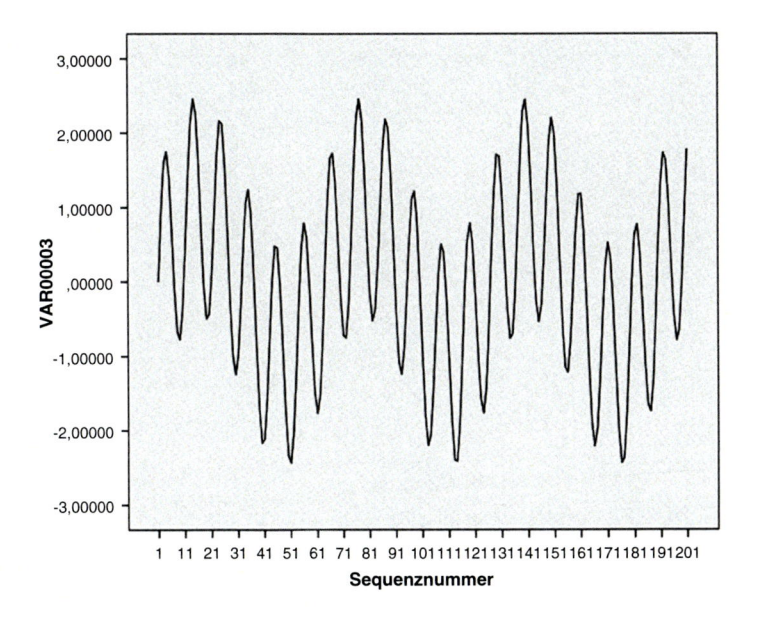

In reality, such "cycles" are often encountered, and indeed partially resemble the concrete oscillations observed in large sections of k-cycle research over longer time series of economic growth or industrial production growth. But a moving average of 11 years clearly detects such a structure

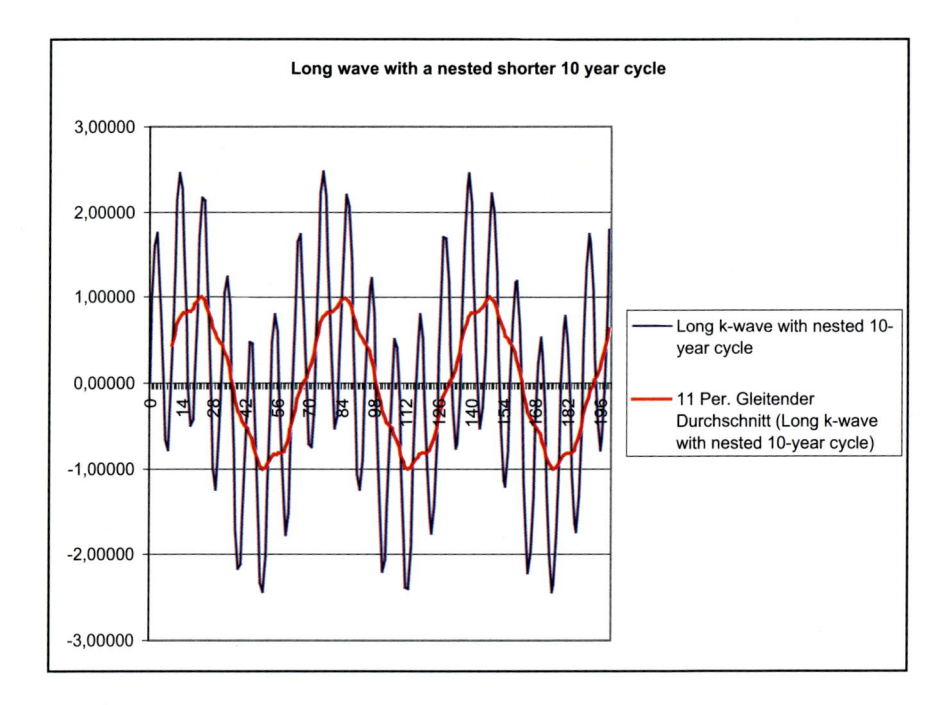

Long wave with a nested shorter 10 year cycle

— Long k-wave with nested 10-year cycle

— 11 Per. Gleitender Durchschnitt (Long k-wave with nested 10-year cycle)

In our case, the sliding or rolling correlation analysis which analyses for each year the correlation of the growth variable with the time axis over the preceding 25 years would also yield a very clear result, reproducing the true underlying 63-year Kondratieff swing

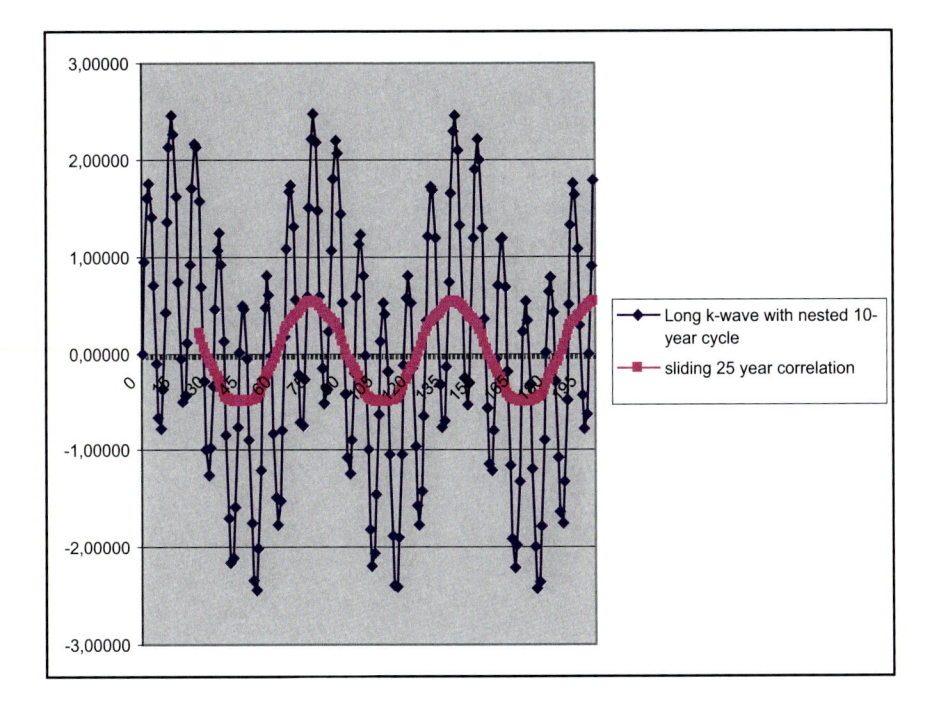

In such a case, the periodogram in spectral analysis again clearly identifies the length of the two cycles—10 years and 63 years, and also truly reflects the different weights assigned to the two time series. The shorter series has a weight of 1.5, while the longer series has a weight of 1:

Plot of the periodogram

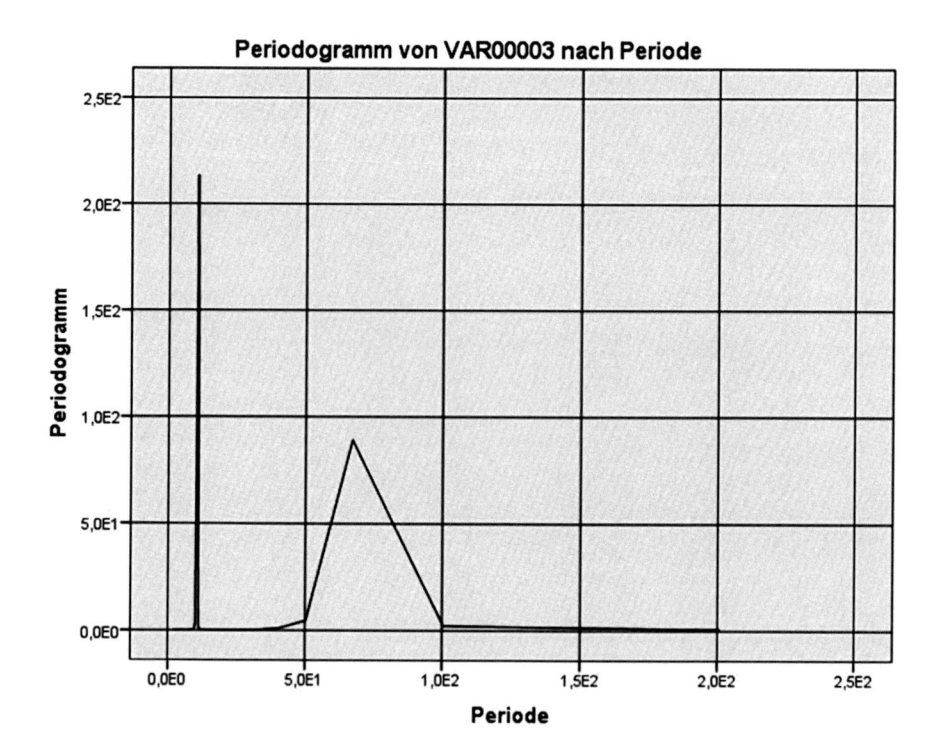

Periodogramm von VAR00003 nach Periode

Appendix B: The Results of Spectral Analysis and Application of Other Statistical... 229

The spectral density diagram for different windows yields the following extremely divergent shapes (3 year window, 5 year window, 11 year window)

3 year window

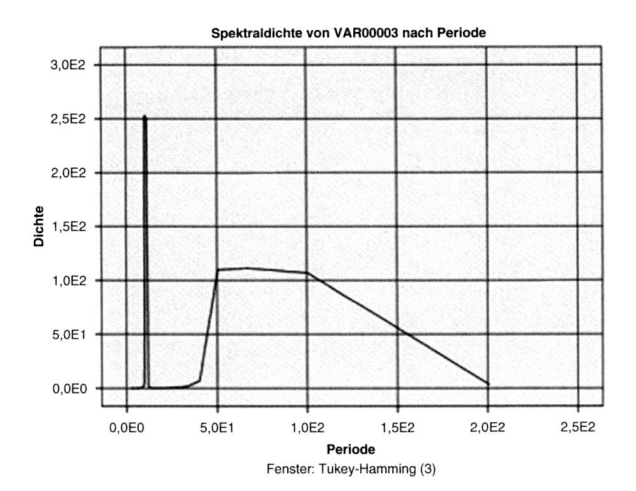

Spektraldichte von VAR00003 nach Periode
Fenster: Tukey-Hamming (3)

5 year window

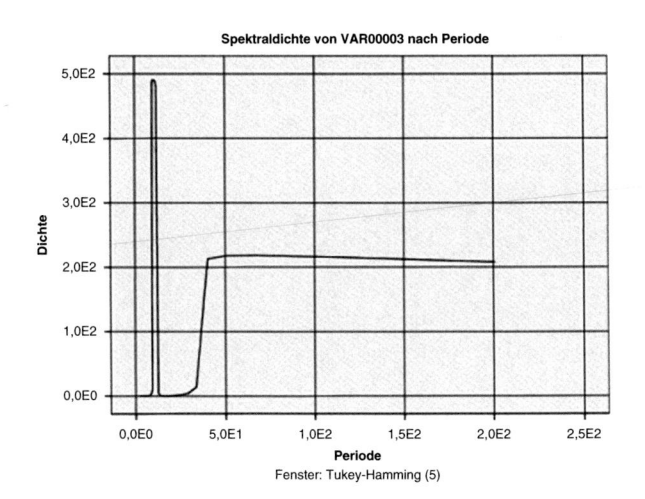

Spektraldichte von VAR00003 nach Periode
Fenster: Tukey-Hamming (5)

11 year window

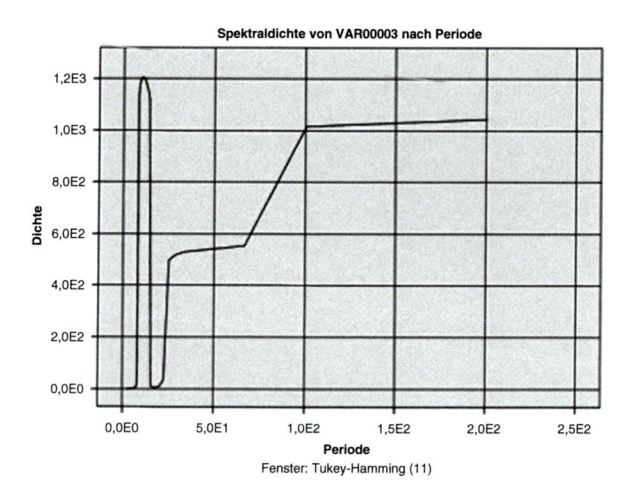

Spektraldichte von VAR00003 nach Periode

Fenster: Tukey-Hamming (11)

The analysis of autocorrelation under such conditions yields the following results about the recurring 10 year fluctuations and the pattern of the longer 63-year trend

Autocorrelation analysis residual plot (ACF autocorrelation plot), showing coefficients and upper and lower bounds of confidence per number of lags

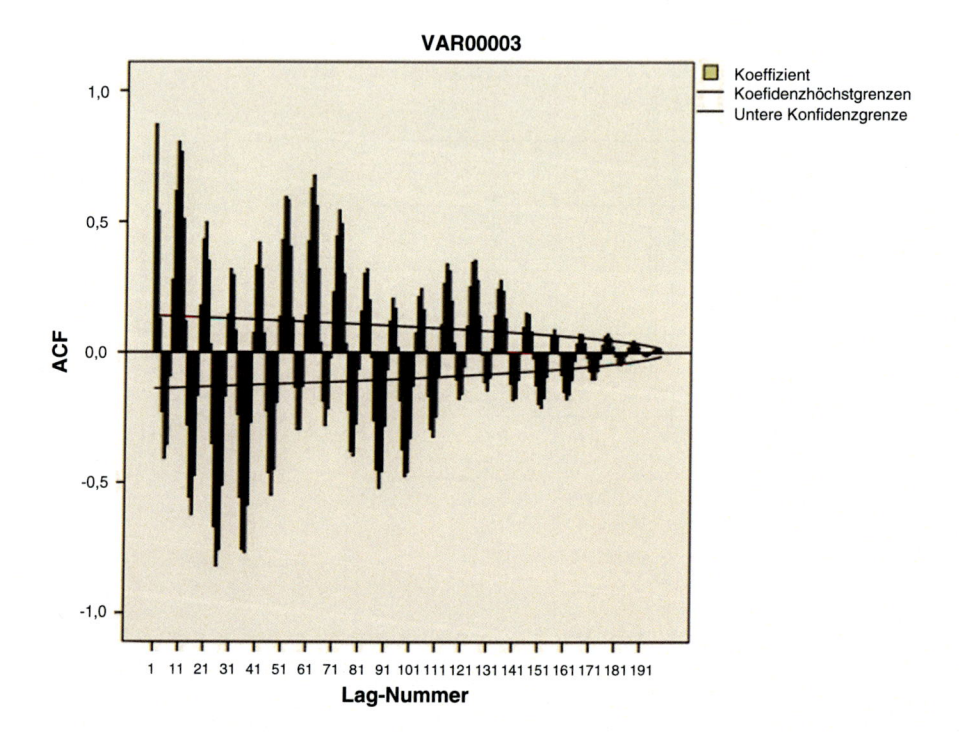

VAR00003
- Koeffizient
- Koefidenzhöchstgrenzen
- Untere Konfidenzgrenze

Appendix B: The Results of Spectral Analysis and Application of Other Statistical... 231

Our main results are to be seen in the following Graphs:

Enter the world of reality—results from the real world economy, 1740 to today

A schematic representation of the global industrial production growth results, based on periodograms of spectral analysis
Plot of the periodogram

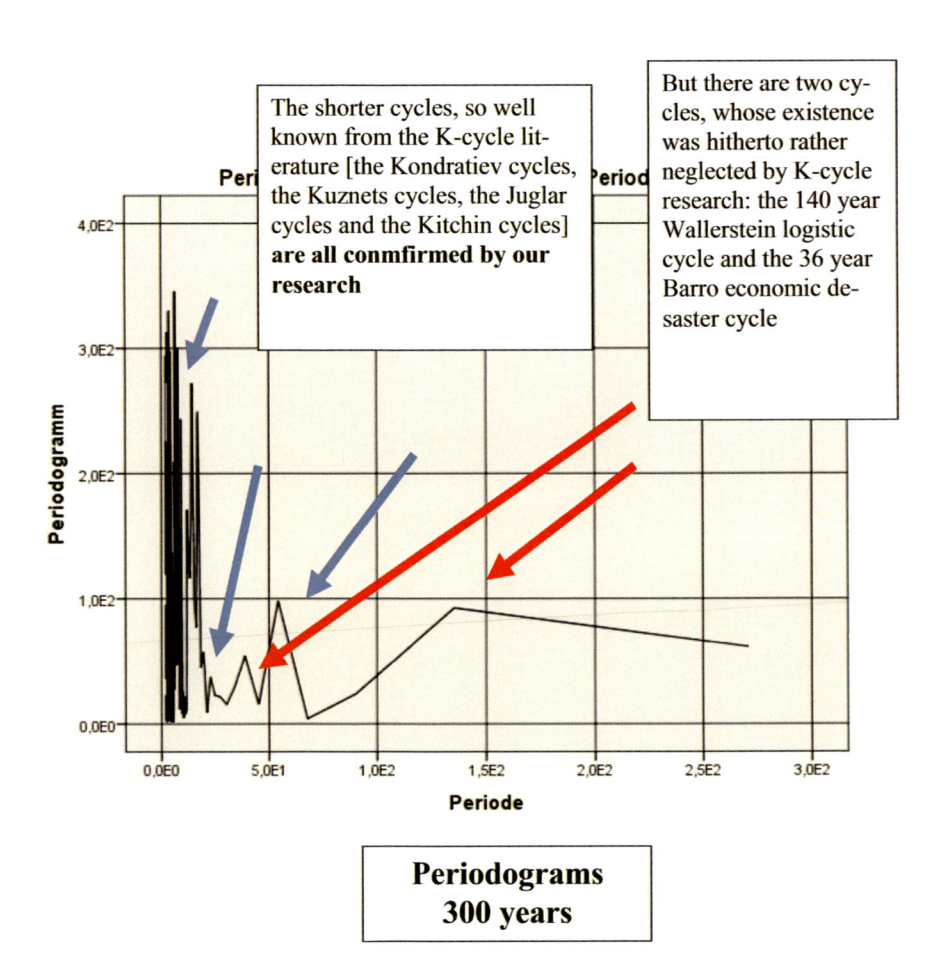

The shorter cycles, so well known from the K-cycle literature [the Kondratiev cycles, the Kuznets cycles, the Juglar cycles and the Kitchin cycles] **are all conmfirmed by our research**

But there are two cycles, whose existence was hitherto rather neglected by K-cycle research: the 140 year Wallerstein logistic cycle and the 36 year Barro economic desaster cycle

**Periodograms
300 years**

The shorter cycles, based on periodograms of spectral analysis
Plot of the periodogram

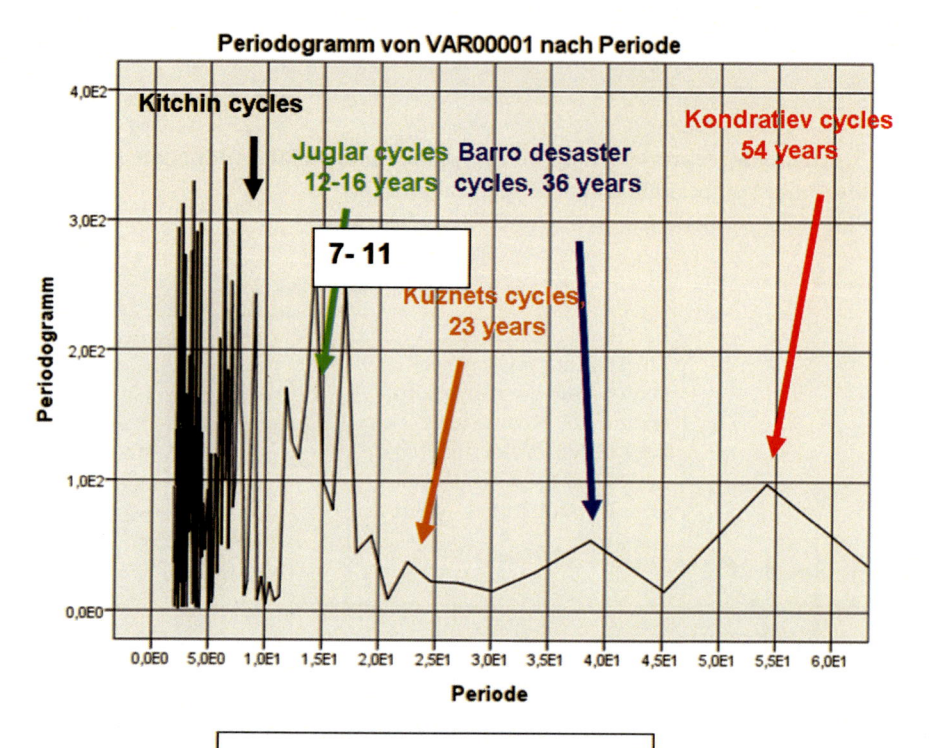

Periodogramm von VAR00001 nach Periode

Kitchin cycles

Juglar cycles **Barro desaster**
12-16 years **cycles, 36 years**

Kondratiev cycles
54 years

7- 11

Kuznets cycles
23 years

60 years

References

Abadir, K., & Talmain, G. (2002). Aggregation, persistence and volatility in a macro model. *Review of Economic Studies, 69*(4), 749–779.
Abel, A. B., & Bernanke, B. S. (2008). *Macroeconomics* (6th ed.). New York: Addison Wesley.
Abramovitz, M. (1961). The nature and significance of Kuznets cycles. *Economic Development and Cultural Change, 9*(3), 225–248.
Acemoglu, D. (2012). *The world our grandchildren will inherit: The rights revolution and beyond (NBER Working Paper 17994)*. Cambridge, MA: National Bureau of Economic Research.
Aftalion, A. (1913). *Les crises périodiques de surproduction*. T. 1 et 2. Paris: Rivière.
Aiginger, K. (2009). *A comparison of the current crisis with the great depression as regards their depth and the policy responses*. Lecture at the NERO-Meeting on 'The causes and consequences of the financial crisis', OECD, Paris, September 21, 2009, WIFO-Lecture, no. 105. Vienna: Austrian Institute for Economic Research. Retrieved from http://karl.aiginger.wifo.ac.at/index.php?id=19.
Akaev, A., Fomin, A., Tsirel, S., & Korotayev, A. (2010). Log-periodic oscillation analysis forecasts the burst of the 'Gold Bubble' in April–June 2011. *Structure and Dynamics, 5*(1), 3–18.
Akaev, A., Korotayev, A., & Fomin, A. (2012). Global inflation dynamics: Regularities and forecasts. *Structure and Dynamics, 5*(3), 3–18.
Akaev, A., Sadovnichii, V., & Korotayev, A. (2011). Explosive rise in gold and oil prices as a precursor of a global financial and economic crisis. *Doklady Mathematics, 83*(2), 1–4.
Akaev, A., Sadovnichy, V., & Korotayev, A. (2012). On the dynamics of the world demographic transition and financial-economic crises forecasts. *The European Physical Journal, 205*, 355–373.
Akamatsu, K. (1961). A theory of unbalanced growth in the world economy. *Weltwirtschaftliches Archiv, 86*(2), 196–217.
Akamatsu, K. (1962). A historical pattern of economic growth in developing countries. *The Developing Economies, 1*, 3–25.
Åkerman, J. (1932). *Economic progress and economic crises*. London: Macmillan.
Alemayehu, B., & Warner, K. E. (2004). The lifetime distribution of health care costs. *Health Services Research, 39*(3), 627–642.
Allen, R. C. (2009). *The British industrial revolution in global perspective*. Cambridge: Cambridge University Press.
Amin, S. (1994). *Re-reading the postwar period: An intellectual itinerary*. New York: Monthly Review Press.

Amin, S., Arrighi, G., Frank, A. G., & Wallerstein, I. (2006). *Transforming the revolution: Social movements and the world-system*. New Delhi: Aakar.

Amsden, A. H. (2004). *The rise of 'the rest'. Challenges to the West from late-industrializing economies*. New York: Oxford University Press.

Arkhangelsky, V., Bogevolnov, J., Goldstone, J., Khaltourina, D., Korotayev, A., Malkov, A., et al. (2015). *Critical 10 years. Demographic Policies of the Russian Federation: Successes and challenges*. Moscow: Russian Presidential Academy Of National Economy and Public Administration (RANEPA).

Arrighi, G. (1995). *The long 20th century. Money, power, and the origins of our times*. London; New York: Verso.

Arrighi, G., & Silver, B. J. (1999). *Chaos and governance in the modern world system*. Minneapolis, MN: University of Minnesota Press.

Arrighi, G., Silver, B. J., & Brewer, B. D. (2003). Industrial convergence, globalization, and the persistence of the North-South divide. *Studies in Comparative International Development, 38*(1), 3–31.

Ashby, R. (1956). *An introduction to cybernetics*. London: Chapman and Hall.

Asset-backedinsecurity. (2008). *Economist*, January 17. Retrieved from http://www.economist.com/node/10533428?story_id=10533428.

Attinà, F. (2005). *State aggregation in defence pacts: Systematic explanations*. Jean Monnet Working Papers in Comparative and International Politics, Jean Monnet Centre EuroMed, Department of Political Studies, University of Catania. Retrieved from http://www.fscpo.unict.it/EuroMed/jmwp56.pdf.

Attinà, F. (2003). Organisation, competition and change of the international system. *International Interactions: Empirical and Theoretical Research in International Relations, 16*(4), 317–333.

Ayres, R. U. (2006). Did the fifth K-wave begin in 1990–92? Has it been aborted by globalization? In T. C. Devezas (Ed.), *Kondratieff waves, warfare and world security* (pp. 57–71). Amsterdam: IOS Press.

Babetskii, I., Komarek, L., & Komarkova, Z. (2007). Financial integration of stock markets among new EU member states and the euro area. *Finance a úvěr. Czech Journal of Economics and Finance, 57*(7–8), 341–362.

Baglioni, A. S., & Cherubini, U. (2010). *Marking-to-market government guarantees to financial systems: An empirical analysis of Europe*. Retrieved November 10, 2010, from http://ssrn.com/abstract=1715405.

Bainbridge, M. S., & Roco, M. C. (2005). *Managing nano-bio-info-cogno innovations: Converging technologies in society*. New York: Springer.

Barr, K. (1979). Long waves: A selective annotated bibliography. *Review, 2*(4), 675–718.

Barro, R. J. (2012). *Convergence and modernization revisited (NBER Working Paper No 18295)*. Cambridge, MA: National Bureau of Economic.

Barro, R. J. (2013). Health and economic growth. *Annals of Economics and Finance, 14*(2), 329–366.

Barro, R. J., Nakamura, E., & Ursúa, J. F. (2011). *Crises and recoveries in an empirical model of consumption disasters*. Cambridge, MA: Harvard University, Department of Economics.

Barro, R. J., & Sala-i-Martin, X. (1991). Convergence across states and regions. *Brookings Papers on Economic Activity, 1*, 107–182.

Barro, R. J., & Ursúa, J. F. (2008). Macroeconomic crises since 1870. *Brookings Papers on Economic Activity, 1*, 255–350.

Bartlett, M. S. (1946). On the theoretical specification of sampling properties of autocorrelated time series. *Journal of Royal Statistical Society, Series B, 8*, 27–27.

Baxter, M., & King, R. (1999). Measuring business cycles: Approximate band-pass filters for economic time series. *Review of Economics and Statistics, 81*, 575–93.

Beck, N. (1991). The illusion of cycles in international relations. *International Studies Quarterly, 35*(4), 455–476.

Beckfield, J. (2006). European integration and income inequality. *American Sociological Review, 71*(6), 964–985.

References

Beer, S. (1967). *Cybernetics and management* (2nd ed.). London: English Universities Press.
Beer, S. (1994). *Decision and control: The meaning of operational research and management cybernetics.* London: John Wiley & Sons.
Bernal, R. (1988). The great depression, colonial policy and industrialization in Jamaica. *Social and Economic Studies, 37*(1/2), 33–64. Retrieved from http://www.richardbernal.net/The_Great_Depression_Colonial_Policy_and_Industrialization_in_Jamaica.pdf.
Bernanke, B., Gertler, M., & Gilchrist, S. (1998). *The financial accelerator in quantitative business cycle framework.* Cambridge, MA: NBER.
Bernstein, E. M. (1940). War and the pattern of business cycles. *American Economic Review, 30*, 524–535.
Berry, B. J. L. (1991). *Long wave rhythms in economic development and political behavior.* Baltimore, MD: Johns Hopkins University Press.
Berry, B. J. L., & Dean, D. J. (2012). Long wave rhythms: A pictorial guide to 220 years of U.S. history, with forecasts. In L. E. Grinin, T. C. Devezas, & A. V. Korotayev (Eds.), *Kondratieff waves. Dimensions and prospects at the dawn of the 21st century* (pp. 107–119). Volgograd: Uchitel.
Berry, B. J. L., Kim, H., & Baker, E. S. (2001). Low-frequency waves of inflation and economic growth: Digital spectral analysis. *Technological Forecasting and Social Change, 68*(1), 63–73.
Berthold, N., & Kullas, M. (2009). *20 Jahre Mauerfall: Konvergenz in Deutschland?* (Discussion Paper Series 105). Julius Maximilian University of Würzburg. Retrieved from http://econstor.eu/bitstream/10419/32490/1/607107391.pdf.
Besomi, D. (2005). *Clément Juglar and the transition from crises theory to business cycle theories.* Paper prepared for a conference on the occasion of the centenary of the death of Clement Juglar, Paris, December 2, 2005.
Beveridge, W. H. (1921). Weather and harvest cycles. *The Economic Journal, 31*, 429–449.
Beveridge, W. H. (1922). Wheat prices and rainfall in Western Europe. *Journal of the Royal Statistical Society, 85*(3), 412–475.
Bhagwati, J. (1995). Trade and wages: Choosing among alternative explanations. *Federal Reserve Bank of New York Economic Policy Review, 1*, 42–47.
Bieshaar, H., & Kleinknecht, A. (1984). Kondratieff long waves in aggregate output? An econometric test. *Konjunkturpolitik, 30*(5), 279–303.
Blalock, H. M. (1972). *Social statistics.* New York: McGraw-Hill.
Blaug, M. (1985). *Economic theory in retrospect* (4th ed.). Cambridge, UK: Cambridge University Press.
Bloomfield, P. (1976). *Fourier analysis of time series.* New York: John Wiley and Sons.
Boccara, P. (2008). *Transformations et crise du capitalisme mondialisé: quelle alternative?* Pantin, Paris: Le Temps des crises.
Bolt, J., & van Zanden, J. L. (2013). *The first update of the Maddison project; re-estimating growth before 1820* (Maddison Project Working Paper No 4). Retrieved from http://www.ggdc.net/maddison/maddison-project/home.htm.
Bornschier, V. (1996). *Western society in transition.* New Brunswick, NJ: Transaction Publishers.
Bornschier, V., & Chase-Dunn, C. K. (1985). *Transnational corporations and underdevelopment.* New York: Praeger.
Box, G. E. P., & Jenkins, G. M. (1976). *Time series analysis: Forecasting and control* (Rev. ed.). San Francisco, CA: Holden-Day.
Braudel, F. (1973). *Capitalism and material life, 1400–1800.* New York: Harper and Row.
Bremmer, I. (2015). *Qué esperamos de EE UU? El Pais.* Retrieved from http://elpais.com/elpais/2015/06/10/opinion/1433926870_545112.html.
Brener, R. (2006). *The economics of global turbulence. The advanced capitalist economies from long boom to long downturn, 1945–2005.* London; New York: Verso.
British Petroleum. (2010). *British Petroleum statistical review of world energy, 1971–2008.* London: Author.
Burns, A. F., & Mitchell, W. C. (1946). *Measuring business cycles.* New York: National Bureau of Economic Research.

Camm, A. J., Malik, M., & Bigger, J. T. (1996). Heart rate variability: Standards of measurement, physiological interpretation, and clinical use. *Circulation, 93*(5), 1043–1065.

Camm, A. J., Malik, M., Bigger, J. T., Breithardt, G., Cerutti, S., Task Force of the European Society of Cardiology, et al. (1996). Heart rate variability standards of measurement, physiological interpretation, and clinical use. *European Heart Journal, 17*, 354–381.

Cardoso, F. H., & Faletto, E. (1971). *Dependencia y desarrollo en América Latina*. Mexico D.F.: Editorial Siglo I.

Cassel, G. (1918). *Theoretische Sozialökonomie*. Leipzig: A. Deichert.

Cassel, G. (1932). *Theory of social economy*. New York: Harcourt.

Chandy, L., & Gertz, G. (2011). With little notice, globalization reduced poverty. *YaleGlobal*, July 5. Retrieved from http://yaleglobal.yale.edu/content/little-notice-globalization-reduced-poverty.

Chase-Dunn, C., & Hall, T. D. (1994). The historical evolution of world-systems. *Sociological Inquiry, 64*, 257–280.

Chase-Dunn, C., & Hall, T. D. (1997). *Rise and demise: Comparing world-systems*. Boulder, CO: Westview.

Chase-Dunn, C., & Grimes, P. (1995). World-systems analysis. *Annual Review of Sociology, 21*, 387–417.

Chu, C. Y. C., & Lee, R. D. (1994). Famine, revolt, and the dynastic cycle: Population dynamics in historic China. *Journal of Population Economics, 7*, 351–378.

Chu, S. H., & Freund, S. (1996). Volatility estimation for stock index options: A GARCH approach. *Quarterly Review of Economics and Finance, 36*(4), 431–450.

CIA. (2013). *The world factbook*. Retrieved from https://www.cia.gov/library/publications/the-world-factbook/geos/xx.html.

Clark, T. E., & West, K. D. (2006). Using out-of-sample mean squared prediction errors to test the martingale difference hypothesis. *Journal of Econometrics, 135*(1–2), 155–186.

Cleary, M. N., & Hobbs, G. D. (1983). The fifty year cycle: A look at the empirical evidence. In C. Freeman (Ed.), *Long waves in the world economy* (pp. 164–182). London: Butterworth.

Cogley, T. (2008). Data filters. In S. N. Durlauf & L. E. Blume (Eds.), *The new Palgrave dictionary of economics* (2nd ed.). Basingstoke: Palgrave Macmillan. Retrieved June 12, 2013, from http://www.dictionaryofeconomics.com/article?id=pde2008_D000255.

Collard, F. (1999). Spectral and persistence properties of cyclical growth. *Journal of Economic Dynamics and Control, 23*(3), 463–488.

Conference Board. (2016). *The conference board total economy database*, January 2016. Retrieved from http://www.conference-board.org/data/economydatabase/.

Cook, R. D. (1977). Detection of influential observations in linear regression. *Technometrics, 19*, 15–18.

Cooper, J. (2006). Of BRICs and brains: Comparing Russia with China, India, and other populous emerging economies. *Eurasian Geography and Economics, 47*(3), 255–284.

Crowley, P. M. (2010). *Long cycles in growth: Explorations using new frequency domain techniques with US data* (Bank of Finland Research Discussion Papers, 6, 2010). Retrieved from http://patrickmcrowley.com/Research/workingpapers.htm.

Cryer, J. D. (1986). *Time series analysis*. Boston, MA: Duxbury Press.

Dator, J. (2006). Alternative futures for K-Waves. In T. C. Devezas (Ed.), *Kondratieff waves, warfare and world security* (pp. 311–317). Amsterdam: IOS Press.

de Grauwe, P., & Ji, Y. (2012). Mispricing of sovereign risk and macroeconomic stability in the Eurozone. *Journal of Common Market Studies, 50*(6), 866–880.

de Groot, B., & Franses, P. H. (2008). Stability through cycles. *Technological Forecasting and Social Change, 75*(3), 301–311.

de Wolff, S. (1924). Prosperitats- und Depressionsperioden. In O. Jenssen (Ed.), *Der Lebendige Marxismus* (pp. 13–43). Jena: Thuringer Verlagsanstalt.

Debande, O. (2006). De-industrialisation. *EIB Papers, 11*(1), 64–83.

Delbeke, J. (1987). Long-term trends in Belgian money supply, 1877–1984. In T. Vasko (Ed.), *The long-wave debate* (pp. 313–325). Berlin: Springer-Verlag.

Dempster, A. P. (1969). *Elements of continuous multivariate analysis*. Reading, MA: Addison-Wesley.

References

Derviş, K. (2012). Convergence, interdependence, and divergence. *Finance and Development, 49*(3), 10–14.

Devezas, T. C. (Ed.). (2006). *Kondratieff waves, warfare and world security*. Amsterdam: IOS Press.

Devezas, T. C. (2010). Crises, depressions, and expansions: Global analysis and secular trends. *Technological Forecasting and Social Change, 77*(5), 739–761.

Devezas, T. C. (2012). The recent crisis under the light of the long wave theory. In L. E. Grinin, T. C. Devezas, & A. V. Korotayev (Eds.), *Kondratieff waves. Dimensions and prospects at the dawn of the 21st century* (pp. 138–175). Volgograd: Uchitel.

Devezas, T. C., & Corredine, J. T. (2001). The biological determinants of long-wave behavior in socioeconomic growth and development. *Technological Forecasting and Social Change, 68*(1), 1–57.

Devezas, T. C., & Corredine, J. T. (2002). The nonlinear dynamics of technoeconomic systems. An informational interpretation. *Technological Forecasting and Social Change, 69*, 317–357.

Devezas, T. C., Linstone, H. A., & Santos, H. J. S. (2005). The growth dynamics of the Internet and the long wave theory. *Technological Forecasting and Social Change, 72*, 913–935.

Devezas, T. C., & Modelski, G. (2003). Power law behavior and world system evolution: A millennial learning process. *Technological Forecasting and Social Change, 70*, 819–859.

DiBacco, T. V., Mason, L. C., & Appy, C. G. (1992). *History of the United States. Vol. 2. Civil war to the present*. Boston, MA: Houghton Mifflin Company.

Dickson, D. (1983). Technology and cycles of boom and bust. *Science, 219*(4587), 933–936.

Diebold, F. X., Kilian, L., & Nerlove, M. (2008). Time series analysis. In S. N. Durlauf & L. E. Blume (Eds.), *The new Palgrave dictionary of economics* (2nd ed.). Basingstoke: Palgrave Macmillan. doi:10.1057/9780230226203.1707. Retrieved June 12, 2013, from http://www.dictionaryofeconomics.com/article?id=pde2008_T000064.

Diebolt, C. (2012). Cliometrics of economic cycles in France. In L. E. Grinin, T. C. Devezas, & A. V. Korotayev (Eds.), *Kondratieff waves. Dimensions and prospects at the dawn of the 21st century* (pp. 120–137). Volgograd: Uchitel.

Diebolt, C., & Doliger, C. (2006). Economic cycles under test: A spectral analysis. In T. C. Devezas (Ed.), *Kondratieff waves, warfare and world security* (pp. 39–47). Amsterdam: IOS Press.

Diebolt, C., & Escudier, J. L. (2002). *Croissance economique dans le long terme*. Paris: L'Harmattan.

Diebold, F. X., Kilian, L., & Nerlove, M. (2010). Time series analysis. In *Macroeconometrics and time series analysis* (pp. 317–342). Basingstoke, UK: Palgrave Macmillan.

Dittmar, R. D., Gavin, W. T., & Kydland, F. E. (2005). Inflation persistence and flexible prices. *International Economic Review, 46*(1), 245–261.

Dosi, G. (1984). *Technical change and industrial transformation*. New York: St. Martin's Press.

Dupriez, L. H. (1947). *Des mouvements economiques generaux* (Vol. 2, Pt. 3). Louvain: Institut de recherches economiques et sociales de l'universite de Louvain.

Dziuban, C. D., & Shirkey, E. C. (1974). When is a correlation matrix appropriate for factor analysis? *Psychological Bulletin, 81*, 358–361.

Eklund, K. (1980). Long waves in the development of capitalism? *Kyklos, 33*(3), 383–419.

Engels, F. (2009 [1845]). *The condition of the working class in England*. Oxford: Oxford University Press.

Erber, G. (2013). *The austerity paradox: I see austerity everywhere, but not in the statistics*. Retrieved February 28, 2013, from http://ssrn.com/abstract=2226319.

Fischer, S., Dornbusch, R., & Schmalensee, R. (1988). *Economics*. New York: McGraw-Hill.

Forrester, J. W. (1977). Growth cycles. *Economist, 125*(4), 525–543.

Forrester, J. W. (1978). *Innovation and the economic long wave (MIT System Dynamics Group working paper)*. Cambridge, MA: MIT Press.

Forrester, J. W. (1981). *The Kondratieff cycle and changing economic conditions (MIT System Dynamics Group working paper)*. Cambridge, MA: MIT Press.

Forrester, J. W. (1985). Economic conditions ahead: Understanding the Kondratieff wave. *Futurist, 19*(3), 16–20.

Frank, A. G. (1967). *Capitalism and underdevelopment in Latin America: Historical studies of Chile and Brazil*. New York: Monthly Review Press.
Frank, A. G. (1990). A theoretical introduction to 5,000 years of world system history. *Review, 13*(2), 155–248.
Frank, A. G. (1993). Bronze Age world system cycles. *Current Anthropology, 34*(4), 383–419.
Frank, A. G. (1998). *ReOrient: Global economy in the Asian age*. Ewing, CA: University of California Press.
Frank, A. G., & Gills, B. K. (Eds.). (1993). *The world system: Five hundred years or five thousand?* London: Routledge.
Freeman, C. (1987). Technical innovation, diffusion, and long cycles of economic development. In T. Vasko (Ed.), *The long-wave debate* (pp. 295–309). Berlin: Springer.
Freeman, C., & Louçã, F. (2001). *As time goes by: From the industrial revolutions to the information revolution*. Oxford: Oxford University Press.
Fuchs, V. (1998). *Provide, provide: The economics of aging (NBER Working Paper no. 6642)*. Cambridge, MA: National Bureau of Economic Research.
Fukuyama, F. (2002). *Our post-human future: Consequences of the biotechnology revolution*. New York: Farrar, Straus, and Giroux.
Fuller, W. A. (1976). *Introduction to statistical time series*. New York: John Wiley and Sons.
Galbraith, J. K. (2012). *Inequality and instability: A study of the world economy just before the Great Crisis*. New York: Oxford University Press.
Garvy, G. (1943). Kondratieff's theory of long cycles. *Review of Economic Statistics, 25*, 1553–1627.
Gelderen, J. van [J. Fedder pseudo]. (1913). Springvloed: Beschouwingen over industrieele ontwikkeling en prijsbeweging (Spring Tides of Industrial Development and Price Movements). De nieuwe tijd, 18.
Gellner, E. (1983). *Nations and nationalism*. Oxford: Blackwell.
Gennaioli, N., La Porta, R., Lopez-de-Silanes, F., & Shleifer, A. (2014). Growth in regions. *Journal of Economic Growth*. Retrieved from http://faculty.tuck.dartmouth.edu/images/uploads/faculty/rafael-laporta/regions.final.submission.with.tables.pdf.
Genzel, R., & Cesarsky, C. J. (2000). Extragalactic results from the infrared space observatory. *Annual Review of Astronomy and Astrophysics, 38*, 761–814.
Gille, B. (1976). Banking and industrialisation in Europe 1730–1914. In C. M. Cipolla (Ed.), *The industrial revolution, 1700–1914* (pp. 255–300). London; New York: Harvester Press; Barnes & Noble.
Ginzburg, A., & Simonazzi, A. (2005). Patterns of industrialization and the flying geese model: The case of electronics in East Asia. *Journal of Asian Economics, 15*(6), 1051–1078.
Glismann, H. H., Rodemer, H., & Wolter, W. (1983). Long waves in economic development: Causes and empirical evidence. In C. Freeman (Ed.), *Long waves in the world economy* (pp. 135–163). London: Butterworth.
Goldstein, J. S. (1985). Kondratiev waves as war cycles. *International Studies Quarterly, 29*(4), 411–444.
Goldstein, J. S. (1987). Long waves in war, production, prices, and wages. New empirical evidence. *Journal of Conflict Resolution, 34*(4), 573–600.
Goldstein, J. S. (1988). *Long cycles: Prosperity and war in the Modern Age*. New Haven, CT: Yale University Press.
Goldstein, J. S. (1991). The possibility of cycles in international relations. *International Studies Quarterly, 35*(4), 477–480.
Goldstein, J. S. (2006). The predictive power of long wave theory, 1989–2004. In T. C. Devezas (Ed.), *Kondratieff waves, warfare and world security* (pp. 137–146). Amsterdam: IOS Press.
Goldstein, J. S. (2011). *Winning the war on war: The decline of armed conflict worldwide*. New York: Dutton/Penguin.
Goldstone, J. A. (2015). Population ageing and global economic growth. In J. A. Goldstone, L. E. Grinin, & A. V. Korotayev (Eds.), *History & mathematics: Political demography & global ageing* (pp. 147–155). Volgograd: Uchitel.

References

Gordon, D. M. (1978). Up and down the long roller coaster. In B. Steinberg (Ed.), *U.S. capitalism in crisis* (pp. 22–34). New York: Economics Education Project of the Union for Radical Political Economics.

Gore, C. (2000). The rise and fall of the Washington consensus as a paradigm for developing countries. *World Development, 28*(5), 789–804.

Gosh, J., Havlik, P., Ribero, M., & Urban, W. (2009). *Models of BRICs' economic development and challenges for EU competitiveness*. Vienna: The Vienna Institute for International Economic Studies.

Gourio, F. (2012). Disaster risk and business cycles. *American Economic Review, 102*(6), 2734–2766.

Granger, C. W. J. (1981). Some properties of time-series data and their use in econometric model specification. *Journal of Econometrics, 16*(1), 121–130.

Grenville, J. A. S. (1999). *Europe Reshaped: 1848–1878*. Somerset, NJ: John Wiley & Sons.

Grinin, A. L., & Grinin, L. E. (2015a). Cybernetic revolution and forthcoming technological transformations (the development of the leading technologies in the light of the theory of production revolutions). In L. E. Grinin & A. V. Korotayev (Eds.), *Evolution: From big bang to nanorobots* (pp. 251–330). Volgograd: Uchitel.

Grinin, A. L., & Grinin, L. E. (2015b). Cybernetic revolution and historical process. *Social Evolution & History, 14*(1), 125–184.

Grinin, A. L., & Grinin, L. E. (2015c). The cybernetic revolution and historical process. In L. E. Grinin, I. V. Ilyin, P. Herrmann, & A. V. Korotayev (Eds.), *Gllobalistics and globalization studies: big history & global history*. Volgograd: 'Uchitel' Publishing House.

Grinin, L. E. (2006). Periodization of history: A theoretic-mathematical analysis. In L. E. Grinin, V. de Munck, & A. V. Korotayev (Eds.), *History and mathematics: Analyzing and modeling global development* (pp. 10–38). Moscow: KomKniga.

Grinin, L. E. (2007a). Production revolutions and periodization of history: A comparative and theoretic-mathematical approach. *Social Evolution and History, 6*(2), 75–120.

Grinin, L. E. (2007b). Production revolutions and the periodization of history. *Herald of the Russian Academy of Sciences, 77*(2), 150–156.

Grinin, L. E. (2008). Globalization and sovereignty: Why do states abandon their sovereign prerogatives? *Age of Globalization, 1*, 22–32.

Grinin, L. E. (2009a). Transformation of sovereignty and globalization. Hierarchy and power in the history of civilisations. In L. Grinin, D. Beliaev, & A. Korotayev (Eds.), *Political aspects of modernity* (pp. 191–224). Moscow: LIBROCOM/URSS.

Grinin, L. E. (2009b). Globalization and the transformation of national sovereignty. In J. Sheffield (Ed.), *Systemic development: Local solutions in a global environment* (pp. 47–53). Goodyear, AZ: ISCE Publishing.

Grinin, L. E. (2010). Which global transformations would the global crisis lead to? *Age of Globalization, 2*, 31–52.

Grinin, L. E. (2011). *The evolution of statehood. From early state to global society*. Saarbrücken: Lambert Academic Publishing.

Grinin, L. E. (2012a). *Macrohistory and globalization*. Volgograd: Uchitel.

Grinin, L. E. (2012b). New foundations of international system or why do states lose their sovereignty in the age of globalization? *Journal of Globalization Studies, 3*(1), 3–38.

Grinin, L. E. (2012c). State and socio-political crises in the process of modernization. *Cliodynamics, 3*(1), 124–157.

Grinin, L. E., Devezas, T. C., & Korotayev, A. V. (2012). Kondratieff's mystery. In L. E. Grinin, T. C. Devezas, & A. V. Korotayev (Eds.), *Kondratieff waves. Dimensions and prospects at the dawn of the 21st century* (pp. 5–22). Volgograd: Uchitel.

Grinin, L. E., & Grinin, A. L. (2013). Global technological transformations. In L. E. Grinin, I. V. Ilyin, & A. V. Korotayev (Eds.), *Globalistics and globalization studies: Theories, research & teaching* (pp. 98–128). Volgograd: Uchitel.

Grinin, L. E., & Grinin, A. L. (2014). The sixth Kondratieff wave and the cybernetic revolution. In L. E. Grinin, T. C. Devezas, & A. V. Korotayev (Eds.), *Kondratieff waves: Juglar – Kuznets – Kondratieff* (pp. 354–378). Volgograd: Uchitel.

Grinin, L.E., & Grinin, A.L. (2016). *The Cybernetic Revolution and the Forthcoming Epoch of Self-Regulating Systems*. Volgograd: Uchitel.

Grinin, L. E., Ilyin, I. V., & Andreev, A. I. (2016). World order in the past, present, and future. *Social Evolution & History, 15*(1), 60–87.

Grinin, L. E., & Korotayev, A. V. (2009). Social macroevolution: Growth of the world system integrity and a system of phase transitions. *World Futures, 65*(7), 477–506.

Grinin, L. E., & Korotayev, A. V. (2010a). Will the global crisis lead to global transformations? Part1. The global financial system: Pros and cons. *Journal of Globalization Studies, 1*(1), 70–89.

Grinin, L. E., & Korotayev, A. V. (2010b). Will the global crisis lead to global transformations? Part 2. The coming epoch of new coalitions. *Journal of Globalization Studies, 1*(2), 166–183.

Grinin, L. E., & Korotayev, A. V. (2012a). Does 'Arab spring' mean the beginning of world system reconfiguration? *World Futures: The Journal of Global Education, 68*(7), 471–505.

Grinin, L. E., & Korotayev, A. V. (2012b). Afroeurasian world-system: Genesis, transformations, characteristics. In S. Babones & C. Chase-Dunn (Eds.), *Routledge handbook of world-systems analysis* (pp. 30–39). London: Routledge.

Grinin, L. E., & Korotayev, A. V. (2014a). Globalization and the shifting of global economic-political balance. In E. Kiss & A. Kiadó (Eds.), *The dialectics of modernity: Recognizing globalization. Studies on the theoretical perspectives of globalization* (pp. 184–207). Budapest: Publisherhouse Arostotelész.

Grinin, L. E., & Korotayev, A. V. (2014b). Globalization shuffles cards of the world pack: In which direction is the global economic-political balance shifting? *World Futures, 70*(8), 515–545.

Grinin, L. E., & Korotayev, A. V. (2014c). Interaction between Kondratieff waves and Juglar cycles. In L. Grinin, T. Devezas, & A. Korotayev (Eds.), *Kondratieff waves. Juglar – Kuznets – Kondratieff* (pp. 25–95). Volgograd: Uchitel.

Grinin, L. E., & Korotayev, A. V. (2014d). The inflationary and deflationary trends in the global economy, or 'the Japanese disease' is spreading. *Journal of Globalization Studies, 5*(2), 152–173.

Grinin, L. E., & Korotayev, A. V. (2015a). *Great divergence and great convergence. A global perspective*. New York: Springer.

Grinin, L. E., & Korotayev, A. V. (2015b). Population ageing in the West and the global financial system. In J. Goldstone, L. E. Grinin, & A. V. Korotayev (Eds.), *History & mathematics: Political demography & global ageing*. Volgograd: Uchitel.

Grinin, L. E., Korotayev, A. V., & Malkov, S. Y. (2010). A mathematical model of Juglar cycles and the current global crisis. In L. Grinin, P. Herrmann, A. Korotayev, et al. (Eds.), *History & mathematics. Processes and models of global dynamics* (pp. 138–187). Volgograd: Uchitel.

Grinin, L. E., Markov, A. V., & Korotayev, A. V. (2009). Aromorphoses in biological and social evolution: Some general rules for biological and social forms of macroevolution. *Social Evolution and History, 8*(2), 6–50.

Grinin, L., & Grinin, A. (2015c). Cybernetic revolution in global perspective. *Journal of Globalization Studies, 6*(2), 119–142.

Haberler, G. (1964 [1937]). *Prosperity and depression. Theoretical analysis of cyclical movements*. Cambridge, MA: Harvard University Press.

Hadjimichalis, C. (2011). Uneven geographical development and socio-spatial justice and solidarity: European regions after the 2009 financial crisis. *European Urban and Regional Studies, 18*(3), 254–274.

Hanahan, D., & Weinberg, R. A. (2000). The hallmarks of cancer. *Cell, 100*(1), 57–70.

Hanahan, D., & Weinberg, R. A. (2011). Hallmarks of cancer: The next generation. *Cell, 144*(5), 646–674.

Hansen, A. H. (1951). *Business cycles and national income*. New York: W. W. Norton.

Harman, H. H. (1976). *Modern factor analysis* (3rd ed.). Chicago, IL: University of Chicago Press.

Haustein, H. D., & Neuwirth, E. (1982). Long waves in world industrial production, energy consumption, innovations, inventions, and patents, and their identification by spectral analysis. *Technological Forecasting and Social Change, 22*(1), 53–89.

Havlik, P., Pindyuk, O., & Stoellinger, R. (2009). *Trade in goods and services between the EU and the BRICs*. Vienna: The Vienna Institute for International Economic Studies.

Hawtrey, R. G. (1926). *Monetary reconstruction* (2nd ed.). London: Longmans.

Hawtrey, R. G. (1928). *Trade and credit* (2nd ed.). London: Longmans.

Held, D., McGrew, A., Goldblatt, D., & Perraton, J. (1999). *Global transformations. Politics, economics and culture*. Stanford, CA: Stanford University Press.

Helenius, A. (2012). Waves on waves: Long waves on the seven seas. In L. E. Grinin, T. C. Devezas, & A. V. Korotayev (Eds.), *Kondratieff waves. Dimensions and prospects at the dawn of the 21st century* (pp. 85–106). Volgograd: Uchitel.

Hicks, J. R. (1946 [1939]). *Value and capital: An inquiry into some fundamental principles of economic theory*. Oxford: Clarendon Press.

High, S. (2013). The wounds of class: A historiographical reflection on the study of deindustrialization, 1973–2013. *History Compass, 11*(11), 994–1007.

Hilferding, R. (1981 [1910]). *Finance capital. A study of the latest phase of capitalist development*. London: Routledge.

Hirooka, M. (2006). *Innovation dynamism and economic growth. A nonlinear perspective*. Cheltenham; Northampton, MA: Edward Elgar.

Hodrick, R. J., & Prescott, E. C. (1996). *Post-war U.S. business cycles: An empirical investigation*. Pittsburgh: Carnegie Mellon University.

Hodrick, R., & Prescott, E. (1997). Postwar U.S. business cycles: An empirical investigation. *Journal of Money, Credit and Banking, 29*, 1–16.

Huang, P. C. C. (2002). Development or involution in eighteenth-century Britain and China? *The Journal of Asian Studies, 61*, 501–538.

Huerta de Soto, J. (2006). *Money, bank credit, and economic cycles*. Auburn, AL: Ludwig von Mises Institute.

Husson, M., & Louça, F. (2012). Late capitalism and neo-liberalism: A perspective on the current phase of the long wave of capitalist development. In L. E. Grinin, T. C. Devezas, & A. V. Korotayev (Eds.), *Kondratieff waves. Dimensions and prospects at the dawn of the 21st century* (pp. 176–187). Volgograd: Uchitel.

IBM. (2011). *IBM-SPSS statistics 20 algorithms*. New York: Armonk. Retrieved from http://www-01.ibm.com/support/docview.wss?uid=swg27021213#en.

IBM. (2014). *IBM SPSS statistics 21 documentation*. New York: Armonk. Retrieved from http://www-01.ibm.com/support/docview.wss?uid=swg27024972#en.

Ibn Khaldūn `Abd al-Rahman. (1958 [1377]). *The Muqaddimah: An introduction to history (Bollingen Series, 43)*. New York: Pantheon Books.

International Monetary Find (IMF). (2014). *World economic outlook database*. Retrieved from http://www.imf.org/external/pubs/ft/weo/2014/01/weodata/index.aspx.

Ito, T. (2001). Growth, crisis, and the future of economic recovery in East Asia. In J. Stiglitz & S. Yusuf (Eds.), *Rethinking the East Asian miracle* (pp. 55–94). New York: Oxford University Press.

Jaeger, J., & Springler, E. (2012). *Oekonomie der Internationalen Entwicklung. Eine kritischer Einfuehrung in die Volkswirtschaftslehre*. Wien: Mandelbaum.

Jotterand, F. (2008). *Emerging conceptual, ethical and policy issues in bionanotechnology* (Vol. 101). Berlin: Springer Science & Business Media.

Jourdon, Ph. (2008). La monnaie unique europeenne et son lien au developpement economique et social coordonne: une analyse cliometrique. Thèse. Montpellier: Universite Montpellier I.

Juglar, C. (1862). *Des Crises Commerciales et de leur retour périodique en France, en Angleterre et aux États-Unis*. Paris: Guillaumin.

Juglar, C. (1889). *Des crises commerciales et de leur retour périodique en France, en Angleterre et aux États-Unis* (2nd ed.). Paris: Alcan.

Junttila, J. (2001). Structural breaks, ARIMA model and Finnish inflation forecasts. *International Journal of Forecasting, 17*(2), 203–230.

Kalecki, M. (1968a). *Theory of economic dynamics; an essay on cyclical and long-run changes in capitalist economy*. New York: Monthly Review Press.

Kalecki, M. (1968b). Trend and business cycles reconsidered. *Economic Journal, 78*(310), 263–276.

Kalecki, M. (1971). *Selected essays on the dynamics of the capitalist economy 1933–1970.* Cambridge: Cambridge University Press.

Kalecki, M., & Feiwel, G. R. (1972). *The last phase in the transformation of capitalism.* New York: Monthly Review Press.

Kasahara, S. (2004). *The flying geese paradigm. A critical study of its application to East Asian regional devleopment* (UNCTAD Discussion Papers, 169, April 2004, United Nations Conference on Trade and Development (UNCTAD), Palais des Nations, CH-1211 Geneva 10, Switzerland). Retrieved from http://unctad.org/en/Docs/osgdp20043_en.pdf.

Keynes, J. M. (1936). *The general theory of employment, interest, and money.* London: Macmillan.

Kindleberger, C. P. (1973). *The world in depression, 1929–1939.* London: Allen Lane and Penguin.

Kissinger, H. (1994). *Diplomacy.* New York: Simon & Schuster.

Kissinger, H. (2001). *Does America need a foreign policy? Toward a diplomacy for the 21st century.* New York: Simon & Schuster.

Kissinger, H. (2014). *World order.* New York: Penguin Press.

Kitchin, J. (1923). Cycles and trends in economic factors. *Review of Economic Statistics, 5*, 10–16.

Klare, M. T. (2015). America's days as a global superpower are numbered. Now what? *The Nation,* May 28. Retrieved from http://www.thenation.com/article/americas-days-global-superpower-are-numbered-now-what/.

Kleinknecht, A. (1981). Innovation, accumulation, and crisis: Waves in economic development? *Review, 4*(4), 683–711.

Kleinknecht, A. (1987). *Innovation patterns in crisis and prosperity: Schumpeter's long cycle reconsidered.* London: Macmillan.

Kleinknecht, A., & van der Panne, G. (2006). Who was right? Kuznets in 1930 or Schumpeter in 1939? In T. C. Devezas (Ed.), *Kondratieff waves, warfare and world security* (pp. 118–127). Amsterdam: IOS Press.

Kojima, K. (2000). The "flying geese" model of Asian economic development: Origin, theoretical extensions, and regional policy implications. *Journal of Asian Economics, 11,* 375–401.

Komarkova, Z., & Komarek, L. (2007). Integration of the foreign exchange markets of the selected EU new member states. *Politicka Ekonomie, 55*(3), 315–333.

Kondratieff, N. D. (1925). The static and the dynamic view of economics. *Quarterly Journal of Economics, 39*(4), 575–583.

Kondratieff, N. D. (1926). Die langen Wellen der Konjunktur. *Archiv für Sozialwissenschaft und Sozialpolitik, 56*(3), 573–609.

Kondratieff, N. D. (1928). Die Preisdynamik der industriellen und landwirtschaftlichen Waren. Zum Problem der relativen Dynamik der Konjunktur. *Archiv fuer Sozialwissenschaften und Sozialpolitik, 60*(1), 1–85.

Kondratieff, N. D. (1935). The long waves in economic life. *Review of Economic Statistics, 17*(6), 105–115.

Kondratieff, N. D. (1984). *The long wave cycle.* New York: Richardson & Snyder.

Kondratiev, N. D. (1998). In W. Samuels, N. Makasheva, & V. Barnett (Eds.), *The works of Nikolai D. Kondratiev* (Vol. 4). London: Pickering and Chatto..

Kondratieff, N. D. (2004 [1922]). *The world economy and its conjunctures during and after the war.* Moscow: International Kondratieff Foundation [first English translation of the original from 1922].

Kopala, M., & Budden, J. (2015). *The dog bone portfolio. A personal Odyssey into the first Kondratieff winter of the twenty-first century.* Toronto; New York: BPS Books.

Korhonen, P. (1994). The theory of the flying geese pattern of development and its interpretations. *Journal of Peace Research, 31*(1), 93–108.

Korhonen, P. (1998). *Japan and the Asia Pacific integration.* London: Routledge.

Korotayev, A. V. (2005). A compact macromodel of world system evolution. *Journal of World-Systems Research, 11*(1), 79–93.

References

Korotayev, A. V. (2006). The world system urbanization dynamics: A quantitative analysis. In P. Turchin, L. Grinin, A. Korotayev, & V. C. de Munck (Eds.), *History & mathematics: Historical dynamics and development of complex societies* (pp. 44–62). Moscow: KomKniga/ URSS.

Korotayev, A. V. (2007a). Compact mathematical models of world system development, and how they can help us to clarify our understanding of globalization processes. In G. Modelski, T. Devezas, & W. R. Thompson (Eds.), *Globalization as evolutionary process: Modeling global change* (pp. 133–160). London: Routledge.

Korotayev, A. V. (2007b). Secular cycles and millennial trends: A mathematical model. In M. G. Dmitriev, A. P. Petrov, & N. P. Tretyakov (Eds.), *Mathematical modeling of social and economic dynamics* (pp. 118–125). Moscow: RUDN.

Korotayev, A. V., & Grinin, L. E. (2012). Kondratieff waves in the world system perspective. In L. E. Grinin, T. C. Devezas, & A. V. Korotayev (Eds.), *Kondratieff waves. Dimensions and prospects at the dawn of the 21st century* (pp. 23–64). Volgograd: Uchitel.

Korotayev, A. V., & Grinin, L. E. (2014). Kondratieff waves in the global studies perspective. In L. Grinin, I. Ilyin, & A. Korotayev (Eds.), *Globalistics and globalization studies: Aspects and dimensions of global views* (pp. 65–98). Volgograd: Uchitel.

Korotayev, A. V., & Khaltourina, D. (2006). *Introduction to social macrodynamics: Secular cycles and millennial trends in Africa*. Moscow: KomKniga/URSS.

Korotayev, A. V., & Komarova, N. L. (2004). A new mathematical model of pre-industrial demographic cycle. In M. G. Dmitriev & A. P. Petrov (Eds.), *Mathematical modeling of social and economic dynamics* (pp. 157–163). Moscow: Russian State Social University.

Korotayev, A. V., Malkov, A. S., & Khaltourina, D. A. (2006a). *Introduction to social macrodynamics: Compact macromodels of the world system growth*. Moscow: KomKniga/URSS.

Korotayev, A. V., Malkov, A., & Khaltourina, D. (2006b). *Introduction to social macrodynamics: Secular cycles and millennial trends*. Moscow: KomKniga/URSS.

Korotayev, A. V., Malkov, S. Y., & Grinin, L. E. (2014). A trap at the escape from the trap? Some demographic structural factors of political instability in modernizing social systems. *History & Mathematics, 4*, 201–267.

Korotayev, A. V., & Tsirel, S. V. (2010). A spectral analysis of world GDP dynamics: Kondratieff waves, Kuznets swings, Juglar and Kitchin cycles in global economic development, and the 2008–2009 economic crisis. *Structure and Dynamics, 4*(1), 3–57. Retrieved from http://www.escholarship.org/uc/item/9jv108xp.

Korotayev, A. V., Zinkina, J., Bogevolnov, J., & Malkov, A. (2011). Global unconditional convergence among larger economies after 1998? *Journal of Globalization Studies, 2*(2), 25–62.

Korotayev, A. V., Zinkina, J., Kobzeva, S., Bogevolnov, J., Khaltourina, D., Malkov, A., et al. (2011). A trap at the escape from the trap? Demographic-structural factors of political instability in modern Africa and West Asia. *Cliodynamics, 2*(2), 276–303.

Korotayev, A. V., Zinkina, J., & Bogevolnov, J. (2011). Kondratieff waves in global invention activity (1900–2008). *Technological Forecasting and Social Change, 78*, 1280–1284.

Korotayev, A., & de Munck, V. (2013). Advances in development reverse inequality trends. *Journal of Globalization Studies, 4*(1), 105–124.

Korotayev, A., & de Munck, V. (2014). Advances in development reverse global inequality trends. *Globalistics and Globalization Studies, 3*, 164–183.

Korotayev, A., Goldstone, J., & Zinkina, J. (2015). Phases of global demographic transition correlate with phases of the great divergence and great convergence. *Technological Forecasting and Social Change, 95*, 163–169.

Korotayev, A., & Zinkina, J. (2014). On the structure of the present-day convergence. *Campus-Wide Information Systems, 31*(2), 41–57.

Korotayev, A., Zinkina, J., Bogevolnov, J., & Malkov, A. (2011b). Unconditional convergence among larger economies. In D. Liu (Ed.), *Great powers, world order and international society: History and future* (pp. 70–107). Changchun: The Institute of International Studies; Jilin University.

Korotayev, A., Zinkina, J., Bogevolnov, J., & Malkov, A. (2012). Unconditional convergence among larger economies after 1998? *Globalistics and Globalization Studies, 1*, 246–280.

Krasilshchikov, V. (2008). *The rise and decline of catching up development. An experience of Russia and Latin America with implications for Asian tigers*. Malaga: Entelequia, Revista Interdisciplinar. Retrieved from http://www.eumed.net/entelequia/en.lib.php?a=b008.

Krasilshchikov, V. (2014). *The Malaise from success: The East Asian 'miracle' revised*. Saarbrücken: Lambert Academic Publishing.

Krugman, P. (1996). *Pop internationalism*. Cambridge, MA: MIT Press.

Krugman, P., & Lawrence, R. Z. (1994). Trade, jobs and wages. *Scientific American, 270*(4), 44–49.

Kuczynski, Th. (1978). *Spectral analysis and cluster analysis as mathematical methods for the periodization of historical processes… Kondratieff cycles—Appearance or reality?* In Proceedings of the seventh international economic history congress, Vol. 2 (pp. 79–86), International Economic History Congress, Edinburgh.

Kuczynski, Th. (1982). *Leads and lags in an escalation model of capitalist development: Kondratieff cycles reconsidered*. In Proceedings of the eighth international economic history congress, Vol. 3, International Economic History Congress, Budapest, Hungary.

Kuczynski, T. (1980). Have there been differences between the growth rates in different periods of the development of the capitalist world economy since 1850? An application of cluster analysis in time series analysis. In J. M. Clubb & E. K. Scheuch (Eds.), *Historical social research* (pp. 300–316). Stuttgart: Klett-Cotta.

Kuhn, P. A. (1978). The taiping rebellion. In D. Twitchett & J. K. Fairbank (Eds.), *The Cambridge history of China. Vol. 10. Part 1. Late Ch'ing, 1800–1911* (pp. 264–317). Cambridge: Cambridge University Press.

Kuznets, S. (1930). *Secular movements in production and prices. Their nature and their bearing upon cyclical fluctuations*. Boston, MA: Houghton Mifflin.

Kuznets, S. (1940). Schumpeters business cycles. *American Economic Review, 30*(2), 157–169.

Kuznets, S. (1958). Long swings in the growth of population and in related economic variables. *Proceeding of the American Philosophical Society, 102*(1), 25–52.

Kuznets, S. (1966). *Modern economic growth: Rate, structure and spread*. New Haven, CT: Yale University Press.

Kuznets, S. S. (1926). *Cyclical fluctuations: Retail and wholesale trade, United States, 1919–1925*. New York: Adelphi.

Kuznets, S. (1976). *Modern economic growth: Rate, structure, and spread*. New Haven/London: Yale University Press.

Kwan, C. H. (1994). *Economic interdependence in the Asia-Pacific region*. London: Routledge.

Kwang-Ching, L. (1978). The Ch'ing restoration. In D. Twitchett & J. K. Fairbank (Eds.), *The Cambridge history of China. Vol. 10. Part 1. Late Ch'ing, 1800–1911* (pp. 409–490). Cambridge: Cambridge University Press.

Kwasnicki, W. (2008). *Kitchin, Juglar and Kuznetz business cycles revisited*. Wroclaw: Institute of Economic Sciences.

Lawrence, R. Z., & Slaughter, M. J. (1993). International trade and American wages in the 1980s: Giant sucking sound or small hiccup. *Brookings Paper on Economic Activity, 2*, 161–226.

Layton, W. T. (1922). *An introduction to the study of prices. With special reference to the history of the nineteenth century*. London: Macmillan.

Lee, K. (2009). Towards a reformulation of core/periphery relationship: A critical reappraisal of the trimodality of the capitalist world-economy in the early 21st century. *Perspectives on Global Development and Technology, 8*(2–3), 263–294.

Lescure, J. (1907). *Des crises générales et périodiques de surproduction*. Paris: L. Larose et Forcel.

Lescure, J. (1912). Les hausses et baisses générales des prix. *Revue d'Economie Politique, 26*(4), 452–490.

Li, M., Xiao, F., & Zhu, A. (2007). Long waves, institutional changes, and historical trends: A study of the long-term movement of the profit rate in the capitalist world economy. *Journal of World-Systems Research, 13*(1), 33–54. Retrieved from http://www.jwsr.org/archive/volume-13-issue-1-2007.

Liang, J., Liu, X., Tu, E., & Whitelaw, N. (1996). Probabilities and lifetime durations of short-stay hospital and nursing home use in the United States, 1985. *Medical Care, 34*(10), 1018–1036.

Linstone, H. A. (2006). The information and molecular ages: Will K-waves persist? In T. C. Devezas (Ed.), *Kondratieff waves, warfare and world security* (pp. 260–269). Amsterdam: IOS Press.
Liu Kwang-Ching (1978). The Ch'ing Restoration. In Twitchett, D., Fairbank, J. K. (eds.), *The Cambridge History of China, 10*(1): Late Ch'ing, 1800–1911 (pp. 409–490). Cambridge, UK: Cambridge University Press.
Louçã, F. (1997). *Turbulence in economics: An evolutionary appraisal of cycles and complexity in historical processess.* Cheltenham; Lyme, CT: Edward Elgar.
Louçã, F., & Reijnders, J. (Eds.). (1999). *The foundations of long wave theory: Models and methodology.* Northampton, MA: Edward Elgar Publishing.
Luxemburg, R. (1964). *The accumulation of capital.* New York: Monthly Review Press.
Lynch, Z. (2004). Neurotechnology and society 2010–2060. *Annals of the New York Academy of Sciences, 1031*, 229–233.
Machiavelli, N. (1996 [1531]). *Discourses on Livy.* Chicago, IL: University of Chicago Press.
Maddison, A. (1995). *Monitoring the world economy, 1820–1992.* Paris: OECD.
Maddison, A. (2001). *Monitoring the world economy: A millennial perspective.* Paris: OECD.
Maddison, A. (2003). *The world economy: Historical statistics.* Paris: Development Centre of the Organisation for Economic Co-operation and Development.
Maddison, A. (2007). *Contours of the world economy, 1–2030 AD: Essays in macro-economic history.* Oxford; New York: Oxford University Press.
Maddison, A. (2010). *World population, GDP and per capita GDP, A.D. 1–2008.* Retrieved from www.ggdc.net/maddison.
Mandel, E. (1995). *Long waves of capitalist development. A Marxist interpretation; based on the Marshall lectures given at the University of Cambridge.* London: Verso.
Mandel, E. (1975). *Late capitalism.* London: New Left Books.
Mandel, E. (1980). *Long waves of capitalist development.* Cambridge: Cambridge University Press.
Mankiw, G. N., Romer, D., & Weil, D. N. (1992). A contribution to the empirics of economic growth. *The Quarterly Journal of Economics, 107*(2), 407–437.
Mankiw, N. G. (2008). *Principles of economics* (5th ed.). Mason, OH: South-Western.
Marchetti, C. (1980). Society as a learning system. Discovery, invention and innovation cycles revisited. *Technological Forecasting and Social Change, 18*(4), 267–282.
Marchetti, C. (1983). Recession 1983: Ten more years to go? *Technological Forecasting and Social Change, 24*, 331–334.
Marchetti, C. (1986). Fifty years pulsation in human affairs. *Futures, 17*(3), 376–388.
Marchetti, C. (1988). Infrastructures for movement: Past and future. In H. Ausubel & R. Herman (Eds.), *Infrastructures for movement: Past and future, in cities and their vital systems* (pp. 146–174). Washington, DC: National Academy Press.
Marchetti, C. (2006). Is history automatic and are wars a la carte? The perplexing suggestions of a system analysis of historical time series. In T. C. Devezas (Ed.), *Kondratieff waves, warfare and world security* (pp. 173–179). Amsterdam: IOS Press.
Markov, A. V., & Korotayev, A. V. (2007). Phanerozoic marine biodiversity follows a hyperbolic trend. *Palaeoworld, 16*, 311–318.
Marx, K., & Engels, F. (2013) (posthumously). *Werke* (free electronic edition). Retrieved from http://www.mlwerke.de/me/default.htm.
Mensch, G. (1979). *Stalemate in technology—Innovations overcome the depression.* New York: Ballinger.
Metz, R. (1992). Re-examination of long waves in aggregate production series. In A. Kleinknecht, E. Mandel, & I. Wallerstein (Eds.), *New findings in long wave research* (pp. 80–119). New York: St. Martin's.
Metz, R. (1998). Langfristige Wachstumsschwankungen—Trends, Zyklen, Strukturbrüche oder Zufall? In H. Thomas & L. A. Nefiodow (Eds.), *Kondratieffs Zyklen der Wirtschaft. An der Schwelle neuer Vollbeschäftigung?* (pp. 283–307). Herford: BusseSeewald.
Metz, R. (2006). Empirical evidence and causation of Kondratieff cycles. In T. C. Devezas (Ed.), *Kondratieff waves, warfare and world security* (pp. 91–99). Amsterdam: IOS Press.

Metz, R. (2008). *Auf der Suche nach den Langen Wellen der Konjunktur*. Stuttgart: Franz Steiner Verlag.

Metz, R. (2011). Do Kondratieff waves exist? How time series techniques can help to solve the problem. *Cliometrica, 5*(3), 205–238.

Microsoft. (1992). *Microsoft EXCEL. Verzeichnis der Funktionen*. Incline Village, NV: Frontline Systems.

Microsoft. (2013). *Liste mit Tabellenfunktionen (nach Kategorie)*. Retrieved from http://office.microsoft.com/de-at/excel-help/liste-mit-tabellenfunktionen-nach-kategorie-HP010079186.aspx#BMstatistical_functions.

Mills, J. (1868). On credit cycles and the origin of commercial panics. *Transactions of the Manchester Statistical Society, 1867–1868*, 5–40.

Minsky, H. P. (1983). The financial instability hypothesis: An interpretation of Keynes and an alternative to 'standard' theory. In J. C. Wood (Ed.), *John Maynard Keynes. Critical assessments* (pp. 282–292). London: Business & Economics.

Minsky, H. P. (1985). The financial instability hypothesis: A restatement. In P. Arestis & T. Skouras (Eds.), *Post-Keynesian economic theory: A challenge to neo-classical economics* (pp. 24–55). Brighton: M. E. Sharpe.

Minsky, H. P. (1986). *Stabilizing an unstable economy*. New Haven, CT: Yale University Press.

Minsky, H. P. (2005). *Induced investment and business cycles*. Cheltenham; Northampton, MA: Edward Elgar.

Mitchell, W. C. (1913). *Business cycles*. Berkeley, CA: University of California Press.

Mitchell, W. C. (1927). *Business cycles: The problem and its setting*. New York: NBER.

Modelski, G. (1987). *Long cycles in world politics*. Seattle, WA: University of Washington Press.

Modelski, G. (2001). What causes K-waves? *Technological Forecasting and Social Change, 68*, 75–80.

Modelski, G. (2006). Global political evolution, long cycles, and K-waves. In T. C. Devezas (Ed.), *Kondratieff waves, warfare, and world security* (pp. 293–302). Amsterdam: IOS Press.

Modelski, G. (2008a). Globalization as evolutionary process. In G. Modelski, W. R. Thompson, & T. Devezas (Eds.), *Globalization as evolutionary process* (pp. 11–29). New York: Routledge.

Modelski, G. (2008b). Innovation and evolution in the world economy. In R. E. Allen (Ed.), *Human ecology economics* (pp. 21–45). New York: Routledge.

Modelski, G. (2012). Kondratieff (K-)waves in the modern world system. In L. Grinin, T. Devezas, & A. Korotayev (Eds.), *Kondratieff waves. Dimensions and prospects at the dawn of the 21st century* (pp. 65–76). Volgograd: Uchitel.

Modelski, G., & Thompson, W. R. (1996). *Leading sectors and world politics: The coevolution of global politics and economics*. Columbia, SC: University of South Carolina Press.

Modelski, G., Thompson, W. R., & Devezas, T. (Eds.). (2008). *Globalization as evolutionary process: Modeling global change*. New York: Routledge.

Moore, H. L. (1914). *Economic cycles: Their law and cause*. New York: Macmillan.

Moore, H. L. (1923). *Generating economic cycles*. New York: Macmillan.

Morgan, M. S. (1991). *The history of econometric ideas*. Cambridge: Cambridge University Press.

Nefedov, S. A. (2004). A model of demographic cycles in traditional societies: The case of ancient China. *Social Evolution and History, 3*(1), 69–80.

Nefiodow, L. (1996). *Der sechste Kondratieff. Wege zur Produktivität und Vollbeschäftigung im Zeitalter der Information (1 Auflage/Edition)*. Sankt Augustin: Rhein-Sieg-Verlag.

Nefiodow, L., & Nefiodow, S. (2014a). The sixth Kondratieff. The growth engine of the 21st century. In L. E. Grinin, T. C. Devezas, & A. V. Korotayev (Eds.), *Kondratieff waves. Juglar – Kuznets – Kondratieff. Yearbook* (pp. 326–353). Volgograd: Uchitel.

Nefiodow, L., & Nefiodow, S. (2014b). *The sixth Kondratieff. The new long wave of the world economy*. Sankt Augustin: Rhein-Sieg-Verlag.

Nisbet, R. (1980). *History of the idea of progress*. New York: Basic Books.

Noren, R. (2011). Towards a more integrated, symmetric and viable EMU. *Journal of Policy Modeling, 33*(6), 821–830.

O'Hara, P. A. (1994). An institutionalist review of long wave theories: Schumpeterian innovation, modes of regulation, and social structures of accumulation. *Journal of Economic Issues, 28*(2), 489–500.

O'Hara, P. A. (2001). Long waves of growth and development. In P. A. O'Hara (Ed.), *Encyclopedia of political economy* (pp. 673–677). London; New York: Routledge.

O'Hara, P. A. (2005). *Growth and development in the global political economy. Social structures of accumulation and modes of regulation*. Oxford; New York: Routledge, Taylor and Francis Group.

OECD. (2001). *The well-being of nations: The role of human and social capital*. Paris: Author.

OECD. (2014a). *Annual survey of large pension funds and public pension reserve funds [Report on pension funds' long-term investments]*. Paris: Author.

OECD. (2014b). *Pension markets in focus*. Paris: Author.

OECD. (2015). *OECD stat: Public pension reserve funds' statistics: Asset allocation*. Retrieved from http://stats.oecd.org/index.aspx?queryid=594.

Ozawa, T. (1992). Foreign direct investment and economic development. *Transnational Corporations, 1*(1), 27–54.

Ozawa, T. (2001). The 'hidden' side of the 'flying-geese' catch-up model: Japan's dirigiste institutional setup and a deepening financial morass. *Journal of Asian Economics, 12*, 471–491.

Ozawa, T. (2004). The Hegelian dialectic and evolutionary economic change. *Global Economy Journal, 4*(1). doi:10.2202/1524-5861.1006. Retrieved from http://www.degruyter.com/view/j/gej.2004.4.1/gej.2004.4.1.1006/gej.2004.4.1.1006.xml?format=INT.

Ozawa, T. (2005). *Institutions, industrial upgrading, and economic performance in Japan: The 'flying-geese' paradigm of catch-up growth*. Cheltenham: Edward Elgar.

Ozawa, T. (2009). *The rise of Asia: The 'flying-geese' theory of tandem growth and regional agglomeration*. Cheltenham: Edward Elgar.

Ozawa, T. (2010). *The (Japan-born) 'flying-geese' theory of economic development revisited and reformulated from a structuralist perspective* (Working Paper No. 291). Center on Japanese Economy and Business, Graduate School of Business, Columbia University. Retrieved October 2010, from http://www.gsb.columbia.edu/cjeb/research.

Ozawa, T. (2013). *The classical origins of Akamatsu's 'flying-geese' theory: A note on a missing link to David Hume (Working Paper Series no. 320)*. New York: Center on Japanese Economy and Business, Columbia University. Retrieved from www.gsb.columbia.edu/cjeb/research.

Papenhausen, C. (2008). Causal mechanisms of long waves. *Futures, 40*, 788–794.

Park, D., & Shin, K. (2015). Impact of population ageing on Asia's future growth. In J. A. Goldstone, L. E. Grinin, & A. V. Korotayev (Eds.), *History & mathematics: Political demography & global ageing* (pp. 107–132). Volgograd: Uchitel.

Perez, C. (1983). Structural change and assimilation of new technologies in the economic and social systems. *Futures, 15*(5), 357–375.

Perez, C. (2002). *Technological revolutions and financial capital: The dynamics of bubbles and golden ages*. Cheltenham: Elgar.

Perez, C. (2010). Technological revolutions and techno-economic paradigms. *Cambridge Journal of Economics, 34*(1), 185–202.

Perez, C. (2011). The advance of technology and major bubble collapses. In A. Linklater (Ed.), *On capitalism: Perspectives from the Engelsberg seminar 2010* (pp. 103–114). Stockholm: Axon Foundation.

Perez, C. (2012). Technological revolutions and the role of government in unleashing golden ages. In L. Grinin, T. Devezas, & A. Korotayev (Eds.), *Kondratieff waves. Dimensions and prospects at the dawn of the 21st century* (pp. 211–218). Volgograd: Uchitel.

Perkins, D. H. (1969). *Agricultural development in China 1368–1968*. Chicago, IL: Aldine.

Perman, R., & Tavera, C. (2005). A cross-country analysis of the Okun's Law coefficient convergence in Europe. *Applied Economics, 37*(21), 2501–2513.

Pigou, A. C. (1929). *Industrial fluctuations* (2nd ed.). London: Macmillan.

Piketty, T. (2014). *Capital in the twenty-first century*. Cambridge, MA: The Belknap Press of Harvard University Press.

Piketty, T., & Zucman, G. (2013). *Capital is back: Wealth-income ratios in rich countries, 1700–2010*. Retrieved from http://piketty.pse.ens.fr/fr/capitalisback.

Pinkerton, S. (2013). The pros and cons of robotic surgery. *The Wall Street Journal*, p. 17. Retrieved from http://www.wsj.com/articles/SB10001424052702304655104579163430371597334.

Polanyi, K. (1944/1957). *The great transformation. The political and economic origins of our time* (Foreword by Robert MacIver). Boston: Beacon Press.

Popper, K. (1961). *The poverty of historicism*. New York: Harper & Row.

Quenouville, M. H. (1949). Approximate tests of correlation in time series. *Journal of the Royal Statistical Society, Series B, 11*, 68–68.

Rasler, K. A., & Thompson, W. R. (1994). *The great powers and global struggle, 1490–1990*. Lexington, KY: University Press of Kentucky.

Rasler, K., & Thompson, W. R. (2009). Globalizaton and north-south inequality, 1870–2000: A factor for convergence, divergence or both? *International Journal of Comparative Sociology, 50*(5–6), 425–451.

Rennstich, J. K. (2002). The new economy, the leadership long cycle and the nineteenth K-wave. *Review of International Political Economy, 9*(1), 150–182.

Reuveny, R., & Thompson, W. R. (2001). Leading sectors, lead economies, and their impact on economic growth. *Review of International Political Economy, 8*, 689–719.

Reuveny, R., & Thompson, W. R. (2004). *Growth, trade and systemic leadership*. Ann Arbor, MI: University of Michigan Press.

Reuveny, R., & Thompson, W. R. (2008). Uneven economic growth and the world economy's north-south stratification. *International Studies Quarterly, 52*, 579–605.

Reuveny, R., & Thompson, W. R. (2009). *Limits to globalization and north-south divergence*. London: Routledge.

Richardson, S. (2011). *PIIGS 'R' us? The coming U.S. debt crisis and what can be done about it University of Calgary – School of Public Policy Communiqué*, 3(2). Retrieved from http://ssrn.com/abstract=1894927.

Robinson, W. I. (2011). Globalization and the sociology of Immanuel Wallerstein: A critical appraisal. *International Sociology, 26*(6), 1–23.

Roehrich, W. (2004). *Die Macht der Religionen. Glaubenskonflikte in der Weltpolitik*. München: C. H. Beck.

Rostow, W. W. (1975). Kondratieff, Schumpeter and Kuznets: Trend periods revisited. *Journal of Economic History, 25*(4), 719–753.

Rostow, W. W. (1978). *The world economy: History and prospect*. Austin, TX: University of Texas Press.

Rothbard, M. N. (1969). *Economic depressions: Causes and cures*. Lansing, MI: Constitutional Alliance of Lansing.

Rothschild, K. W. (1995). *Economic method, theory and policy: Selected essays of Kurt W. Rothschild* (J. E. King, Ed.). Aldershot; Brookfield, WI: E. Elgar Pub.

Rothschild, K. W. (2003). *Die politischen Visionen großer Ökonomen*. Zuerich: Wallstein.

Rowthorn, R., & Ramaswany, R. (1997). *Deindustrialization: Causes and implications* (IMF Working Paper no. 42). Retrieved from http://www.imf.org/external/pubs/ft/wp/wp9742.pdf.

Rummel, R. J. (1970). *Applied factor analysis*. Evanston, IL: Northwestern University Press.

Sala-i-Martin, X. X. (2006). The world distribution of income: Falling poverty and ... convergence, period. *The Quarterly Journal of Economics, 121*(2), 351–397.

Samuelson, P. A., & Nordhaus, W. D. (2005). *Economics* (18th ed.). New York: McGraw-Hill.

Samuelson, P. A., & Nordhaus, W. D. (2009). *Macroeconomics* (19th ed.). New York: McGraw-Hill.

Schäfer, U. (2009). *Der Crash des Kapitalismus*. Frankfurt: Campus Verlag.

Schroeppel, Ch., & Nakajima, M. (2002). *The changing interpretation of the flying geese model of economic development*. German Institute for Japanese Studies, Japanstudien, 14. Retrieved from http://contemporary-japan.org/back_issues/japanstudien_14_japan_als_fallbeispiel/dij-jb14-Schroeppel-Nakajima.pdf.

References

Schulmeister, S. (2013). Muehsal der Wahr-Nehmung. In K. Eicker-Wolf, G. Quaißer, & U. Thöne (Eds.), *Bildungschancen und Verteilungsgerechtigkeit* (pp. 15–60). Marburg: Metropolis Verlag.

Schumpeter, J. A. (1934). *The theory of economic development: An inquiry into profits, capital, credit, interest, and the business cycle*. Cambridge, MA: Harvard University Press.

Schumpeter, J. A. (1939). *Business cycles: A theoretical, historical, and statistical analysis of the capitalist process*. New York; London: McGraw-Hill Book.

Schumpeter, J. A. (1949 [1911]). *The theory of economic development: An inquiry into profits, capital, credit, interest and the business cycle*. Cambridge, MA: Harvard University Press.

Schumpeter, J. A. (1954). *History of economic analysis*. London: George Allen & Unwin.

Schumpeter, J. A. (2010). *The nature and essence of economic theory*. New Brunswick, NJ: Transaction Publishers.

Seers, D., Schaffer, B., & Kiljunen, M. L. (Eds.). (1979). *Underdeveloped Europe: Studies in core-periphery relations*. Atlantic Highlands, NJ: Humanities Press.

Seers, D., Vaitsos, C. V., & Kiljunen, M. L. (Eds.). (1980). *Integration and unequal development: The experience of the EEC*. New York: St. Martin's Press.

Seers, D., Vaitsos, C. V., & Kiljunen, M. L. (Eds.). (1982). *The second enlargement of the EEC: The integration of unequal partners*. New York: St. Martin's Press.

Senge, P. M. (1982). *The economic long wave: A survey of evidence (MIT System Dynamics Group working paper)*. Cambridge, MA: MIT Press.

Shinohara, M. (1982). *Industrial growth, trade, and dynamic patterns in the Japanese economy*. Tokyo: University of Tokyo Press.

Shiode, N., Li, C., Batty, M., Longley, P., & Maguire, D. (2004). The impact and penetration of location-based services. In H. A. Karimi & A. Hammad (Eds.), *Telegeoinformatics: Location-based computing and services* (pp. 349–366). Boca Raton, FL: CRC Press.

Shostak, F. (2002). *Where we are, where we are headed*. Paper presented at the 'Boom, Bust, and Future' Seminar at Ludwig von Mises Institute, Auburn, AL, January 18–19, 2002.

Sidaway, J. D. (2012). Geographies of development: New maps, new visions? *Professional Geographer, 64*(1), 49–62.

Silberling, N. J. (1943). *The dynamics of business: An analysis of trends, cycles, and time relationships in American economic activity since 1700 and their bearing upon governmental and business policy*. New York: McGraw-Hill.

Silverberg, G. (2006). Long waves in global warfare and maritime hegemony? A complex system perspective. In T. C. Devezas (Ed.), *Kondratieff waves, warfare and world security [Proceedings of the NATO Advanced Research Workshop on the Influence of Chance Events and Socioeconomic Long Waves in the New Arena of Asymmetric Warfare, Covilhã, Portugal, 14–18 February, 2005]* (pp. 154–164). Amsterdam: IOS Press.

Simiand, F. (1932). *Les fluctuations économiques à longue période et la crise mondiale*. Paris: Lib. Felix Alcan.

Skousen, M. (1993). *Who predicted the 1929 crash? The meaning of Ludwig von Mises* (pp. 247–283). Norwell, MA: Kluwer Academic Publishers.

Smith, R. J., & Taylor, A. M. R. (2001). Recursive and rolling regression-based tests of the seasonal unit root hypothesis. *Journal of Econometrics, 105*(2), 309–336.

Solomou, S. N. (2008a). Kondratieff cycles. In S. N. Durlauf & L. E. Blume (Eds.), *The new Palgrave dictionary of economics* (2nd ed.). Basingstoke: Palgrave Macmillan. doi:10.1057/9780230226203.0902. Retrieved from http://www.dictionaryofeconomics.com/article?id=pde2008_K000037.

Solomou, S. N. (2008b). Kuznets swings. In S. N. Durlauf & L. E. Blume (Eds.), *The new Palgrave dictionary of economics* (2nd ed.). Basingstoke: Palgrave Macmillan. doi:10.1057/9780230226203.0908. Retrieved from http://www.dictionaryofeconomics.com/article?id=pde2008_K000045.

Solow, R. M. (1956). A contribution to the theory of economic growth. *Quarterly Journal of Economics, 70*(1), 65–94.

Sornette, D. (2003). *Why stock markets crash. Critical events in complex financial systems.* Princeton, NJ: Princeton University Press.
Spence, M. (2011). *The next convergence: The future of economic growth in a multispeed world.* New York: Farrar, Straus and Giroux.
Spiethoff, A. (1925). *Kriesen. Handwörterbuch der Staatswissenschaften. Bd. 6. 4 Aufl. (S. 8–91).* Jena: Verlag von Gustav Fischer.
SPSS. (1999). *Trends 10.0.* Chicago, IL: Marketing Department, SPSS Inc. Retrieved from http://www.bf.lu.lv/grozs/Datorlietas/SPSS/SPSS%20Trends%2010.0.pdf.
Steindl, J. (1952). *Maturity and stagnation in American capitalism.* Oxford: Basil Blackwell.
Steindl, J. (1979). Stagnation theory and stagnation policy. *Cambridge Journal of Economics, 3*, 1–14.
Steindl, J. (1990). *Economic papers 1941–88.* Basingstoke: MacMillan.
Sterman, J. D. (1985). *The economic long wave: Theory and evidence.* Cambridge, MA: MIT Press.
Sterman, J. D. (1986). The economic long wave: Theory and evidence. *System Dynamics Review, 2*(2), 87–125.
Stiglitz, J. E. (2015). America in the way. *Project Syndicate*, August 6. Retrieved from http://www.project-syndicate.org/commentary/us-international-development-finance-by-joseph-e--stiglitz-2015-08.
Stiglitz, J. E. (2002). *Globalization and its discontents.* New York: W. W. Norton.
Tang, C. F. (2010). The money-prices nexus for Malaysia: New empirical evidence from the time-varying cointegration and causality tests. *Global Economic Review, 39*(4), 383–403.
Tausch, A. (2006a). *From the 'Washington' towards a 'Vienna consensus'? A quantitative analysis on globalization, development and global governance.* Buenos Aires: Centro Argentino de Estudios Internacionales.
Tausch, A. (2006b). Global terrorism and world political cycles. In L. Grinin, V. C. de Munck, & A. Korotayev (Eds.), *History and mathematics: Analyzing and modeling global development* (pp. 99–126). Moscow: KomKniga/URSS.
Tausch, A. (2007). War cycles. *Social Evolution and History, 6*(2), 39–74.
Tausch, A. (2010). Towards yet another age of creative destruction? *Journal of Globalization Studies, 1*(1), 104–130.
Tausch, A. (2012). The 'four economic freedoms' and life quality. General tendencies and some hard lessons for EU-27 Europe. *Journal of Globalization Studies, 2*(3), 79–97.
Tausch, A. (2013). Inequality, migration, and 'smart' survival performance. *Social Evolution and History, 12*(1), 77–101.
Tausch, A., & Ghymers, C. (2007). *From the 'Washington' towards a 'Vienna consensus'? A quantitative analysis on globalization, development and global governance.* Hauppauge, NY: Nova Science Publishers.
Tausch, A., & Heshmati, A. (2011). Re-orient? Understanding contemporary shifts in the global political economy. *Journal of Globalization Studies, 2*(2), 89–128.
Tausch, A., & Heshmati, A. (2014). Labour migration and 'smart public health'. In L. Grinin & A. Korotayev (Eds.), *History and mathematics: Trends and cycles* (pp. 268–280). Volgograd: Uchitel.
Tausch, A., Heshmati, A., & Bajalan, C. S. J. (2010). On the multivariate analysis of the 'Lisbon process'. In L. Grinin, P. Herrmann, A. Korotayev, & A. Tausch (Eds.), *History and mathematics: Processes and models of global dynamics* (pp. 92–137). Volgograd: Uchitel.
Tausch, A., & Jourdon, P. (2011). *Trois essais pour une économie politique du 21e siècle: Mondialisation, gouvernance mondiale, marginalisation.* Paris: L'Harmattan.
Tausch, A., & Prager, F. (1992). *Towards a socio-liberal theory of world development.* Basingstoke; New York: Macmillan/St. Martin's Press.
Ternyik, S. I. (2012). K-periodicity, space-time structures and world economics. In L. Grinin, T. Devezas, & A. Korotayev (Eds.), *Kondratieff waves. Dimensions and prospects at the dawn of the 21st century* (pp. 77–84). Volgograd: Uchitel.
Thompson, W. R. (1988). *On global war: Historical-structural approaches to world politics.* Columbia, SC: University of South Carolina Press.

Thompson, W. R. (1990). Long waves, technological innovation, and relative decline. *International Organization, 44*(2), 201–233.
Thompson, W. R. (2000). *The emergence of a global political economy*. London: Routledge.
Thompson, W. R. (2007). The Kondratieff wave as global social process. In G. Modelski & R. A. Denemark (Eds.), *World system history, encyclopedia of life support systems, UNESCO*. Oxford: EOLSS Publishers.
Thompson, W. R. (2012). Energy, K-waves, lead economies, and their interpretation/implications. In L. Grinin, T. Devezas, & A. Korotayev (Eds.), *Kondratieff waves. Dimensions and prospects at the dawn of the 21st century* (pp. 188–210). Volgograd: Uchitel.
Thompson, W. R., & Zuk, L. G. (1982). War, inflation, and the Kondratieff long wave. *Journal of Conflict Resolution, 26*(4), 621–644.
Tugan-Baranovsky, M. I. (1954). Periodic industrial crises. *Annals of the Ukrainian Academy of Arts and Sciences in the United States, 3*(3), 745–802.
Turchin, P. (2003). *Historical dynamics: Why states rise and fall*. Princeton, NJ: Princeton University Press.
Turchin, P. (2005a). Dynamical feedbacks between population growth and sociopolitical instability in agrarian states. *Structure and Dynamics, 1*, 49–69.
Turchin, P. (2005b). *War and peace and war: Life cycles of imperial nations*. New York: Pi Press.
Turchin, P., & Korotayev, A. (2006). Population density and warfare: A reconsideration. *Social Evolution and History, 5*(2), 121–158.
Turchin, P., & Nefedov, S. (2009). *Secular cycles*. Princeton, NJ: Princeton University Press.
Tylecote, A. (1992). *The long wave in the world economy*. London: Routledge.
U.S. Bureau of the Census. (2016). *World population information*. Retrieved from http://www.census.gov/ipc/www/idb/worldpopinfo.php.
Umpleby, S. A., & Dent, E. B. (1999). The origins and purposes of several traditions in systems theory and cybernetics. *Cybernetics and Systems: An International Journal, 30*, 79–103.
UN Population Division. (2016). *UN population division database*. Retrieved January 17, 2016, from http://www.un.org/esa/population.
University of Texas Inequality (UTIP) Project. (2013). *Estimated household income inequality data set*. Retrieved from http://utip.gov.utexas.edu/data.html.
Usher, D. (1989). The dynastic cycle and the stationary state. *The American Economic Review, 79*, 1031–1044.
van der Zwan, A. (1980). On the assessment of the Kondratieff cycle and related issues. In S. K. Kuipers & G. J. Lanjouw (Eds.), *Prospects of economic growth* (pp. 183–222). Amsterdam: North-Holland.
van Duijn, J. J. (1979). The long wave in economic life. *De Economist, 125*(4), 544–576.
van Duijn, J. J. (1981). Fluctuations in innovations over time. *Futures, 13*(4), 264–275.
van Duijn, J. J. (1983). *The long wave in economic life*. Boston, MA: Allen and Unwin.
Van Ewijk, C. (1982). A spectral analysis of the Kondratieff cycle. *Kyklos, 35*(3), 468–499.
Velleman, P. F., & Welsch, R. E. (1981). Efficient computing of regression diagnostics. *American Statistician, 35*, 234–242.
Vernengo, M. (2006). Technology, finance, and dependency: Latin American radical political economy in retrospect. *Review of Radical Political Economics, 38*, 551–558.
Vernon, R. (1966). International investment and international trade in the product cycle. *Quarterly Journal of Economics, 80*(2), 190–207.
Vernon, R. (1971). *Sovereignty at bay: The multinational spread of US enterprises*. New York: Basic Books.
Vogelsang, T. J. (2008). Spectral analysis. In S. N. Durlauf & L. E. Blume (Eds.), *The new Palgrave dictionary of economics* (2nd ed.). Basingstoke: Palgrave Macmillan. doi:10.1057/9780230226203.1588. Retrieved from http://www.dictionaryofeconomics.com/article?id=pde2008_S000201.
von Foerster, H., & Zopf, G. (Eds.). (1962). *Principles of self-organization*. New York: Pergamon Press.
von Hayek, F. A. (1931). *Prices and production*. London: Routledge.
von Hayek, F. A. (1933). *Monetary theory and the trade cycle*. London: Jonathan Cape.

von Mises, L. (1981 [1912]). *The theory of money and credit*. Indianapolis, IN: Liberty Fund.
Wallerstein, I. (1974, 1980, 1988). *The modern world-system*, 3 vols. New York: Academic Press.
Wallerstein, I. (1984). Economic cycles and socialist policies. *Futures, 16*(6), 579–585.
Wallerstein, I. (1987). World-systems analysis. In A. Giddens & J. Turner (Eds.), *Social theory today* (pp. 309–324). Cambridge: Polity Press.
Wallerstein, I. (2000). *The essential Wallerstein*. New York: The New Press.
Weber, R. P. (1981). Society and economy in the Western world system. *Social Forces, 59*(4), 1130–1148.
Wiener, N. (1948). *Cybernetics, or control and communication in the animal and the machine*. Cambridge, MA: MIT Press.
Wilenius, M., & Casti, J. (2015). Seizing the X-events. The sixth K-wave and the shocks that may upend it. *Technological Forecasting and Social Change, 94*, 335–349.
Wind, S. L. (2011). *Eurozone sovereign debt crisis*. Retrieved from http://dx.doi.org/10.2139/ssrn.1966315.
Wirth, M. (Ed.). (1883). *Geschichte der Handelskrisen*. 3 verm. und verb. Auflage. J.D. Sauerlander's Verlag.
World Bank. (2016). *World development indicators online*. Washington, DC: Author. Retrieved from http://data.worldbank.org/indicator/.
World Intellectual Property Organization (WIPO). (2012a). *Statistics on patents. Total number of patent grants by resident and non-resident (1985–2008)*. Retrieved from http://www.wipo.int/export/sites/www/ipstats/en/statistics/patents/xls/wipo_pat_grant_total_from_1985.xls.
World Intellectual Property Organization (WIPO). (2012b). *Statistics on patents. Patent grants by patent office by resident and non-resident*. Retrieved from http://www.wipo.int/export/sites/www/ipstats/en/statistics/patents/xls/wipo_pat_grant_from_1883_table.xls.
Yamazawa, I. (1990). *Economic development and international trade: The Japanese model*. Honolulu, Hawaii: East-West Center.
Zakaria, F. (2008). *The post-American world*. New York; London: W.W. Norton.
Zarnowitz, V. (1985). Recent work on business cycles in historical perspective: Review of theories and evidence. *Journal of Economic Literature, 23*(2), 523–580.
Zinkina, J., Malkov, A., & Korotayev, A. (2014). A mathematical model of technological, economic, demographic and social interaction between the center and periphery of the world system. In K. Mandal, N. Asheulova, & S. G. Kirdina (Eds.), *Socio-economic and technological innovations: Mechanisms and institutions* (pp. 135–147). New Delhi: Narosa Publishing House.
Zinn, H. (1995). *A people's history of the United States: 1492–present*. New York: Harper Perennial.
Zivot, E., & Wang, J. (2006). *Modeling financial time series with s-plus, second edition, with Jiahui Wang*. Heidelberg; Berlin; New York: Springer.
Абалкин, Л. (1992). *Научное наследие Н. Д. Кондратьева и современность*. М.: Институт экономики РАН.
Абель, Э., и Бернанке, Б. (2008). *Макроэкономика*. 5-е изд. СПб.: Питер.
Аврамов, Р. (1992). Теория длинных волн: исторический контекст и методологические проблемы. *Вопросы экономики, 10*, 63–68.
Акаев, А. А. (2010). Современный финансово-экономический кризис в свете теории инновационно-технологического развития экономики и управления инновационным процессом. В: Халтурина, Д. А., и Коротаев, А. В. (ред.), *Системный мониторинг глобального и регионального развития* (с. 230–258). М.: ЛИБРОКОМ/URSS.
Акаев, А. А. (2011). Математические основы инновационно-циклической теории экономического развития Кондратьева – Шумпетера. *Вестник института экономики РАН, 2*, 39–60.
Акаев, А. А. (2012). Математические основы инновационно-циклической теории экономического развития Шумпетера – Кондратьева. В: Акаев, А. А., Гринберг, Р. С., Гринин, Л. Е., Коротаев, А. В., и Малков, С. Ю. (ред.), *Кондратьевские волны: аспекты и перспективы* (с. 110–135). Волгоград: Учитель.

Акаев, А. А. (2015). *От эпохи Великой дивергенции к эпохе Великой конвергенции. Математическое моделирование и прогнозирование долгосрочного технологического и экономического развития мировой динамики*. М.: URSS.

Акаев, А. А., Румянцева, С. Ю., Сарыгулов, А. И., и Соколов, В. Н. (2011). *Экономические циклы и экономический рост*. СПб.: Изд-во Политехн. ун-та.

Акаев, А. А., и Садовничий, В. А. (2010). О новой методологии долгосрочного циклического прогнозирования динамики развития мировой и российской экономики. В: Акаев, А. А., Коротаев, А. В., и Малинецкий, Г. Г. (ред.), *Прогноз и моделирование кризисов и мировой динамики* (с. 5–69). М.: ЛКИ/URSS.

Архангельский, В. Н., Божевольнов, Ю. В., Голдстоун, Д., Зверева, Н. В., Зинькина, Ю. В., Коротаев, А. В., Малков, А. С., Рыбальченко, С. И., Рязанцев, С. В., Стек, Ф., Халтурина, Д. А., Шульгин, С. Г., и Юрьев, Е. Л. (2014). *Через 10 лет будет поздно. Демографическая политика Российской Федерации: вызовы и сценарии*. М.: Институт научно-общественной экспертизы; РАНХиГС при Президенте РФ; Рабочая группа «Семейная политика и детство» Экспертного совета при Правительстве РФ.

Благих, И. А. (1993). К 100-летию со дня рождения Н. Д. Кондратьева. *Вестник РАН* 2: 112–121.

Благих, И. А. (1994). Николай Кондратьев – экономист, мыслитель, гражданин. *Вестник РАН, 64*(2), 138–146.

Бобровников, А. В. (2004). *Макроциклы в экономике стран Латинской Америки*. М.: Институт Латинской Америки РАН.

Бунятян, М. А. (1915). *Экономические кризисы. Опыт морфологии и теории периодических экономических кризисов и теории конъюнктуры*. М.: Мысль.

Бурстин, Д. (1993а). *Американцы. Колониальный опыт*. М.: Прогресс-Литера.

Бурстин, Д. (1993б). *Американцы. Национальный опыт*. М.: Прогресс-Литера.

Варга, Е. С. (1937). *Мировые экономические кризисы 1848–1935 гг.* Т. 1. М.: ОГИЗ.

Варга, Е. С. (1974). *Капитализм после Второй мировой войны*. М.: Наука.

Глазьев, С. Ю. (1993). *Теория долгосрочного технико-экономического развития*. М.: ВлаДар.

Глазьев, С. Ю. (2009). Мировой экономический кризис как процесс смены технологических укладов. *Вопросы экономики, 3,* 26–32.

Горбунов. С. В., и Шутов, Г. К. (1994). *Узник 'Святого монастыря'*. Иваново: Галка.

Гринин, А. Л., и Гринин, Л. Е. (2013). Кибернетическая революция и грядущие технологические трансформации (развитие ведущих технологий в свете теории производственных революций). В: Гринин, Л. Е., Коротаев, А. В., и Марков, А. В. (ред.), *Эволюция Земли, жизни, общества, разума* (с. 167–239). Волгоград: Учитель.

Гринин, А. Л., и Гринин, Л. Е. (2015). Кибернетическая революция и исторический процесс (технологии будущего в свете теории производственных революций). *Философия и общество, 1,* 17–47.

Гринин, Л. Е. (2003). *Производительные силы и исторический процесс* (2-е изд.). Волгоград: Учитель.

Гринин, Л. Е. (2005). Глобализация и национальный суверенитет. *История и современность, 1,* 6–31.

Гринин, Л. Е. (2006а). *Производительные силы и исторический процесс* (3-е изд.). М.: КомКнига/URSS.

Гринин, Л. Е. (2006б). Методологические основания периодизации истории. *Философские науки, 8,* 117–123.

Гринин, Л. Е. (2007а). Некоторые размышления по поводу природы законов, связанных с демографическими циклами (к постановке проблемы определения общих методологических подходов к анализу демографических циклов). В: Турчин, П. В., Гринин, Л. Е., Малков, С. Ю., и Коротаев, А. В. (ред.), *История и математика: Концептуальное пространство и направления поиска* (с. 219–246). М.: ЛКИ/ URSS.

Гринин, Л. Е. (2007б). Производственные революции и периодизация истории. *Вестник Российской Академии наук, 77*(4), 309–315.

Гринин, Л. Е. (2008а). Глобализация и модели трансформации суверенности в западных и незападных странах. В: Кульпин, Э. С. (ред.), *Человек и природа: «Вызов и ответ»* (с. 56–88). М.: ИАЦ-Энергия.

Гринин, Л. Е. (2008б). Глобализация и процессы трансформации национального суверенитета. *Век глобализации, 1,* 86–97.

Гринин, Л. Е. (2008в). Национальный суверенитет и процессы глобализации (вводные замечания). *Полис, 1,* 123–133.

Гринин, Л. Е. (2008г). Национальный суверенитет в век глобализации. В: Ильин, М. В., и Кудряшова, И. В. (ред.), *Суверенитет. Трансформация понятий и практик* (с. 104–128). М.: МГИМО-Университет.

Гринин, Л. Е. (2008д). Нежеланное дитя глобализации. Заметки о кризисе. *Век глобализации, 2,* 46–53.

Гринин, Л. Е. (2009а). Приведет ли глобальный кризис к глобальным изменением? *Век глобализации, 2,* 117–140.

Гринин, Л. Е. (2009б). Глобальный кризис как кризис перепроизводства денег. *Философия и общество, 1,* 5–32.

Гринин, Л. Е. (2009в). Современный кризис: новые черты и классика жанра. *История и современность, 1,* 3–32.

Гринин, Л.Е. (2009г). Психология экономических кризисов. *Историческая психология и социальная история, 2,* 75–99.

Гринин, Л. Е. (2009д). *Государство и исторический процесс: Политический срез исторического процесса.* М.: ЛИБРОКОМ/URSS.

Гринин, Л. Е. (2010а). Вербальная модель соотношения длинных кондратьевских волн и среднесрочных жюгляровских циклов. В: Коротаев, А. В., Малков, С. Ю., и Гринин, Л. Е. (ред.), *История и математика: Анализ и моделирование глобальной динамики* (с. 44–111). М.: ЛИБРОКОМ/URSS.

Гринин, Л. Е. (2010б). Мальтузианско-марксова «ловушка» и русские революции. *История и математика. О причинах Русской революции* / Ред. Л. Е. Гринин, А. В. Коротаев, С. Ю. Малков, с. 198–224. М.: ЛКИ/URSS

Гринин, Л. Е. (2011). Мальтузианские и модернизационные ловушки. *Проблемы экономической истории: теория и практика. Профессорский сборник научных статей, посвященный 60-летию С. А. Нефедова* / Ред. В. В. Запарий, (с. 95–119). Екатеринбург: ООО «Издательство УМЦ-УПИ).

Гринин, Л. Е. (2012а). Реконфигурация мира, или наступающая эпоха новых коалиций (возможные сценарии ближайшего будущего). *История и современность, 2,* 3–27.

Гринин, Л. Е. (2012б). Кондратьевские волны, технологические уклады и теория производственных революций. В: Акаев, А. А., Гринберг, Р. С., Гринин, Л. Е., Коротаев, А. В., и Малков, С. Ю. (ред.), *Кондратьевские волны: аспекты и перспективы* (с. 222–262). Волгоград: Учитель.

Гринин, Л. Е. (2013а). Динамика кондратьевских волн в свете теории производственных революций. В: Гринин, Л. Е., Коротаев, А. В., и Малков, С. Ю. (ред.), *Кондратьевские волны: палитра взглядов* (с. 31–83). Волгоград: Учитель.

Гринин, Л. Е. (2013б). Глобализация тасует карты (Куда сдвигается глобальный экономико-политический баланс мира). *Век глобализации, 2,* 63–78.

Гринин, Л. Е. (2013в). «Дракон» и «тигр»: модели развития и перспективы. *Историческая психология и социология истории, 1,* 111–133.

Гринин, Л. Е. (2013г). Модели развития Китая и Индии. *Государственная служба, 2,* 87–90.

Гринин, Л. Е. (2013д). Технологический аспект социальной эволюции. В: Гринин, Л. Е., Коротаев, А. В., Марков, А. В. (отв. ред.), *Эволюция Земли, жизни, общества, разума* (с. 98–166). Волгоград: Учитель.

Гринин, Л. Е. (2014). Индия и Китай: модели развития и перспективы в мире. *Комплексный системный анализ, математическое моделирование и прогнозирование развития стран БРИКС: Предварительные результаты* / Отв. ред. А. А. Акаев, А. В. Коротаев, С. Ю. Малков, (с. 246–276). М.: КРАСАНД.

Гринин, Л. Е. (2015). Новый мировой порядок и эпоха глобализации. Ст. 1. Американская гегемония: апогей и ослабление. Что дальше? *Век глобализации, 2*, 3–17.

Гринин, Л. Е. (2016). Новый мировой порядок и эпоха *глобализации*. Статья вторая. Возможности и перспективы формирования нового мирового порядка. *Век глобализации, 1*, 3–27.

Гринин, Л. Е., и Гринин, А. Л. (2015а). Кибернетическая революция и шестой технологический уклад. В: Гринин, Л. Е., Коротаев, А. В., и Бондаренко, В. М. (ред.), *Кондратьевские волны: наследие и современность* (с. 51–74). Волгоград: Учитель.

Гринин, Л. Е., и Гринин, А. Л. (2015б). *От рубил до нанороботов. Мир на пути к эпохе самоуправляемых систем (история технологий и описание их будущего).* Волгоград: Учитель.

Гринин, Л. Е., и Гринин, А. Л. (2015в). Кибернетическая революция и шестой технологический уклад. *Историческая психология и социология истории, 8*(1), 172–197.

Гринин, Л. Е., Исаев, Л. М., и Коротаев, А. В. (2016). *Революции и нестабильность на Ближнем Востоке* (2-е изд.). М.: Московская редакция издательства «Учитель».

Гринин, Л. Е., и Коротаев, А. В. (2009а). *Социальная макроэволюция: Генезис и трансформации Мир-Системы.* М.: ЛИБРОКОМ.

Гринин, Л. Е., и Коротаев, А. В. (2009б). Урбанизация и политическая нестабильность: к разработке математических моделей политических процессов. *Полис, 4*, 34–52.

Гринин, Л. Е., и Коротаев, А. В. (2010). *Глобальный кризис в ретроспективе. Краткая история подъемов и кризисов: от Ликурга до Алана Гринспена.* М.: ЛИБРОКОМ/URSS.

Гринин, Л. Е., и Коротаев, А. В. (2012). *Циклы, кризисы, ловушки современной Мир-Системы. Исследование кондратьевских, жюгляровских и вековых циклов, глобальных кризисов, мальтузианских и постмальтузианских ловушек.* М.: ЛКИ/URSS.

Гринин, Л. Е., и Коротаев, А. В. (2013а). Николай Кондратьев. Жизнь. Судьба. Наследие. В: Гринин, Л. Е., Коротаев, А. В., и Малков, С. Ю. (ред.), *Кондратьевские волны: палитра взглядов* (с. 9–22). Волгоград: Учитель.

Гринин, Л. Е., и Коротаев, А. В. (2013б). *Социальная макроэволюция: генезис и трансформация Мир-Системы* (2-е изд.). М.: Либроком.

Гринин, Л. Е., и Коротаев, А. В. (2014а). Безнадежная попытка опровергнуть Кондратьева. Ответ на статью А. С. Смирнова. Предварительные комментарии. В: Гринин, Л. Е., и Коротаев, А. В. (ред.), *Кондратьевские волны: длинные и среднесрочные циклы: ежегодник* (с. 74–92). Волгоград: Учитель

Гринин, Л. Е., и Коротаев, А. В. (2014б). В защиту Н. Д. Кондратьева. Постраничные комментарии к статье А. С. Смирнова. Предварительные комментарии. В: Гринин, Л. Е., и Коротаев, А. В. (ред.), *Кондратьевские волны: длинные и среднесрочные циклы: ежегодник* (с. 170–275). Волгоград: Учитель.

Гринин, Л. Е., и Коротаев, А. В. (2014в). Инфляционные и дефляционные тренды мировой экономики, или распространение «японской болезни». В: Гринин, Л. Е., и Коротаев, А. В. (ред.), *История и Математика: аспекты демографических и социально-экономических процессов* (с. 229–253). Волгоград: Учитель.

Гринин, Л. Е., и Коротаев, А. В. (2014г). Взаимосвязь длинных и среднесрочных циклов (кондратьевских волн и жюгляровских циклов). В: Гринин, Л. Е., и Коротаев, А. В. (ред.), *Кондратьевские волны: длинные и среднесрочные циклы* (с. 15–73). Волгоград: Учитель.

Гринин, Л. Е., и Коротаев, А. В. (2015а). Дефляция как болезнь современных развитых стран. В: Садовничий, В. А., Акаев, А. А., Малков, С. Ю., и Гринин, Л. Е. (ред.), *Анализ и моделирование мировой и страновой динамики: методология и базовые модели* (с. 241–270). М.: Моск. ред. изд-ва «Учитель».

Гринин, Л. Е., и Коротаев, А. В. (2015б). Глобальное старение населения и глобальная финансовая система. В: Гринин, Л. Е., Коротаев, А. В., и Бондаренко, В. М. (ред.), *Кондратьевские волны: наследие и современность* (с. 107–133). Волгоград: Учитель.

Гринин, Л. Е., Коротаев, А. В., и Малков, С. Ю. (Ред.). (2010). *О причинах Русской революции.* М.: ЛКИ/URSS

Гринин, Л. Е., Коротаев, А. В., и Цирель, С. В. (2011). *Циклы развития современной Мир-Системы*. М.: ЛИБРОКОМ/URSS.

Гринин, Л. Е., Малков, С. Ю, Гусев, В. А., и Коротаев, А. В. (2009). Некоторые возможные направления развития теории социально-демографических циклов и математические модели выхода из «мальтузианской ловушки». В: С. Ю. Малков, Л. Е. Гринин, А. В. Коротаев (ред.) *История и математика. Процессы и модели* (с. 134–210). М.: ЛИБРОКОМ/URSS.

Гринин, Л. Е., Малков, С. Ю., и Коротаев, А. В. (2010а). Математическая модель среднесрочного экономического цикла. В: Садовничий, В. А., Акаев, А. А., Малинецкий, Г. Г., и Коротаев, А. В. (ред.), *Прогноз и моделирование кризисов и мировой динамики* (с. 292–304). М.: ЛИБРОКОМ/URSS.

Гринин, Л. Е., Малков, С. Ю., и Коротаев, А. В. (2010б). Математическая модель среднесрочного экономического цикла и современный глобальный кризис. В: Малков, С. Ю., Гринин, Л. Е., и Коротаев, А. В. (ред.), *История и Математика: Эволюционная историческая макродинамика* (с. 233–284). М.: ЛИБРОКОМ.

Гринспен, А. (2009). *Эпоха потрясений: Проблемы и перспективы мировой финансовой системы* (изд. 2-е). М.: Альпина Бизнес Букс.

Дорнбуш, Р., и Фишер, С. (1997). *Макроэкономика*. М.: МГУ.

Доронин, И. Г. (2003). Мировые фондовые рынки. В: Королев, И. С. (ред.), *Мировая экономика: глобальные тенденции за 100 лет* (с. 101–133). М.: Экономистъ.

Ефимкин А. П. 1991. *Дважды реабилитированные: Н. Д. Кондратьев, Л. Н. Юровский*. М. – Л.: Финансы и статистика.

Зиновьев, А. А. (2003). *Глобальный человейник*. М.: Эксмо.

Илюшечкин, В. П. (1967). *Крестьянская война тайпинов*. М.: Наука.

Капелюшников, Р. И. (2012). *Сколько стоит человеческий капитал России?* М.: НИУ ВШЭ.

Кассель, Г. (1925). *Теория конъюнктур*. М.: Тип. ЦУП ВСНХ.

Каутский, К. (1918). *Золото, деньги и дороговизна*. Пг.: Книга.

Каутский, К., и Бауэр, О. (1923). *Изложение 2-го тома «Капитала» Карла Маркса*. М.

Киссинджер, Г. (2015). *Мировой порядок*. Москва: АСТ.

Клинов, В. Г. (2008). Мировая экономика: прогноз до 2050 г. *Вопросы экономики, 5*, 62–79.

Ковальчук, М. В. (2011). Конвергенция наук и технологий – прорыв в будущее. *Российские нанотехнологии, 6*(1–2). Retrieved from http://www.nrcki.ru/files/nbik01.pdf.

Кондратьев, Н. Д. (1918а). *На пути к голоду. Большевики у власти: Социально-политические итоги Октябрьского переворота*. М..

Кондратьев, Н. Д. (1918б). Год революции с экономической точки зрения. Год русской революции, 1917–1918. М.).

Кондратьев, Н. Д. (1922). *Мировое хозяйство и его конъюнктура во время и после войны*. Вологда: Областное отделение Государственного издательства.

Кондратьев, Н. Д. (1923). *Михаил Иванович Туган-Барановский*. Петроград: Колос.

Кондратьев, Н. Д. (1924). К вопросу о понятиях экономической статики, динамики и конъюнктуры. *Социалистическое хозяйство*. Кн. 2.

Кондратьев, Н. Д. (1925). Большие циклы конъюнктуры. *Вопросы конъюнктуры, 1*(1), 28–79.

Кондратьев, Н. Д. (1926б). Проблема предвидения. *Вопросы конъюнктуры*. Т. 2. Вып. 2.

Кондратьев, Н. Д. (1926в). *Мировое хозяйство. 1919–1925 гг.: Современное положение и основные тенденции развития*. М. – Л.: ЦУП ВСНХ СССР.

Кондратьев, Н. Д. (1927). Критические заметки о плане развития народного хозяйства. *Плановое хозяйство, 4*.

Кондратьев, Н. Д. (1928). *Большие циклы конъюнктуры. Доклады и их обсуждение в Институте экономики*. М.: Институт экономики.

Кондратьев, Н. Д. (1988). Проблема предвидения. *Экономика и математические методы, 24*(2).

Кондратьев, Н. Д. (1991а). *Основные проблемы экономической статики и динамики*. М.: Наука.

Кондратьев, Н. Д. (1991б). Письма Н. Д. Кондратьева Е. Д. Кондратьевой (1932–1938). *Основные проблемы экономической статики и динамики* (с. 535–561). М.: Наука.

Кондратьев, Н. Д. (1993а). *Избранные сочинения*. М.: Экономика.

Кондратьев, Н. Д. (1993б). *Особое мнение*. Избранные произведения в 2-х книгах. М.: Наука.

Кондратьев, Н. Д. (1993в [1925]). Большие циклы конъюнктуры. В: Кондратьев Н. Д., *Избранные сочинения*, с. 24–83. М.: Экономика.

Кондратьев, Н. Д. (2002 [1926]). *Большие циклы конъюнктуры и теория предвидения*. М.: Экономика.

Королев, И. С. (2003). (Ред.). *Мировая экономика: глобальные тенденции за 100 лет*. М.: Экономистъ.

Коротаев, А. В. (2006). *Долгосрочная политико-демографическая динамика Египта: циклы и тенденции*. М.: Вост. лит-ра.

Коротаев, А. В. (2007а). Демографические циклы и социально-экономическая история России. *Личность. Культура. Общество*, 3(37), 380–385.

Коротаев, А. В. (2007б). О некоторых особенностях средневековых египетских и иных политико-демографических циклов. *Восток, 1,* 5–15.

Коротаев, А. В. (2013). Структура современной глобальной конвергенции: количественный анализ. *Эконометрические методы в исследовании глобальных процессов*. М.: Анкил. С. 101–111.

Коротаев, А. В. (2014). Великая дивергенция, Великая конвергенция и глобальный демографический переход. *Мировая экономика ближайшего будущего: откуда ждать инновационного рывка?* / Ред. В. М. Бондаренко. (с. 101–111) М. – Волгоград: Международный фонд Н. Д. Кондратьева – Учитель.

Коротаев, А. В. (2015а). К математическому моделированию процессов Великой дивергенции и Великой конвергенции. *Социофизика и социоинженерия* / Ред. Ю. Л. Словохотов. М.: МГУ, 2015. С. 16–17.

Коротаев, А. В. (2015б). Математическое моделирование процессов Великой дивергенции и Великой конвергенции. *Информационный бюллетень Ассоциации «История и компьютер», 44,* 97–102.

Коротаев, А. В. (2015в). Глобальный демографический переход и фазы дивергенции – конвергенции центра и периферии Мир-Системы. *Вестник Института экономики Российской академии наук, 1,* 149–162.

Коротаев, А. В., и Божевольнов, Ю. В. (2010). Некоторые общие тенденции экономического развития Мир-Системы. В: Акаев, А. А., Коротаев, А. В., и Малинецкий, Г. Г. (ред.), *Прогноз и моделирование кризисов и мировой динамики* (с. 161–172). М.: ЛКИ/URSS.

Коротаев, А. В., и Божевольнов, Ю. В. (2012). Сценарии демографического будущего России. В: Акаев, А. А., Коротаев, А. В., Малинецкий, Г. Г., и Малков, С. Ю. (ред.), *Моделирование и прогнозирование глобального, регионального и национального развития* (с. 436–461). М.: ЛИБРОКОМ/URSS.

Коротаев, А. В., и Гринин, Л. Е. (2012). Кондратьевские волны в мир-системной перспективе. В: Акаев, А. А., Гринберг, Р. С., Гринин, Л. Е., Коротаев, А. В., и Малков, С. Ю. (ред.), *Кондратьевские волны: аспекты и перспективы* (с. 58–109). Волгоград: Учитель.

Коротаев, А. В., и Гринин, Л. Е. (2013). Н. Д. Кондратьев и кондратьевские волны в мировой техноинновационной активности. *Экономическая наука современной России, 2,* 128–140.

Коротаев, А. В., Зинькина, Ю. В., Халтурина, Д. А., Зыков, В. А., Шульгин, С. Г., и Фоломеева, Д. А. (2015). Перспективы демографической динамики России. В: Садовничий, В. А., Акаев, А. А., Малков, С. Ю., и Гринин, Л. Е. (ред.), *Анализ и моделирование мировой и страновой динамики: методология и базовые модели* (с. 192–240). М.: Учитель.

Коротаев, А. В., Комарова, Н. Л., и Халтурина, Д. А. (2007). *Законы истории. Вековые циклы и тысячелетние тренды. Демография. Экономика. Войны*. М.: КомКнига/URSS.

Коротаев, А. В., Малков, А. С., Божевольнов, Ю. В., и Халтурина, Д. А. (2010). К системному анализу глобальной динамики: взаимодействие центра и периферии Мир-Системы. В:

Абылгазиев, И. И., Ильин, И. В., и Шестова, Т. Л. (ред.), *Глобалистика как область научных исследований и сфера преподавания* (с. 228–242). М.: МАКС Пресс.

Коротаев, А. В., и Халтурина, Д. А. (2009). *Современные тенденции мирового развития*. М.: Либроком/URSS.

Коротаев, А. В., Халтурина, Д. А., и Божевольнов, Ю. В. (2010). *Законы истории. Вековые циклы и тысячелетние тренды. Демография. Экономика. Войны* (3-е изд.). М.: ЛКИ/URSS.

Коротаев, А. В., Халтурина, Д. А., и Божевольнов, Ю. В. (2011). Математическое моделирование и прогнозирование демографического будущего России: пять сценариев. В: Садовничий, В. А., Акаев, А. А., Коротаев, А. В., и Малинецкий, Г. Г. (ред.), *Сценарий и перспектива развития России* (с. 196–219). М.: Ленанд/URSS.

Коротаев, А. В., Халтурина, Д. А., Кобзева, С. В., и Зинькина, Ю. В. (2011). Ловушка на выходе из ловушки? О некоторых особенностях политико-демографической динамики модернизирующихся систем. *Проекты и риски будущего. Концепции, модели, инструменты, прогнозы* / Ред. А. А. Акаев, А. В. Коротаев, Г. Г. Малинецкий, С. Ю. Малков, с. 45–88. М.: Красанд/URSS.

Коротаев, А. В., Халтурина, Д. А., Малков, А. С., Божевольнов, Ю. В., Кобзева, С. В., и Зинькина, Ю. В. (2010). *Законы истории. Математическое моделирование и прогнозирование мирового и регионального развития* (3-е изд.). М.: ЛКИ/URSS.

Коротаев, А. В., и Цирель, С. В. (2010а). Кондратьевские волны в мировой экономической динамике. В: Халтурина, Д. А., и Коротаев, А. В. (ред.), *Системный мониторинг глобального и регионального развития* (с. 189–229). М.: ЛИБРОКОМ/URSS.

Коротаев, А. В., и Цирель, С. В. (2010б). Кондратьевские волны в мир-системной экономической динамике. В: Акаев, А. А., Коротаев, А. В., Малинецкий, Г. Г. (ред.), *Прогноз и моделирование кризисов и мировой динамики* (с. 5–69). М.: ЛКИ/URSS.

Куряев, А. В. (2005). (Ред.). *Экономический цикл: анализ австрийской школы*. Челябинск: Социум.

Лазуренко, С. (1992). Проблемы долговременных колебаний экономической динамики. *Вопросы экономики, 10,* 69–75.

Лан, В. И. (1975). *США: от испано-американской до Первой мировой войны*. М.: Наука.

Лан, В. И. (1976). *США: от Первой мировой до Второй мировой войны*. М.: Наука.

Лан, В. И. (1978). *США в военные и послевоенные годы*. М.: Наука.

Ланкастер, К. (1993). Перемены и новаторство в технологии потребления. В: Гальперин, В. М. (ред.), *Теория потребительского поведения и спроса* (с. 326–336). СПб.: Экономическая школа.

Ларин, В. Л. (1986). *Повстанческая борьба народов Юго-Западного Китая в 50–70-х годах XIX века*. М.: Наука.

Лескюр, Ж. (1908). *Общие и периодические промышленные кризисы*. СПб.: Общественная польза.

Маевский, В. И. (1992). О характере длинных волн. *Вопросы экономики, 10,* 58–62

Маевский, В. И. (1997). *Введение в эволюционную макроэкономику*. М.: Япония сегодня.

Малаховский, К. В. (1971). *История Австралийского союза*. М.: Наука.

Малков, А. С., Божевольнов, Ю. В., Халтурина, Д. А., и Коротаев, А. В. (2010). К системному анализу мировой динамики: взаимодействие центра и периферии Мир-Системы. В: Акаев, А. А., Коротаев, А. В., и Малинецкий, Г. Г. (ред.), *Прогноз и моделирование кризисов и мировой динамики* (с. 234–248). М.: ЛКИ/URSS.

Малков, А. С., Коротаев, А. В., и Божевольнов, Ю. В. (2010). Математическое моделирование взаимодействия центра и периферии Мир-Системы. В: Акаев, А. А., Коротаев, А. В., и Малинецкий, Г. Г. (ред.), *Прогноз и моделирование кризисов и мировой динамики* (с. 277–286). М.: ЛКИ/URSS.

Марков, А. В., и Коротаев, А. В. (2009). *Гиперболический рост в живой природе и обществе*. М.: Либроком/URSS.

Маркс, К. (1960 [1867]). Капитал. Т. 1. В: Маркс, К., и Энгельс, Ф., *Сочинения,* т. 23 (2-е изд.). М.: Политиздат.

Маркс, К. (1961). *Капитал.* Т. 2 [1893], Т.3 [1894]. В: Маркс, К., и Энгельс, Ф., *Сочинения*, т. 24–25. (2-е изд.). М.: Политиздат.

Мельянцев, В. А. (2009). *Развитые и развивающиеся страны в эпоху перемен.* М.: ИД «Ключ-С».

Меньшиков, С. М., и Клименко, Л. А. (1989). *Длинные волны в экономике. Когда общество меняет кожу.* М.: Международные отношения.

Мендельсон, Л. А. (1959–1964). *Теория и история экономических кризисов и циклов.* Т. 1–3. М.: Издательство социально-экономической литературы.

Мизес, Л. фон. (2005). *Человеческая деятельность: трактат по экономической теории.* Челябинск: Социум.

Митчелл, У. (1930). *Экономические циклы. Проблема и ее постановка.* М.: Госиздат.

Модельски, Дж., и Томпсон, У. (1992). Волны Кондратьева, развитие мировой экономики и международная политика. *Вопросы экономики, 10,* 49–57.

Мотылев, В. Е. (1923). Законы тенденции нормы процента к понижению. *Вестник социалистической академии, 3,* 134–158.

Моуги, Р. 1992. Развитие процесса длинноволновых колебаний. *Вопросы экономики, 10,* 76–78.

Мэнкью, Н. Г. (1994). *Макроэкономика.* М.: МГУ.

Непомнин, О. Е. (2005). *История Китая: Эпоха Цин. XVII – начало XX века.* М.: Вост. лит-ра.

Осинский, Н. (1923а). Мировое хозяйство в оценке наших экономистов. *Красная Новь, 2.* М.

Осинский, Н. (1923б). Мировое хозяйство и кризисы: Профессор Кондратьев защищается, профессор Кондратьев нападает. *Социалистическое хозяйство, 6–8,* 25–27.

Пантин, В. И. (1996). *Циклы и ритмы истории.* Рязань: Аракс.

Пантин, В. И., и Лапкин, В. В. (2006). *Философия исторического прогнозирования: ритмы истории и перспективы мирового развития в первой половине XXI века.* Дубна: Феникс+.

Перес, К. (2011). *Технологические революции и финансовый капитал. Динамика пузырей и периодов процветания.* М.: Дело.

Плакиткин, Ю. А. (2011). Исследование динамики патентных заявок как инструмент анализа инновационного развития энергетики. В: Акаев, А. А., Коротаев, А. В., Малинецкий, Г. Г., Малков, С. Ю. (ред.), *Проекты и риски будущего: Концепции, модели, инструменты, прогнозы* (с. 323–336). М.: Красанд.

Полетаев, А. В., и Савельева, И. М. (1993). *Циклы Кондратьева и развитие капитализма (опыт междисциплинарного исследования).* М.: Наука.

Полтерович, В. (2009). Гипотеза об инновационной паузе и стратегия модернизации. *Вопросы экономики, 6,* 4–23.

Попов, В. А. (1978). Некоторая стабилизация консервативного правления и нарастание экономической экспансии (июль 1960–1970 г.). В: Попов, В. А. (ред.), *История Японии (1945–1975)* (с. 249–307). М.: Наука.

Прайд, В., и Коротаев, А. (Ред.) (2008). *Новые технологии и продолжение эволюции человека?* М.: ЛКИ/URSS.

Румянцева, С. Ю. (2003). *Длинные волны в экономике: многофакторный анализ.* СПб.: Изд-во СПУ.

Садовничий, В. А., Акаев А. А., Коротаев А. В., и Малков, С. Ю. (2014). *Комплексное моделирование и прогнозирование развития стран БРИКС в контексте мировой динамики.* М.: Наука.

Сакс, Дж. Л., и Ларрен, Ф. Б. (1996). *Макроэкономика. Глобальный подход.* М.: Дело.

Самуэльсон, П. Э. (1994). *Экономика:* в 2 т. М.: Алгон.

Самуэльсон, П. Э, и Нордхаус, В. Д. (2009). *Макроэкономика* (изд. 18-е). М.: Вильямс.

Севостьянов, Г. Н. (Ред.) (1983). *История США.* Т. 1. *1607–1877.* М.: Наука.

Симонов, В. В., Фигуровская, Н. К. (1991). Николай Дмитриевич Кондратьев (краткая биография). *Основные проблемы экономической статики и динамики* / Н. Д. Кондратьев, (с. 524–534). М.: Наука.

Симонов, В. В., Фигуровская Н. К. (1993). Великий перелом (дело Трудовой крестьянской партии. *Особое мнение. Избранные произведения* в 2-х книгах / Н. Д. Кондратьев. Книга 2, 573–608. М.: Наука.

Смит, А. (1935). *Исследование о природе и причинах богатства народов.* Т. 2. М.; Л.

Сорокин, П. (1992). О так называемых факторах социальной эволюции. В: Сорокин, П. (ред.), *Человек. Цивилизация. Общество* (с. 521–531). М.: Издательство политической литературы.

Суэтин, А. (2009). О причинах современного финансового кризиса. *Вопросы экономики, 1*, 40–51.

Тауш, А. (2002). Европейский Союз и будущая мировая система. *Европа, 2*(3), 23–62.

Тауш, А. (2003). Европейская перспектива: по пути к созданию «общего средиземноморского дома» и интегрированию положительного потенциала общественного развития ислама. *Европа, 4*(9), 87–109.

Тауш, А. (2007). Европейский союз: «град на холме» и Лиссабонская стратегия. *Мировая экономика и международные отношения, 50*(3), 65–72.

Тауш, А. (2008). «Разрушительное созидание?» (Рассуждения в духе Шумпетера о некоторых трендах и Лиссабонском процессе в Европе). *Мировая экономика и международные отношения, 10,* 34–41.

Тауш, А. (2009). Евроислам. Миф или реальность? Количественный анализ по данным «Всемирной программы изучения ценностей». *Европа, 1*(26), 121–151.

Тауш, А. (2012). Геостратегические соображения по поводу циклов Кондратьева, глобализации и войн. *Мировая экономика и международные отношения, 10,* 105–114.

Теслер, Г. С. (2004). *Новая кибернетика.* Киев: Логос.

Трахтенберг, И. А. (1963 [1939]). *Денежные кризисы (1821–1938 гг.).* М.: Изд-во АН СССР.

Троцкий, Л. Д. (1923). О кривой капиталистического развития. *Вестник Социалистической академии, 4,* 3–12.

Туган-Барановский, М. (1894). *Промышленные кризисы в современной Англии, их причины и ближайшие влияния на народную жизнь.* СПб.: Типография И. Н. Скороходова

Туган-Барановский, М. И. (1998 [1917]) Бумажные деньги и металл. В: Туган-Барановский М. И. *Экономические очерки,* с. 284–422. М.: РОССПЭН.

Туган-Барановский, М. И. (2008 [1913]). *Периодические промышленные кризисы.* М.: Директмедиа Паблишинг.

Фишер, С., Дорбуш, Р., и Шмалензи, Р. (1993). *Экономика.* М.: Дело.

Фридман, М. (2002). *Основы монетаризма.* М.: ТЕИС.

Хаберлер, Г. (2008). *Процветание и депрессия. Теоретический анализ циклических колебаний.* Челябинск: Социум.

Халтурина, Д. А., и Коротаев, А. В. (2010). Системный мониторинг глобального и регионального развития. В: Халтурина, Д. А., и Коротаев, А. В. (ред.), *Системный мониторинг: Глобальное и региональное развитие* (с. 11–188). М.: ЛИБРОКОМ/URSS.

Хансен, Э. (1959). *Экономические циклы и национальный доход.* М.: Изд-во ин. лит-ры.

Хикс, Дж. Р. (1993). *Стоимость и капитал.* М.: Прогресс.

Штефан, Е. (2008). Пенсионные фонды США потеряли два триллиона долларов. *Новый регион 2,* 8 октября. Retrieved from http://www.nr2.ru/economy/199830.html.

Шумпетер, Й. (1982). *Теория экономического развития.* М.: Прогресс.

Щеглов, С. И. (2009). Циклы Кондратьева в 20 веке, или Как сбываются экономические прогнозы. Retrieved from http://schegloff.livejournal.com/242360.html#cutid1.

Яковец, Ю. В. (2001). *Наследие Н. Д. Кондратьева: взгляд из XXI века.* М.: МФК.

Яковец, Ю. В. (2002а). Наследие Н. Д. Кондратьева: взгляд из XXI века. В: Кондратьев, Н. Д., *Избранные труды* (с. 708–736). М.: Экономика.

Яковец, Ю. В. (2002б). *Научное наследие Н.Д. Кондратьева в контексте развития российской и мировой социально-экономической мысли.* М.: МФК.

Index

A
Ageing population
  age structure, 163
  Cybernetic Revolution, 179
  elderly people, 165
  financial system, 169, 170
  Japan, 165
  life expectancy, 163
  massive acceleration, 163
  pensioners and pension funds, 171–179
  percentage of, 162
  problems, 166
  retirement age, 164
  sixth technological paradigm, 167–169
  types, 172
  young population, 173
Agrarian revolution, 145, 146
Akamatsu Waves
  Akamatsu cycles, 112
  Arrighi's Center-Periphery model
    BRICS countries, 127
    global income convergence, 123
    Great Depression, 124, 126
    industrial innovations, 122
    Maddison data, 122
    product innovations, 122
    profit-oriented innovations, 121
    purchasing power parity, 126
    real GDP per capita declines, 124–126
    resilience, 127
    triade, 123
  auto centered development, 112
  center-periphery structure, 111
  economic convergence, 113, 128

economic disasters, 128
flying geese model
  advanced differentiation, 117
  Akamatsu cycles, 120
  Akamatsu's analysis in 1961, 117
  Akamatsu's theory, 114
  Bornschier's dependency theory, 118
  characteristic structure, 117
  complementary, 116
  degree of freedom, 121
  development stages, 114, 115
  differentia specifica, 119
  discrepancy, 118
  falling period, 116
  Hegelian dialectic, 118
  income convergence, 114
  industry and agriculture, 114
  innovations, 115
  Kondratieff cycles, 119, 121
  Kondratieff's theory, 114
  Maddison's database, 115, 116
  old and waning economic cycle, 115
  tendencies, 116
  wild-geese flying, 117
Global Maps, 133, 137–139
Maddison data, 112
PIIGS countries, 113
re-analysis, 112
World System
  archaic and tectonic structure, 135
  convergence data, 129
  correlation analysis, 130
  cross-national characteristics, 129
  depth-analysis, 134

Index

Akamatsu Waves (*cont.*)
  divergence process, 134
  evidence, 133
  inegalitarian neoliberalism, 136
  information, 134
  K-cycles, 131, 132
  Maddison's dataset, 129, 130
  neoliberalism, 134
  Piketty data, 135, 136
  proven cycle length, 129
  trend diagnosis, 136
  "U" shaped, 135
  world-systems research, 113
Arrighi's Center-Periphery model
  BRICS countries, 127
  global income convergence, 123
  Great Depression, 124, 126
  industrial innovations, 122
  Maddison data, 122
  product innovations, 122
  profit-oriented innovations, 121
  purchasing power parity, 126
  real GDP per capita declines, 124–126
  resilience, 127
  triade, 123

B

Bornschier's dependency theory, 118
BRICS countries, 127

C

Crisis approaches, 56
Cybernetic Revolution, 146, 147
Cyclical dynamics
  Akamatsu's theory, 16
  bankruptcy, 4
  competition for resources, 1
  components, 2
  Core growth rates, 13
  economic cycles, 5–11
  economic turnover, 4
  English, German, and Russian, 11
  environmental constraints, 1, 2
  Great Convergence, 16
  Great Depression, 15, 17
  Industrial Revolution, 3
  Kondratieff waves, 2, 3, 12, 13
  long-term economic development, 11
  medium-term Juglar cycles, 3, 4, 13, 14
  nonlinear fashion, 1
  population ageing, 19, 20
  PRIO data, 21
  production principles and revolutions, 17–19
  purchasing power per capita, 17
  steady and continuous expansion, 3
  trade and economic relations, 4
  World System, 14, 15

D

Deindustrialization, 53
Devezas–Corredine model, 27

E

Economic convergence, 113, 128
Economic disasters, 128

F

Financial system, 169, 170
Flying geese model
  advanced differentiation, 117
  Akamatsu cycles, 120
  Akamatsu's analysis in 1961, 117
  Akamatsu's theory, 114
  Bornschier's dependency theory, 118
  characteristic structure, 117
  complementary, 116
  degree of freedom, 121
  development stages, 114, 115
  differentia specifica, 119
  discrepancy, 118
  falling period, 116
  Hegelian dialectic, 118
  income convergence, 114
  industry and agriculture, 114
  innovations, 115
  Kondratieff cycles, 119, 121
  Kondratieff's theory, 114
  Maddison's database, 115, 116
  old and waning economic cycle, 115
  tendencies, 116
  wild-geese flying, 117

G

Globalization, 176
Global Maps, 133, 137–139
Global trading system, 108
Glass-Steagall Act, 66
Great Convergence, 16
Great Depression, 15, 17, 124, 126

Index

I
Industrial Production Principle, 150
Industrial revolution, 146
Innovation-based approach, 70
Investment-based approach, 70

J
Juglar cycles (J-cycles)
  achievement, 56
  activities, 67
  aggregate demand changes, 61
  business optimism, 102
  classical theory, 60
  clusters, 88, 89
  crisis theory, 56
  cycles stems, 91
  depression, 65, 90
  depressive pause, 102, 103
  direction of changes
    amplitude and periodicity, 107
    GDP, 107
    global trading system, 108
    gold deposits, 108
    K-wave phases, 108
    organic synthesis, 108
    price changes, 109
    upswing and downswing phases, 108
    upswing/downswing dynamics, 107
  economic crises theory, 59
  economic cycle scheme, 56, 91, 92
  emergence and resolution, 92–94
  equilibrium, 60
  factors, 65
  features, 67
  financial assets, 65
  fluctuations, 57
  Glass-Steagall Act, 66
  growth factors, exhaustion of, 100, 101
  Keynesian revolution, 60
  Keynesian theory, 61
  K-waves (*see* Kondratieff waves (K-waves))
  medium-term cycle
    contraction, 62
    cyclical crises, 64
    depression/stagnation phase, 63, 64
    expansion phase, 62–64
    features, 64
    recession phase, 64
    recovery phase, 63
    respective analysis, 62
    sharp transitions, 65
  metallic standard, 66
  monetary theories, 58, 61
  non-monetary direction, 59
  over-accumulation theory, 58
  production structure, 58
  psychological theories, 59
  rational expectations, 62
  role of the state, 109
  Spiethoff's table, 90
  substantial synthesis, 62
  Tugan-Baranovsky's opinion, 57
  under-consumption theory, 58
  upswing, boom and overheating, 66
  upswings and recessions, 90
  World System Core, 60
  World System dimension
    innovations, 104, 105
    intensive modernization, 104
    K-wave synchronicity, 106
    socioeconomic crises, 104

K
Kitchin cycles, 6, 7
Kondratieff cycles, 119, 121
Kondratieff's theory, 114
Kondratieff waves (K-waves)
  analysis, 69
  annual growth rates, 31, 33–38, 41, 43
  annual world GDP growth rates, 76, 80
  A-phases and B-phases, 72, 73, 76–78, 80–84, 95, 96
    anti-crisis social innovations, 98
    blind-alley innovations, 97
    downswing phase innovators, 97
    limitation, 99, 100
    modernization processes, 98
    outsourcing, 99
    respective technological paradigms, 97
    U.S. Congress, 96
  average growth rate, 38–40
  broad modeling approach, 76
  characteristic period, 74–76
  characteristics change, 73
  clusters, 88, 89
  component, 71
  Core and Periphery, 46, 47
  correlation, 76–79
  Cybernetic Revolution
    MANBRIC-technology, 158–160
    self-regulating systems, 156–158
  depression, 81, 90
  downswings, 71, 72
  duration, 78, 79

Kondratieff waves (K-waves) (*cont.*)
   economic development, 51
   economic indicators, 69
   1810/1817–1844/1851, 47
   1844/1851–1870/1875, 48
   1870/1875–1890/1896, 48
   1890/1896–1914/1928, 48
   evidence support, 29
   fifth K-wave, 82, 154, 155
   fourth K-wave, 153, 154
   GDP dynamics, 30
   halves, 83
   Industrial Production Principle, 150
   innovation-based approach, 70, 104, 105
   intensive modernization, 104
   investment-based approach, 70
   K-wave synchronicity, 106
   late 1780s/early 1790s–1810/1817, 47
   long-term inflation/deflation trends, 73, 74
   long-term process, 69
   long-term trend curves, 29
   macroeconomic indicators, 29
   Maddison/World Bank empirical
      estimates, 31
   1914/1928–1939/1950, 49
   1939/1950–1968/1974, 49
   1968/1974–1984/1991, 49
   1984/1991–2001/2007, 49, 50
   periodic fluctuations, 68
   phases, 25
   post-World War II dynamics, 26, 30, 32
   pre-1870 period, 39–41
   Pre-1945/50 World GDP Data, 33, 34, 37, 38
   production principle, 143, 144, 147, 149
   production revolution, 144–146, 150, 152
   socioeconomic crises, 104
   stylized facts, 76
   synthetic theory, 70
   technological innovation processes, 42–44
   2001/2007–2017/2020, 50
   types, 69
   unanimity, 68
   upswings, 52–54, 71, 72, 90
   USA producer price index, 28
   US Congress, 94
   verbal model (*see* Verbal model)
   vs. warfare, 75
   world economic dynamics
      Beveridge Report, 25
      cluster-of-innovation, 26, 27
      decline phases, 24
      Devezas–Corredine model, 27
      Paper Money and Metal, 25
      pattern, 27
      post-World War 1, 25
      production and communication, 26
      redshift data, 25
      world-system dynamics, 27
   world-system approach, 44, 45

L
Life expectancy, 163

M
Maddison's database, 115, 116
Medium-term cycle
   contraction, 62
   cyclical crises, 64
   depression/stagnation phase, 63, 64
   expansion phase, 62–64
   features, 64
   recession phase, 64
   recovery phase, 63
   respective analysis, 62
   sharp transitions, 65

N
Nonlinear fashion, 1

P
Pensioners, 171–179
Pension funds, 171–179
PIIGS countries, 113
Profit-oriented innovations, 121
Purchasing power parity (PPP), 126

R
Random factors, 56
Recession phase, 64
Recovery phase, 63

S
Scientific-cybernetic production principle, 149–155
Spiethoff's table, 90
Synthetic theory, 70

T
Tugan-Baranovsky's opinion, 57

U
University of Texas Inequality Project (UTIP), 135
US Congress, 94

V
Verbal model
 characteristic period, 85
 development, 87
 innovation and modernization trends, 86
 phase alteration, 87, 88
 pising prices and profit margins, 85
 principles, 87
 technical and social innovations, 86
 trend's change, 85
 upswings and downswings, 85
 upward and downward, 85
 World System, 86

W
World economic dynamics
 Beveridge Report, 25
 cluster-of-innovation, 26, 27
 decline phases, 24
 Devezas–Corredine model, 27
 Paper Money and Metal, 25
 pattern, 27
 post-World War 1, 25
 production and communication, 26
 redshift data, 25
 world-system dynamics, 27
The World Economy during and after the War, 6
World System
 archaic and tectonic structure, 135
 convergence data, 129
 correlation analysis, 130
 cross-national characteristics, 129
 depth-analysis, 134
 divergence process, 134
 evidence, 133
 inegalitarian neoliberalism, 136
 information, 134
 K-cycles, 131, 132
 Maddison's dataset, 129, 130
 neoliberalism, 134
 Piketty data, 135, 136
 proven cycle length, 129
 trend diagnosis, 136
 "U" shaped, 135
 verbal model, 86
World System Core, 13, 46–47

Y
Young population, 173